CREDITS

D&D 4th Edition Design Team
Rob Heinsoo, Andy Collins, James Wyatt

D&D 4th Edition Final Development Strike Team
Bill Slavicsek, Mike Mearls, James Wyatt

Monster Manual Design
Mike Mearls, Stephen Schubert, James Wyatt

Monster Manual Development
Andy Collins, Mike Mearls, Stephen Radney-MacFarland,
Peter Schaefer, Stephen Schubert

Monster Manual Editing
Greg Bilsland, Jennifer Clarke Wilkes, Jeremy Crawford,
Julia Martin, Christopher Perkins

Monster Manual Managing Editing
Christopher Perkins

Additional Design and Development
Richard Baker, Greg Bilsland, Logan Bonner, Bart Carroll,
Michele Carter, Jennifer Clarke Wilkes, Bruce R. Cordell,
Jeremy Crawford, Jesse Decker, Michael Donais,
Robert Gutschera, Gwendolyn F. M. Kestrel, Peter Lee,
Julia Martin, Kim Mohan, David Noonan, Christopher Perkins,
Matthew Sernett, Chris Sims, Ed Stark, Rodney Thompson,
Rob Watkins, Steve Winter, Chris Youngs

Director of R&D, Roleplaying Games/Book Publishing
Bill Slavicsek

D&D Story Design and Development Manager
Christopher Perkins

D&D System Design and Development Manager
Andy Collins

D&D Senior Art Director
Stacy Longstreet

Cover Illustrations
Wayne Reynolds (front), **Brian Hagan** (back)

Special Thanks to Brandon Daggerhart, keeper of Shadowfell

Graphic Designers
Keven Smith, Leon Cortez, Emi Tanji

Additional Graphic Design
Karin Powell, Mari Kolkowsky,
Shauna Wolf Narciso, Ryan Sansaver

Concept Artists
Dave Allsop, Christopher Burdett, Adam Gillespie,
Lars Grant-West, David Griffith, Lee Moyer, William O'Connor

Interior Illustrations
Dave Allsop, Steve Argyle, Daren Bader, Zoltan Boros &
Gabor Szikszai, Miguel Coimbra, Stephen Crowe, Jason A.
Engle, Carl Frank, Lars Grant-West, David Griffith, Espen
Grundetjern, Fred Hooper, Ralph Horsley, Heather Hudson,
Michael Komarck, Doug Kovacs, Ron Lemen, Todd Lockwood,
Warren Mahy, Izzy Medrano, Raven Mimura, Jorge Molina, Jim
Nelson, William O'Connor, Saejin Oh, Steve Prescott, RK Post,
Wayne Reynolds, Richard Sardinha, Marc Sasso, Ron Spears,
Chris Stevens, Anne Stokes, Arnie Swekel, Jean Pierre Targete,
Francis Tsai, Eric Vedder, Adam Vehige, Pete Venters, Franz
Vohwinkel, Eva Widermann, Sam Wood, Ben Wootten, Kevin
Yan, James Zhang, Jim Zubkavich

D&D Brand Team
Liz Schuh, Scott Rouse, Sara Girard, Kierin Chase,
Martin Durham, Linae Foster

Publishing Production Specialists
Angelika Lokotz, Erin Dorries, Moriah Scholz,
Christopher Tardiff

Prepress Manager
Jefferson Dunlap

Imaging Technicians
Travis Adams, Bob Jordan, Sven Bolen

Production Manager
Cynda Callaway

Building on the Design of Previous Editions by
E. Gary Gygax, Dave Arneson (1st Edition and earlier);
David "Zeb" Cook (2nd Edition); **Jonathan Tweet, Monte Cook,**
Skip Williams, Richard Baker, Peter Adkison (3rd Edition)

Dedicated to the memory of E. Gary Gygax

620-21720720-001 EN
9 8 7 6 5 4 3 2 1
First Printing: June 2008
ISBN: 978-0-7869-4852-9

U.S., CANADA, ASIA, PACIFIC,
& LATIN AMERICA
Wizards of the Coast, Inc.
P.O. Box 707
Renton WA 98057-0707
+1-800-324-6496

EUROPEAN HEADQUARTERS
Hasbro UK Ltd
Caswell Way
Newport, Gwent NP9 0YH
GREAT BRITAIN
Please keep this address for your records

WIZARDS OF THE COAST,
BELGIUM
't Hofveld 6D
1702 Groot-Bijgaarden
Belgium
+32 2 467 3360

VISIT OUR WEBSITE AT WWW.WIZARDS.COM/DND

CONTENTS

Monsters A to Z

WELCOME TO the *Monster Manual*. It joins the *Player's Handbook* and *Dungeon Master's Guide* to form the core rules for the DUNGEONS & DRAGONS *Roleplaying Game!*

The *Monster Manual* offers a rich collection of monsters designed to challenge player characters (PCs) of every level. This introduction explains how to read each monster's statistics. Refer to the glossary on pages 280-283 for definitions of common terms that are not spelled out in a monster's statistics block.

Lists of monsters by level and role appear on pages 284-287 to assist you in tailoring encounters to the level and abilities of the player characters.

A monster's statistics are presented in a format that makes them easy to use right off the page. Each statistics block is divided into sections, as shown in the example below.

Monster Name	**Level # Role**
Size origin type (keyword)	XP #

Initiative +#   **Senses** Perception +#; special senses
Aura Name (Keyword) aura #; effect.
HP #; **Bloodied** #
AC #; **Fortitude** #, **Reflex** #, **Will** #
Saving Throws +#
Speed #
Action Points #

[Type] Power Name (action; recharge) ✦ **Keyword(s)**
   Reach; range, area, or targets; attack bonus vs. target defense; effect. *Miss:* effect (if any). Secondary attack or effect.

[Type] Power Name (action; recharge) ✦ **Keyword(s)**
   Reach; range, area, or targets; attack bonus vs. target defense; effect. *Miss:* effect (if any). Secondary attack or effect.

Alignment   **Languages**
Skills skill name +#, skill name +#
Str score (+#)   **Dex** score (+#)   **Wis** score (+#)
Con score (+#)   **Int** score (+#)   **Cha** score (+#)
Equipment armor, shield, weapons, other gear

MONSTER NAME

Every monster has a unique name. Related monsters can have similar names, such as the hobgoblin soldier and the hobgoblin archer.

LEVEL AND ROLE

The level of the monster and the role it fills are given in the top right-hand corner of the statistics block. The *Dungeon Master's Guide* explains more about monster level and role and how to build encounters using them.

LEVEL

A monster's level summarizes how tough it is in an encounter. It determines most of the monster's numerical statistics as well as the experience point (XP) award the PCs earn for defeating the monster.

Role

A monster's role describes its preferred combat tactics, much as a character class's role suggests tactics for PCs. Monster roles are **artillery**, **brute**, **controller**, **lurker**, **skirmisher**, and **soldier**. These roles are discussed in the *Dungeon Master's Guide*.

A monster might have the **leader** keyword in parentheses, indicating that it grants some sort of boon to its allies in combat, such as a beneficial aura.

Size, Origin, and Type

Each monster has a size, origin, and type, listed in that order. Some monsters also have one or more keywords in parentheses.

Size

A monster's size determines the space it occupies, as well as its reach.

Monster Size	Space	Reach
Tiny	–	0
Small	1	1
Medium	1	1
Large	2 × 2	1 (long) or 2 (tall)
Huge	3 × 3	2 (long) or 3 (tall)
Gargantuan	4 × 4 or larger	3 (long) or 4 (tall)

Space: This is the number of squares the creature occupies on the battle grid. Tiny creatures have no Space entry because they work a little differently: Four Tiny creatures can fit in a single square.

Reach: Large, Huge, and Gargantuan creatures often have exceptional reach and can attack enemies that are not adjacent to them. A creature's reach depends in part on whether it has a tall form, standing upright, or a long form that is oriented lengthwise. Tall creatures often reach farther than long ones. A creature's reach is built into its melee powers.

A Tiny creature has 0 reach; it cannot attack outside its own space.

A creature with reach greater than 1 still can't make opportunity attacks against nonadjacent creatures unless it has *threatening reach* (see page 283).

Origin

A monster's origin summarizes its place in the D&D cosmology. Origins are **aberrant**, **elemental**, **fey**, **immortal**, **natural**, and **shadow**. These terms are defined in the glossary.

Type

A creature's type summarizes some basic things about its appearance and behavior. Types are **animate**, **beast**, **humanoid**, and **magical beast**. These terms are defined in the glossary.

Keywords

Some monsters have keywords that further define them. These keywords represent groups of monsters, such as **angel**, **demon**, **devil**, **dragon**, and **undead**. Others indicate that a creature is made up of or strongly linked to a certain type of elemental force: **air**, **cold**, **earth**, **fire**, or **water**. Monsters can have more than one keyword.

If the monster's name doesn't include its race, the race is added after the monster's type and keywords. For example, the snaketongue assassin is categorized as a "Medium natural humanoid (shapechanger), human."

Experience Points (XP)

This entry gives the experience point award for defeating the monster.

Initiative

The monster's initiative modifier appears here.

Senses

Every monster has a Perception check modifier. Some monsters also have special senses that allow them to detect enemies in unusual situations, such as darkvision or tremorsense; these are defined in the glossary.

Aura

An aura is a passive ability that takes effect when another creature comes within a certain distance of the monster. Not all monsters have auras. For more information on auras, see the glossary.

Hit Points (HP)

Damage a monster takes is subtracted from its hit points.

HP: The monster's total hit points.

Bloodied: Half the monster's total hit points. If the monster's current hit points are equal to or less than this value, the monster is considered bloodied.

Defenses

This line of the monster's statistics block lists the monster's Armor Class (**AC**) and its **Fortitude**, **Reflex**, and **Will** defenses.

Immune/Resist/ Vulnerable

This line appears if certain attacks have reduced or increased effects against the monster.

Saving Throws

If the monster has a bonus to saving throws, that entry appears above its speed entry.

Speed

This is the number of squares the monster can move with a single move action. Alternative movement modes, such as fly, climb, or swim, are listed as well.

Action Points

Elite and solo monsters have action points they can use to take extra actions, just as PCs do. If a monster has action points, it is noted here. Unlike PCs, a monster can spend more than one action point in a single encounter, but like PCs, they can't spend one in a surprise round.

ATTACK POWERS

Attack powers are presented so that basic attacks appear first, followed by the monster's other powers.

TYPE

Each power has an icon that indicates what type of attack it is: **melee** (✦), **ranged** (↗), **close** (↔), or **area** (✹).

Basic Attack: The first attack presented is always the monster's basic attack (usually a melee attack). Some monsters have several basic attacks. A basic attack has a circle around its icon: **melee basic attack** (✦) or **ranged basic attack** (↗).

Monsters use their basic attacks when making opportunity attacks or when using powers that allow a basic attack.

ACTION

This states the kind of action required to use the power: **standard**, **move**, **minor**, **immediate interrupt**, **immediate reaction**, or **free**. Most immediate actions trigger on a specific event, which is described following the action type.

Some powers, especially secondary effects that trigger when the main power hits, do not have an action type. They take place as part of the action required for the main attack, or they simply occur in response to a trigger.

Sustain: The monster can sustain the power's effect until the start of its next turn, usually as a standard or minor action. If the power requires an attack roll, the attack must succeed before the monster can sustain the power.

RECHARGE

Some powers can be used only once in a given encounter. Others recharge during the encounter, allowing the monster to use them again.

At-will: The monster can use an at-will power as often as it wants.

Encounter: The power can be used once per encounter and recharges after a short rest.

Daily: The power can be used only once per day and recharges after an extended rest.

Recharge ⚀ ⚁ ⚂ ⚃ ⚄: The power has a random chance of recharging during each round of combat. At the start of the monster's turn, roll 1d6. If the roll is one of the die results shown, the power is recharged and the monster can use it again that turn. The power also recharges after a short rest.

Recharges when . . . : The power recharges under a specific circumstance, such as when the monster is first bloodied, when it bloodies a foe, and so forth. The power also recharges after a short rest.

KEYWORD(S)

Certain powers have one or more keywords. Monsters and characters might have a special immunity, resistance, or vulnerability to attacks with a particular keyword, such as fire or poison. Attack power keywords are described in the glossary.

REACH

If the monster has an unusual reach, its melee attack entries include a reach number.

RANGE, AREA, OR TARGETS

Ranged, close, and area attacks specify a range and area of effect in squares. Any kind of attack power might specify targets.

ATTACK BONUS

This is the modifier to the d20 die roll when the monster attacks. Some powers are automatic hits.

TARGET DEFENSE

An attack targets AC, Fortitude, Reflex, or Will. Powers that grant a benefit to allies do not attack a defense.

EFFECT

This section describes what happens if the attack hits.

The most common result of a hit is damage, which occurs instantaneously. Many powers also produce conditions or ongoing damage. These effects might end when the affected creature makes a successful saving throw ("save ends") or have a stated duration. Typical durations are until the end of the attacking creature's next turn or until the end of the encounter.

Some powers deal damage that combines two or more damage types. The target must have resistance or immunity to all the specified damage types to reduce or ignore all the damage.

MISS

Sometimes a power has a reduced effect on a miss; this is stated after the main effect.

SECONDARY ATTACK/AFTEREFFECT

Sometimes when a power hits, it triggers a secondary attack. A few powers have effects that grow worse each time a saving throw is failed, or that have lingering aftereffects even after a successful saving throw. Such effects work the same way as those produced by PCs' powers; see the *Player's Handbook* for more information.

ALIGNMENT

A monster's alignment is not rigid, and exceptions can exist to the general rule. Chapter 2 of the *Player's Handbook* contains detailed information on the various alignments.

SKILLS

This line shows only trained skills or skills in which the monster has a racial bonus. A monster's Perception score appears elsewhere in its statistics and isn't repeated here.

ABILITY SCORES

This section shows the monster's six ability scores, presented so that each vertical pair contributes to one of the three defenses (Fortitude, Reflex, and Will). Following each score in parentheses is the adjusted ability score modifier including one-half the monster's level, which is useful whenever the monster needs to make an untrained skill check or an ability check.

HEALING SURGES

Monsters, like PCs, have healing surges. However, few monsters have a power that lets them spend a healing surge. The number of healing surges a monster has is based on its level: 1–10, one healing surge; 11–20, two healing surges; 21 or higher, three healing surges.

Because they rarely come into play, healing surges are not included in a monster's statistics block.

ABOLETHS ARE HULKING AMPHIBIOUS CREATURES that hail from the Far Realm, a distant and unfathomable plane. They live in the Underdark, swimming through drowned crannies or creeping through lightless tunnels and leaving trails of slimy mucus in their wake. Malevolent and vile, aboleths bend humanoid creatures to their will, and more powerful aboleths can transform their minions into slimy horrors.

Aboleth Lasher	Level 17 Brute
Large aberrant magical beast (aquatic)	XP 1,600

Initiative +11   **Senses** Perception +14; darkvision
Mucus Haze aura 5; enemies treat the area within the aura as difficult terrain.
HP 200; **Bloodied** 100
AC 29; **Fortitude** 27, **Reflex** 25, **Will** 25
Speed 5, swim 10
⊕ **Tentacle** (standard; at-will)
   Reach 2; +20 vs. AC; 2d8 + 8 damage (4d8 + 8 damage against a dazed target), and the target is dazed (save ends).
Combat Advantage
   An aboleth lasher makes an extra tentacle attack against any enemy it has combat advantage against.
Alignment Evil   **Languages** Deep Speech, telepathy 20
Skills Arcana +19, Dungeoneering +19, Insight +19
Str 26 (+16)   **Dex** 16 (+11)   **Wis** 22 (+14)
Con 20 (+13)   **Int** 23 (+14)   **Cha** 17 (+11)

ABOLETH LASHER TACTICS

The aboleth lasher relies on its *mucus haze* to hinder its opponents' movement while simultaneously using it to gain combat advantage with its allies. Once it covers an enemy with slime, it uses its tentacles to flay the hapless creature to death.

Aboleth Slime Mage	Level 17 Artillery (Leader)
Large aberrant magical beast (aquatic)	XP 1,600

Initiative +11   **Senses** Perception +15; darkvision
Mucus Haze aura 5; enemies treat the area within the aura as difficult terrain.
HP 128; **Bloodied** 64
AC 31; **Fortitude** 28, **Reflex** 28, **Will** 29
Speed 5, swim 10
⊕ **Tentacle** (standard; at-will)
   Reach 2; +19 vs. AC; 1d8 + 6 damage (3d8 + 6 damage against a dazed target), and the target is dazed (save ends).
⌁ **Slime Orb** (standard; at-will) ✦ **Psychic**
   Ranged 10; +22 vs. Reflex; 2d8 + 7 psychic damage, and the target is slowed (save ends).
⌁ **Dominate** (standard; at-will) ✦ **Charm**
   Ranged 10; targets a dazed humanoid; +20 vs. Will; the target is dominated (save ends). An aboleth slime mage can dominate only one creature at a time.
✴ **Slime Burst** (standard; encounter) ✦ **Psychic**
   Area burst 4 within 10; targets enemies; +17 vs. Reflex; 2d8 + 7 psychic damage, and the target is immobilized (save ends). *Aftereffect:* The target is slowed (save ends).
Alignment Evil   **Languages** Deep Speech, telepathy 20
Skills Arcana +19, Dungeoneering +20, Insight +20
Str 23 (+14)   **Dex** 16 (+11)   **Wis** 25 (+15)
Con 20 (+13)   **Int** 23 (+14)   **Cha** 20 (+13)

ABOLETH SLIME MAGE TACTICS

An aboleth slime mage prefers to have its underlings fight for it. When pressed into combat, it relies on its *mucus haze* to keep opponents away while it blasts them with ranged attacks. It uses *slime orb* and *slime burst* to slow its enemies' approach and tries to dominate one of them as soon as possible.

Aboleth Overseer	Level 18 Elite Controller (Leader)
Large aberrant magical beast (aquatic)	XP 4,000

Initiative +12   **Senses** Perception +16; darkvision
Mucus Haze aura 5; enemies treat the area within the aura as difficult terrain.
HP 348; **Bloodied** 174
AC 35; **Fortitude** 33, **Reflex** 31, **Will** 33
Saving Throws +2
Speed 5, swim 10
Action Points 1
⊕ **Tentacle** (standard; at-will)
   Reach 2; +22 vs. AC; 1d8 + 8 damage (3d8 + 8 damage against a dazed target), and the target is dazed (save ends).
↞ **Psychic Slime** (standard; recharges when first bloodied) ✦ **Psychic**
   Close burst 10; targets enemies; +20 vs. Will; 2d8 + 8 psychic damage, and the target is dazed (save ends).
⌁ **Dominate** (standard; at-will) ✦ **Charm**
   Ranged 10; targets a dazed humanoid; +20 vs. Will; the target is dominated (save ends). An aboleth overseer can dominate only one creature at a time.
⌁ **Enslave** (standard; at-will) ✦ **Charm, Psychic**
   Ranged 5; targets a dominated creature; +20 vs. Will; 6d8 + 8 psychic damage. A target reduced to 0 hit points or fewer by this attack doesn't die but becomes enslaved in preparation for the Aboleth Servitor ritual. Enslaved targets are dominated, and only the death of the overseer can end this domination. Once a creature is enslaved, an aboleth overseer is free to dominate other creatures.
Invisibility (minor; encounter) ✦ **Illusion**
   The aboleth overseer and one ally within 10 squares of it turn invisible until the end of the aboleth overseer's next turn.
Alignment Evil   **Languages** Deep Speech, telepathy 20
Skills Arcana +20, Dungeoneering +21, Insight +21
Str 26 (+17)   **Dex** 16 (+12)   **Wis** 25 (+16)
Con 22 (+15)   **Int** 23 (+15)   **Cha** 22 (+15)

ABOLETH OVERSEER TACTICS

An aboleth overseer uses *psychic slime* to hinder its enemies and then selects a target to dominate, preferably one that is greatly injured so that it can use its *enslave* ability on the creature. The overseer then forces the enslaved creature to fight its former allies while it attempts to dominate others.

ABOLETH LORE

A character knows the following information with a successful Dungeoneering check.

DC 20: Aboleths lair in the deepest reaches of the Underdark, having slipped into the world from the Far Realm. However, lone aboleths can be found closer to the world's surface, haunting ruins, deep lakes, and old temples without hope or want of companionship. In many of these places, kuo-toas serve them.

DC 25: Aboleths communicate via telepathy. They can speak and understand Deep Speech.

An aboleth overseer and its aboleth servitors

DC 30: Sometimes aboleths live together as a brood or even in a collection of broods. Aboleth overseers also populate their lairs with humanoids that they've enslaved and transformed into slimy minions.

ABOLETH SERVITOR

A HUMANOID IS TRANSFORMED INTO AN ABOLETH SERVITOR by way of a ritual. When a creature transforms into an aboleth servitor, its skin becomes a clear, slimy membrane that allows it to swim and breathe in water.

Aboleth Servitor	Level 16 Minion
Medium aberrant humanoid (aquatic)	XP 350

Initiative +10 **Senses** Perception +8; darkvision
HP 1; a missed attack never damages a minion.
AC 30; **Fortitude** 28, **Reflex** 23, **Will** 21
Speed 6, swim 6
⊕ **Slam** (standard; at-will)
  +19 vs. AC; 7 damage.
Aboleth Devotion
  An aboleth servitor gains a +2 bonus to attack rolls against enemies in an aboleth's *mucus haze* aura. If an aboleth servitor is ever more than 10 squares from its aboleth master, the servitor becomes dazed, weakened, and immobilized until its master moves within 10 squares of it.
Alignment Unaligned **Languages** Common
Str 24 (+15) **Dex** 15 (+10) **Wis** 10 (+8)
Con 20 (+13) **Int** 10 (+8) **Cha** 10 (+8)

ABOLETH SERVITOR TACTICS

The servitor remains within 10 squares of its aboleth master and exists only to protect its master from harm.

ENCOUNTER GROUPS

Kuo-toas serve aboleths willingly, but powerful aboleths also fashion servitors from dominated and defeated foes.

Level 17 Encounter (XP 7,950)
✦ 1 aboleth slime mage (level 17 artillery)
✦ 2 aboleth lashers (level 17 brute)
✦ 9 kuo-toa guards (level 16 minion)

Level 18 Encounter (XP 10,200)
✦ 1 aboleth overseer (level 18 controller)
✦ 1 nabassu gargoyle (level 18 lurker)
✦ 1 savage minotaur (level 16 brute)
✦ 8 aboleth servitors (level 16 minion)

ABOMINATION

ABOMINATIONS ARE LIVING WEAPONS that were created during the ancient cosmic war between the gods and the primordials. Some of these creations were enormous, others small. Some were singular beings of terrific power, while others were legion. A few abominations stand apart as failed or incomplete divine experiments that have either been locked away or forgotten.

ASTRAL STALKER

DEVIOUS AND BATTLE-HUNGRY HUNTERS, astral stalkers savor challenge and renown. Many of them serve as assassins and bounty hunters, and an astral stalker might pursue its quarry simply to test its mettle against a worthy foe.

Astral Stalker		Level 22 Elite Lurker
Medium immortal humanoid		XP 8,300

Initiative +23   **Senses** Perception +18; blindsight 10
HP 314; **Bloodied** 157
AC 38; **Fortitude** 32, **Reflex** 38, **Will** 32
Saving Throws +2
Speed 10, climb 6
Action Points 1

⊕ **Claw** (standard; at-will)
    +27 vs. AC; 2d6 + 8 damage, and the astral stalker can choose to designate the target as its quarry (see *stalker's quarry*).

⊗ **Throat Dart** (standard; at-will) ✦ **Poison**
    Ranged 5/10; +29 vs. AC; 1d10 + 8 damage, and the target takes ongoing 5 poison damage and is slowed (save ends both). *First Failed Save:* The target is immobilized instead of slowed (save ends). *Second Failed Save:* The target is stunned instead of immobilized (save ends).

✝ **Quick Claws** (standard; at-will)
    Against a slowed or an immobilized target, the astral stalker makes two claw attacks.

Combat Advantage
    The astral stalker's melee attacks deal an extra 2d6 damage against any target it has combat advantage against.

Invisibility (standard; at-will) ✦ **Illusion**
    The astral stalker turns invisible until it attacks.

Stalker's Quarry (minor; at-will)
    The astral stalker knows the exact location of a creature it has designated as its quarry. The astral stalker can have only one quarry at a time, but the power works across any distance and even crosses planar boundaries.

Alignment Evil	**Languages** Supernal	
Skills Stealth +24		
Str 22 (+17)	**Dex** 26 (+19)	**Wis** 15 (+13)
Con 19 (+15)	**Int** 8 (+10)	**Cha** 10 (+11)

ASTRAL STALKER TACTICS

An astral stalker relies on its *invisibility* and stealth to catch prey by surprise. It has poisonous bone darts in its throat that it can eject with deadly accuracy. It uses these darts to disorient and incapacitate enemies. Once one or more foes are slowed or immobilized, the stalker lunges into melee and uses its *quick claws* ability against its chosen quarry. If its quarry shakes off the darts' debilitating effects, the stalker retreats and turns invisible again, returning to ranged attacks and repeating the same strategy.

ASTRAL STALKER LORE

A character knows the following information with a successful Religion check.

    DC 25: Although created as instruments of the gods in their war against the primordials, astral stalkers survive still. They're now a race unto themselves, inhabiting the Astral Sea. Astral stalkers gather in small tribes, and leadership of a tribe falls to the astral stalker with the best hunting trophies.

ENCOUNTER GROUPS

Astral stalkers often hunt in pairs or small groups if they seek particularly elusive game. They have also been known to sell their services to other beings.

Level 22 Encounter (XP 21,400)
✦ 1 astral stalker (level 22 elite lurker)
✦ 2 war devils (level 22 brute)
✦ 6 legion devil legionnaires (level 21 minion)

ATROPAL

ATROPALS ARE CALAMITOUS BEINGS scorned by life. They now exist only to bring destruction and despair to everything around them.

ATROPAL LORE

A character knows the following information with a successful Religion check.

    DC 25: Atropals are unfinished godlings that had enough of a divine spark to rise as undead. A few atropals roam freely across the planes, while others are sealed away in separate realms or buried beneath the ruins of dead civilizations.

ENCOUNTER GROUPS

An atropal gathers undead to it and might have a squad of abyssal ghouls or vampire spawn at its disposal. Vampire lords, liches, and dracoliches all have reason to value an atropal ally.

WAYNE REYNOLDS

Level 28 Encounter (XP 70,000)
- ✦ 1 atropal (level 28 elite brute)
- ✦ 2 sorrowsworn reapers (level 27 soldier)
- ✦ 2 shadowraven swarms (level 27 brute)

Atropal	Level 28 Elite Brute
Large immortal magical beast (undead)	XP 26,000

Initiative +18   **Senses** Perception +20; darkvision

Shroud of Death (Necrotic) aura 5; at the beginning of the atropal's turn, undead allies within the aura regain 20 hit points, and living creatures in the aura take 10 necrotic damage. Radiant damage to the atropal ends its *shroud of death*. The atropal can restore the aura as a minor action.

HP 634; **Bloodied** 317

AC 42; **Fortitude** 42, **Reflex** 37, **Will** 40

Immune disease, necrotic, poison; **Vulnerable** 10 radiant

Saving Throws +2

Speed fly 9 (hover)

Action Points 1; see also *atropos burst*

ⓐ **Necrotizing Touch** (standard; at-will) ✦ **Necrotic**

    Reach 2; +29 vs. Reflex; 2d10 + 10 damage, and the target takes ongoing 15 necrotic damage and a -2 penalty to attack rolls, and the target loses any resistance or immunity to necrotic damage (save ends all).

⟳ **Atropos Burst** (standard; recharges when a living creature drops to 0 hit points within the atropal's aura) ✦ **Necrotic**

    Close burst 5; +27 vs. Reflex; 4d8 + 5 necrotic damage, and the target loses 1 healing surge. The atropal gains 1 action point if it hits any creatures with *atropos burst*.

Alignment Evil   **Languages** Supernal

Skills Insight +25, Religion +19

Str 30 (+24)	**Dex** 18 (+18)	**Wis** 22 (+20)
Con 27 (+22)	**Int** 10 (+14)	**Cha** 20 (+19)

ATROPAL TACTICS

An atropal floats toward living creatures and tries to envelop as many of them as it can with its *shroud of death* aura. It relies on its hit points and speed to outlast and outmaneuver its opponents. Once surrounded, it uses *atropos burst* and then spends an action point to make a *necrotizing touch* against the most wounded creature. It continues to attack this foe with its *necrotizing touch*, hoping to slay the creature and recharge its *atropos burst*.

BLOOD FIEND

VICIOUS, BLOODTHIRSTY PREDATORS, blood fiends have a countenance so terrifying that they can stop other creatures in their tracks with a baleful glare. They have keen senses and hunt anything for food or sport.

BLOOD FIEND LORE

A character knows the following information with a successful Arcana check.

    DC 25: Blood fiends are feral killers that feed on the blood of living creatures. Although they originated in the Elemental Chaos, they can be found just about any place where living prey is plentiful.

ENCOUNTER GROUPS

Blood fiends travel in packs. They also find common ground with mighty elementals, such as efreets and demons, and forces of death, such as death giants.

Level 23 Encounter (XP 25,500)
- ✦ 3 blood fiends (level 23 soldier)
- ✦ 1 efreet cinderlord (level 23 artillery)
- ✦ 1 efreet flamestrider (level 23 skirmisher)

Blood Fiend	Level 23 Soldier
Medium elemental humanoid	XP 5,100

Initiative +21   **Senses** Perception +23; darkvision
HP 220; **Bloodied** 110
AC 41; **Fortitude** 36, **Reflex** 34, **Will** 32
Immune fear
Speed 8, fly 10

⊕ **Claws** (standard; at-will)
  +28 vs. AC; 2d8 + 10 damage.

† **Bloodthirsty Bite** (standard; at-will) ✦ **Healing**
  Requires combat advantage; +28 vs. AC; 1d8 + 10 damage, and the target is grabbed and takes ongoing 10 damage (until escape). Also, the blood fiend regains 10 hit points.

↞ **Terror Gaze** (minor; at-will) ✦ **Fear**
  Close blast 3; +24 vs. Will; the target is immobilized (save ends).

Combat Advantage
  The blood fiend gains combat advantage against any living, bloodied enemy.

Alignment Chaotic evil   **Languages** Primordial
Skills Intimidate +24

Str 30 (+21)	**Dex** 26 (+19)	**Wis** 24 (+18)
Con 28 (+20)	**Int** 22 (+17)	**Cha** 27 (+19)

BLOOD FIEND TACTICS

A blood fiend uses its *terror gaze* at the beginning of each round, attempting to immobilize foes. It then turns its attention to a weak foe, tearing it to pieces with its sharp talons. The creature relentlessly attacks one foe until its prey is dead and it can select a new target.

Blood fiends are fearless adversaries and do not flee under any circumstances.

PHANE

PHANES CAN MANIPULATE TIME, which they use to sow chaos among mortals. Occasionally they form pacts with powerful beings that share their destructive propensities.

Consisting of coalescent mist, this creature has the lower body of a hunting cat and the torso, arms, and head of a humanoid. The air ripples around the creature, and though it moves with feline grace, it seems as though it can barely hold itself together.

PHANE TACTICS

A phane uses its great speed to stay out of range of opponents while targeting them with *wizening ray*. If forced into close combat, a phane uses either its *temporal touch* or *wizening tempest* to slow or stun enemies so it can withdraw safely and attack from a distance.

PHANE LORE

A character knows the following information with a successful Religion check.

DC 25: Phanes are native to the Astral Sea, but they are found throughout the cosmos, walking the space between moments, ever on the hunt for prey.

ENCOUNTER GROUPS

Phanes aren't choosy about their allies. Legend tells of them working with sorrowsworn, nightwalkers, powerful demons and devils, and mighty fey.

Level 26 Encounter (XP 46,000)
- ✦ 1 phane (level 26 elite controller)
- ✦ 2 sorrowsworn soulrippers (level 25 skirmisher)
- ✦ 2 dread wraiths (level 25 lurker)

CHRIS STEVENS AND KEVIN YAN/IZZY MEDRANO

Phane — Level 26 Elite Controller

Phane	Level 26 Elite Controller
Large immortal magical beast	XP 18,000

Initiative +23   **Senses** Perception +25; darkvision

HP 478; **Bloodied** 239

AC 41; **Fortitude** 38, **Reflex** 41, **Will** 38

Resist insubstantial

Saving Throws +2

Speed 10, fly 10

Action Points 1

⊕ **Temporal Touch** (standard; at-will)

Reach 2; +29 vs. Reflex; 2d8 + 10 damage, and the target is slowed until the end of the phane's next turn. The phane shifts 4 squares before or after making this attack.

↗ **Wizening Ray** (standard; at-will)

Ranged 10; +29 vs. Fortitude; 2d6 + 9 damage, and the target is dazed and weakened (save ends both). *Aftereffect:* The target is weakened (save ends). The target appears elderly until the effects of the *wizening ray* end.

↙ **Wizening Tempest** (standard, usable only while bloodied; at-will)

Close burst 1; phanes are immune; +29 vs. Fortitude; 2d6 + 10 damage, and the target is stunned (save ends). *Aftereffect:* The target is dazed and weakened (save ends both). The target appears elderly until the effects of the *wizening tempest* end.

Temporal Fugue (minor; at-will)

By moving backward and forward in time, a phane can remove one effect afflicting it.

Alignment Unaligned		**Languages** Supernal
Str 24 (+20)	**Dex** 30 (+23)	**Wis** 25 (+20)
Con 23 (+19)	**Int** 28 (+22)	**Cha** 22 (+19)

TARRASQUE

A TERRIFYING EMBODIMENT OF WANTON DESTRUCTION, the tarrasque attacks without motivation or purpose—unless that purpose is to obliterate all life.

TARRASQUE TACTICS

The tarrasque tramples enemies as it wades into battle. It uses *fury of the tarrasque* as often as it can, alternating between *rend-ing bite* and *tail slap* until bloodied, then using *frenzy*. Not one to conserve its power, the tarrasque spends its action points in the opening rounds of combat to make additional attacks.

TARRASQUE LORE

A character knows the following information with a successful Arcana check.

DC 25: The tarrasque is a living engine of destruction created by the primordials to obliterate the works of the gods. It sleeps within the world's core, stirring occasionally. When it wakes, it burrows up to the surface and begins a continent-wide rampage.

DC 30: The tarrasque is inexorably bound to the world, such that the most one can hope for is to lay the creature to rest, forcing it to sleep within the world's core for many years before it stirs again. However, ancient texts postulate that the tarrasque could be destroyed permanently were it somehow coaxed or tricked into leaving the world.

Tarrasque — Level 30 Solo Brute

Tarrasque	Level 30 Solo Brute
Gargantuan elemental magical beast	XP 95,000

Initiative +23   **Senses** Perception +19; blindsight 20

Earthbinding aura 40; any flying creature in the aura has its fly speed reduced to 1 and maximum altitude reduced to 20 feet (putting it within the tarrasque's reach). Any creature above this altitude at the end of its turn falls to an altitude of 20 feet automatically.

HP 1,420; **Bloodied** 710

AC 43; **Fortitude** 49, **Reflex** 38, **Will** 32

Immune charm, fear; **Resist** 10 to all damage

Saving Throws +5

Speed 8, burrow 8, climb 8

Action Points 2

Elder of Annihilation

The tarrasque's attacks ignore all resistances.

⊕ **Bite** (standard; at-will)

Reach 3; +34 vs. AC; 1d12 + 16 damage, and ongoing 15 damage (save ends).

✦ **Fury of the Tarrasque** (standard, not usable while bloodied; recharge ⚄ ⚅)

The tarrasque makes a bite attack and one of the following attacks:

  ✦ **Rending Bite:** reach 3; +34 vs. AC; 3d12 + 16 damage, plus the target takes a -5 penalty to AC until the end of the tarrasque's next turn.

  ✦ **Tail Slap:** reach 3; cannot use against the same target it attacked with its bite; +32 vs. Fortitude; 3d12 + 16 damage, plus the target is pushed 4 squares and knocked prone.

✦ **Trample** (standard; at-will)

The tarrasque can move up to its speed and enter enemies' spaces. This movement provokes opportunity attacks, and the tarrasque must end its move in an unoccupied space. When it enters an enemy's space, the tarrasque makes a trample attack: +33 vs. Reflex; 1d12 + 16 damage, and the target is knocked prone.

↙ **Frenzy** (standard, usable only while bloodied; at-will)

Close burst 3; the tarrasque makes a bite attack against each creature within the burst.

Eternal Slumber

When the tarrasque is reduced to 0 hit points, it sinks back into the world's core and slumbers once again.

Alignment Unaligned		**Languages** –
Str 42 (+31)	**Dex** 26 (+23)	**Wis** 18 (+19)
Con 36 (+28)	**Int** 3 (+11)	**Cha** 7 (+13)

ARNIE SWEKEL

Most deities have angel servants. Although their appearances can vary, all angels are vaguely humanoid in form, with masculine or feminine features and lower bodies that trail off into flowing energy.

Angels exist as expressions of the Astral Sea, sentient energy in humanoid form. They most often serve the gods, so some believe that the gods created them. In reality, angels are powerful astral beings who appeared during the first moments of the creation of the Astral Sea. Different types of angels have different callings; they are literally manifestations of celestial vocations. Perhaps it was the needs of the gods that caused the astral stuff to spew them forth, but it was not a conscious act of creation. During the great war between the gods and the primordials, angels offered themselves as warriors to the gods that best encompassed their callings, and today they continue to act as mercenary forces for anyone willing to meet their price—be it wealth, or power, or a cause worthy of their attention.

Angels are more involved in the world and other planes than deities and exarchs. They act both openly and secretly, often acting as emissaries, generals, and even assassins.

ANGEL OF BATTLE

Angels of battle command angels of valor, but they also lead cadres of mortals in combat.

Angel of Battle	Level 15 Skirmisher (Leader)
Large immortal humanoid (angel)	XP 1,200

Initiative +13   **Senses** Perception +11

Angelic Presence Attacks against the angel of battle take a -2 penalty unless the angel is bloodied.

HP 296; **Bloodied** 148

AC 29; **Fortitude** 27, **Reflex** 25, **Will** 28

Immune fear; **Resist** 10 radiant

Speed 8, fly 12 (hover); see also *mobile melee attack* and *storm of blades*

⊕ **Falchion** (standard; at-will) ✦ **Weapon**

    Reach 2; +21 vs. AC; 1d10 + 5 damage (crit 2d10 + 16).

↓ **Mobile Melee Attack** (standard; at-will)

    An angel of battle can move up to half its speed and make one melee basic attack at any point during that movement. The angel doesn't provoke opportunity attacks when moving away from the target of its attack.

✤ **Storm of Blades** (standard; encounter)

    Razor-sharp blades explode from the angel's wings. Close burst 3; +19 vs. AC; 6d8 + 7 damage. After using this ability, the angel of battle has a fly speed of 2 (hover) until the end of the encounter.

Chosen Foe (free, after making a falchion attack; at-will)

    Once during its turn, an angel of battle can illuminate an enemy it hits with a falchion attack, bathing the enemy in light as bright as a torch and granting the angel's allies combat advantage against that enemy until the start of the angel's next turn.

Alignment Any	**Languages** Supernal	
Skills Intimidate +19		
Str 23 (+13)	**Dex** 19 (+11)	**Wis** 18 (+11)
Con 20 (+12)	**Int** 15 (+9)	**Cha** 25 (+14)

Equipment falchion

ANGEL OF BATTLE TACTICS

An angel of battle employs a combination of airborne and ground-based tactics. Against tough adversaries, the angel uses *chosen foe* and takes to the air, using its reach to stay out of melee attack range. The angel reserves *storm of blades* for the end of battle, when it believes it will no longer need to fly, either because death or victory is imminent.

ANGEL OF BATTLE LORE

A character knows the following information with a successful Religion check.

DC 20: As their name implies, angels of battle lead forces into combat. More powerful than angels of valor, angels of battle fulfill a similar function but are called upon to fight greater threats.

DC 25: When a god sends an angel of battle to tend to a situation, it's unlikely the god desires to deliver a message or negotiate. Angels of battle are harbingers for war.

ENCOUNTER GROUPS

A typical encounter includes one angel of battle supported by two angels of protection and several angel of valor minions. Angels of battle also act as leaders in mixed groups of devout creatures in the service of a god.

Level 15 Encounter (XP 6,000)
✦ 1 angel of battle (level 15 skirmisher)
✦ 2 angels of protection (level 14 soldier)
✦ 8 angel of valor veterans (level 16 minion)

ANGEL OF PROTECTION

ANGELS OF PROTECTION SERVE AS BODYGUARDS for important persons and others who summon them. They also guard temples and other sites tied to the deities they serve.

Angel of Protection	Level 14 Soldier
Medium immortal humanoid (angel)	XP 1,000

Initiative +12   **Senses** Perception +11

Angelic Presence Attacks against the angel of protection take a -2 penalty until the angel is bloodied.

Angelic Shield aura 5; enemies treat the area within the aura as difficult terrain as long as the angel's *angelic presence* is active and the angel is within 5 squares of its ward (see below).

HP 141; **Bloodied** 70

AC 30; **Fortitude** 26, **Reflex** 24, **Will** 25

Immune fear; **Resist** 10 radiant

Speed 6, fly 8 (hover)

ⓐ **Greatsword** (standard; at-will) ✦ **Radiant, Weapon**
+19 vs. AC; 1d10 + 6 damage plus 5 radiant damage.

Ward (standard; at-will)
An angel of protection designates a creature within 5 squares of it as its ward. When the angel is within 5 squares of its ward, the ward takes only half damage from melee and ranged attacks; the angel of protection takes the rest. While the angel is adjacent to its ward, the ward gains a +2 bonus to AC. A creature can be the ward of only one angel of protection at a time. If multiple angels designate the same creature as their ward, it becomes the ward of the last angel that designated it as so.

Alignment Any	**Languages** Supernal

Skills Insight +16, Intimidate +14

Str 22 (+13)	**Dex** 17 (+10)	**Wis** 19 (+11)
Con 21 (+12)	**Int** 12 (+8)	**Cha** 14 (+9)

Equipment plate armor, greatsword

ANGEL OF PROTECTION TACTICS

An angel of protection guards its chosen or appointed ward faithfully. Barring dire circumstances, the angel stays within 5 squares of its ward (preferably adjacent to it) and remains there until the ward dies (at which point the angel either designates another ward or, lacking another creature to protect, fights until slain).

ANGEL OF PROTECTION LORE

A character knows the following information with a successful Religion check.

DC 20: An angel of protection never steps outside the role of guardian and caretaker. Its ward is often chosen for it, either by its god or by the one who summons it. It is said that no angel of protection has ever left its ward except by being killed in that ward's defense.

DC 25: Normally, only a god or powerful servitor of a god can assign duties to an angel of protection. Sometimes, simple prayer is enough to gain such protection for a brief period. If such a prayer is ever answered, it is important that the recipient be careful not to use the angel's talents in a way that fails to serve its true master.

ENCOUNTER GROUPS

A typical encounter might include one angel of protection and its ward, or three or four angels of protection plus the creatures in their care.

Level 14 Encounter (XP 5,200)
✦ 2 angels of protection (level 14 soldier)
✦ 1 eidolon (level 13 controller)
✦ 3 dragonborn raiders (level 13 skirmisher)

ANGEL OF VALOR

ANGELS OF VALOR, THOUGH COURAGEOUS AND FIERCE, are the weakest and the most numerous of angels called to serve a given deity.

Angel of Valor		Level 8 Soldier
Medium immortal humanoid (angel)		XP 350

Initiative +10 **Senses** Perception +6
Angelic Presence Attacks against the angel of valor take a -2 penalty until the angel is bloodied.
HP 88; **Bloodied** 44
AC 24; **Fortitude** 22, **Reflex** 20, **Will** 19
Immune fear; **Resist** 10 fire, 10 radiant
Speed 6, fly 9 (hover)
⊕ **Longsword** (standard; at-will) ✦ **Weapon**
  +13 vs. AC; 1d8 + 6 damage.
⊣ **Dagger** (standard; at-will) ✦ **Weapon**
  +13 vs. AC; 1d4 + 6 damage.
⊣ **Blade Flurry** (standard; at-will) ✦ **Weapon**
  The angel of valor makes a longsword attack and a dagger attack.
⟻ **Lightning Strike** (standard; encounter) ✦ **Lightning**
  Close burst 1; targets enemies; +11 vs. Fortitude; 1d8 + 4 lightning damage, and the target is dazed until the end of the angel of valor's next turn.
Fiery Blades (minor, usable only while bloodied; at-will) ✦ **Fire**
  Until the start of the angel of valor's next turn, the angel of valor's weapons deal fire damage and attack the target's Reflex defense instead of AC.
Alignment Any **Languages** Supernal
Skills Intimidate +12

Str 23 (+10)	**Dex** 18 (+8)	**Wis** 14 (+6)
Con 16 (+7)	**Int** 11 (+4)	**Cha** 16 (+7)

Equipment chainmail, longsword, dagger

Angel of Valor Cohort		Level 11 Minion
Medium immortal humanoid (angel)		XP 150

Initiative +9 **Senses** Perception +7
HP 1; a missed attack never damages a minion.
AC 25; **Fortitude** 25, **Reflex** 23, **Will** 22
Immune fear; **Resist** 10 fire, 10 radiant
Speed 6, fly 9 (hover)
⊕ **Greatsword** (standard; at-will) ✦ **Fire, Weapon**
  +16 vs. AC; 6 fire damage.
Alignment Any **Languages** Supernal

Str 23 (+11)	**Dex** 18 (+9)	**Wis** 14 (+7)
Con 16 (+8)	**Int** 11 (+5)	**Cha** 16 (+8)

Equipment chainmail, greatsword

Angel of Valor Veteran		Level 16 Minion
Medium immortal humanoid (angel)		XP 350

Initiative +12 **Senses** Perception +10
HP 1; a missed attack never damages a minion.
AC 30; **Fortitude** 30, **Reflex** 27, **Will** 26
Immune fear; **Resist** 10 fire, 10 radiant
Speed 6, fly 9 (hover)
⊕ **Greatsword** (standard; at-will) ✦ **Fire, Weapon**
  +21 vs. AC; 7 fire damage.
Alignment Any **Languages** Supernal

Str 24 (+15)	**Dex** 18 (+12)	**Wis** 14 (+10)
Con 18 (+12)	**Int** 12 (+9)	**Cha** 16 (+11)

Equipment chainmail, greatsword

Angel of Valor Legionnaire		Level 21 Minion
Medium immortal humanoid (angel)		XP 800

Initiative +14 **Senses** Perception +12
HP 1; a missed attack never damages a minion.
AC 35; **Fortitude** 35, **Reflex** 31, **Will** 30
Immune fear; **Resist** 10 fire, 10 radiant
Speed 6, fly 9 (hover)
⊕ **Greatsword** (standard; at-will) ✦ **Fire, Weapon**
  +26 vs. AC; 9 fire damage.
Alignment Any **Languages** Supernal

Str 26 (+18)	**Dex** 18 (+14)	**Wis** 14 (+12)
Con 18 (+14)	**Int** 12 (+11)	**Cha** 16 (+13)

Equipment chainmail, greatsword

ANGEL OF VALOR TACTICS

Angels of valor employ straightforward melee tactics, wading into the fray and making use of a combination of basic attacks and powers. Angels of valor collaborate well with others of their kind, flanking enemies and concentrating their attacks on the most powerful opponent.

ANGEL OF VALOR LORE

A character knows the following information with a successful Religion check.

  DC 15: Angels of valor are the soldiers of the gods, serving in vast armies and following the commands of mortal priests or more powerful angels. When a cleric needs numbers to get the job done, angels of valor offer the best aid.

DC 20: When a devout worshiper of a particular god does something to delight that god, such as showing valor in the god's name, an angel of valor might be dispatched to reward the worshiper. An appropriate reward might include a magic item or even the service of the angel of valor for 10 days.

ENCOUNTER GROUPS
Angels of valor fill out mixed groups of creatures in the service of a particular god or a powerful cleric.

Level 8 Encounter (XP 1,700)
✦ 2 angels of valor (level 8 soldier)
✦ 1 shadar-kai warrior (level 8 soldier)
✦ 1 doppelganger assassin (level 8 lurker)
✦ 1 shadar-kai witch (level 7 controller)

Level 11 Encounter (XP 3,350)
✦ 4 angel of valor cohorts (level 11 minion)
✦ 2 stone-eye basilisks (level 12 soldier)
✦ 1 snaketongue celebrant (level 11 controller)
✦ 6 snaketongue zealots (level 12 minion)

ANGEL OF VENGEANCE
ANGELS OF VENGEANCE STRIKE DOWN THOSE who wrong a deity. They also punish disloyalty and failure among the devout.

Angel of Vengeance	Level 19 Elite Brute
Large immortal humanoid (angel)	XP 4,800

Initiative +13   **Senses** Perception +16
HP 446; **Bloodied** 223
AC 34; **Fortitude** 33, **Reflex** 29, **Will** 33; see also *cloak of vengeance*
Immune disease, fear; **Resist** 15 cold, 15 fire, 15 radiant; see also *coldfire pillar*
Saving Throws +2
Speed 8, fly 12 (hover); see also *sign of vengeance*
Action Points 1
⚔ **Longsword** (standard; at-will) ✦ **Cold, Fire, Weapon**
   Reach 2; +25 vs. AC; 1d10 + 9 damage plus 1d8 fire damage plus 1d8 cold damage.
‡ **Double Attack** (standard; at-will) ✦ **Cold, Fire, Weapon**
   The angel of vengeance makes two longsword attacks.
⤴ **Sign of Vengeance** (minor; encounter) ✦ **Teleportation**
   Ranged sight; the angel of vengeance places an invisible sign upon the target. Until the end of the encounter, as a move action, the angel can teleport adjacent to the target.
⟵ **Coldfire Pillar** (free, when first bloodied; encounter) ✦ **Cold, Fire, Polymorph**
   The angel transforms into a 30-foot-high pillar of blue flame. Close burst 2; +23 vs. Reflex; 1d8 + 9 cold damage plus 1d8 + 9 fire damage. The angel of vengeance is immune to all damage until the start of its next turn.
Cloak of Vengeance (until bloodied) ✦ **Cold, Fire**
   Attacks against the angel of vengeance take a -2 penalty until the angel is bloodied. While *cloak of vengeance* is in effect, a creature that makes a successful melee attack against the angel takes 1d8 fire damage and 1d8 cold damage.
Alignment Any   **Languages** Supernal
Skills Insight +21, Intimidate +22
Str 27 (+17)   **Dex** 18 (+13)   **Wis** 25 (+16)
Con 23 (+15)   **Int** 19 (+13)   **Cha** 26 (+17)
Equipment plate armor, 2 longswords

ANGEL OF VENGEANCE TACTICS
An angel of vengeance focuses on a single target. It evokes its *sign of vengeance* at the start of battle, then teleports to the target and spends an action point to use *double attack* against the foe. The angel continues its relentless pursuit of the target, paying little heed to events around it.

ANGEL OF VENGEANCE LORE
A character knows the following information with a successful Religion check.

DC 20: Deities send angels of vengeance to punish those who have defied or angered them. A god might also send an angel of vengeance to test one who is in danger of falling off the deity's path, showing no mercy for failure.

DC 25: Influential members of a clergy use a ritual to call forth their deity's wrath in the form of one of these angels.

ENCOUNTER GROUPS
Angels of vengeance appear alone or in pairs, sometimes aided by angels of valor or angels of battle.

Level 19 Encounter (XP 13,600)
✦ 2 angels of vengeance (level 19 elite brute)
✦ 5 angel of valor legionnaires (level 21 minion)

ARCHON

ARCHONS ARE MILITARISTIC CREATURES native to the Elemental Chaos. Vaguely humanoid in form, they serve powerful primordial entities as well as various elemental lords and princelings.

Archons trace back to an ancient time when the world had hardly been formed, when primordial beings battled the gods for control of creation. In this cataclysmic conflict, the deities marshaled armies of angels and cadres of exarchs, and though the primordials could call forth titanic beasts and giants, they could not muster a true military to face their enemies until they found the means by which elemental creatures could be reshaped and hammered into soldiers. The warriors formed through this process were the first archons.

Two kinds of archons are presented here: fire archons and ice archons. These soldiers are bent on returning the world to the rule and whim of the primordials, and fire archons and ice archons have no issues working together to achieve their common goal.

(Left to right) fire archon ash disciple, emberguard, and blazesteel

FIRE ARCHON EMBERGUARD

FIRE ARCHON EMBERGUARDS SERVE AS GUARDIANS in temples, tombs, and other locations with strong ties to the elements (fire in particular). They also guard portals leading to the Elemental Chaos and serve as infantry in elemental armies.

Fire Archon Emberguard		Level 12 Brute
Medium elemental humanoid (fire)		XP 700

Initiative +12   **Senses** Perception +13
Ember Cloud (Fire) aura 1; any creature that begins its turn in the aura takes 5 fire damage.
HP 151; **Bloodied** 75
AC 24; **Fortitude** 21, **Reflex** 22, **Will** 18
Immune disease, poison; **Resist** 30 fire
Speed 8
⊕ **Greataxe** (standard; at-will) ✦ **Fire, Weapon**
    +13 vs. AC; 1d12 + 3 damage (crit 2d12 + 15) plus 1d10 fire damage.
↯ **Immolating Strike** (standard; recharge ⚁ ⚂ ⚃) ✦ **Fire, Weapon**
    Requires greataxe; +13 vs. AC; 1d12 + 3 damage (crit 2d12 + 15) plus 1d10 fire damage, and ongoing 5 fire damage (save ends).
Alignment Chaotic evil   **Languages** Primordial
| **Str** 17 (+9) | **Dex** 22 (+12) | **Wis** 14 (+8) |
| **Con** 21 (+11) | **Int** 14 (+8) | **Cha** 12 (+7) |
Equipment plate armor, greataxe

FIRE ARCHON EMBERGUARD TACTICS

Emberguards prefer to wade into melee combat, hacking enemies with their greataxes, saving their *immolating strike* for particularly irksome foes.

EMBERGUARD LORE

A character knows the following information with a successful Arcana check.

DC 20: Emberguards protect temples, tombs, and other locations where fire is prevalent.

DC 25: A cloud of embers surrounds the emberguard, burning foes that get too close.

ABOUT ARCHONS

The archons presented here are but a small sampling of the archons that exist. In addition to a multitude of fire archons and ice archons, the Elemental Chaos is home to archons composed of (or combining) other elements as well. Air archons, earth archons, and water archons are commonplace, but one doesn't have to travel far in the Elemental Chaos to find crystal archons, slime archons, and storm archons.

Archons of different elements freely associate with one another, although bereft of strong leadership they are prone to infighting. A typical archon army is a jumble of many different kinds of archons, just as the Elemental Chaos is a jumble of many different elements and energy types.

When an archon dies, all that remains is its armor, and sometimes its weapons. Some archons, such as ice archons, wield weapons that melt away when the archon dies.

JIM NELSON

FIRE ARCHON BLAZESTEEL

ILL-TEMPERED AND EASILY PROVOKED, archon blazesteels serve as shock troopers in elemental armies. They are also employed as bodyguards by powerful efreets and fire titans.

Fire Archon Blazesteel	Level 19 Soldier
Medium elemental humanoid (fire)	XP 2,400

Initiative +18   **Senses** Perception +12
HP 182; **Bloodied** 91; see also *wounded fireburst*
AC 35; **Fortitude** 33, **Reflex** 32, **Will** 28
Immune disease, poison; **Resist** 30 fire
Speed 8

ⓐ **Scimitar** (standard; at-will) ✦ **Fire, Weapon**
+25 vs. AC; 1d8 + 8 damage (crit 2d8 + 16) plus 1d8 fire damage, and the target is marked until the end of the blazesteel's next turn.

↺ **Wounded Fireburst** (when first bloodied and again when the blazesteel is reduced to 0 hit points) ✦ **Fire**
Close burst 2; +21 vs. Reflex; 10 fire damage, and ongoing 5 fire damage (save ends).

Combat Advantage ✦ **Fire**
The blazesteel makes a single extra scimitar attack and deals an extra 1d8 fire damage against any enemy it has combat advantage against.

Alignment Chaotic evil	**Languages** Primordial	
Str 26 (+17)	**Dex** 24 (+16)	**Wis** 16 (+12)
Con 22 (+15)	**Int** 14 (+11)	**Cha** 15 (+11)

Equipment plate armor, scimitar

FIRE ARCHON BLAZESTEEL TACTICS

Blazesteels try to close ranks around an enemy and gain the extra attack through combat advantage and deal extra damage from flanking. Tough and resilient warriors, they become more emboldened once they are bloodied, using *wounded fireburst* to ignite their enemies in flames.

BLAZESTEEL LORE

A character knows the following information with a successful Arcana check.

DC 20: Blazesteels like to concentrate their attacks on singular foes, flanking whenever possible.

DC 25: When a fire archon blazesteel is bloodied, it unleashes a burst of searing flame. It also gains its fiery revenge by unleashing a similar burst when slain.

FIRE ARCHON ASH DISCIPLE

FIRE ARCHON ASH DISCIPLES BELIEVE IN THE PURITY OF FLAME and dream of the day when fire immolates and cleanses the world.

Fire Archon Ash Disciple	Level 20 Artillery
Medium elemental humanoid (fire)	XP 2,800

Initiative +18   **Senses** Perception +13
HP 150; **Bloodied** 75; see also *death embers*
AC 33; **Fortitude** 33, **Reflex** 34, **Will** 29
Immune disease, poison; **Resist** 30 fire
Speed 8; see also *flame step*

ⓐ **Flaming Fist** (standard; at-will) ✦ **Fire**
+20 vs. Reflex; 1d8 + 5 fire damage, and ongoing 5 fire damage (save ends).

✻ **Rain of Fire** (standard; encounter) ✦ **Fire**
Area burst 1 within 10; +23 vs. Reflex; 2d8 + 8 fire damage, and ongoing 5 fire damage (save ends). *Miss:* Half damage, and no ongoing damage.

↺ **Flame Wave** (standard; encounter) ✦ **Fire**
Close blast 5; +23 vs. Reflex; 2d8 + 8 fire damage, and the target is pushed 2 squares and takes ongoing 10 fire damage (save ends).

↺ **Cinder Burst** (standard; encounter) ✦ **Fire**
Close burst 5; +23 vs. Fortitude; 2d8 + 8 fire damage, and the target is blinded (save ends).

↺ **Death Embers** (when reduced to 0 hit points) ✦ **Fire**
As the effect of *cinder burst*. The ash disciple is consumed in the burst, leaving only its metallic robes behind.

Flame Step (move; at-will) ✦ **Teleportation**
The ash disciple can teleport to within 3 squares of any fire creature within 20 squares of it.

Alignment Chaotic evil	**Languages** Primordial	
Str 20 (+15)	**Dex** 27 (+18)	**Wis** 16 (+13)
Con 24 (+17)	**Int** 14 (+12)	**Cha** 15 (+12)

Equipment scale armor (metal robes)

FIRE ARCHON ASH DISCIPLE TACTICS

An ash disciple uses *rain of fire* against distant targets, and then uses *flame step* to position itself where it can unleash a *flame wave* or *cinder burst*. Once bloodied, the ash disciple tries to get close to its enemies so that it catches as many of them as possible with *death embers*.

ASH DISCIPLE LORE

A character knows the following information with a successful Arcana check.

DC 20: The presence of one or more ash disciples can have a sympathetic and noticeable effect on local weather patterns, including prolonged heat waves and droughts.

DC 25: An ash disciple can hurl fire, unleash pounding waves of heat, and engulf its enemies in a blinding cloud of cinders. It explodes in a burst of fiery embers when slain.

ICE ARCHON HAILSCOURGE

This archon hurls shards of ice and besieges foes with storms of fist-sized hailstones.

DESCRIPTION

The hailscourge wears ice armor but carries no weapons. It conjures blades of ice similar in shape to shuriken and hurls them at distant enemies.

Ice Archon Hailscourge	Level 16 Artillery
Medium elemental humanoid (cold)	XP 1,400

Initiative +11 **Senses** Perception +10
HP 120; **Bloodied** 60
AC 30; **Fortitude** 28, **Reflex** 27, **Will** 26
Immune disease, poison; **Resist** 20 cold
Speed 6 (ice walk)
(♦) **Slam** (standard; at-will) ✦ **Cold**
   +19 vs. AC; 1d6 + 4 cold damage.
(➵) **Ice Shuriken** (standard; at-will) ✦ **Cold**
   Ranged 6/12; +21 vs. AC; 1d6 + 4 damage plus 1d6 cold damage.
➵ **Double Attack** (standard; at-will) ✦ **Cold**
   The ice archon hailscourge makes two *ice shuriken* attacks.
✵ **Hail Storm** (standard; recharge ⚄ ⚅) ✦ **Cold**
   Area burst 1, 2, 3, or 4 within 20; +21 vs. AC; 2d8 + 4 cold damage. *Miss:* Half damage. The ice archon hailscourge determines the exact burst radius of the *hail storm*.
Frost Shield (immediate interrupt, when attacked by a ranged, a close, or an area attack; encounter) ✦ **Cold**
   The ice archon hailscourge gains resist 20 to all damage against the triggering attack.

Alignment Chaotic evil   **Languages** Primordial
Str 18 (+12)   **Dex** 16 (+11)   **Wis** 14 (+10)
Con 18 (+12)   **Int** 14 (+10)   **Cha** 15 (+10)
Equipment plate armor

ICE ARCHON HAILSCOURGE TACTICS

The ice archon hailscourge unleashes its *hail storm* as often as it can, reducing the storm's radius as needed to avoid harming its allies. While it waits for this power to recharge, it hurls *ice shuriken* at its enemies.

HAILSCOURGE LORE

A character knows the following information with a successful Arcana check.

DC 20: A hailscourge prefers ranged combat over melee combat. Hailscourges serve as artillery in elemental armies.

DC 25: The ice archon hailscourge pummels its enemies with fist-sized chunks of ice that rain down from above. It can also conjure and hurl jagged shards of ice resembling shuriken.

ICE ARCHON RIMEHAMMER

Ice archon rimehammers make fine enforcers and are often used as bodyguards by powerful elemental beings. They are not blindingly loyal, however, and they abandon their masters if treated poorly.

Ice Archon Rimehammer	Level 19 Soldier
Medium elemental humanoid (cold)	XP 2,400

Initiative +15   **Senses** Perception +12
Icy Ground (Cold) aura 1; enemies treat the area within the aura as difficult terrain.
HP 185; **Bloodied** 92
AC 35; **Fortitude** 35, **Reflex** 32, **Will** 31
Immune disease, poison; **Resist** 30 cold
Speed 6 (ice walk)
(♦) **Maul** (standard; at-will) ✦ **Cold, Weapon**
   +25 vs. AC; 2d6 + 7 damage plus 1d6 cold damage, and the target is slowed (save ends). Against a slowed target, the rimehammer deals an extra 2d6 cold damage.

Alignment Chaotic evil   **Languages** Primordial
Str 24 (+16)   **Dex** 18 (+13)   **Wis** 16 (+12)
Con 25 (+16)   **Int** 14 (+11)   **Cha** 15 (+11)
Equipment plate armor, maul

ICE ARCHON RIMEHAMMER TACTICS

This archon uses its *icy ground* aura to hinder foes that are trying to flank it. It otherwise engages in melee, using its maul to slow enemies and the *icy ground* to hinder their movement even further.

RIMEHAMMER LORE

A character knows the following information with a successful Arcana check.

DC 20: The ice archon rimehammer takes its name from the icy maul it wields. The weapon is so numbingly cold that those it strikes are barely able to walk.

DC 25: These archons are usually found in the service of frost giants, ice archon frostshapers, and similar creatures. However, they have been known to serve other creatures with ties to the Elemental Chaos, including such unlikely masters as efreets and fire giants.

ICE ARCHON FROSTSHAPER

As heartless and merciless as a winter storm, the ice archon frostshaper seeks to turn the world into a frigid wasteland. The creature can conjure ice out of thin air and shape it to serve its whims.

Ice Archon Frostshaper	Level 20 Controller (Leader)
Medium elemental humanoid (cold)	XP 2,800

Initiative +14   **Senses** Perception +14
Icy Aura (Cold) aura 5 (not active while bloodied); cold creatures in the aura gain regeneration 10. Enemies treat the area within the aura as difficult terrain.
HP 190; **Bloodied** 95
AC 34; **Fortitude** 32, **Reflex** 28, **Will** 32
Immune disease, poison; **Resist** 30 cold
Speed 6 (ice walk)
(↓) **Ice Blade** (standard; at-will) ✦ **Cold, Weapon**
    +23 vs. AC; 2d6 + 8 cold damage.
(➶) **Ice Javelin** (standard; at-will) ✦ **Cold, Weapon**
    Ranged 5; +23 vs. AC; 2d6 + 8 cold damage, plus the target is slowed until the end of the frostshaper's next turn.
(❄) **Icy Burst** (standard; recharges when the frostshaper hits with a melee attack) ✦ **Cold**
    Area burst 1 within 5; +23 vs. AC; 3d8 + 8 cold damage, plus the target is slowed (save ends). *Miss:* Half damage, and the target is not slowed.
Alignment Chaotic evil   **Languages** Primordial
Skills Intimidate +23
Str 26 (+18)   **Dex** 19 (+14)   **Wis** 18 (+14)
Con 22 (+16)   **Int** 14 (+12)   **Cha** 27 (+18)

ICE ARCHON FROSTSHAPER TACTICS

The ice archon frostshaper relies on its *icy aura* to hinder enemies. It begins battle by closing to within 5 squares of foes so it can unleash an *icy burst* and make its enemies suffer the combined effects of slow and difficult terrain. The frostshaper follows up with basic attacks until one of these is successful, at which point it uses *icy burst* again.

FROSTSHAPER LORE

A character knows the following information with a successful Arcana check.

DC 20: Jagged shards of ice crystallize on the ground around the ice archon frostshaper, making it hard for enemies to reach it.

DC 25: A frostshaper often retains the services of one or more ice archon rimehammers, using them as bodyguards and enforcers. A very powerful elemental being or primordial might have a frostshaper advisor or even frostshaper commanders leading their armies.

ARCHON ENCOUNTER GROUPS

Archons work with elemental creatures of all types, and they have no aversion to working with creatures not of their element. For example, it's not unheard of for an efreet to have a contingent of ice archon mercenaries among their other soldiers.

(Top to bottom) ice archon frostshaper and rimehammer

Level 12 Encounter (XP 3,600)
✦ 2 fire archon emberguards (level 12 brute)
✦ 1 beholder eye of flame (level 13 elite artillery)
✦ 1 firelasher elemental (level 11 skirmisher)

Level 18 Encounter (XP 10,800)
✦ 2 ice archon hailscourges (level 16 artillery)
✦ 1 elder white dragon (level 17 solo brute)

Level 19 Encounter (XP 13,200)
✦ 1 ice archon frostshaper (level 20 controller)
✦ 2 ice archon rimehammers (level 19 soldier)
✦ 2 rimefire griffons (level 20 skirmisher)

Level 21 Encounter (XP 17,100)
✦ 2 ice archon frostshapers (level 20 controller)
✦ 1 efreet flamestrider (level 23 skirmisher)
✦ 1 fire titan (level 21 elite soldier)

JIM NELSON

These fire-infused dwarves often serve fire giants or fire titans, either out of obedience or devotion. However, some azers live free and pursue their own goals, for good or evil.

AZER LORE

A character knows the following information with a successful Arcana check.

DC 15: Long ago, all dwarves were slaves to the giants and titans. Today's dwarves are the descendants of those who freed themselves. Azers are dwarves that did not escape captivity before they were corrupted and transformed into fiery beings by their overlords. Although a few have escaped captivity since, most azers remain bound to their fire giant masters to this day.

Azer foot soldier

ENCOUNTER GROUPS

Azers work with other fire creatures as well as nonelemental creatures. In fire giant strongholds, azers perform menial tasks better suited to smaller hands, and they act as a front line in defense.

Level 14 Encounter (XP 5,000)
- 2 azer foot soldiers (level 14 soldier)
- 2 salamander lancers (level 14 brute)
- 1 salamander firetail (level 14 skirmisher)

Level 15 Encounter (XP 6,050)
- 6 azer warriors (level 17 minion)
- 2 azer ragers (level 15 brute)
- 1 immolith demon (level 15 controller)

Level 17 Encounter (XP 8,000)
- 1 azer taskmaster (level 17 controller)
- 1 azer beastlord (level 17 soldier)
- 8 azer warriors (level 17 minion)
- 1 firebred hell hound (level 17 brute)

Azer Warrior		**Level 17 Minion**
Medium elemental humanoid (fire)		XP 400

Initiative +11   **Senses** Perception +12
Warding Flame (**Fire**) Any enemy adjacent to two or more azers at the start of its turn takes 5 fire damage.
HP 1; a missed attack never damages a minion.
AC 31; **Fortitude** 30, **Reflex** 26, **Will** 27
Resist 20 fire
Speed 5
⚔ **Warhammer** (standard; at-will) ✦ **Fire, Weapon**
    +20 vs. AC; 7 fire damage, and ongoing 3 fire damage (save ends).

Alignment Unaligned	**Languages** Giant	
Str 21 (+13)	**Dex** 17 (+11)	**Wis** 18 (+12)
Con 23 (+14)	**Int** 11 (+8)	**Cha** 16 (+11)

Equipment chainmail, light shield, warhammer

AZER WARRIOR TACTICS

Azer warriors try to surround enemies and scorch them with their *warding flame*.

Azer Foot Soldier		**Level 14 Soldier**
Medium elemental humanoid (fire)		XP 1,000

Initiative +12   **Senses** Perception +11
Warding Flame (**Fire**) Any enemy adjacent to two or more azers at the start of its turn takes 5 fire damage.
HP 141; **Bloodied** 70
AC 30; **Fortitude** 28, **Reflex** 26, **Will** 27
Resist 30 fire
Speed 5
⚔ **Warhammer** (standard; at-will) ✦ **Fire, Weapon**
    +20 vs. AC; 1d10 + 4 damage plus 1d8 fire damage, and the target is marked until the end of the azer foot soldier's next turn.

Alignment Unaligned	**Languages** Giant	
Str 19 (+11)	**Dex** 16 (+10)	**Wis** 18 (+11)
Con 21 (+12)	**Int** 11 (+7)	**Cha** 15 (+9)

Equipment scale armor, light shield, warhammer

AZER FOOT SOLDIER TACTICS

These azers maneuver to flank their foes, gaining the benefits of their *warding flame* power in addition to combat advantage.

Azer Rager		**Level 15 Brute**
Medium elemental humanoid (fire)		XP 1,200

Initiative +9   **Senses** Perception +9
Warding Flame (**Fire**) Any enemy adjacent to two or more azers at the start of its turn takes 5 fire damage.
HP 181; **Bloodied** 90
AC 27; **Fortitude** 28, **Reflex** 25, **Will** 24
Immune fear; **Resist** 30 fire
Speed 6
⚔ **Spiked Gauntlet** (standard; at-will) ✦ **Fire, Weapon**
    +18 vs. AC; 1d6 + 6 damage, and ongoing 5 fire damage (save ends).
↫ **Chains of Flame** (standard, usable only while bloodied; encounter) ✦ **Fire**
    Close burst 5; +17 vs. Reflex; 3d8 + 5 fire damage. Enemies adjacent to an azer or with ongoing fire damage are immobilized until the end of the azer rager's next turn.

Alignment Unaligned	**Languages** Giant	
Str 22 (+13)	**Dex** 15 (+9)	**Wis** 14 (+9)
Con 21 (+12)	**Int** 11 (+7)	**Cha** 15 (+9)

Equipment scale armor, spiked gauntlets

Azer Rager Tactics

An azer rager attacks foes with its spiked gauntlets wreathed in fire. Once bloodied, it lets loose a furious howl and uses *chains of flame*.

Azer Taskmaster		Level 17 Controller (Leader)
Medium elemental humanoid (fire)		XP 1,600

Initiative +12   **Senses** Perception +14
Warding Flame (Fire) Any enemy adjacent to two or more azers at the start of its turn takes 5 fire damage.
HP 165; **Bloodied** 82
AC 31; **Fortitude** 28, **Reflex** 27, **Will** 29
Resist 30 fire
Speed 5
⊕ **Scourge** (standard; at-will) ✦ **Fire, Weapon**
     +22 vs. AC; 1d6 + 5 damage plus 2d6 fire damage.
Clinging Flames (immediate reaction, when an enemy within 5 squares of the azer taskmaster takes fire damage; at-will) ✦ **Fire**
     The enemy takes ongoing 5 fire damage (save ends).

Alignment Unaligned	**Languages** Giant	
Str 20 (+13)	**Dex** 18 (+12)	**Wis** 22 (+14)
Con 21 (+13)	**Int** 14 (+10)	**Cha** 16 (+11)

Equipment chainmail, scourge

Azer Taskmaster Tactics

The azer taskmaster uses *clinging flames* and orders its servants into battle. Beyond that, it is a capable fighter that lashes foes with its flaming scourge.

Azer Beastlord		Level 17 Soldier (Leader)
Medium elemental humanoid (fire)		XP 1,600

Initiative +13   **Senses** Perception +12
Warding Flame (Fire) Any enemy adjacent to two or more azers at the start of its turn takes 5 fire damage.
HP 167; **Bloodied** 83
AC 32; **Fortitude** 31, **Reflex** 28, **Will** 29
Resist 30 fire
Speed 5
⊕ **Battleaxe** (standard; at-will) ✦ **Fire, Weapon**
     +22 vs. AC; 1d10 + 5 damage plus 1d8 fire damage, and the target is marked until the end of the azer beastlord's next turn.
On My Command (standard; encounter)
     Each allied elemental beast within 5 squares of the azer beastlord makes a basic attack as a free action, provided the elemental beast is flanking an enemy and can both see and hear the azer beastlord.
Spur the Beast (minor; at-will)
     One allied elemental beast within 5 squares of the azer beastlord recharges an encounter or daily power of the beastlord's choice.

Alignment Unaligned	**Languages** Giant	
Str 21 (+13)	**Dex** 17 (+11)	**Wis** 18 (+12)
Con 23 (+14)	**Int** 11 (+8)	**Cha** 16 (+11)

Equipment chainmail, light shield, battleaxe

Azer Beastlord Tactics

An azer beastlord is rarely encountered without elemental beasts of its level or lower. The beastlord waits until its charges are locked in battle before joining the fray, helping the beasts maneuver into flanking positions so that it can take advantage of its *on my command* power.

(Left to right) azer beastlord, azer taskmaster, and azer rager

FRANZ VOHWINKEL (2)

23

BALHANNOTH

A cunning subterranean hunter, the balhannoth distorts nearby reality with its very presence.

Balhannoth	Level 13 Elite Lurker
Large aberrant magical beast (blind)	XP 1,600

Initiative +18 **Senses** Perception +16; blindsight 10
HP 216; **Bloodied** 108
AC 28; **Fortitude** 27, **Reflex** 26, **Will** 24
Immune gaze, illusion
Saving Throws +2
Speed 4, climb 4 (spider climb); see also *reality shift*
Action Points 1
⊕ **Tentacle** (standard; at-will)
    Reach 3; +17 vs. AC; 1d8 + 9 damage.
↺ **Whipping Tentacles** (standard; at-will)
    Close burst 3; targets enemies; +17 vs. AC; 1d8 + 9 damage, and the target slides to any other square of the balhannoth's choosing within the burst area.
Combat Advantage
    The balhannoth deals an extra 2d8 damage against any target it has combat advantage against.
Invisibility (minor; at-will) ✦ **Illusion**
    The balhannoth can turn invisible until the end of its next turn. It turns visible if it takes a standard action.
Reality Shift (move; at-will) ✦ **Teleportation**
    The balhannoth can teleport 10 squares. Enemies adjacent to the balhannoth before it teleports are dazed until the end of its next turn. The balhannoth automatically gains combat advantage against creatures it teleports adjacent to.

Alignment Chaotic evil **Languages** Deep Speech
Skills Stealth +19
Str 29 (+15) **Dex** 27 (+14) **Wis** 20 (+11)
Con 24 (+13) **Int** 3 (+2) **Cha** 8 (+5)

BALHANNOTH TACTICS

The balhannoth is opportunistic and sometimes waits for hours in ambush or stalks prey across many miles. Once it decides to attack, the balhannoth uses *reality shift* to teleport adjacent to its prey and uses its *whipping tentacles* to pull some enemies closer while pushing others back. It continues to use *reality shift* in subsequent rounds, dazing enemies that get too close and teleporting to more advantageous locations.

BALHANNOTH LORE

A character knows the following information with a successful Dungeoneering check.

DC 20: In the deep earth, a balhannoth travels along ceilings and across rocky formations. It comes to the ground only to kill prey, doing so by teleporting to within striking distance of its quarry.

DC 25: Balhannoths rarely assemble in large groups. They have no society, but they can be found among other sentient species living in the Underdark.

DC 30: Balhannoths don't make sounds or otherwise verbally communicate. They locate prey through some form of extrasensory perception. A trained balhannoth responds to spoken commands, but balhannoths react most favorably to creatures that communicate using telepathy.

ENCOUNTER GROUPS

An indiscriminate predator, a balhannoth hunts alone or with another of its kind. No creature is safe in a balhannoth's hunting grounds.

Some Underdark races capture and train balhannoths. A wild balhannoth can be subdued and tamed only by a creature that has telepathy, such as an aboleth or a mind flayer. Otherwise, the creature must be raised from birth to accept a master. Kuo-toas commonly raise balhannoths in this way, while drow, grimlocks, and minotaur cabalists do so less often.

Level 13 Encounter (XP 4,000)
✦ 1 balhannoth (level 13 elite lurker)
✦ 3 grimlock berserkers (level 13 brute)

Level 13 Encounter (XP 4,200)
✦ 1 balhannoth (level 13 elite lurker)
✦ 2 kuo-toa marauders (level 12 skirmisher)
✦ 2 kuo-toa harpooners (level 14 soldier)

BANSHRAE

Banshraes are sly fey with insectlike features that view humans and similar creatures as objects of amusement and sources of wealth. The kindest banshrae is an impish trickster, while the worst is a terrifying, bloodthirsty killer that toys with victims before slaying them.

Banshrae Dartswarmer		Level 11 Artillery
Medium fey humanoid		XP 600

Initiative +11   **Senses** Perception +7; low-light vision
HP 89; **Bloodied** 44
AC 23; **Fortitude** 20, **Reflex** 23, **Will** 22
Speed 8
⊕ **Slam** (standard; at-will)
+13 vs. AC; 1d8 + 3 damage.
↗ **Blowgun Dart** (standard; at-will) ✦ **Weapon**
Ranged 5/10; +16 vs. AC; 1d10 + 6 damage, and the target is dazed and takes a -2 penalty to attack rolls (save ends both).
↞ **Dart Flurry** (standard; recharge ⚄ ⚅ ⚁) ✦ **Weapon**
Close blast 5; +16 vs. AC; 1d10 + 6 damage, plus the target is dazed and takes a -2 penalty to attack rolls (save ends both).
Alignment Unaligned   **Languages** telepathy 20
Str 16 (+8)   **Dex** 22 (+11)   **Wis** 15 (+7)
Con 17 (+8)   **Int** 14 (+7)   **Cha** 20 (+10)
Equipment blowgun, darts

Banshrae Dartswarmer Tactics

This creature avoids melee, preferring to fire darts from its blowgun or catch multiple foes in a *dart flurry*.

Banshrae Warrior		Level 12 Skirmisher
Medium fey humanoid		XP 700

Initiative +14   **Senses** Perception +8; low-light vision
HP 121; **Bloodied** 60
AC 26; **Fortitude** 22, **Reflex** 24, **Will** 22
Speed 8
⊕ **Slam** (standard; at-will)
+17 vs. AC; 1d8 + 4 damage.
† **Staggering Palm** (standard; recharges after the use of *mantid dance*)
+17 vs. AC; 2d8 + 4 damage, plus the target is stunned until the end of the banshrae warrior's next turn.
↗ **Blowgun Dart** (standard; at-will) ✦ **Weapon**
Ranged 5/10; +17 vs. AC; 1d4 + 6 damage.
Melee Agility (minor, usable immediately after hitting with a melee attack; at-will)
The banshrae warrior shifts 1 square.
Mantid Dance (move; recharge ⚄ ⚅ ⚁)
Until the end of its next turn, the banshrae warrior gains a +2 bonus to all defenses and all noncritical ranged attacks automatically miss it.
Skirmish +2d8
If, on its turn, the banshrae warrior ends its move at least 4 squares away from its starting point, it deals an extra 2d8 damage on its melee attacks until the start of its next turn.
Alignment Unaligned   **Languages** telepathy 20
Str 18 (+10)   **Dex** 23 (+12)   **Wis** 15 (+8)
Con 17 (+9)   **Int** 14 (+8)   **Cha** 20 (+11)
Equipment blowgun, darts

Banshrae Warrior Tactics

This banshrae moves like a hunting insect, using its *skirmish* ability to deal extra damage. In close combat, the warrior uses *staggering palm* and then, if its enemy is stunned, withdraws to a safer position without risking an opportunity attack. The banshrae then employs *mantid dance* to limit attackers' success at ranged attacks while recharging *staggering palm* so it can repeat the strategy.

Banshrae Lore

A character knows the following information with a successful Arcana check.

DC 20: Banshraes are cold-hearted fey with insectoid features. They do not speak, communicating only via telepathy.

DC 25: All banshraes love singing and the sound of wind instruments—although they have no way to sing or play such instruments themselves. Stories speak of murderous banshraes turned aside by a song and impish banshraes calmed by a tune.

Encounter Groups

Banshraes work with any creature willing to tolerate their sinister and egotistical inclinations. Such creatures commonly include other fey, such as ignoble eladrin, satyrs, dryads, hags, and even unicorns.

Level 12 Encounter (XP 3,900)
✦ 2 banshrae dartswarmers (level 11 artillery)
✦ 1 banshrae warrior (level 12 skirmisher)
✦ 1 ettin spirit-talker (level 12 elite controller)
✦ 1 iron gorgon (level 11 soldier)

BASILISK

Basilisks are predatory reptiles that hunt with a deadly gaze attack. They are not malicious creatures, but their gaze makes them widely feared.

Venom-Eye Basilisk		Level 10 Artillery
Large natural beast (reptile)		XP 500

Initiative +6　　**Senses** Perception +11
HP 87; **Bloodied** 43
AC 27; **Fortitude** 25, **Reflex** 22, **Will** 21
Immune poison
Speed 6

⊕ **Bite** (standard; at-will)
　　+15 vs. AC; 1d8 + 4 damage.

❊ **Venomous Gaze** (standard; at-will) ✦ **Gaze, Poison**
　　Area burst 1 within 10; +15 vs. Fortitude; 2d6 poison damage, and ongoing 5 poison damage (save ends). As long as the target is taking ongoing poison damage from this attack, the target deals 2 poison damage to all creatures adjacent to it at the start of its turn.

Alignment Unaligned　　**Languages** —
Skills Stealth +11

Str 19 (+9)	**Dex** 12 (+6)	**Wis** 13 (+6)
Con 21 (+10)	**Int** 2 (+1)	**Cha** 8 (+4)

Venom-eye Basilisk Tactics

This basilisk has a weak bite attack, but its *venomous gaze* can affect multiple creatures at once, and at quite a distance. Green mist issues from the eyes of creatures poisoned by the basilisk's gaze.

Basilisk Lore

A character knows the following information with a successful Nature check.

DC 15: Basilisks are strangely evolved drakes. As such, they can be domesticated and trained.

DC 20: The venom-eye basilisk's poisonous gaze is empowered by the beast's spirit. The creature itself isn't venomous; consequently, the venom can't be captured and used for other purposes.

DC 25: A stone-eye basilisk's jaws are so strong that it can chew up and devour creatures it has petrified with its gaze.

Stone-Eye Basilisk		Level 12 Soldier
Large natural beast (reptile)		XP 700

Initiative +9　　**Senses** Perception +13
Baleful Gaze Any creature within 5 squares of the stone-eye basilisk that attacks the basilisk is slowed until the end of its next turn. This effect doesn't rely on the target seeing the basilisk.
HP 126; **Bloodied** 63
AC 28; **Fortitude** 26, **Reflex** 22, **Will** 22
Immune petrification
Speed 4

⊕ **Bite** (standard; at-will)
　　+17 vs. AC; 2d8 + 5 damage.

⬅ **Petrifying Gaze** (standard; at-will) ✦ **Gaze**
　　Close blast 3; +17 vs. Fortitude; the target is slowed (save ends). *First Failed Save:* The target is immobilized (save ends). *Second Failed Save:* The target is petrified (no save).

Alignment Unaligned　　**Languages** —
Skills Stealth +12

Str 20 (+11)	**Dex** 12 (+7)	**Wis** 14 (+8)
Con 22 (+12)	**Int** 2 (+2)	**Cha** 8 (+5)

Stone-eye Basilisk Tactics

A stone-eye basilisk tries to affect multiple targets with its *petrifying gaze*, sometimes waiting in ambush until opponents draw close together. The creature resorts to its bite attack only against foes that consistently resist its gaze.

Encounter Groups

A small pack of wild basilisks is called a clutch. Like a wolf pack, a clutch coordinates to hunt and its members live together in a communal den. Tamed basilisks can be found among various humanoids.

Level 11 Encounter (XP 3,400)
✦ 2 venom-eye basilisks (level 10 artillery)
✦ 4 mezzodemons (level 11 soldier)

Level 12 Encounter (XP 3,700)
✦ 2 stone-eye basilisks (level 12 soldier)
✦ 1 feygrove choker (level 12 lurker)
✦ 1 briar witch dryad (level 13 elite controller)

BAT

Normal bats are innocuous wild animals that feed on mammals, insects, reptiles, or fruit. Monstrous bats, on the other hand, are fearsome predators that attack just about anything without provocation.

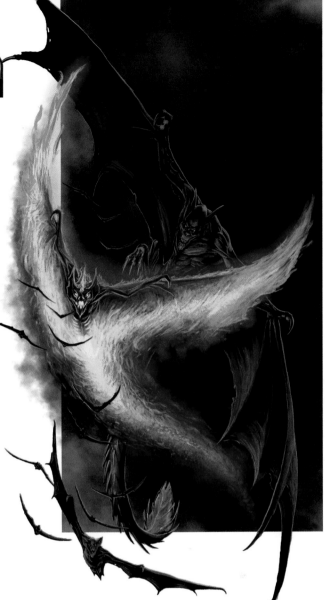

Shadowhunter Bat		Level 3 Lurker
Medium shadow beast		XP 150

Initiative +9 **Senses** Perception +7; darkvision
HP 38; **Bloodied** 19
AC 17; **Fortitude** 14, **Reflex** 17, **Will** 12
Speed 2 (clumsy), fly 8; see also *flyby attack*
(+) **Tail Slash** (standard; at-will)
  +8 vs. AC; 1d6 + 4 damage. In dim light or darkness, a shadowhunter bat gains a +2 bonus to the attack roll and deals an extra 6 damage.
╪ **Flyby Attack** (standard; at-will)
  The shadowhunter bat flies up to 8 squares and makes one melee basic attack at any point during that movement. The bat doesn't provoke opportunity attacks when moving away from the target of the attack.
Alignment Unaligned **Languages** –
Skills Stealth +10
Str 13 (+2) **Dex** 18 (+5) **Wis** 13 (+2)
Con 14 (+3) **Int** 2 (–3) **Cha** 11 (+1)

SHADOWHUNTER BAT TACTICS

A shadowhunter bat uses *flyby attack* to dart out of the shadows, strike an opponent, and move back into the shadows without taking an opportunity attack. However, it prefers to catch prey in complete darkness, where its attacks are more lethal.

Fire Bat		Level 5 Skirmisher
Medium elemental beast (fire)		XP 200

Initiative +8 **Senses** Perception +8
HP 60; **Bloodied** 30
AC 20; **Fortitude** 15, **Reflex** 20, **Will** 13
Resist 10 fire
Speed 2 (clumsy), fly 8; see also *fiery swoop*
(+) **Fiery Touch** (standard; at-will) ✦ **Fire**
  +6 vs. Reflex; 1d6 + 4 fire damage, and ongoing 5 fire damage (save ends).
╪ **Fiery Swoop** (standard; at-will) ✦ **Fire**
  The fire bat shifts up to 4 squares and can move through occupied squares as it moves. It makes a melee basic attack against any creature whose space it enters. The fire bat cannot attack a target more than once in this fashion, and it must end its movement in an unoccupied square.
Alignment Unaligned **Languages** –
Str 6 (+0) **Dex** 19 (+6) **Wis** 12 (+3)
Con 12 (+3) **Int** 2 (–2) **Cha** 7 (+0)

FIRE BAT TACTICS

Fire bats use *fiery swoop* to strike multiple targets in a round while avoiding opportunity attacks.

BAT LORE

A character knows the following information with a successful Arcana check.

DC 15: Fire bats are native to the Elemental Chaos, but they now live in the world. They can be domesticated and are often found alongside azer beastlords and other fire creatures.

DC 15: Shadowhunter bats linger near places touched by the Shadowfell. They hunt alone or in small groups, sometimes acting at the behest of other shadow creatures or undead masters.

ENCOUNTER GROUPS

Bats frequently cohabit dungeons alongside other monstrous denizens.

Level 3 Encounter (XP 750)
✦ 2 shadowhunter bats (level 3 lurker)
✦ 1 goblin hexer (level 3 controller)
✦ 2 goblin skullcleavers (level 3 brute)

BATTLEBRIAR

BATTLEBRIARS ARE DEADLY LIVING PLANTS purposefully grown to serve in military capacities. They can destroy massed formations of lesser troops, storm defended embankments, and bring down fortifications.

Warthorn Battlebriar	Level 14 Controller
Large natural animate (plant)	XP 1,000

Initiative +8   **Senses** Perception +9
Grasping Thorns aura 2; enemies treat the area within the aura as difficult terrain; at the start of the warthorn battlebriar's turn, enemies in the aura take 5 damage.
HP 141; **Bloodied** 70
AC 28; **Fortitude** 28, **Reflex** 23, **Will** 24
Speed 6
(+) **Claw** (standard; at-will)
    Reach 2; +19 vs. AC; 1d8 + 6 damage, and the target is pulled 1 square.
(<) **Thorn Burst** (standard; at-will)
    Close burst 2; +17 vs. Reflex; 2d8 + 1 damage, plus the target is slowed until the end of the warthorn battlebriar's next turn.
Threatening Reach
    A warthorn battlebriar can make opportunity attacks against all enemies within its reach (2 squares).

Alignment Unaligned	**Languages** —	
Str 23 (+13)	**Dex** 13 (+8)	**Wis** 15 (+9)
Con 21 (+12)	**Int** 3 (+3)	**Cha** 12 (+8)

WARTHORN BATTLEBRIAR TACTICS

A warthorn battlebriar moves close to foes and sprays them with a *thorn burst*. It attempts to keep foes locked in melee combat and uses its *grasping thorns* aura to hinder opponents trying to flank it or escape.

BATTLEBRIAR LORE

A character knows the following information with a successful Nature check.

DC 20: Many powerful entities use battlebriars as living siege engines. However, battlebriars sometimes escape the control of their commanders and roam as autonomous agents of destruction.

DC 25: Battlebriars don't feed like an animal might. They can survive like plants do, and thus make excellent eternal guardians.

ENCOUNTER GROUPS

Battlebriars often guard fey strongholds. Elemental creatures employ them as well, so a battlebriar might be part of a hill giant enclave.

Level 14 Encounter (XP 5,400)
✦ 1 warthorn battlebriar (level 14 controller)
✦ 2 cyclops ramblers (level 14 skirmisher)
✦ 3 hill giants (level 13 brute)

Earthrage Battlebriar	Level 28 Elite Brute
Huge elemental animate (plant)	XP 26,000

Initiative +19   **Senses** Perception +17; tremorsense 5
Grasping Vines aura 3; at the start of the battlebriar's turn, enemies in the aura are pulled 1 square.
HP 634; **Bloodied** 317
AC 42; **Fortitude** 44, **Reflex** 38, **Will** 36
Saving Throws +2
Speed 8, burrow 6
Action Points 1
(+) **Claw** (standard; at-will)
    Reach 3; +32 vs. AC; 2d12 + 11 damage, and the target is slowed until the end of the earthrage battlebriar's next turn.
(+) **Trample** (standard; at-will)
    The earthrage battlebriar can move up to its speed and enter enemies' spaces. This movement provokes opportunity attacks, and the battlebriar must end its move in an unoccupied space. When it enters an enemy's space, the battlebriar makes a trample attack: +30 vs. Reflex; 1d12 + 22 damage, and the target is knocked prone.
Threatening Reach
    The earthrage battlebriar can make opportunity attacks against all enemies within its reach (3 squares).

Alignment Unaligned	**Languages** —	
Str 32 (+25)	**Dex** 20 (+19)	**Wis** 17 (+17)
Con 27 (+22)	**Int** 3 (+10)	**Cha** 16 (+17)

EARTHRAGE BATTLEBRIAR TACTICS

This battlebriar likes to bury itself, use tremorsense to detect foes passing overhead, and erupt from the ground suddenly to catch them by surprise. On the open battlefield, it enters combat by trampling enemies, spending its action point (if necessary) to move as far as it can. It then resorts to claw attacks, using its *grasping vines* to pull enemies closer and its threatening reach to attack those who retreat.

ARNIE SWEKEL

BEAR

Even in a world filled with monsters, bears present a threat. Monstrous varieties, such as the cave bear and the dire bear, are vicious predators and territorial menaces.

Cave Bear	Level 6 Elite Brute
Medium natural beast	XP 500

Initiative +4   **Senses** Perception +5; darkvision
HP 170; **Bloodied** 85
AC 20; **Fortitude** 21, **Reflex** 17, **Will** 18
Saving Throws +2
Speed 8
Action Points 1
⊕ **Claw** (standard; at-will)
   +10 vs. AC; 1d8 + 5 damage.
↤ **Cave Bear Frenzy** (standard; recharge ⚄ ⚅)
   Close burst 1; targets enemies; +10 vs. AC; 1d8 + 5 damage.
Alignment Unaligned   **Languages** –

Str 20 (+8)	**Dex** 13 (+4)	**Wis** 14 (+5)
Con 15 (+5)	**Int** 2 (–1)	**Cha** 12 (+4)

CAVE BEAR TACTICS

The cave bear wades into combat, often beginning with a charge. The creature claws foes with reckless abandon, using *cave bear frenzy* if it's adjacent to two or more targets.

BEAR LORE

A character knows the following information with a successful Nature check.

DC 15: Bears generally live in forests and caves. Cave bears are ferocious predators that make their lairs deep underground and are accustomed to darkness. Dire bears are savage hunters that eat humanoids as readily as game animals.

DC 20: Dire bears typically maul prey with their claws or crush them to death with their thick, bestial arms.

Dire Bear	Level 11 Elite Brute
Large natural beast	XP 1,200

Initiative +8   **Senses** Perception +9
HP 276; **Bloodied** 138
AC 25; **Fortitude** 25, **Reflex** 22, **Will** 23
Saving Throws +2
Speed 8
Action Points 1
⊕ **Claw** (standard; at-will)
   Reach 2; +15 vs. AC; 2d8 + 6 damage.
† **Maul** (standard; at-will)
   The dire bear makes two claw attacks. If both claw attacks hit the same target, the dire bear makes a secondary attack against the target. *Secondary Attack:* +13 vs. AC; the target is grabbed (until escape).
† **Ursine Crush** (standard; at-will)
   The cave bear deals 4d8 + 6 damage to a grabbed creature (no attack roll required).
Alignment Unaligned   **Languages** –

Str 23 (+11)	**Dex** 16 (+8)	**Wis** 18 (+9)
Con 18 (+9)	**Int** 2 (+1)	**Cha** 16 (+8)

DIRE BEAR TACTICS

A dire bear has reach and tries to grab its prey after making a successful claw attack. Against a grabbed creature, it uses *ursine crush*. The first time it uses its *maul* attack, it spends an action point to make a second *maul* attack against the same target that round.

ENCOUNTER GROUPS

Bears are encountered alone or in small groups. Some humanoids domesticate bears as guard animals. Similarly, larger humanoids (such as hill giants and ettins) keep dire bear pets.

Level 6 Encounter (XP 1,250)
✦ 2 cave bears (level 6 elite brute)
✦ 1 bugbear strangler (level 6 lurker)

Level 11 Encounter (XP 3,050)
✦ 1 dire bear (level 11 elite brute)
✦ 1 ettin spirit-talker (level 12 elite controller)
✦ 3 ogre thugs (level 11 minion)

JIM NELSON

BEETLE

Beetles usually feed on carrion, but monstrous varieties rarely pass up a warm meal.

Fire Beetle		Level 1 Brute
Small natural beast		XP 100

Initiative +1 **Senses** Perception +0
HP 32; **Bloodied** 16
AC 13; **Fortitude** 13, **Reflex** 12, **Will** 11
Resist 10 fire
Speed 6
⊕ **Bite** (standard; at-will)
  +5 vs. AC; 2d4 + 2 damage.
⟻ **Fire Spray** (standard; recharge ⚄ ⚅) ✦ Fire
  Close blast 3; +4 vs. Reflex; 3d6 fire damage.

Alignment Unaligned	**Languages** –	
Str 14 (+2)	**Dex** 12 (+1)	**Wis** 10 (+0)
Con 12 (+1)	**Int** 1 (−5)	**Cha** 8 (−1)

Fire Beetle Tactics

A fire beetle uses its *fire spray* power if several enemies clump together; otherwise, it relies on bite attacks.

Tangler Beetle		Level 5 Controller
Large natural beast		XP 200

Initiative +2 **Senses** Perception +3; darkvision
HP 62; **Bloodied** 31
AC 19; **Fortitude** 17, **Reflex** 13, **Will** 14
Speed 6
⊕ **Bite** (standard; at-will)
  Reach 2; +10 vs. AC; 1d10 + 4 damage.
⤤ **Entangling Spittle** (standard; recharge ⚄ ⚄ ⚅)
  Ranged 5; +8 vs. Reflex; the target is immobilized (save ends).

Alignment Unaligned	**Languages** –	
Str 18 (+6)	**Dex** 10 (+2)	**Wis** 12 (+3)
Con 14 (+4)	**Int** 1 (−3)	**Cha** 8 (+1)

Tangler Beetle Tactics

The tangler beetle uses globs of entangling spittle to immobilize targets. It then uses its reach to bite immobilized prey.

Rot Scarab Swarm		Level 8 Soldier
Medium shadow beast (swarm)		XP 350

Initiative +9 **Senses** Perception +7; darkvision
Swarm Attack aura 1; the rot scarab swarm makes a basic attack as a free action against each enemy that begins its turn in the aura.
HP 88; **Bloodied** 44
AC 22; **Fortitude** 21, **Reflex** 21, **Will** 19
Resist half damage from melee and ranged attacks; **Vulnerable** 10 against close and area attacks
Speed 8, climb 8
⊕ **Swarm of Mandibles** (standard; at-will) ✦ Necrotic
  +12 vs. Reflex; 1d8 + 5 necrotic damage, and ongoing 5 necrotic damage (save ends).

Alignment Unaligned	**Languages** –	
Str 20 (+9)	**Dex** 16 (+7)	**Wis** 16 (+7)
Con 16 (+7)	**Int** 1 (−1)	**Cha** 11 (+4)

Rot Scarab Swarm Tactics

Rot scarab swarms emerge from dark hidden places to catch prey by surprise.

Beetle Lore

A character knows the following information with a successful skill check.

Nature DC 15: A fire beetle has two fiery glands that continue to glow for 1d12 hours after the beetle's death; these can be removed and used as torches.

Nature DC 15: Tangler beetle saliva is sticky enough to hold fast a giant, but it dries and loses its stickiness a few minutes after exposure to air.

Arcana DC 15: Rot scarabs gather in tombs and graveyards.

Encounter Groups

Humanoids use fire beetles and tangler beetles for light and protection, respectively. Rot scarabs inhabit the Shadowfell and places touched by death.

Level 1 Encounter (XP 500)
✦ 2 fire beetles (level 1 brute)
✦ 1 kobold slinger (level 1 artillery)
✦ 2 kobold skirmishers (level 1 skirmisher)

JIM NELSON

BEHEMOTH

A BEHEMOTH IS AN OMNIVOROUS REPTILIAN BEAST that relies on its size and ferocity to drive off or defeat its enemies.

MACETAIL BEHEMOTH

WILD MACETAIL BEHEMOTHS aggressively defend their territory, but macetail hatchlings can be domesticated for use as pack animals.

Macetail Behemoth		Level 7 Soldier
Large natural beast (reptile)		XP 300
Initiative +8	**Senses** Perception +5	
HP 82; **Bloodied** 41		
AC 23; **Fortitude** 23, **Reflex** 18, **Will** 18		
Speed 5		
⊕ **Tail Bludgeon** (standard; at-will)		
Reach 2; +14 vs. AC; 1d10 + 6 damage, and the target is marked until the end of the macetail behemoth's next turn.		
⟵ **Tail Sweep** (standard; recharge ⚄ ⚅ ⚅)		
Close burst 1; +12 vs. Reflex; 1d10 + 6 damage, and the target is knocked prone if it is Medium size or smaller.		
Alignment Unaligned	**Languages** –	
Str 22 (+9)	**Dex** 16 (+6)	**Wis** 14 (+5)
Con 18 (+7)	**Int** 2 (-1)	**Cha** 6 (+1)

MACETAIL BEHEMOTH TACTICS

A macetail behemoth charges headlong into battle, smashing foes with its tail and using *tail sweep* when it has multiple opponents adjacent to it.

BEHEMOTH LORE

A character knows the following information with a successful Nature check.

DC 15: Behemoths are notoriously ill-tempered and territorial beasts, attacking anything that intrudes upon their lairs or feeding grounds.

BLOODSPIKE BEHEMOTH

THESE ILL-TEMPERED BEHEMOTHS can be trained to pull heavy carts and siege engines, but even domesticated specimens can be difficult to control.

Bloodspike Behemoth		Level 9 Brute
Large natural beast (reptile)		XP 400
Initiative +5	**Senses** Perception +7	
HP 118; **Bloodied** 59; see also *bloodied sweep*		
AC 21; **Fortitude** 24, **Reflex** 18, **Will** 20		
Speed 5		
⊕ **Spiked Tail** (standard; at-will)		
Reach 2; +13 vs. AC; 2d6 + 7 damage, and ongoing 5 damage (save ends).		
⟵ **Tail Sweep** (standard; recharge ⚄ ⚅ ⚅)		
Close burst 1; +11 vs. Reflex; 1d8 + 7 damage, and the target is knocked prone if it is Medium size or smaller.		
⟵ **Bloodied Sweep** (free, when first bloodied; encounter)		
Close burst 1; +13 vs. Fortitude; 1d8 + 7 damage, and ongoing 5 damage (save ends).		
Alignment Unaligned	**Languages** –	
Str 24 (+11)	**Dex** 12 (+5)	**Wis** 16 (+7)
Con 18 (+8)	**Int** 2 (+0)	**Cha** 6 (+2)

BLOODSPIKE BEHEMOTH TACTICS

A bloodspike charges into battle and impales foes with its spiked tail. It panics when surrounded or bloodied, using its *tail sweep* or *bloodied sweep* to take down foes.

ENCOUNTER GROUPS

In the wild, behemoths live in small herds. Some humanoids, particularly hobgoblins and troglodytes, domesticate behemoths as war beasts.

Level 7 Encounter (XP 1,450)
- ✦ 1 macetail behemoth (level 7 soldier)
- ✦ 1 troglodyte curse chanter (level 8 controller)
- ✦ 2 troglodyte maulers (level 6 soldier)
- ✦ 1 troglodyte impaler (level 7 artillery)

Few monsters evoke greater terror than the dread beholder, an avaricious tyrant that fires terrible rays from its eyestalks.

Beholder Eye of Flame		Level 13 Elite Artillery
Large aberrant magical beast		XP 1,600

Initiative +11 **Senses** Perception +15; all-around vision, darkvision

Eyes of the Beholder aura 5; at the start of each enemy's turn, if that creature is within the aura and in the eye of flame's line of sight, the eye of flame uses one random *eye ray* power against that creature.

HP 240; **Bloodied** 102; see also *fiery burst*

AC 26; **Fortitude** 26, **Reflex** 27, **Will** 28

Saving Throws +2

Speed fly 6 (hover)

Action Points 1

⊕ **Bite** (standard; at-will)
+18 vs. AC; 2d6 damage.

⌁ **Central Eye** (minor; at-will)
Ranged 8; the target gains vulnerable 10 fire, and any attack that deals fire damage to the target also deals ongoing 5 fire damage (save ends both).

⌁ **Eye Rays** (standard; at-will) ✦ see text
The eye of flame can use up to two *eye ray* powers (chosen from the list below), at least one of which must be a *fire ray*. Each power must target a different creature. Using eye rays does not provoke opportunity attacks.
1—Fire Ray (Fire): Ranged 8; +17 vs. Reflex; 2d8 + 6 fire damage.
2—Telekinesis Ray: Ranged 8; +17 vs. Fortitude; the target slides 4 squares.
3—Fear Ray (Fear): Ranged 8; +17 vs. Will; the target moves its speed away from the eye of flame by the safest route possible and takes a -2 penalty to attack rolls (save ends).

⬳ **Fiery Burst** (when first bloodied and again when the eye of flame is reduced to 0 hit points) ✦ **Fire**
Close burst 2; +17 vs. Reflex; 2d8 + 6 fire damage.

Alignment Evil	**Languages** Deep Speech	
Str 10 (+6)	**Dex** 20 (+11)	**Wis** 19 (+10)
Con 18 (+10)	**Int** 14 (+8)	**Cha** 23 (+12)

Eye of Flame Tactics

Each round, the eye of flame targets a creature with its *central eye* power followed by a *fire ray*. It attacks another creature with either a second *fire ray* or one of its other rays.

Eye Tyrant Tactics

A beholder tries to stay close enough to use its *eyes of the beholder* power while floating out of the reach of melee attacks. Once bloodied, the beholder uses *eye ray frenzy*.

Beholder Lore

A character knows the following information with a successful Dungeoneering check.

DC 20: Eyes of flame are less egotistical than beholder eye tyrants and will work with one another. They often serve more powerful beholder masters.

DC 25: Beholder eye tyrants consider themselves to be paragons of creation, and they like to rule over "lesser" creatures. An eye tyrant's ego prevents it from getting along with others of its kind.

Beholder Eye Tyrant		Level 19 Solo Artillery
Large aberrant magical beast		XP 12,000

Initiative +16 **Senses** Perception +17; all-around vision, darkvision

Eyes of the Beholder aura 5; at the start of each enemy's turn, if that foe is within the aura and in the eye tyrant's line of sight, the eye tyrant uses one random *eye ray* power against that creature.

HP 900; **Bloodied** 450

AC 33; **Fortitude** 30, **Reflex** 32, **Will** 34

Saving Throws +5

Speed fly 4 (hover)

Action Points 2

⊕ **Bite** (standard; at-will)
+24 vs. AC; 2d6 + 1 damage.

⌁ **Central Eye** (minor; at-will)
Ranged 20; +25 vs. Will; the target is dazed until the end of the beholder's next turn.

⌁ **Eye Rays** (standard; at-will) ✦ see text
The eye tyrant can use up to two different *eye ray* powers (chosen from the list below). Each power must target a different creature. Using eye rays does not provoke opportunity attacks.
1—Searing Ray (Radiant): Ranged 10; +22 vs. Reflex; 2d8 + 9 radiant damage.
2—Withering Ray (Necrotic): Ranged 10; +22 vs. Fortitude; 1d8 + 9 damage, and ongoing 10 necrotic damage (save ends).
3—Sleep Ray (Sleep): Ranged 10; +22 vs. Will; the target falls unconscious (save ends).
4—Telekinesis Ray: Ranged 10; +22 vs. Fortitude; the target slides 4 squares.
5—Hold Ray: Ranged 10; +22 vs. Reflex; the target is restrained (save ends).
6—Confusion Ray (Charm): Ranged 10; +22 vs. Will; the target charges its nearest ally and makes a melee basic attack against it.
7—Fear Ray (Fear, Psychic): Ranged 10; +22 vs. Will; 1d8 + 9 psychic damage, and the target moves its speed away from the beholder by the safest route possible.
8—Petrifying Ray: Ranged 10; +22 vs. Fortitude; the target is slowed (save ends). *First Failed Save:* The target is immobilized instead of slowed (save ends). *Second Failed Save:* The target is petrified (no save).
9—Death Ray (Necrotic): Ranged 10; +22 vs. Fortitude; 1d8 + 9 necrotic damage, and if the target is bloodied it is dazed (save ends). *First Failed Save:* The target is dazed and weakened (save ends). *Second Failed Save:* The target dies.
10—Disintegrate Ray: Ranged 10; +22 vs. Fortitude; 2d10 + 9 damage, and ongoing 2d20 damage (save ends). *Aftereffect:* Ongoing 2d6 damage (save ends).

⌁ **Eye Ray Frenzy** (standard, usable only while bloodied; recharge ⚅) ✦ see text
As *eye rays* above, except the eye tyrant makes four eye ray attacks.

Alignment Evil	**Languages** Deep Speech	
Str 12 (+10)	**Dex** 24 (+16)	**Wis** 17 (+12)
Con 20 (+14)	**Int** 22 (+15)	**Cha** 28 (+18)

Encounter Groups

Beholders use a wide range of minions and strike alliances with other powerful monsters. Eyes of flame prefer to fight behind a group of submissive soldiers or brutes.

Level 13 Encounter (XP 4,000)
✦ 1 beholder eye of flame (level 13 elite artillery)
✦ 3 hill giants (level 13 brute)

BERBALANG

BERBALANGS CONSUME THE FLESH AND BONES of dead humanoids, acquiring the lost memories of those upon whom they feast. They also have the power to manifest psychic duplicates of themselves.

Berbalang	Level 10 Solo Skirmisher
Medium immortal humanoid	XP 2,500

Initiative +13   **Senses** Perception +6
AC 25; **Fortitude** 22, **Reflex** 25, **Will** 21; see also *psychic deflection*
HP 408; **Bloodied** 204
Saving Throws +5
Speed 6, fly 8
Action Points 2

(✦) **Claw** (standard; at-will)
+14 vs. AC; 1d8 + 6 damage.

Summon Duplicate (minor, not usable while bloodied; at-will)
✦ **Conjuration, Psychic**

The berbalang manifests an exact duplicate of itself in an unoccupied adjacent square. It can have no more than four duplicates at once, and duplicates cannot summon other duplicates. When a duplicate appears, it makes an initiative check and joins the battle on that initiative count. All damage a duplicate deals is treated as psychic damage.

A duplicate has the same statistics as the berbalang except for its hit points. When the berbalang manifests a duplicate, the berbalang loses one-quarter of its current hit points and the duplicate appears with that quantity of hit points. The berbalang's maximum number of hit points remains the same.

Duplicates last until the berbalang reaches 0 hit points, absorbs them, or uses *sacrifice*. A duplicate must stay within 10 squares of the berbalang at all times or it disappears.

Absorb Duplicate (standard, at-will) ✦ **Healing**
The berbalang absorbs a duplicate adjacent to it and regains 50 hit points.

Berbalang Sneak Attack
A berbalang or a duplicate that flanks an enemy with another duplicate deals an extra 1d8 damage on melee attacks against that enemy.

⁜ **Sacrifice** (standard; at-will) ✦ **Psychic**
Area burst 1 centered on a duplicate; the berbalang can cause one of its duplicates to explode in a burst of psychic gore; +11 vs. Fortitude; 2d8 + 6 psychic damage, plus the target is dazed (save ends). *Miss:* No damage, but the target is dazed (save ends). *Hit or Miss:* The berbalang takes 25 damage.

Psychic Deflection (immediate reaction, when the berbalang is damaged by an attack; at-will) ✦ **Psychic**
The berbalang can deflect the damage it takes from an attack to one of its duplicates. Any effects or secondary attacks included in the attack are also deflected to the duplicate. The damage a duplicate takes in this way is considered psychic damage.

Alignment Evil	**Languages** Supernal	
Str 16 (+8)	**Dex** 22 (+11)	**Wis** 13 (+6)
Con 14 (+7)	**Int** 14 (+7)	**Cha** 15 (+7)

BERBALANG TACTICS

A surprised berbalang uses *summon duplicate* at the start of battle, and if faced with several opponents, it might spawn a third or a fourth duplicate using its initial standard and move actions as well. Conversely, if it hears enemies approaching, it spawns duplicates out of initiative, before the battle begins.

The duplicates try to maneuver around enemies to gain the benefit of their *berbalang sneak attack*.

When the berbalang is bloodied, it increasingly uses *absorb duplicate* and *sacrifice*. A berbalang fearing its death retreats and uses a duplicate to block pursuit.

BERBALANG LORE

A character knows the following information with a successful Religion check.

DC 20: Berbalangs consume the flesh of dead humanoids. They do not differentiate between those recently dead and those dead for centuries.

DC 25: Berbalangs absorb the memories of the corpses they eat and relive significant portions of those memories while asleep. This absorption of dead memories gives berbalangs the nutrition they require. There are some remote villages where the dead are not interred, but instead are given to a resident berbalang as part of a bargain made by the village elders. When too few deaths occur naturally, a sacrifice is determined by lot to satisfy the deal.

ENCOUNTER GROUPS

Berbalangs are solitary, but they occasionally share their lairs with various tomb-dwellers.

Level 12 Encounter (XP 3,500)
✦ 1 berbalang (level 10 solo skirmisher)
✦ 1 gibbering mouther (level 10 controller)
✦ 1 skeletal tomb guardian (level 10 brute)

ANNE STOKES

BOAR

These wild cousins of the domestic pig can be found in any wilderness location, from cold hinterlands to tropical rain forests. When incensed, they become mindless, destructive animals.

Dire Boar	Level 6 Brute
Large natural beast (mount)	XP 250

Initiative +3 **Senses** Perception +2
HP 85; **Bloodied** 42; see also *death strike*
AC 17; **Fortitude** 21, **Reflex** 17, **Will** 16
Speed 8
⊕ **Gore** (standard; at-will)
  +9 vs. AC; 1d10 + 4 damage, or 1d10 + 9 damage against a prone target.
† **Death Strike** (when reduced to 0 hit points)
  The dire boar makes a gore attack.
† **Rabid Charger** (while mounted by a friendly rider of 6th level or higher; at-will) ✦ **Mount**
  When it charges, the dire boar makes a gore attack in addition to its rider's charge attack; see also *furious charge*.
Furious Charge
  When a dire boar charges, its gore deals an extra 5 damage, pushes the target 2 squares, and knocks the target prone on a hit.

Alignment Unaligned		**Languages** —
Str 19 (+7)	**Dex** 10 (+3)	**Wis** 9 (+2)
Con 15 (+5)	**Int** 2 (-1)	**Cha** 8 (+2)

DIRE BOAR TACTICS

A dire boar begins battle with a *furious charge*, aiming to knock an opponent prone. The creature attacks with wild abandon, fighting until slain.

ENCOUNTER GROUPS

All boars can be found in small groups called sounders. Domesticated dire boars can be found among all sorts of humanoids.

Level 5 Encounter (XP 1,150)
✦ 1 dire boar (level 6 brute)
✦ 1 orc eye of Gruumsh (level 5 controller)
✦ 4 orc berserkers (level 4 brute)

Thunderfury Boar	Level 15 Brute
Large fey beast	XP 1,200

Initiative +9 **Senses** Perception +8
HP 182; **Bloodied** 91
AC 27; **Fortitude** 29, **Reflex** 20, **Will** 20
Speed 8
⊕ **Gore** (standard; at-will)
  +18 vs. AC; 2d8 + 7 damage, or 3d8 + 7 damage while the thunderfury boar is bloodied.
† **Death Strike** (when reduced to 0 hit points)
  The thunderfury boar makes a gore attack.
↞ **Thunderfury** (standard; recharge ⚄ ⚅) ✦ **Thunder**
  Close burst 2; +17 vs. Fortitude; 2d8 + 6 thunder damage, and the target is knocked prone. *Miss:* Half damage, and the target is not knocked prone.
Thunderous Charge ✦ **Thunder**
  The thunderfury boar deals an extra 10 thunder damage when it charges.

Alignment Unaligned		**Languages** —
Str 24 (+14)	**Dex** 15 (+9)	**Wis** 12 (+8)
Con 22 (+13)	**Int** 5 (+4)	**Cha** 9 (+6)

THUNDERFURY BOAR TACTICS

This boar enters battle with a *thunderous charge* and uses *thunderfury* as often as it can. Those who flee from the boar are likely to incite the beast's wrath, and it pursues a fleeing enemy without regard for opportunity attacks.

BOAR LORE

A character knows the following information with a successful skill check.

  Nature DC 15: Dire boars are omnivores that roam wild in many landscapes, but sometimes humanoids domesticate them for use in battle. Domesticating a dire boar is difficult, and they remain fierce and dangerous even to their trainers. Dwarves refer to their domesticated dire boar mounts as thundertusks.

  Arcana DC 20: Thunderfury boars are native to the Feywild. They are too fierce for true domestication, but they are sometimes kept and goaded into battle by canny fey.

BODAK

Bodaks are heartless creatures that kill for the sake of killing, serving their own desires or the desires of an even crueler master.

Bodak Skulk		Level 16 Lurker
Medium shadow humanoid (undead)		XP 1,400

Initiative +16   **Senses** Perception +10; darkvision
Agonizing Gaze (Fear, Gaze, Necrotic) aura 5; a creature in the aura that makes a melee or a ranged attack against the bodak skulk takes 5 necrotic damage before the attack roll is made and takes a -2 penalty to the attack roll.
HP 124; **Bloodied** 62
AC 29; **Fortitude** 29, **Reflex** 27, **Will** 29
Immune disease, poison; **Resist** 15 necrotic; **Vulnerable** 5 radiant; a bodak skulk that takes radiant damage cannot weaken a target until the end of its next turn.
Speed 6
⊕ **Slam** (standard; at-will) ✦ **Necrotic**
  +21 vs. AC; 1d6 + 5 damage plus 2d6 necrotic damage, and the target is weakened until the end of the bodak skulk's next turn.
⌁ **Death Gaze** (standard; encounter) ✦ **Gaze, Necrotic**
  Ranged 10; targets a living creature; +19 vs. Fortitude; if the target is weakened, it is reduced to 0 hit points; otherwise, the target takes 1d6 + 6 necrotic damage and loses 1 healing surge.
Spectral Form (standard; at-will)
  The bodak skulk turns invisible and gains the insubstantial and phasing qualities . It can do nothing but move in its spectral form, and it can return to its normal form as a free action.

Alignment Evil	**Languages** Common	
Str 21 (+13)	**Dex** 19 (+12)	**Wis** 15 (+10)
Con 22 (+14)	**Int** 6 (+6)	**Cha** 23 (+14)

BODAK SKULK TACTICS

The bodak skulk approaches foes undetected using *spectral form* and then waits for an opportunity to gain combat advantage. When it's poised to attack, the bodak reverts to normal form and attempts to weaken a foe with its slam attack. It fixes its *death gaze* on the first enemy it weakens.

Bodak Reaver		Level 18 Soldier
Medium shadow humanoid (undead)		XP 2,000

Initiative +16   **Senses** Perception +17; darkvision
Agonizing Gaze (Fear, Gaze, Necrotic) aura 5; a creature in the aura that makes a melee or a ranged attack against the bodak reaver takes 5 necrotic damage before the attack roll is made and takes a -2 penalty to the attack roll.
HP 175; **Bloodied** 87
AC 31; **Fortitude** 31, **Reflex** 30, **Will** 31
Immune disease, poison; **Resist** 20 necrotic; **Vulnerable** 5 radiant; a bodak reaver that takes radiant damage can't weaken a target until the end of its next turn.
Speed 5
⊕ **Greataxe** (standard; at-will) ✦ **Necrotic, Weapon**
  +23 vs. AC; 1d12 + 6 damage (crit 2d12 + 18) plus 1d8 necrotic damage, and the target is dazed and weakened (save ends both).
⌁ **Death Gaze** (standard; encounter) ✦ **Gaze, Necrotic**
  Ranged 10; targets a living creature; +20 vs. Fortitude; if the target is weakened, it is reduced to 0 hit points; otherwise, the target takes 1d6 + 6 necrotic damage and loses 1 healing surge.
Death Drinker
  If a living creature is reduced to 0 hit points within 5 squares of the bodak reaver, the reaver gains a +1 bonus to attack rolls until the end of its next turn, as well as 15 temporary hit points.

Alignment Evil	**Languages** Common	
Str 22 (+15)	**Dex** 21 (+14)	**Wis** 16 (+12)
Con 23 (+15)	**Int** 10 (+9)	**Cha** 23 (+15)
Equipment plate armor, greataxe		

BODAK REAVER TACTICS

This bodak reaver wades into combat wielding its greataxe and taking advantage of its *death gaze*. A bodak reaver sometimes slays allied minions to reap the benefits of its *death drinker* power.

BODAK LORE

A character knows the following information with a successful skill check.

  Arcana DC 20: Bodaks are undead humanoids with strong ties to the Shadowfell. Its visage is so ghastly that it can kill with a look.

  Religion DC 30: When a nightwalker slays a humanoid, that nightwalker can ritually transform the slain creature's body and spirit into a bodak. The bodak then acts at the nightwalker's behest, serving whomever its master dictates.

ENCOUNTER GROUPS

An enslaved bodak collaborates with other shadow or undead creatures.

Level 18 Encounter (XP 10,000)
✦ 2 bodak reavers (level 18 soldier)
✦ 1 cambion hellfire magus (level 18 artillery)
✦ 2 slaughter wights (level 18 brute)

BONECLAW

BONECLAWS ARE MAGICALLY CONSTRUCTED UNDEAD built to hunt and slay the living. Liches, deathpriests of Orcus, shadar-kai necromancers, and other vile individuals use them as guards and agents. Their skewerlike claws contract and extend from moment to moment, sometimes instantly reaching a length of 10 feet or more before slowly contracting.

Boneclaw	Level 14 Soldier
Large shadow animate (undead)	XP 1,000

Initiative +15   **Senses** Perception +13; darkvision
HP 136; **Bloodied** 68; see also *necrotic pulse*
AC 30; **Fortitude** 24, **Reflex** 27, **Will** 25
Immune disease, poison; **Resist** 20 necrotic; **Vulnerable** 5 radiant
Speed 8

⊕ **Claw** (standard; at-will)
     Reach 3; +20 vs. AC; 1d12 + 6 damage.
⟵ **Necrotic Pulse** (free, when first bloodied; encounter) ✦ **Healing**, **Necrotic**
     Close burst 10; undead allies in the burst regain 10 hit points, and enemies in the burst take 10 necrotic damage.

Relentless Opportunist
     If the boneclaw hits with an opportunity attack, it can make another opportunity attack against the same target during the current turn.

Threatening Reach
     The boneclaw can make opportunity attacks against all enemies within its reach (3 squares).

Alignment Evil	**Languages** Common	
Skills Intimidate +16, Stealth +18		
Str 17 (+10)	**Dex** 23 (+13)	**Wis** 12 (+8)
Con 16 (+10)	**Int** 10 (+7)	**Cha** 18 (+11)

BONECLAW TACTICS

A boneclaw impales foes with its claws, relying on its threatening reach to discourage enemies from fleeing.

BONECLAW LORE

A character knows the following information with a successful skill check.

Religion DC 20: Boneclaws are intelligent undead constructs that enjoy hunting and slaying living creatures.

Arcana DC 25: One creates a boneclaw by means of a dark ritual that binds a powerful evil soul to a specially prepared amalgamation of undead flesh and bone. The exact ritual is a closely guarded secret known only to a handful of liches and necromancers. Cabals that wish to possess the knowledge of boneclaw creation have resorted to diplomacy, theft, and clandestine warfare to acquire the ritual.

Religion DC 30: Although rumor holds that the first boneclaws were created by a powerful lich in the service of Vecna, the truth is that a coven of hags led by a powerful night hag named Grigwartha created the first boneclaw over a century ago. They invented a ritual that combines the flesh and bones from ogres along with the trapped soul of an oni. Although the materials can vary, the ritual is the same among those who know it.

Arcana DC 35: Grigwartha trades her knowledge of the boneclaw creation ritual for favors she can later call upon. As such, she has a vast network of individuals and creatures that owe her a debt for the ritual.

ENCOUNTER GROUPS

Boneclaws can appear in any setting, always serving evil. They act as guardians, soldiers, and even assassins.

Level 14 Encounter (XP 5,000)
✦ 2 boneclaws (level 14 soldier)
✦ 1 lich (level 14 elite controller)
✦ 1 shield guardian (level 14 soldier)

BULETTE

Heavily armored predators that burrow through the earth, bulettes hunt for morsels to slake their appetite and once satisfied, retreat underground.

Bulette	Level 9 Elite Skirmisher
Large natural beast	XP 800

Initiative +7   **Senses** Perception +5; darkvision, tremorsense 20
HP 204; **Bloodied** 102; see also *second wind*
AC 27; **Fortitude** 26, **Reflex** 21, **Will** 21
Saving Throws +2
Speed 6, burrow 6; see also *earth furrow*
Action Points 1
⊕ **Bite** (standard; at-will)
   Before it bites, the bulette can make a standing long jump (as a free action) without provoking opportunity attacks; +14 vs. AC; 2d6 + 7 damage, or 4d6 + 7 damage against a prone target.
↞ **Rising Burst** (standard; at-will)
   Close burst 2; the bulette sprays rock and dirt into the air when it rises out of the ground; +13 vs. AC; 1d6 + 7 damage.
↧ **Earth Furrow** (move; at-will)
   The bulette moves up to its burrow speed just below the surface of the ground, avoiding opportunity attacks as it passes underneath other creatures' squares. As it burrows beneath the space of a Medium or smaller creature on the ground, the bulette makes an attack against the creature: +8 vs. Fortitude; on a hit, the target is knocked prone.
Ground Eruption
   The squares into which a bulette surfaces and the squares it leaves when it burrows underground become difficult terrain.
Second Wind (standard; encounter) ✦ **Healing**
   The bulette spends a healing surge and regains 51 hit points. It gains a +2 bonus to all defenses until the start of its next turn.

Alignment Unaligned	**Languages** –

Skills Athletics +16, Endurance +15

Str 24 (+11)	**Dex** 13 (+5)	**Wis** 12 (+5)
Con 22 (+10)	**Int** 2 (+0)	**Cha** 8 (+3)

Bulette Tactics

A bulette hides underground and uses its tremorsense to detect prey. First it burrows beneath its opponents, using *earth furrow* to knock them prone and *rising burst* when it surfaces. It then spends an action point to leap toward and bite the nearest prone target. When bloodied, the creature burrows underground and uses its *second wind*.

Dire Bulette	Level 18 Elite Skirmisher
Huge natural beast	XP 4,000

Initiative +13   **Senses** Perception +13; darkvision, tremorsense 20
HP 360; **Bloodied** 180; see also *second wind*
AC 36; **Fortitude** 33, **Reflex** 29, **Will** 29
Saving Throws +2
Speed 8, burrow 8; see also *earth furrow*
Action Points 1
⊕ **Bite** (standard; at-will)
   Before it bites, the dire bulette can make a standing long jump (as a free action) without provoking opportunity attacks; +23 vs. AC; 2d8 + 10 damage, or 4d8 + 10 damage if the target is prone.
↞ **Rising Burst** (standard; at-will)
   Close burst 2; the dire bulette sprays rock and dirt into the air when it rises out of the ground; +22 vs. AC; 1d8 + 10 damage.
↧ **Earth Furrow** (move; at-will)
   The dire bulette moves up to its burrow speed just below the surface of the ground, avoiding opportunity attacks as it passes underneath other creatures' squares. As it burrows beneath the space of a Large or smaller creature on the ground, the dire bulette makes an attack against the creature: +17 vs. Fortitude; on a hit, the target is knocked prone.
Ground Eruption
   The squares into which a dire bulette surfaces and the squares it leaves when it burrows underground become difficult terrain.
Second Wind (standard; encounter) ✦ **Healing**
   The dire bulette spends a healing surge and regains 90 hit points. The dire bulette gains a +2 bonus to all defenses until the start of its next turn.

Alignment Unaligned	**Languages** –

Skills Athletics +24, Endurance +23

Str 30 (+19)	**Dex** 15 (+11)	**Wis** 18 (+13)
Con 28 (+18)	**Int** 5 (+6)	**Cha** 12 (+10)

Bulette Lore

A character knows the following information with a successful Nature check.

   DC 15: Bulettes are sometimes called landsharks. They dwell in earthen cysts underground, in caves, or sometimes even aboveground. They rarely burrow much deeper than a few dozen feet.

Encounter Groups

Bulettes are solitary creatures, but they have been known to surface and join a battle in progress.

Level 9 Encounter (XP 2,000)
✦ 1 bulette (level 9 elite skirmisher)
✦ 3 trolls (level 9 brute)

BEN WOOTTEN

CAMBION

Cambions are the offspring of devils and depraved or unwitting mortals, inheriting the worst traits of each parent.

Cambion Hellsword	Level 8 Brute
Medium immortal humanoid (devil)	XP 350

Initiative +8   **Senses** Perception +7; darkvision
HP 106; **Bloodied** 53
AC 20; **Fortitude** 20, **Reflex** 18, **Will** 21
Resist 10 fire
Speed 6, fly 8 (clumsy)

⊕ **Greatsword** (standard; at-will) ✦ **Fire, Weapon**
+10 vs. AC; 1d10 + 5 damage, and ongoing 5 fire damage (save ends).

Whirlwind Charge
When a hellsword charges an enemy, it can make a greatsword attack against each enemy within its reach at the end of its charge.

Triumphant Surge
The cambion hellsword gains 5 temporary hit points each time it bloodies an enemy or reduces an enemy to 0 hit points or fewer.

Alignment Evil   **Languages** Common, Supernal
Skills Athletics +13, Intimidate +14
| **Str** 20 (+9) | **Dex** 18 (+8) | **Wis** 16 (+7) |
| **Con** 16 (+7) | **Int** 10 (+4) | **Cha** 21 (+9) |

Equipment chainmail, greatsword

HELLSWORD TACTICS

A cambion hellsword charges toward a group of opponents and use its *whirlwind charge* power. The hellsword then focuses on one opponent it perceives as weaker than the rest, hoping to bloody or slay the target and reap the benefit of its *triumphant surge*.

Cambion Hellfire Magus	Level 18 Artillery
Medium immortal humanoid (devil)	XP 2,000

Initiative +14   **Senses** Perception +13; darkvision
HP 130; **Bloodied** 65
AC 30 (34 against ranged attacks); **Fortitude** 27, **Reflex** 30 (34 against ranged attacks), **Will** 32
Resist 15 fire
Speed 6, fly 8 (clumsy)

⊕ **Quarterstaff** (standard; at-will) ✦ **Weapon**
+20 vs. AC; 1d8 + 2 damage.

⊕ **Hellfire Ray** (standard; at-will) ✦ **Fire**
Ranged 20; +22 vs. Reflex; 2d8 + 8 fire damage, and the target is knocked prone.

✳ **Soulscorch** (standard; recharge ⚄ ⚅) ✦ **Fire**
Area burst 1 within 10; +22 vs. Reflex; 1d10 + 8 fire damage, and ongoing 5 fire damage (save ends).

Soul Mantle
A mantle of soul energy protects the hellfire magus, giving it a +4 bonus to AC and Reflex defense against ranged attacks (already included in its statistics).

Alignment Evil   **Languages** Common, Supernal
Skills Arcana +20, Bluff +22, Diplomacy +22
| **Str** 14 (+11) | **Dex** 20 (+14) | **Wis** 19 (+13) |
| **Con** 16 (+12) | **Int** 22 (+15) | **Cha** 27 (+17) |

Equipment robes, quarterstaff

HELLFIRE MAGUS TACTICS

A hellfire magus targets enemies with its *hellfire ray*, knocking opponents prone and allowing allies to gain combat advantage. Against tightly gathered foes, the hellfire magus uses *soulscorch*.

CAMBION LORE

A character knows the following information with a successful Religion check.

DC 15: Some cambions are born to human mothers and raised as vicious children in the natural world, while others are born to succubi or other devils and reared in the Nine Hells.

ENCOUNTER GROUPS

Diabolical cambions frequently serve as bodyguards, lieutenants, or advisors to formidable evil beings, particularly devils.

Level 8 Encounter (XP 1,800)
✦ 4 cambion hellswords (level 8 brute)
✦ 1 succubus (level 9 controller)

Level 18 Encounter (XP 10,400)
✦ 2 cambion hellfire magi (level 18 artillery)
✦ 1 rakshasa noble (level 19 controller)
✦ 2 rockfire dreadnought elementals (level 18 soldier)

ANNE STOKES

CARRION CRAWLER

CARRION CRAWLERS FEED ON CORPSES but don't always limit their diet to the dead. They are aggressive scavengers feared for their paralyzing tentacles.

Carrion Crawler	Level 7 Controller
Large aberrant beast	XP 300

Initiative +6   **Senses** Perception +5; darkvision
HP 81; **Bloodied** 40
AC 20; **Fortitude** 19, **Reflex** 18, **Will** 17
Speed 6, climb 6 (spider climb)

(+) **Tentacles** (standard; at-will) ✦ **Poison**
Reach 2; +10 vs. Fortitude; 1d4 + 5 damage, and the target takes ongoing 5 poison and is slowed (save ends both). *First Failed Save:* The target is immobilized instead of slowed (save ends). *Second Failed Save:* The target is stunned instead of immobilized (save ends). Saving throws made against the carrion crawler's paralytic tentacles take a -2 penalty.

✦ **Bite** (standard; at-will)
+12 vs. AC; 1d10 + 5 damage.

Alignment Unaligned	**Languages** —	
Str 20 (+8)	**Dex** 16 (+6)	**Wis** 14 (+5)
Con 17 (+6)	**Int** 2 (-1)	**Cha** 16 (+6)

CARRION CRAWLER TACTICS
Carrion crawlers (regardless of size) guard their food and eagerly attack trespassers. The crawlers have no tactical sense but instinctively focus on one or two opponents at a time, relying solely on the efficacy of their poisonous tentacles. Carrion crawlers generally make bite attacks only against stunned targets.

CARRION CRAWLER LORE
A character knows the following information with a successful Dungeoneering check.

DC 15: Carrion crawlers might be the result of some mad wizard's experiment. They feed on carrion (hence the name) but aggressively attack whatever wanders into their feeding grounds.

DC 25: Carrion crawlers lay their eggs in corpses or mounds of offal. When the eggs hatch, hundreds of baby crawlers burst forth and begin gorging on one another. Thankfully, their poison is too weak at that age to harm anyone, and only a handful of them survive to adulthood.

ENCOUNTER GROUPS
Humanoid creatures and aberrant creatures sometimes use carrion crawlers to dispose of waste. Some even manage to train the crawlers as mounts or guard beasts.

Level 7 Encounter (XP 1,500)
✦ 2 carrion crawlers (level 7 controller)
✦ 3 otyughs (level 7 soldier)

Enormous Carrion Crawler	Level 17 Elite Controller
Huge aberrant beast	XP 3,200

Initiative +12   **Senses** Perception +11; darkvision
HP 332; **Bloodied** 166; see also *tentacle flurry*
AC 32; **Fortitude** 31, **Reflex** 30, **Will** 29
Saving Throws +2
Speed 6, climb 6 (spider climb)
Action Points 1

(+) **Tentacles** (standard; at-will) ✦ **Poison**
Reach 3; +20 vs. Fortitude; 2d4 + 7 damage, and the target takes ongoing 10 poison damage and is slowed (save ends both). In addition, the target is pulled 1 square. *First Failed Save:* The target is immobilized instead of slowed (save ends). *Second Failed Save:* The target is stunned instead of immobilized (save ends). Saving throws made against the enormous carrion crawler's paralytic tentacles take a -5 penalty.

✦ **Bite** (standard; at-will)
+22 vs. AC; 2d8 + 7 damage.

↔ **Tentacle Flurry** (standard; recharges when first bloodied) ✦ **Poison**
Close blast 3; +20 vs. Fortitude; 1d4 + 5 damage, and the target takes ongoing 5 poison damage and is slowed (save ends both). *First Failed Save:* The target is immobilized instead of slowed (save ends). *Second Failed Save:* The target is stunned instead of immobilized (save ends). Saving throws made against the enormous carrion crawler's paralytic tentacles take a -5 penalty.

Threatening Reach
The enormous carrion crawler can make opportunity attacks against all enemies within its reach (3 squares).

Alignment Unaligned	**Languages** —	
Str 25 (+15)	**Dex** 18 (+12)	**Wis** 16 (+11)
Con 22 (+14)	**Int** 4 (+5)	**Cha** 18 (+12)

DAVID GRIFFITH

CHIMERA

CHIMERAS HAVE A DRAGON'S EYE FOR TREASURE and line their caves with the baubles and bones of slaughtered prey. They survive well in any climate, provided there's abundant food.

Chimera		Level 15 Elite Brute
Large natural magical beast		XP 2,400

Initiative +10   **Senses** Perception +14; all-around vision, darkvision

HP 366; **Bloodied** 183; see also *bloodied breath*

AC 27; **Fortitude** 29, **Reflex** 23, **Will** 24

Resist 10 fire

Saving Throws +2

Speed 6, fly 10 (clumsy), overland flight 15

Action Points 1

⊕ **Lion's Bite** (standard; at-will)
+18 vs. AC; 2d8 + 7 damage.

↯ **Ram's Charge** (standard; at-will)
The chimera makes a charge attack; +19 vs. AC; 1d10 + 11 damage, and the target is pushed 1 square or knocked prone.

↯ **Triple Threat** (standard; at-will)
The chimera makes the following three melee attacks, each one against a different target:
Lion's Bite +18 vs. AC; 2d8 + 7 damage.
Dragon's Bite +18 vs. AC; 3d6 + 7 damage.
Ram's Gore +18 vs. AC; 1d10 + 7 damage, and the target is knocked prone.

✦ **Dragon Breath** (standard; encounter) ✦ **Fire**
Close blast 5; +16 vs. Reflex; 2d6 + 3 damage, and ongoing 10 fire damage (save ends).

✦ **Bloodied Breath** (free, when first bloodied; encounter)
The chimera recharges and uses *dragon breath*.

Alignment Unaligned   **Languages** Common, Draconic

Str 24 (+14)	**Dex** 17 (+10)	**Wis** 14 (+9)
Con 23 (+13)	**Int** 5 (+4)	**Cha** 17 (+10)

CHIMERA TACTICS

A chimera begins combat by charging the nearest foe and using its *ram's charge*. The chimera then maneuvers itself so that it can employ its *triple threat* or *dragon's breath* power. The first time it uses its *triple threat* power, it spends an action point to use it again on the same turn. The chimera unleashes its *dragon's breath* again when first bloodied, targeting the closest and largest group of foes.

CHIMERA LORE

A character knows the following information with a successful Nature check.

DC 20: Chimeras are belligerent carnivores that dwell in caves and plunder the countryside for food. Despite having three heads, they're not terribly smart.

DC 25: Despite their low intelligence, chimeras can be trained to serve as guards or mounts.

A chimera's dragon head resembles that of a red dragon, although other chromatic dragon heads are possible. The type of damage the chimera's breath weapon deals changes depending on the color of the dragon head (for example, acid damage for the black dragon head), and the chimera's resistance changes to that damage type as well.

ENCOUNTER GROUPS

Chimeras are often encountered in pairs or trios. Smarter creatures sometimes train chimeras and use them as pets or guardians.

Level 15 Encounter (XP 6,000)
✦ 2 chimeras (level 15 elite brute)
✦ 2 hill giants (level 13 brute)

Level 15 Encounter (XP 6,400)
✦ 1 chimera (level 15 elite brute)
✦ 1 azer taskmaster (level 17 controller)
✦ 6 azer warriors (level 17 minion)

CHOKER

Chokers strangle unwary passersby with their long tentacle arms, then loot the corpses for food and valuable trinkets.

Cavern Choker		Level 4 Lurker
Small natural humanoid		XP 175

Initiative +9   **Senses** Perception +3; darkvision
HP 42; **Bloodied** 21
AC 17 (see also *chameleon hide*); **Fortitude** 15, **Reflex** 15, **Will** 13
Speed 6, climb 6 (spider climb)
⊕ **Tentacle Claw** (standard; at-will)
  Reach 2; +9 vs. AC; 1d8 + 3 damage, and the target is grabbed (until escape). A target trying to escape the grab takes a -4 penalty to the check.
† **Choke** (standard; at-will)
  Grabbed target only; +9 vs. Fortitude; 1d8 + 3 damage.
Body Shield (immediate interrupt, when targeted by a melee or a ranged attack against Reflex or AC; recharges when the choker makes a successful *tentacle claw* or *choke* attack)
  The cavern choker makes its grabbed victim the target instead. The choker cannot use this power to redirect attacks made by a creature it is currently grabbing.
Chameleon Hide (minor; at-will)
  The cavern choker gains concealment until the start of its next turn. It can't use this power while grabbing a creature or while grabbed.

Alignment Unaligned	**Languages** Common	
Skills Stealth +10		
Str 17 (+5)	**Dex** 17 (+5)	**Wis** 13 (+3)
Con 12 (+3)	**Int** 6 (+0)	**Cha** 6 (+0)

CAVERN CHOKER TACTICS

This choker strikes with surprise and uses its reach to full advantage. The choker holds on to its victim as long as possible, using *body shield* to protect itself while choking its grabbed prey.

Feygrove Choker		Level 12 Lurker
Medium fey humanoid		XP 700

Initiative +14   **Senses** Perception +7; low-light vision
HP 91; **Bloodied** 45
AC 24; **Fortitude** 22, **Reflex** 22, **Will** 19
Speed 8 (forest walk), climb 8 (spider climb)
⊕ **Tentacle Claw** (standard; at-will)
  Reach 3; +17 vs. AC; 2d6 + 4 damage, and the target is grabbed (until escape). A target trying to escape the grab takes a -4 penalty to the check. The feygrove choker can grab up to 2 creatures at once.
† **Choke** (standard; at-will)
  Up to 2 grabbed targets; +17 vs. Fortitude; 2d8 + 4 damage. The feygrove choker makes a separate attack against each grabbed target.
✵ **Vine Fetter** (standard; recharge ⚅)
  Area burst 3 within 10; nearby vines animate and snare the feygrove choker's enemies; +15 vs. Reflex; the target is restrained (save ends).
Body Shield (immediate interrupt, when targeted by a melee or a ranged attack against Reflex or AC; recharges when the choker makes a successful *tentacle claw* or *choke* attack)
  The feygrove choker makes its grabbed victim the target instead. The choker cannot use this power to redirect attacks made by a creature it is currently grabbing.
Chameleon Hide (minor; at-will)
  The feygrove choker gains concealment until the start of its next turn. It can't use this power while grabbing a creature or while grabbed.

Alignment Unaligned	**Languages** Elven	
Skills Stealth +15		
Str 19 (+10)	**Dex** 18 (+10)	**Wis** 13 (+7)
Con 13 (+7)	**Int** 6 (+4)	**Cha** 6 (+4)

FEYGROVE CHOKER TACTICS

The creature hides among trees and flora with the aid of its *chameleon hide*, striking when prey comes within reach. When confronted with multiple enemies, the feygrove choker uses *vine fetter* to restrain as many of them as possible while it chokes one or two targets.

CHOKER LORE

A character knows the following information with a successful Arcana or Nature check.

  DC 15: A choker's arms and legs contain multiple knobby joints of cartilage, which allow them to flex and coil almost like tentacles. Thus, a choker's movements are rolling and fluid.

ENCOUNTER GROUPS

Chokers don't hang around with other lurkers, but they do share territory with creatures of other roles. Goblins, gnolls, and other evil humanoids use chokers as sentries and assassins, paying them with food and treasure.

Level 4 Encounter (XP 950)
✦ 2 cavern chokers (level 4 lurker)
✦ 3 hobgoblin soldiers (level 3 soldier)
✦ 1 hobgoblin warcaster (level 3 controller)

IZZY MEDRANO

CHUUL

A chuul lurks in underground lakes, still ponds, dank grottos, and murky cesspools, patiently waiting for prey to happen by.

Chuul	Level 10 Soldier
Large aberrant magical beast (aquatic)	XP 500

Initiative +10   **Senses** Perception +9; darkvision
HP 109; **Bloodied** 54
AC 27; **Fortitude** 26, **Reflex** 20, **Will** 21
Speed 6, swim 6
(+) **Claw** (standard; at-will)
    Reach 2; +17 vs. AC; 1d6 + 6 damage, or 3d6 + 6 damage against an immobilized creature.
‡ **Double Attack** (standard; at-will) ✦ **Poison**
    The chuul makes two claw attacks. If both claw attacks hit a single target, the chuul makes a secondary attack against the same target with its tentacles. *Secondary Attack:* +14 vs. Fortitude; the target is immobilized (save ends).
Tentacle Net ✦ **Poison**
    A creature hit by a chuul's opportunity attack is immobilized until the end of the chuul's next turn.
Alignment Unaligned   **Languages** Deep Speech
Str 22 (+11)   **Dex** 16 (+8)   **Wis** 18 (+9)
Con 21 (+10)   **Int** 4 (+2)   **Cha** 14 (+7)

CHUUL TACTICS

The chuul hides just below the surface of a murky pool patiently waiting for prey. When the time is right, it emerges quickly, clamps its huge pincers around its foe, and paralyzes the victim with its poisonous mouth tentacles.

Chuul Juggernaut	Level 23 Elite Soldier
Huge aberrant magical beast (aquatic)	XP 10,200

Initiative +17   **Senses** Perception +17; darkvision
Psychic Moan (Psychic) aura 1; a chuul juggernaut exudes a constant hum of psychic energy. Enemies in the aura take a –2 penalty to Will defense and gain vulnerable 5 psychic.
HP 434; **Bloodied** 217
AC 39; **Fortitude** 37, **Reflex** 31, **Will** 33
Saving Throws +2
Speed 7, swim 7
Action Points 1
(+) **Claw** (standard; at-will)
    Reach 3; +30 vs. AC; 2d8 + 8 damage, or 5d8 + 8 damage against an immobilized creature.
‡ **Double Attack** (standard; at-will) ✦ **Poison**
    The chuul juggernaut makes two claw attacks. If both claw attacks hit a single target, the chuul juggernaut makes a secondary attack against the same target with its tentacles. *Secondary Attack:* +28 vs. Fortitude; the target is immobilized (save ends).
⤸ **Psychic Lure** (standard; at-will) ✦ **Psychic**
    Ranged 10; +29 vs. Will; 2d10 + 3 psychic damage, and the target is pulled 5 squares.
Tentacle Net ✦ **Poison**
    A creature hit by a chuul juggernaut's opportunity attack is immobilized until the end of the juggernaut's next turn.
Alignment Unaligned   **Languages** Deep Speech
Str 27 (+19)   **Dex** 19 (+15)   **Wis** 22 (+17)
Con 25 (+18)   **Int** 4 (+8)   **Cha** 16 (+14)

CHUUL JUGGERNAUT TACTICS

This creature is bold, gladly leaving the safety of its watery den in pursuit of prey. If it immobilizes a foe, it spends its action point to make another *double attack* against the same target. If it can't reach enemies with its melee attacks, it uses *psychic lure* to pull an enemy into its reach.

CHUUL LORE

A character knows the following information with a successful Dungeoneering check.

    DC 15: A chuul devours nearly all of its captured prey except for the creature's brain. Brains are both distasteful and poisonous to chuuls, but they eat everything else, even going to the trouble of peeling away bits of skull.

ENCOUNTER GROUPS

Chuuls are often found living in and around mind flayer settlements, disposing of brainless corpses left behind by their illithid masters. Chuuls are also trained to work by other monsters, such as troglodytes or grimlocks.

Level 10 Encounter (XP 2,500)
✦ 2 chuuls (level 10 soldier)
✦ 1 feymire crocodile (level 10 elite soldier)
✦ 1 bog hag (level 10 skirmisher)

Level 23 Encounter (XP 25,500)
✦ 1 chuul juggernaut (level 23 elite soldier)
✦ 3 blood fiend abominations (level 23 soldier)

COLOSSUS

Like a massive golem, a colossus exists to carry out its creator's will. A colossus is a massive animated statue, often humanoid in shape and fashioned in the likeness of a god or another mighty entity.

Godforged Colossus	Level 29 Elite Brute
Huge immortal animate (construct)	XP 30,000

Initiative +19   **Senses** Perception +26

Reverberating Presence (Psychic) aura 5; an enemy that starts its turn in the aura takes 20 psychic damage.

HP 662; **Bloodied** 331

AC 43; **Fortitude** 48, **Reflex** 40, **Will** 45

Immune disease, fear, poison, sleep; **Resist** 30 force, 30 psychic

Saving Throws +2

Speed 10

Action Points 1

⊕ **Force Weapon** (standard; at-will) ✦ **Force, Psychic, Weapon**
Reach 3; +32 vs. AC; 4d12 + 15 force damage, and the colossus makes a secondary attack against the same target. *Secondary Attack:* +25 vs. Will; 3d6 psychic damage, and the target is stunned until the end of the godforged colossus's next turn.

⊕ **Defensive Strike** (immediate reaction, when an enemy moves adjacent to the godforged colossus; recharge ⚄ ⚅) ✦ **Psychic**
+32 vs. AC; 4d12 + 15 damage plus 3d6 psychic damage, and the colossus makes a secondary attack against the same target. *Secondary Attack:* +30 vs. Fortitude; the target is pushed 5 squares, knocked prone, and dazed (save ends).

↗ **Force Missile** (standard; at-will) ✦ **Force**
Ranged 20; +30 vs. Reflex; 3d10 + 3 force damage, and the target is pushed 5 squares.

⬔ **Voice of the Demiurge** (standard; encounter) ✦ **Psychic**
Close burst 10; targets enemies; +26 vs. Will; 3d8 + 11 psychic damage, and the target is stunned until the end of the godforged colossus' next turn.

Alignment Unaligned	**Languages** –	
Str 40 (+29)	**Dex** 21 (+19)	**Wis** 34 (+26)
Con 31 (+24)	**Int** 4 (+11)	**Cha** 17 (+17)

Godforged Colossus Tactics

This colossus uses *voice of the demiurge* when surrounded by several enemies. The creature then makes melee attacks, using *force missile* only if it has no targets within reach.

Colossus Lore

A character knows the following information with a successful Arcana or Religion check.

DC 25: Animating a colossus requires constructing the statue and then imbuing it with "life" through an epic ritual. This sort of power is rare, but well within the abilities of creatures such as demon lords and divine exarchs.

Encounter Groups

A city's greatest statue might be its key defender, a god's enormous idol could attack those who defile the deity's temple, or a pair of great sculptures might serve as guardians of another creature's lair.

Level 28 Encounter (XP 66,00)
✦ 1 godforged colossus (level 29 elite brute)
✦ 4 dragonborn champions (level 26 soldier)

Level 29 Encounter (XP 85,000)
✦ 1 godforged colossus (level 29 elite brute)
✦ 3 sorrowsworn reapers (level 27 soldier)
✦ 2 shadowraven swarms (level 27 brute)

CROCODILE

CROCODILES ARE STEALTHY, COLD-EYED PREDATORS that inhabit rivers, lakes, fens, and other wetlands.

Visejaw Crocodile		Level 4 Soldier
Large natural beast (reptile)		XP 175

Initiative +5   **Senses** Perception +3; low-light vision
HP 58; **Bloodied** 29
AC 20; **Fortitude** 19, **Reflex** 14, **Will** 15
Speed 6, swim 8
⊕ **Bite** (standard; at-will)
  +10 vs. AC; 1d8 + 4 damage, and the target is grabbed (until escape). The visejaw crocodile cannot make bite attacks while grabbing a creature, but it can use *clamping jaws.*
✦ **Clamping Jaws** (standard; at-will)
  If a visejaw crocodile begins its turn with a target grabbed in its jaws, it makes an attack against the grabbed creature: +10 vs. AC; 2d8 + 4 damage. *Miss:* Half damage.
Alignment Unaligned   **Languages** –
Skills Stealth +8
Str 18 (+6)   **Dex** 12 (+3)   **Wis** 13 (+3)
Con 18 (+6)   **Int** 2 (–2)   **Cha** 7 (+0)

VISEJAW CROCODILE TACTICS

A visejaw crocodile waits in hiding until prey comes close and then makes a vicious bite attack. The creature uses *clamping jaws* in subsequent rounds, shifting back toward the water with its move action.

WARREN MAHY

Feymire Crocodile		Level 10 Elite Soldier
Huge fey beast (reptile)		XP 1,000

Initiative +9   **Senses** Perception +8; low-light vision
Feymire aura 2; enemies treat the area within the aura as difficult terrain.
HP 216; **Bloodied** 108
Regeneration 5 (if the feymire crocodile takes fire damage, its regeneration doesn't function on its next turn)
AC 28; **Fortitude** 29, **Reflex** 21, **Will** 24
Saving Throws +2
Speed 6, swim 8
Action Points 1
⊕ **Bite** (standard; at-will)
  Reach 2; +17 vs. AC; 2d8 + 6 damage, plus the target is grabbed (until escape). The feymire crocodile cannot make bite attacks while grabbing a creature, but it can use *clamping jaws.*
✦ **Clamping Jaws** (standard; at-will)
  If a feymire crocodile begins its turn with a target grabbed in its jaws, it makes an attack against the grabbed creature: +17 vs. AC; 3d8 + 6 damage. *Miss:* Half damage.
✦ **Swallow** (standard; at-will)
  The feymire crocodile attempts to swallow a bloodied Medium or smaller creature it is grabbing; +15 vs. Fortitude; on a hit, the target is swallowed and restrained (no save) and takes 10 damage on subsequent rounds at the start of the crocodile's turn. The swallowed creature can make melee basic attacks only, and only with one-handed or natural weapons. If the feymire crocodile dies, any creature trapped in the gullet can escape as a move action, ending that action in a square formerly occupied by the crocodile.
Alignment Unaligned   **Languages** –
Skills Stealth +12
Str 22 (+11)   **Dex** 15 (+7)   **Wis** 17 (+8)
Con 20 (+10)   **Int** 5 (+2)   **Cha** 8 (+4)

FEYMIRE CROCODILE TACTICS

A feymire crocodile uses the same tactics as the visejaw crocodile with one exception: It attempts to swallow a foe at the first opportunity.

CROCODILE LORE

A character knows the following information with a successful skill check.

    Nature DC 15: Creatures caught in a visejaw crocodile's tooth-lined mouth are savaged until they manage to tear themselves loose or are killed.

    Arcana DC 20: A feymire crocodile hails from the untamed marshlands of the Feywild, although they inhabit worldly swamps as well. The crocodile constantly extends roots and tendrils into its surrounding environment to draw nourishment from it.

ENCOUNTER GROUPS

Crocodiles are often tamed by lizardfolk and other swamp dwellers.

Level 4 Encounter (XP 900)
✦ 1 visejaw crocodile (level 4 soldier)
✦ 3 greenscale hunter lizardfolk (level 4 skirmisher)
✦ 1 greenscale darter lizardfolk (level 5 lurker)

CYCLOPS

Cyclopses are one-eyed giants originally from the Feywild. They usually act as servitors to more powerful masters with dark ambitions.

Cyclops Guard	Level 14 Minion
Large fey humanoid	XP 250

Initiative +8   Senses Perception +13; truesight 6
HP 1; a missed attack never damages a minion.
AC 27; Fortitude 26, Reflex 23, Will 23
Speed 6

(↷) **Battleaxe** (standard; at-will) ✦ **Weapon**
    Reach 2; +17 vs. AC; 7 damage.
✝ **Evil Eye** (immediate reaction, when a melee attack misses the cyclops guard; at-will)
    The cyclops guard makes a melee basic attack against the attacker.

Alignment Unaligned   **Languages** Elven
Str 22 (+11)   **Dex** 16 (+8)   **Wis** 17 (+8)
Con 20 (+10)   **Int** 11 (+5)   **Cha** 11 (+5)
Equipment hide armor, heavy shield, battleaxe

Cyclops Guard Tactics

Cyclops guards surround an enemy, using their reach to full advantage. Then they close ranks and use *evil eye* against enemies who attempt to attack them.

Cyclops Warrior	Level 16 Minion
Large fey humanoid	XP 350

Initiative +11   Senses Perception +18; truesight 6
HP 1; a missed attack never damages a minion.
AC 32; Fortitude 31, Reflex 27, Will 29
Speed 6

(↷) **Battleaxe** (standard; at-will) ✦ **Weapon**
    Reach 2; +22 vs. AC; 8 damage.
✝ **Evil Eye** (immediate reaction, when a melee attack misses the cyclops warrior; at-will)
    The cyclops warrior makes a melee basic attack against the attacker.

Alignment Unaligned   **Languages** Elven
Str 25 (+15)   **Dex** 16 (+11)   **Wis** 20 (+13)
Con 22 (+14)   **Int** 10 (+8)   **Cha** 13 (+9)
Equipment hide armor, heavy shield, battleaxe

Cyclops Warrior Tactics

Cyclops warriors are usually assigned to protect artillery or controller creatures. If their charge is attacked, they quickly leap into action and use tactics similar to the cyclops guards.

Cyclops Impaler	Level 14 Artillery
Large fey humanoid	XP 1,000

Initiative +10   Senses Perception +16; truesight 6
HP 111; Bloodied 55
AC 28; Fortitude 28, Reflex 25, Will 26
Speed 8

(↷) **Spear** (standard; at-will) ✦ **Weapon**
    Reach 2; +19 vs. AC; 1d10 + 6 damage.
↗ **Spear** (standard; at-will) ✦ **Weapon**
    Ranged 10/20; +19 vs. AC; 1d10 + 6 damage.
↗ **Impaling Volley** (standard; recharge ⚅⚅) ✦ **Weapon**
    The cyclops impaler makes 2 ranged spear attacks against different targets no more than 2 squares apart; range 10; +19 vs. AC; 2d6 + 6 damage, and ongoing 5 damage (save ends).
↗ **Evil Eye** (minor; at-will)
    Ranged sight; the cyclops impaler gains a +2 bonus to ranged attacks made against the target. It can designate only one target with its *evil eye* at a time.

Alignment Unaligned   **Languages** Elven
Skills Athletics +18
Str 23 (+13)   **Dex** 16 (+10)   **Wis** 19 (+11)
Con 21 (+12)   **Int** 10 (+7)   **Cha** 12 (+8)
Equipment leather armor, 12 spears (in sheaf over back)

Cyclops Impaler Tactics

A cyclops impaler uses its *evil eye* every round and hurls spears at its designated target from a safe distance. Whenever possible, it uses *impaling volley*.

Cyclops Rambler — Level 14 Skirmisher
Large fey humanoid — XP 1,000

Initiative +12   **Senses** Perception +16; truesight 6
Mocking Eye aura 10; an enemy in the aura that makes an opportunity attack against any target takes a -5 penalty to the attack roll.
HP 141; **Bloodied** 70
AC 29; **Fortitude** 28, **Reflex** 25, **Will** 26
Speed 8
⊕ **Greatsword** (standard; at-will) ✦ **Weapon**
Reach 2; +20 vs. AC; 1d12 + 6 damage.
↭ **Evil Eye** (minor; at-will)
Ranged 20; the cyclops rambler can designate only one target with its *evil eye* at a time. It can move 2 squares any time it shifts from a square adjacent to the designated target.
Feywild Alacrity (free, when the cyclops rambler hits the target of its *evil eye* power; recharge ⚄)
The cyclops rambler gains an extra move action, which it must use before the end of its turn.
Alignment Unaligned   **Languages** Elven
Str 23 (+13)   **Dex** 16 (+10)   **Wis** 19 (+11)
Con 21 (+12)   **Int** 10 (+7)   **Cha** 12 (+8)
Equipment chainmail, greatsword

CYCLOPS RAMBLER TACTICS
A cyclops rambler is a masterful skirmisher, using its *evil eye* power to move around its enemies and confound their opportunity attacks.

Cyclops Hewer — Level 16 Soldier
Large fey humanoid — XP 1,400

Initiative +13   **Senses** Perception +18; truesight 6
HP 158; **Bloodied** 79
AC 33; **Fortitude** 31, **Reflex** 27, **Will** 29
Speed 8
⊕ **Battleaxe** (standard; at-will) ✦ **Weapon**
Reach 2; +23 vs. AC; 1d12 + 7 damage.
↭ **Evil Eye** (minor; at-will)
Ranged 20; the cyclops hewer can designate only one target with its *evil eye* at a time and gains the following effects:
✦ If the designated target misses one of the cyclops hewer's allies with a melee attack, the cyclops hewer can make a melee basic attack against that enemy as an immediate reaction.
✦ If the designated target moves out of the cyclops hewer's reach, the cyclops hewer can shift 1 square toward the target as an immediate reaction.
Alignment Unaligned   **Languages** Elven
Str 25 (+15)   **Dex** 16 (+11)   **Wis** 20 (+13)
Con 22 (+14)   **Int** 10 (+8)   **Cha** 13 (+9)
Equipment chainmail, light shield, battleaxe

CYCLOPS HEWER TACTICS
A cyclops hewer uses its *evil eye* and then charges headlong into battle, cutting down enemies in its way.

(Left to right) cyclops impaler, cyclops hewer, and cyclops rambler

ZOLTAN BOROS & GABOR SZIKSZAI

Cyclops Battleweaver — Level 17 Skirmisher
Large fey humanoid   XP 1,600

Initiative +14   **Senses** Perception +18; truesight 6
HP 165; **Bloodied** 82
AC 31; **Fortitude** 30, **Reflex** 28, **Will** 29
Speed 8

⊕ **Glaive** (standard; at-will) ✦ Weapon
Reach 2; +22 vs. AC; 1d10 + 6 damage.

� **Sweeping Glaive** (standard; at-will) ✦ Weapon
Requires glaive; close blast 2; +22 vs. AC; 1d10 + 6 damage, and the target is pushed 1 square and knocked prone.

↗ **Evil Eye** (minor; at-will)
Ranged 20; the cyclops battleweaver can designate only one target with its *evil eye* at a time. The target takes a -2 penalty to its speed.

Effect Transfer (immediate interrupt, when the cyclops battleweaver suffers an effect that a save can end; encounter)
The effect instead applies to the target of the battleweaver's *evil eye*.

Alignment Unaligned   **Languages** Elven
Str 23 (+14)   **Dex** 18 (+12)   **Wis** 20 (+13)
Con 21 (+13)   **Int** 10 (+8)   **Cha** 12 (+9)
Equipment chainmail, glaive

Cyclops Battleweaver Tactics

At the start of combat, the cyclops battleweaver uses *evil eye* to confound a highly mobile enemy. It relies on its *sweeping glaive* power to push enemies back so that it can move around the battlefield without provoking opportunity attacks, and it uses *effect transfer* to shrug off one debilitating effect.

Cyclops Storm Shaman — Level 17 Artillery
Large fey humanoid   XP 1,600

Initiative +11   **Senses** Perception +17; truesight 6
HP 128; **Bloodied** 64
AC 29; **Fortitude** 28, **Reflex** 26, **Will** 27
Speed 8; see also wind flight

⊕ **Quarterstaff** (standard; at-will) ✦ Thunder, Weapon
Reach 2; +22 vs. AC; 2d4 + 4 damage plus 1d8 thunder damage.

↗ **Tempest Orb** (standard; at-will) ✦ Lightning, Thunder
Ranged 20; +20 vs. Reflex; 2d8 + 6 lightning and thunder damage.

↗ **Evil Eye** (minor; at-will)
Ranged 20; +20 vs. Fortitude; the target gains vulnerable 5 to thunder damage and vulnerable 5 to lightning damage (save ends both effects).

❖ **Storm Burst** (standard; encounter) ✦ Lightning, Thunder, Zone
Area burst 2 within 10; the power creates a zone that lasts until the end of the encounter. Enemies within the zone at the start of their turns take 2d8 lightning damage. Uncovered flames are doused and ongoing fire damage ends immediately within the zone.

Wind Flight (minor; encounter)
The cyclops storm shaman gains a fly speed of 8 (hover) until the end of its next turn. If it doesn't land before then, it crashes.

Alignment Unaligned   **Languages** Elven
Str 18 (+12)   **Dex** 16 (+11)   **Wis** 19 (+12)
Con 20 (+13)   **Int** 14 (+10)   **Cha** 15 (+10)
Equipment leather armor, quarterstaff

Cyclops Storm Shaman Tactics

The cyclops storm shaman catches as many enemies as possible in its *storm burst* before targeting foes individually with its *evil eye* and *tempest orb* powers. If pressed, it uses *wind flight* to fly to a safer location or enters the *storm burst's* zone and uses it for protection.

Cyclops Lore

A character knows the following information with a successful Arcana check.

DC 20: Cyclopses are the willing subjects of fomorians, whom they view as the rightful lords of the Feywild. Indeed, cyclopses believe that fomorians are divine. Thus cyclopses are the fomorians' most valued subjects, serving as bodyguards, soldiers, and artisans—roles that fomorians consider beneath them, but which they don't trust to faithless subjects or slaves.

DC 25: Cyclopses are master craftspeople, and in the depths of the Feywild's Underdark, their most storied elders are hard at work forging implements of immense power for their fomorian masters. Magical rings, swords with blades of lightning, and shields that can turn a dragon's breath—these and more are gifts cyclopses lay at the feet of those they consider gods.

DC 30: Cyclopses sometimes wander the world at the behest of their masters. They do so to fulfill various purposes, but they often make war on elves and despoil eladrin holdings. On some occasions, cyclopses ally with drow. Whenever such an alliance occurs, rumors resurface of an ancient agreement between fomorians and drow referred to as the "Declaration of Eschatos." The exact nature of this agreement and the lore it keeps safe, if any, is unknown. Whatever the hidden specifics of the accords, it seems that cyclopses aid the drow in minor raids and other evil enterprises.

DC 35: Cyclopses formed on the Feywild as an unforeseen echo of ogres in the world. It is said that fomorians shaped and taught them, much as the ancient titans formed and influenced the world's giants.

Encounter Groups

Cyclopses are usually encountered with other cyclopses and fomorians. They readily work with other evil fey as directed by their dark lords.

Level 12 Encounter (XP 3,800)
✦ 4 cyclops guards (level 14 minion)
✦ 2 drow warriors (level 11 lurker)
✦ 1 drow blademaster (level 13 elite skirmisher)

Level 17 Encounter (XP 8,000)
✦ 2 cyclops battleweavers (level 17 skirmisher)
✦ 2 thunderfury boars (level 15 brute)
✦ 1 fomorian warrior (level 17 elite soldier)

Level 17 Encounter (XP 8,000)
✦ 1 cyclops storm shaman (level 17 artillery)
✦ 2 cyclops battleweavers (level 17 skirmisher)
✦ 1 chimera (level 15 elite brute)

Level 17 Encounter (XP 9,600)
✦ 2 cyclops hewers (level 16 soldier)
✦ 2 cyclops impalers (level 14 artillery)
✦ 1 fomorian painbringer (level 19 elite controller)

DARK ONE

NATIVE TO THE SHADOWFELL, dark ones are sly, murderous creatures clad in black garments. They come to the world with sinister schemes, take and learn what they can, and slink back into the gloom.

Dark Creeper	Level 4 Skirmisher
Small shadow humanoid	XP 175

Initiative +8 **Senses** Perception +4; darkvision
HP 54; **Bloodied** 27; see also *killing dark*
AC 18 (see also *dark step*); **Fortitude** 15, **Reflex** 17, **Will** 15
Speed 6

⊕ **Dagger** (standard; at-will) ✦ **Weapon**
+9 vs. AC; 1d4 + 4 damage.

⤳ **Dagger** (standard; at-will) ✦ **Weapon**
Ranged 5/10; +9 vs. AC; 1d4 + 4 damage.

↩ **Killing Dark** (when reduced to 0 hit points)
Close burst 1; targets enemies; each target is blinded (save ends). When slain, a dark creeper explodes in a spout of darkness.

Combat Advantage
The dark creeper deals an extra 1d6 damage on melee and ranged attacks against any target it has combat advantage against.

Dark Step (move; at-will)
The dark creeper moves up to 4 squares, gains a +4 bonus to AC against opportunity attacks, and gains combat advantage against any target that it ends its move adjacent to.

Alignment Unaligned **Languages** Common
Skills Stealth +11, Thievery +11
| **Str** 11 (+2) | **Dex** 18 (+6) | **Wis** 14 (+4) |
| **Con** 14 (+4) | **Int** 13 (+3) | **Cha** 13 (+3) |
Equipment black garments, 5 daggers

DARK CREEPER TACTICS

A dark creeper doesn't enter combat unless it clearly has something to gain, in which case it uses *dark step* to move up to an enemy, gain combat advantage, and stab it.

DARK ONE LORE

A character knows the following information with a successful Arcana check.

DC 15: Dark ones live among shadar-kai, much the way as halflings find their place among populations of humans, dwarves, and elves. Dark ones prefer to dwell in homes that are at least partially underground.

ENCOUNTER GROUPS

Dark ones often serve shadar-kai and intelligent undead as agents, assassins, envoys, messengers, and spies. They can be found among various Underdark dwellers.

Level 5 Encounter (XP 1,000)
✦ 3 dark creepers (level 4 skirmisher)
✦ 2 shadowhunter bats (level 3 lurker)
✦ 1 deathlock wight (level 4 controller)

Dark Stalker	Level 10 Lurker
Small shadow humanoid	XP 500

Initiative +14 **Senses** Perception +7; darkvision
HP 81; **Bloodied** 40; see also *killing dark*
AC 24 (see also *dark step*); **Fortitude** 21, **Reflex** 24, **Will** 23
Speed 6

⊕ **Scimitar** (standard; at-will) ✦ **Weapon**
+15 vs. AC; 1d8 + 5 damage (crit 1d8 + 13).

⤳ **Dagger** (standard; at-will) ✦ **Weapon**
Ranged 5/10; +15 vs. AC; 1d4 + 5 damage.

❋ **Dark Fog** (standard; sustain minor; encounter) ✦ **Zone**
Area burst 4 within 10; creates a zone of darkness that blocks line of sight (creatures with darkvision ignore this effect).

↩ **Killing Dark** (when reduced to 0 hit points)
Close burst 1; targets enemies; each target is blinded (save ends). When slain, a dark creeper explodes in a spout of darkness.

Combat Advantage
The dark stalker deals an extra 2d6 damage on melee and ranged attacks against any target it has combat advantage against.

Dark Step (move; at-will)
The dark stalker moves up to 4 squares, gains a +4 bonus to AC against opportunity attacks, and gains combat advantage against any target that it ends its move adjacent to.

Invisibility (minor; recharge ⚁ ⚂ ⚃ ⚄) ✦ **Illusion**
The dark stalker becomes invisible until the end of its next turn.

Alignment Unaligned **Languages** Common
Skills Stealth +15, Thievery +15
| **Str** 12 (+6) | **Dex** 21 (+10) | **Wis** 14 (+7) |
| **Con** 15 (+7) | **Int** 14 (+7) | **Cha** 19 (+9) |
Equipment black garments, scimitar, 4 daggers

DARK STALKER TACTICS

A dark stalker uses its *dark fog* power to block enemies' line of sight. It then uses *invisibility* and moves to gain combat advantage against a ripe target. If battle turns against the dark stalker, it uses *invisibility* again (provided the power has recharged) to retreat safely.

DEATH KNIGHT

Death knights were powerful warriors who accepted eternal undeath rather than face the end of their mortal existence. With their souls bound to the weapons they wield, death knights command necrotic power in addition to their undiminished martial prowess.

A death knight's armor and weapons are the same items it used in life, but their appearance is often transformed into deadly echoes of their past forms. Its armor is fire-blackened, etched with blasphemous runes, and often adorned with bloodstained spikes. Its weapon—which contains the death knight's soul—is still brightly polished but crackles with dark necrotic energy.

"Death knight" is a monster template that can be applied to nonplayer characters. See the *Dungeon Master's Guide* for rules on creating new death knights using the template.

DEATH KNIGHT LORE

A character knows the following information with a successful Religion check.

DC 20: Death knights are skeletal warriors who retain the intelligence and combat skills they had in life. They often lead other undead soldiers in a war against the living.

DC 25: A death knight carries its soul in its weapon, which has the power to become ghostly and pass through armor as if it was not there. If you take a death knight's weapon, you daze and weaken it. A death knight's soul weapon dazes and weakens anyone else who wields it as long as the death knight has not been destroyed. If you break a death knight's weapon, the death knight can restore it with a touch.

DC 30: The ritual to become a death knight is said to have originated with Orcus, Demon Prince of the Undead. Many death knights gained access to the ritual by contacting Orcus or his servants directly, but some discovered the ritual through other means.

ENCOUNTER GROUPS

Death knights often lead other undead into battle against the living.

Level 16 Encounter (XP 7,600)
✦ 1 human death knight (level 17 elite soldier)
✦ 2 abyssal ghouls (level 16 skirmisher)
✦ 2 sword wraiths (level 17 lurker)

Level 24 Encounter (XP 33,750)
✦ 1 dragonborn death knight (level 25 elite soldier)
✦ 1 fell wyvern (level 24 skirmisher)
✦ 1 great flameskull (level 24 artillery)
✦ 6 abyssal ghoul myrmidons (level 23 minion)

Death Knight (Human Fighter)	Level 17 Elite Soldier
Medium natural humanoid (undead)	XP 3,200

Initiative +11   **Senses** Perception +8; darkvision
Marshal Undead aura 10; lower-level undead allies in the aura gain a +2 bonus to their attack rolls.
AC 35; **Fortitude** 32, **Reflex** 26, **Will** 27
HP 264; **Bloodied** 132; see also *second wind*
Immune disease, poison; **Resist** 10 necrotic; **Vulnerable** 10 radiant
Saving Throws +2
Speed 5
Action Points 1

⊕ **Soulsword** (standard; at-will) ✦ **Necrotic, Weapon**
+23 vs. AC; 1d8 + 12 damage plus 5 necrotic damage (plus an extra 2d6 necrotic damage on a critical hit).

† **Containing Strike** (standard; at-will) ✦ **Necrotic, Weapon**
Requires soulsword; +23 vs. AC; 1d8 + 12 plus 5 necrotic damage, and the death knight can make a melee basic attack as an immediate interrupt against the target if the target shifts on its next turn.

† **Warrior's Challenge** (standard; encounter) ✦ **Necrotic, Weapon**
Requires soulsword; +23 vs. AC; 3d8 + 12 plus 5 necrotic damage, and the target is pushed 2 squares. All enemies within 2 squares of the target are marked until the end of the death knight's next turn.

⬅ **Unholy Flames** (standard; recharge ⚄ ⚅) ✦ **Fire, Necrotic**
Close burst 2; +19 vs. Reflex; 6d8 + 12 fire and necrotic damage to living creatures. Undead creatures within the burst (including the death knight) deal an extra 2d6 fire damage with melee attacks until the end of the death knight's next turn.

Combat Challenge
Every time the death knight attacks an enemy, whether that attack hits or misses, the death knight can mark that target. The mark lasts until the end of the death knight's next turn. In addition, whenever an adjacent enemy shifts, the death knight makes a melee basic attack against that enemy (as an immediate interrupt).

Second Wind (standard; encounter) ✦ **Healing**
The death knight spends a healing surge and regains 66 hit points. The death knight gains a +2 bonus to all defenses until the start of its next turn.

Alignment Evil	**Languages** Common	
Str 20 (+13)	**Dex** 12 (+9)	**Wis** 11 (+8)
Con 18 (+12)	**Int** 13 (+9)	**Cha** 14 (+10)

Equipment plate armor, light shield, soulsword (longsword)

HUMAN DEATH KNIGHT TACTICS

This death knight uses *containing strike* and *combat challenge* round after round. If its allies are taking a beating, the death knight uses *warrior's challenge* to draw attacks, spending an action point to use *second wind* if necessary. The death knight uses *unholy flames* when surrounded by multiple allies and enemies.

Death Knight (Dragonborn Paladin) Level 25 Elite Soldier

Medium natural humanoid (undead)   XP 14,000

Initiative +16   **Senses** Perception +14; darkvision

Marshal Undead aura 10; lower-level undead allies in the aura gain
a +2 bonus to their attack rolls.

HP 373; **Bloodied** 186; see also *second wind*

AC 41; **Fortitude** 39, **Reflex** 34, **Will** 37

Immune disease, poison; **Resist** 15 necrotic; **Vulnerable** 15 radiant

Saving Throws +2

Speed 5

Action Points 1

(+) **Soulsword** (standard; at-will) ✦ **Necrotic, Weapon**
+31 vs. AC; 1d8 + 16 damage plus 5 necrotic damage (plus an
extra 3d6 necrotic damage on a critical hit).

✦ **Valiant Strike** (standard; at-will) ✦ **Necrotic, Weapon**
Requires soulsword; +31 vs. AC, with a +1 bonus to the attack
roll for each adjacent ally; 2d8 + 16 plus 5 necrotic damage.

✦ **Terrifying Smite** (standard; encounter) ✦ **Fear, Weapon**
Requires soulsword; +31 vs. AC; 3d8 + 16 damage, and the
target is pushed 5 squares and can't move closer to the death
knight on its next turn.

↗ **Divine Challenge** (minor; at-will) ✦ **Necrotic**
Ranged 5; the target is marked until the death knight uses this
power against another target. If the target makes an attack that
doesn't include the death knight as a target, the target takes a -2
penalty on attack rolls and 14 necrotic damage.

↩ **Unholy Flames** (standard; recharge ⚃ ⚅) ✦ **Fire, Necrotic**
Close burst 2; +27 vs. Reflex; 6d8 + 14 fire and necrotic damage
to living creatures. Undead creatures within the area (including
the death knight) deal an extra 2d6 fire damage with melee
attacks until the end of the death knight's next turn.

Second Wind (standard; encounter) ✦ **Healing**
The death knight spends a healing surge and regains 93 hit
points. The death knight gains a +2 bonus to all defenses until
the start of its next turn.

Alignment Evil	**Languages** Common, Draconic	
Str 25 (+19)	**Dex** 14 (+14)	**Wis** 14 (+14)
Con 15 (+14)	**Int** 13 (+13)	**Cha** 21 (+17)

Equipment plate armor, heavy shield, soulsword (longsword)

Dragonborn Death Knight Tactics

This death knight issues a *divine challenge* every round and
stays adjacent to one or more of its allies to maximize the
effectiveness of its *valiant strike* power. When swarmed by
multiple melee combatants, it uses *terrifying smite* against
the toughest-looking target or *unholy flames* against the lot
of them. It spends its action point to use *second wind* once
bloodied.

SOUL WEAPON

The ritual of becoming a death knight requires its caster
to bind his immortal essence into the weapon used in
the ritual. If this soul weapon is broken or destroyed, the
death knight can restore it to perfect condition by touch
as a minor action.

A death knight is dazed and weakened while it doesn't
have possession of its soul weapon. Any creature other
than the death knight is dazed and weakened while
carrying the soul weapon.

The soul weapon loses its soul weapon properties when
the death knight is destroyed.

In their many and varied forms, demons are living engines of annihilation. They embody the destructive forces of chaos. All things tend to decay into entropy, but demons exist to hurry that process along.

Fear and mercy are utterly alien to demons' minds. Hate and savagery are their only masters, destruction their only pleasure. They care nothing for plans or structure, banding together only in rampaging hordes, not nations or legions. There is nothing subtle about them: They are not manipulators or schemers, nor are they tempters or bargain makers. While a demonic presence might turn mortals toward corruption through indirect influence, demons do not actively lure other creatures toward evil; they burn them alive or rip them to quivering shreds.

Sometimes powerful beings attempt to summon demons to do their will, hoping to harness demonic strength for their own purposes. But demons are not easily bent to their summoners' will; when a demon appears in the midst of combat, it is with the boundless fury and power of an elemental.

Personal power, wealth, prestige, and even survival are not important to demons–their only goal is to destroy as much as they can before they themselves are destroyed. And then, born anew in the depths of the Abyss, they rise again to continue the destruction.

BALOR

Few demons are more formidable than the cruel balor. Weaker demons obey the balor's commands out of fear of being torn asunder.

THE BIRTH OF THE ABYSS

In the earliest days of creation, even before the gods and primordials began their terrible war, one god was not content with sharing power–he wanted absolute control over the nascent universe. This god, whose name is spoken only in panicked whispers, sought a source of power he could use to gain total dominion over the unfolding realms of creation. Somewhere in the infinite expanse of space, he found the weapon he sought in the form of a tiny shard of utter evil.

The touch of the shard drove this god to madness, corrupting him so completely that he was no longer recognizable as his former self. Nevertheless, he carried the crystalline fragment into the depths of the universe–into the lowest reaches of the primordial vastness that would one day become the Elemental Chaos–and planted it there.

Evil took root like a foul seed of corruption, burrowing deep into the unshaped matter of the Elemental Chaos and spreading unholy tendrils far and wide. A yawning chasm of infinite gloom and despair opened up at the lowest pit of creation, swallowing all matter and light, defiling anything that drew near.

The Abyss was born.

The evil of the Abyss corrupted even some of the mighty primordials–Demogorgon, Baphomet, Orcus–and reshaped them into the likeness of pure destructive evil. The mad god hoped to wield these demonic princes as weapons in his war of conquest, but they would not bend to his will or any but their own.

So he left the Abyss and marshaled other elemental forces in his bid for domination, but the other gods overcame him, chaining him forever in a secret place known only to them.

Now he is called the Chained God, or by his demented followers, the Elder Elemental Eye. His only desire is to escape his prison, and he rarely spares a thought for the realm he inadvertently created.

But the Abyss remains, a festering cyst beneath the Elemental Chaos. Within its lightless depths, demons erupt into birth, live out their short and violent lives, and are reabsorbed into the darkness. Demon princes rule their petty Abyssal domains, scheming to destroy the gods and all their works. The god Lolth hides in the Demonweb Pits, corrupted and perhaps driven mad by the same power that shattered the Chained God and made the first demon princes.

And somewhere far beneath all imagining, the crystalline Heart of the Abyss still beats its unceasing cadence of evil.

Balor	Level 27 Elite Brute
Huge elemental humanoid (demon)	XP 22,000

Initiative +17   **Senses** Perception +23; truesight 6

Flaming Body (Fire) aura 2 (aura 3 while the balor is bloodied); enemies that start their turns in the aura takes 10 fire damage (20 fire damage while the balor is bloodied).

HP 624; **Bloodied** 312; see also *death burst*

AC 42; **Fortitude** 46, **Reflex** 39, **Will** 40

Immune fear; **Resist** 40 fire, 20 variable (3/encounter; see glossary)

Saving Throws +2

Speed 8, fly 12 (clumsy)

Action Points 1

⊕ **Lightning Sword** (standard; at-will) ✦ **Lightning, Weapon**
     Reach 3; +32 vs. AC; 2d10 + 10 lightning damage, or 3d10 + 30 lightning damage on a critical hit.

⨥ **Flame Whip** (standard; at-will) ✦ **Fire, Weapon**
     Reach 5; +30 vs. Reflex; 3d8 + 5 fire damage, and ongoing 5 fire damage (save ends). Also, the target is pulled into an unoccupied space adjacent to the balor.

⨥ **Fire and Lightning** (standard; at-will) ✦ **Fire, Lightning, Weapon**
     The balor makes a lightning sword attack and a flame whip attack.

Demonic Accuracy (free, when the balor misses with an attack; encounter)
     The balor rerolls the attack and gains a +5 bonus to the roll.

⬗ **Death Burst** (when reduced to 0 hit points) ✦ **Fire**
     The balor explodes in a burst of flame: close burst 10; +29 vs. Reflex; 7d10 fire damage. *Miss:* Half damage. The balor and its weapons are completely destroyed.

Alignment Chaotic evil   **Languages** Abyssal, Common

Skills Bluff +20, Insight +23, Intimidate +20

Str 30 (+23)	Dex 19 (+17)	Wis 21 (+18)
Con 32 (+24)	Int 12 (+14)	Cha 14 (+15)

Balor Tactics

The fearless balor concentrates its attacks on single targets and does not allow itself to be distracted. It uses its *demonic accuracy* power when particularly infuriated by an opponent. The balor uses its *flame whip* to pull enemies within reach of its sword. The first time it's able to attack with both weapons on its turn, it spends an action point to do it again. A balor rarely retreats from battle, fighting until destroyed.

Balor Lore

A character knows the following information with a successful Arcana check.

DC 25: Balors answer directly to demon lords and other creatures of tremendous power. However, a few balors are mighty enough to hold their own as minor princelings of the Abyss, answering to no one.

DC 30: Some balors lurk in the deepest reaches of the natural world, bound against their will or preparing to rage against creation at the first opportunity.

Encounter Groups

Balors prefer the company of creatures that are near their own level but not above it. They sometimes work in pairs, but a natural sense of rivalry breaks up such alliances before long.

Level 26 Encounter (XP 54,000)
 ✦ 1 balor demon (level 27 elite brute)
 ✦ 1 thunderblast cyclone elemental (level 26 elite artillery)
 ✦ 2 efreet pyresingers (level 25 controller)

BARLGURA

BARLGURAS ARE DRIVEN BY A SAVAGE BLOODLUST that can be slaked only in combat, where they can tear apart their foes with bare claws.

Barlgura	Level 8 Brute
Large elemental beast (demon)	XP 350

Initiative +7   **Senses** Perception +12; low-light vision

HP 108; **Bloodied** 54; see also *savage howl*

AC 19; **Fortitude** 20, **Reflex** 17, **Will** 17

Resist 10 variable (1/encounter; see glossary)

Speed 8, climb 8

⊕ **Slam** (standard; at-will)
     Reach 2, +10 vs. AC; 1d8 + 6 damage, or 2d8 + 6 damage if the barlgura is bloodied.

⨥ **Double Attack** (standard; at-will)
     The barlgura makes two slam attacks.

Savage Howl (free, when first bloodied; encounter)
     The barlgura and all allies within 5 squares of the barlgura gain a +2 bonus to attack rolls until the end of the barlgura's next turn.

Alignment Chaotic evil   **Languages** Abyssal

Skills Athletics +15

Str 22 (+10)	Dex 16 (+7)	Wis 16 (+7)
Con 18 (+8)	Int 6 (+2)	Cha 12 (+5)

Barlgura Tactics

A barlgura charges into battle, using its *double attack* to pummel its opponents.

(Top, left to right)
glabrezu, evistro, barlgura

BARLGURA LORE

A character knows the following information with a successful Arcana check.

DC 15: Barlguras are favored by the demon prince Demogorgon, who enjoys their primitive, bestial savagery. Their presence in the world is often a sign of a hidden cult of the so-called Prince of Demons.

ENCOUNTER GROUPS

Barlguras often fight alongside demon cultists, other demons, and powerful elemental beings.

Level 9 Encounter (XP 2,000)
- ✦ 1 barlgura demon (level 8 brute)
- ✦ 2 gnoll claw fighters (level 6 skirmisher)
- ✦ 3 gnoll marauders (level 6 brute)
- ✦ 2 gnoll huntmasters (level 5 artillery)

Level 11 Encounter (XP 3,200)
- ✦ 4 barlgura demons (level 8 brute)
- ✦ 2 minotaur warriors (level 10 soldier)
- ✦ 1 minotaur cabalist (level 13 controller)

EVISTRO

EVISTROS CRAVE CARNAGE and rampage across planes and worlds in enormous hordes, leaving devastation in their wake.

Evistro (Carnage Demon)		Level 6 Brute
Medium elemental magical beast (demon)		XP 250

Initiative +4   **Senses** Perception +4
HP 90; **Bloodied** 45
AC 16; **Fortitude** 18, **Reflex** 14, **Will** 14
Resist 10 variable (1/encounter; see glossary)
Speed 6
⊕ **Claws** (standard; at-will)
  +9 vs. AC; 1d8 + 5 damage.
↯ **Destructive Bite** (minor; at-will)
  Bloodied target only; +8 vs. AC; 1d6 + 5 damage.
Carnage
  The carnage demon gains a +1 bonus to melee attacks if it has one or more allies adjacent to its target (+3 if one of these allies is another carnage demon). This bonus stacks with combat advantage.
Alignment Chaotic evil   **Languages** Abyssal
Str 21 (+8)   **Dex** 12 (+4)   **Wis** 12 (+4)
Con 20 (+8)   **Int** 5 (+0)   **Cha** 7 (+1)

EVISTRO TACTICS

In addition to attacking with its claws, a carnage demon can use its *destructive bite* against a bloodied foe. It stays close to its allies to reap the benefit of its *carnage* power.

EVISTRO LORE

A character knows the following information with a successful Arcana check.

DC 15: Rituals known to demon-worshiping cultists and certain depraved wizards can summon evistros to the world. However, evistros are notoriously difficult to control—usually, the best their summoner can accomplish is to send them out to wreak havoc. Sometimes, though, they turn on their summoner before extending their rampage.

ENCOUNTER GROUPS

Evistros are most commonly encountered in packs of their own kind, led by other demons, or backed by the demonic cultists that summoned them into the world.

Level 6 Encounter (XP 1,250)
- ✦ 3 evistro demons (level 6 brute)
- ✦ 2 gnoll claw fighters (level 6 skirmisher)

Level 6 Encounter (XP 1,250)
- ✦ 4 evistro demons (level 6 brute)
- ✦ 1 harpy (level 6 controller)

GLABREZU

GLABREZUS ARE CUNNING BRUTES that use magic as well as brawn to slaughter everything that stands in their way.

Glabrezu	Level 23 Elite Brute
Huge elemental humanoid (demon)	XP 10,200

Initiative +14   **Senses** Perception +18; truesight 6
HP 520; **Bloodied** 260; see also *arcane fury*
AC 39; **Fortitude** 42, **Reflex** 37, **Will** 37
Resist 20 variable (3/encounter; see glossary)
Saving Throws +2
Speed 8, fly 8
Action Points 1
⊕ **Pincer Claw** (standard; at-will)
  Reach 3; +26 vs. AC; 2d8 + 8 damage.
↯ **Double Attack** (standard; at-will)
  The glabrezu makes two pincer claw attacks. If both claws hit the same target, the target is grabbed (until escape) if the glabrezu so chooses.
↗ **Abyssal Bolt** (minor; at-will)
  Ranged 10; +24 vs. Reflex; 3d4 + 7 damage.
⇜ **Blasphemous Word** (minor; encounter) ✦ **Psychic**
  Close burst 5; targets enemies; +24 vs. Will; 1d12 + 7 psychic damage, and the target is dazed until the end of the glabrezu's next turn.
⇜ **Chaos Word** (minor; recharge ⚄⚅)
  Close burst 5; targets enemies; +24 vs. Fortitude; 1d12 + 7 damage. This damage bypasses all resistances.
Arcane Fury (free, when first bloodied; encounter)
  The glabrezu teleports 8 squares, recharges its *blasphemous word* and *chaos word* powers, and makes an *abyssal bolt*, *blasphemous word*, or *chaos word* attack.
Alignment Chaotic evil   **Languages** Abyssal, Common
Skills Arcana +23, Bluff +19, Intimidate +19
Str 26 (+19)   **Dex** 17 (+14)   **Wis** 14 (+13)
Con 20 (+16)   **Int** 24 (+18)   **Cha** 16 (+14)

GLABREZU TACTICS

Unlike mortal spellcasters, glabrezus do not cower behind minions and armored comrades while they cast their foul magic; they wade into the thick of combat and shout out their magic with wild abandon.

A glabrezu moves close to its enemies and unleashes both a *blasphemous word* and a *word of chaos*. After this initial onslaught, it targets a weak-looking opponent with its pincer claws. If the glabrezu is bloodied, it teleports a safe distance and hurls *abyssal bolts* (missiles of crackling purple energy), exchanging move actions and standard actions to do this up to three times in a round.

(Left to right)
goristro, immolith, hezrou

GLABREZU LORE

A character knows the following information with a successful Arcana check.

DC 25: Glabrezus use their high intelligence to sow discord. They also like to goad their allies into ever-greater acts of depravity and violence.

DC 30: When a demon as wicked as a glabrezu lingers too long in the world, its corruption spreads. Crops are stunted, animals die, people sicken, and the sky itself seems to darken. Only when the demon is driven off or slain is the natural order restored.

ENCOUNTER GROUPS

Though they often lead groups of other demons, glabrezus could hardly be termed generals—they lead by example, spearheading the devastation. More often, though, glabrezus are brought to the world by incredibly powerful and destructive villains.

Level 23 Encounter (XP 25,500)
✦ 1 glabrezu demon (level 23 elite brute)
✦ 1 earthwind ravager elemental (level 23 controller)
✦ 2 blood fiend abominations (level 23 soldier)

GORISTRO

GORISTROS ARE LIVING SIEGE ENGINES capable of destroying castles and laying waste to entire cities. With a tremendous roar they surge forth, obliterating everything in their path.

Goristro	Level 19 Elite Brute
Huge elemental humanoid (demon)	XP 4,800

Initiative +10　　**Senses** Perception +17; darkvision
HP 450; **Bloodied** 225; see also *raging frenzy*
AC 31; **Fortitude** 34, **Reflex** 27, **Will** 29
Resist 20 variable (2/encounter; see glossary)
Saving Throws +2
Speed 8
Action Points 1

✦ **Slam** (standard; at-will)
　Reach 3; +22 vs. AC; 2d10 + 8 damage.

✦ **Double Attack** (standard; at-will)
　The goristro makes two slam attacks.

✦ **Goristro Stomp** (immediate reaction, when a nonadjacent enemy moves adjacent to the goristro; recharge ⚄ ⚅ ⚅)
　The goristro makes an attack against the enemy: +22 vs. AC; 4d8 + 8 damage, and the target is knocked prone.

✦ **Goring Charge** (standard; at-will)
　The goristro makes a charge attack: +23 vs. AC; 3d10 + 8 damage, and the target is pushed 2 squares and knocked prone.

✦ **Raging Frenzy** (immediate reaction, when attacked by an adjacent enemy while bloodied; at-will)
　The goristro makes a frenzied gore attack against the enemy: +22 vs. AC; 2d8 + 8 damage.

Alignment Chaotic evil		**Languages** Abyssal
Str 27 (+17)	**Dex** 12 (+10)	**Wis** 17 (+12)
Con 25 (+16)	**Int** 6 (+7)	**Cha** 12 (+10)

Goristro Tactics

The goristro makes a *goring charge* toward the nearest enemy. Once in battle, it makes slam attacks against those it perceives as the most physically challenging and uses *goristro stomp* on enemies that get too close. The goristro becomes much more dangerous when bloodied, using *raging frenzy* each time it's attacked by an adjacent enemy.

Goristro Lore

A character knows the following information with a successful Arcana check.

DC 20: Goristros are the favored servitors of Baphomet, the Horned Lord (demon lord of minotaurs). They are numerous in the Abyss and the Elemental Chaos, but thankfully rare in the natural world.

Encounter Groups

Baphomet's minotaur cultists often summon goristros from the Abyss to guard their enclaves or take their sacrifices to the Horned Lord.

Level 18 Encounter (XP 11,800)
✦ 1 goristro demon (level 19 elite brute)
✦ 2 savage minotaurs (level 16 brute)
✦ 3 abyssal ghouls (level 16 skirmisher)

HEZROU

As obedient as they are loathsome, hezrous eagerly serve more powerful demons and summoners who encourage and reward their destructive behavior.

Hezrou	Level 22 Brute
Large elemental humanoid (demon)	XP 4,150

Initiative +16   **Senses** Perception +16; darkvision
Noxious Stench (Poison) aura 2; enemies in the aura take a -2 penalty to attack rolls. While the hezrou is bloodied, enemies within its aura are also weakened.
HP 255; **Bloodied** 127
AC 34; **Fortitude** 36, **Reflex** 32, **Will** 32
Resist 20 variable (2/encounter; see glossary)
Speed 6; see also *demonic step* below
(+) **Slam** (standard; at-will)
    Reach 2; +25 vs. AC; 2d10 + 9 damage.
‡ **Bite** (standard; at-will)
    Reach 2; +25 vs. AC; 2d8 + 9 damage.
‡ **Combination Attack** (standard; at-will)
    The hezrou makes one slam attack and one bite attack.
Demonic Step
    The hezrou ignores difficult terrain, seeming to phase through it.
Alignment Chaotic evil   **Languages** Abyssal
Skills Stealth +21
Str 28 (+20)   **Dex** 20 (+16)   **Wis** 20 (+16)
Con 25 (+18)   **Int** 8 (+10)   **Cha** 16 (+14)

Hezrou Tactics

A hezrou lumbers into melee, pummeling and biting enemies while overwhelming them with its *noxious stench*.

Hezrou Lore

A character knows the following information with a successful Arcana check.

DC 25: Hezrous are numerous, expendable, powerful, and able to stay focused on the simple tasks they are given. As demons go, they're fairly easy to please provided there's abundant food that they can kill.

Encounter Groups

Hezrous can be found alongside virtually any creature that can match its power and approach its appetite for destruction.

Level 22 Encounter (XP 21,075)
✦ 2 hezrou demons (level 22 brute)
✦ 1 deathpriest hierophant (level 21 elite controller)
✦ 5 abyssal ghoul myrmidons (level 23 minion)

IMMOLITH

The spirits of deceased demons sometimes fuse together as they fall back into the Abyss that spawned them. The event is unpredictable, and the result is a horrid demonic entity called an immolith.

Immolith	Level 15 Controller
Large elemental magical beast (demon, fire, undead)	XP 1,200

Initiative +10   **Senses** Perception +9
Flaming Aura (Fire) aura 1; any creature that enters or starts its turn in the aura takes 10 fire damage.
HP 153; **Bloodied** 76
AC 27; **Fortitude** 28, **Reflex** 24, **Will** 25
Immune disease, fire, poison; **Resist** 15 variable (2/encounter; see glossary); **Vulnerable** 10 radiant
Speed 6
(+) **Claw** (standard; at-will) ✦ Fire
    Reach 4; +20 vs. AC; 1d8 + 7 fire damage, and ongoing 5 fire damage (save ends).
‡ **Fiery Grab** (standard; at-will) ✦ Fire
    The immolith makes a claw attack (see above) against a Large or smaller target. On a hit, the target slides into a square adjacent to the immolith and is grabbed (until escape). While grabbed, the target loses any resistance it has to fire. An immolith can hold up to five grabbed creatures using this power.
⌁ **Deathfire Curse** (minor; at-will) ✦ Fire
    Ranged 10; +18 vs. Will; the target is slowed (save ends).
    Aftereffect: The target takes ongoing 5 fire damage (save ends).
Vigor of the Grave (minor 1/round; at-will) ✦ Healing
    Close burst 5; undead in the burst (including the immolith) regain 5 hit points.
Alignment Chaotic evil   **Languages** Abyssal
Str 22 (+13)   **Dex** 16 (+10)   **Wis** 15 (+9)
Con 25 (+14)   **Int** 9 (+6)   **Cha** 18 (+11)

Immolith Tactics

The immolith issues a *deathfire curse* at the beginning of each round to slow an enemy. Then, with its standard action, it uses *fiery grab* to drag an enemy into its *flaming aura*. If an immolith doesn't need to move, it issues another *deathfire curse* with its remaining move action. It repeats these tactics round after round, using *vigor of the grave* whenever possible to heal itself and nearby undead allies.

IMMOLITH LORE

A character knows the following information with a successful Arcana check.

DC 20: Few demons despise the living more than immoliths. Thus, they are often encountered in the company of powerful undead creatures including liches and vampires.

ENCOUNTER GROUPS

Immoliths are most commonly found in the company of undead, other demons, or both.

Level 14 Encounter (XP 5,800)
✦ 1 immolith demon (level 15 controller)
✦ 2 vrock demons (level 13 skirmisher)
✦ 4 mezzodemons (level 11 soldier)
✦ 6 horde ghouls (level 13 minion)

MARILITH

THIS SIX-ARMED, SERPENTINE TERROR delights in hacking enemies to pieces with its swords, doing so with horrifying ease and astonishing grace.

MARILITH LORE

A character knows the following information with a successful Arcana check.

DC 25: Mariliths are obsessed with martial skill, and they take trophy weapons from particularly fierce opponents, which they hide in secret caches–sometimes in the depths of the Abyss, sometimes in the world.

Marilith	Level 24 Elite Skirmisher
Large elemental humanoid (demon)	XP 12,100

Initiative +22 **Senses** Perception +21; darkvision
HP 440; **Bloodied** 220
AC 38 (42 when using *shroud of steel*); **Fortitude** 36, **Reflex** 35, **Will** 33
Resist 20 variable (3/encounter; see glossary)
Saving Throws +2
Speed 8
Action Points 1

⚔ **Scimitar** (standard; at-will) ✦ **Weapon**
Reach 2; +29 vs. AC; 2d10 + 9 damage (crit 6d10 + 29).

✦ **Hacking Blades** (free, when an adjacent enemy misses the marilith with a melee attack; at-will) ✦ **Weapon**
The marilith makes a scimitar attack against the enemy.

✦ **Shroud of Steel** (standard; at-will) ✦ **Weapon**
The marilith makes two scimitar attacks and uses its other scimitars to parry incoming attacks, gaining a +4 bonus (+1 per scimitar) to AC until the start of its next turn.

✦ **Weapon Dance** (standard; recharges when first bloodied) ✦ **Weapon**
The marilith makes six scimitar attacks. Each time it hits, the marilith shifts 1 square.

Alignment Chaotic evil **Languages** Abyssal
Skills Bluff +23, Insight +21, Intimidate +23, Stealth +25
Str 28 (+21) **Dex** 26 (+20) **Wis** 19 (+16)
Con 20 (+17) **Int** 14 (+14) **Cha** 22 (+18)
Equipment 6 scimitars

(Left to right)
marilith, mezzodemon, vrock

Marilith Tactics

The marilith uses *shroud of steel* each round, switching to *weapon dance* when it wants to maneuver to a new location or quickly take down a bloodied foe. Once bloodied, it uses *weapon dance* again and then spends its action point to use *shroud of steel*.

Encounter Groups

When yuan-ti turn from the worship of Zehir and embrace Demogorgon or some other demon prince, they display a particular affinity for mariliths.

Level 23 Encounter (XP 28,700)
✦ 1 marilith demon (level 24 elite skirmisher)
✦ 4 hezrou demons (level 22 brute)

MEZZODEMON

These insectoid demons are something of a mystery. While they delight in killing, their priorities lie with the accumulation of treasure.

Mezzodemon	Level 11 Soldier
Large elemental humanoid (demon)	XP 600

Initiative +9   **Senses** Perception +13; darkvision
HP 113; **Bloodied** 56
AC 27; **Fortitude** 25, **Reflex** 22, **Will** 23
Resist 20 poison, 10 variable (2/encounter; see glossary)
Speed 6
⊕ **Trident** (standard; at-will) ✦ **Weapon**
  Requires trident; reach 2; +18 vs. AC; 1d8 + 5 damage.
↟ **Skewering Tines** (standard; at-will) ✦ **Weapon**
  Reach 2; +18 vs. AC; 1d8 + 5 damage, ongoing 5 damage and the target is restrained (save ends both). While the target is restrained, the mezzodemon can't make trident attacks.
↞ **Poison Breath** (standard; recharge ⚄ ⚅) ✦ **Poison**
  Close blast 3; targets enemies; +16 vs. Fortitude; 2d6 + 3 poison damage, and ongoing 5 poison damage (save ends).
Alignment Chaotic evil   **Languages** Abyssal
Skills Intimidate +11
Str 20 (+10)   **Dex** 15 (+7)   **Wis** 16 (+8)
Con 17 (+8)   **Int** 10 (+5)   **Cha** 13 (+6)
Equipment trident

Mezzodemon Tactics

Unlike other demons, the mezzodemon is a cautious foot soldier that is unopposed to fleeing when bloodied or heavily outnumbered. It attacks with its trident and uses *skewering tines* to restrain and further injure its foe. The mezzodemon likes to holds its prey in place while it breathes a cloud of poison on it and other nearby enemies.

Mezzodemon Lore

A character knows the following information with a successful Arcana check.

DC 20: In the eons since they were spawned in the Abyss, mezzodemons (sometimes referred to as mezzoloths) have spread throughout the planes. They are more likely than other demons to establish lairs and infest specific areas, rather than rampage across realms in monstrous hordes.

DC 25: Mezzodemons lust after gold and other valuables. Because of this, mezzodemons often work for pay alone and have a mercenary reputation.

Encounter Groups

As the mercenaries of the Abyss, mezzodemons are found serving as frontline troops for a wide variety of wealthy creatures, even those not normally associated with demons.

Level 11 Encounter (XP 3,200)
✦ 2 mezzodemons (level 11 soldier)
✦ 2 drow warriors (level 11 lurker)
✦ 1 drow arachnomancer (level 13 artillery)

VROCK

With demonic glee, vrocks swoop down upon their victims and tear them to pieces, cackling madly and relishing their victims' screams.

Vrock	Level 13 Skirmisher
Large elemental humanoid (demon)	XP 800

Initiative +12   **Senses** Perception +13; darkvision
HP 132; **Bloodied** 66; see also *spores of madness*
AC 27; **Fortitude** 25, **Reflex** 23, **Will** 23
Resist 10 variable (2/encounter; see glossary)
Speed 6, fly 8; see also *flyby attack*
⊕ **Claw** (standard; at-will)
  Reach 2; +18 vs. AC; 2d8 + 6 damage.
↟ **Flyby Attack** (standard; at-will)
  The vrock flies up to 8 squares and makes one claw attack at any point during that movement. The vrock doesn't provoke opportunity attacks when moving away from the target of the attack.
↞ **Stunning Screech** (standard; recharge ⚅)
  Close burst 3; deafened creatures are immune; +17 vs. Fortitude; the target is stunned until the end of the vrock's next turn.
↞ **Spores of Madness** (free, when first bloodied; encounter)
  ✦ **Poison**
  Close burst 2; demons are immune; +16 vs. Will; 1d10 + 4 poison damage, and the target is dazed (save ends).
Alignment Chaotic evil   **Languages** Abyssal
Skills Bluff +15, Insight +13
Str 23 (+12)   **Dex** 19 (+10)   **Wis** 15 (+8)
Con 20 (+11)   **Int** 12 (+7)   **Cha** 19 (+10)

Vrock Tactics

This demon uses *flyby attack* to make swooping attacks against foes before landing to make basic claw attacks. It uses its *stunning screech* when surrounded and its *spores of madness* when first bloodied.

Vrock Lore

A character knows the following information with a successful Arcana check.

DC 20: Vrocks have a reputation for disloyalty, often abandoning their posts and forsaking one master to join another whom they view as more powerful. They also like to plot against their superiors, although these schemes rarely amount to anything.

Encounter Groups

Vrocks associate with demonic cults, and sometimes with giants and evil fey.

Level 13 Encounter (XP 4,000)
✦ 2 vrock demons (level 13 skirmisher)
✦ 1 briar witch dryad (level 13 elite controller)
✦ 1 hill giant (level 13 brute)

DESTRACHAN

THIS BLIND BEAST STALKS THROUGH DUNGEONS, relying on its other senses to detect prey. When it finds something it can eat, the destrachan blasts it with skullcracking waves of sound.

Destrachan		Level 9 Artillery
Large aberrant magical beast (blind)		XP 400

Initiative +8   **Senses** Perception +11; blindsight 10
HP 80; **Bloodied** 40
AC 22; **Fortitude** 24, **Reflex** 21, **Will** 20
Immune gaze
Resist 10 thunder
Speed 6, climb 3
⊕ **Claw** (standard; at-will)
  +14 vs. AC; 1d8 + 4 damage.
↗ **Sound Pulse** (standard; at-will) ✦ **Thunder**
  Ranged 10; +13 vs. Reflex; 2d6 + 5 thunder damage.
↤ **Bellowing Blast** (standard; recharge ⚁ ⚂ ⚃ ⚄) ✦ **Thunder**
  Close blast 5; +13 vs. Fortitude; 2d6 + 5 thunder damage, and
  the target is dazed (save ends).
Alignment Evil   **Languages** Deep Speech
Skills Bluff +9, Stealth +13
Str 18 (+8)   **Dex** 18 (+8)   **Wis** 14 (+6)
Con 20 (+9)   **Int** 7 (+2)   **Cha** 10 (+4)

DESTRACHAN TACTICS

The stealthy destrachan can sense prey within 10 squares of it and prefers to attack at range using its *sound pulse* power. It uses *bellowing blast* against close targets.

Destrachan Far Voice		Level 15 Artillery
Large aberrant magical beast (blind)		XP 1,200

Initiative +12   **Senses** Perception +14; blindsight 20
HP 122; **Bloodied** 61
AC 28; **Fortitude** 32, **Reflex** 27, **Will** 25
Immune gaze
Resist 15 thunder
Speed 8, climb 4
⊕ **Claw** (standard; at-will)
  +20 vs. AC; 1d8 + 6 damage.
↗ **Sound Pulse** (standard; at-will) ✦ **Thunder**
  Ranged 10; +19 vs. Reflex; 2d8 + 8 thunder damage.
↤ **Bellowing Blast** (standard; recharge ⚁ ⚂ ⚃ ⚄) ✦ **Thunder**
  Close blast 5; +19 vs. Fortitude; 2d6 + 8 thunder damage, and
  the target is dazed (save ends).
↤ **Reverberate** (standard; encounter) ✦ **Thunder**
  Close burst 2; +19 vs. Fortitude; 2d8 + 8 thunder damage, and
  the target is stunned (save ends). *Miss:* Half damage, and the
  target is dazed until the end of the destrachan far voice's next
  turn.
Alignment Evil   **Languages** Deep Speech
Skills Bluff +12, Stealth +17
Str 23 (+13)   **Dex** 20 (+12)   **Wis** 15 (+9)
Con 26 (+15)   **Int** 10 (+7)   **Cha** 11 (+7)

DESTRACHAN FAR VOICE TACTICS

The destrachan far voice favors ranged attacks over melee and uses *reverberate* against enemies that come too close.

DESTRACHAN LORE

A character knows the following information with a successful Dungeoneering check.

DC 15: A destrachan can learn to imitate sounds it hears often, such as ambient dungeon noises and guttural sounds made by other creatures. The creature uses such noises to cover its footsteps or trick prey into thinking it's something far less threatening (this requires a successful Bluff check).

ENCOUNTER GROUPS

A destrachan is attracted to other aberrant creatures, such as chuuls, gibbering mouthers, and gricks. A destrachan might also ally itself with drow, grimlocks, hags, medusas, trolls, onis, troglodytes, and other humanoids.

Level 9 Encounter (XP 1,950)
✦ 2 destrachans (level 9 artillery)
✦ 2 foulspawn berserkers (level 9 soldier)
✦ 1 foulspawn grue (level 8 controller)

Level 15 Encounter (XP 6,200)
✦ 1 destrachan far voice (level 15 artillery)
✦ 2 drider fanglords (level 14 brute)
✦ 1 drow priest (level 15 controller)
✦ 3 drow warriors (level 11 lurker)

BEN WOOTTEN

DEVIL

MALEVOLENT AND CORRUPT, devils are the rebellious servants of the gods now living in the Nine Hells, one of the darkest dominions on the Astral Sea. Devils come in many varieties, from the sly imp to the mighty archdevils known as the Lords of the Nine, each a ruler of one of the Nine Hells. The greatest of these infernal lords is the god Asmodeus, prince of Nessus, the ninth hell. Long ago, Asmodeus was a powerful divine servant who chose to rebel against the god he served. At the head of an army of like-minded creatures, Asmodeus slew his divine master. For their betrayal, he and his followers were cursed with monstrous forms and imprisoned within the fuming ruin of the murdered god's dominion.

Devils can leave the Nine Hells, but it is very difficult for them to do so. They can be sent forth by mighty archdevils through costly infernal magic, or travel through rare and well-hidden magical portals (usually only a few at a time when conditions are right). However, most devils outside of the Nine Hells have been brought to the natural world by evil mortals employing dark rituals.

Devils lust for the souls of mortals; each mortal spirit devils enslave undermines the gods' sway over mortalkind and adds to the Nine Hells' power. Devils torment and consume captured souls to fuel the mightiest of their infernal works, including evil constructs and terrible invocations. Devils compete fiercely to gather souls in order to earn favor and status within the infernal order, but they all work together toward the common goal of gathering souls for the Nine Hells. Some devils seek to drive mortals into surrendering their souls through tyranny, despair, or terror; some seek to destroy the servants of good-aligned gods and tear down their works; and still others are tempters and deceivers who inflame mortal ambition, desire, greed, or pride.

Long ago, Asmodeus and his vassals forged dark pacts with various evil deities. Devils are therefore commonly found serving Bane, Gruumsh, Tiamat, Torog, and Vecna. Devils carefully honor their bargains—but they are extremely good at giving reckless mortals exactly what they ask for, and few of those who bargain with devils escape the final payment.

BEARDED DEVIL

FIERCE WARRIORS OF THE NINE HELLS, bearded devils are used as guards and assault troops by more powerful devils or evil mortals. They are violent, wrathful creatures that relish battle.

Bearded Devil (Barbazu)		Level 13 Soldier
Medium immortal humanoid (devil)		XP 800

Initiative +10   **Senses** Perception +14; darkvision
Beard Tendrils aura 1; enemies that begin their turns adjacent to the bearded devil take 5 damage.
HP 129; **Bloodied** 64; see also *battle frenzy*
AC 29; **Fortitude** 25, **Reflex** 22, **Will** 23
Resist 20 fire
Speed 6
✛ **Glaive** (standard; at-will) ✦ **Weapon**
    Reach 2; +18 vs. AC; 2d4 + 5 damage, and the target is marked until the end of the bearded devil's next turn and takes ongoing 5 damage (save ends).
✛ **Claw** (standard; at-will)
    +18 vs. AC; 1d6 + 5 damage.
Battle Frenzy
    While the bearded devil is bloodied, it gains a +2 bonus to attack rolls and deals an extra 5 damage with its melee attacks.
Devilish Teamwork
    Allies adjacent to the bearded devil gain a +2 power bonus to AC.

Alignment Evil	**Languages** Supernal	
Skills Intimidate +11		
Str 20 (+11)	**Dex** 15 (+8)	**Wis** 16 (+9)
Con 17 (+9)	**Int** 10 (+6)	**Cha** 11 (+6)

Equipment glaive

BEARDED DEVIL TACTICS

The bearded devil is a straightforward melee combatant trained to protect adjacent allies using its *devilish teamwork*. It makes claw attacks only if it loses its glaive.

BEARDED DEVIL LORE

A character knows the following information with a successful Religion check.

(Left to right) chain devil, bone devil, and bearded devil

JEAN PIERRE TARGETE

DC 20: Bearded devils (also known as barbazus) are among the weakest devils, but they are savage and dangerous fighters. The bearded devil's glaive is a vicious weapon that inflicts horrible bleeding wounds.

DC 25: Bearded devils are followers, not leaders, and usually serve as bodyguards or assault troops. They rarely seek to tempt or lure mortals, preferring straightforward slaughter and terror instead.

ENCOUNTER GROUPS

Bearded devils are usually little more than infernal muscle for a smarter devil or villain.

Level 13 Encounter (XP 4,000)
+ 3 bearded devils (level 13 soldier)
+ 2 yuan-ti malison sharp-eyes (level 13 artillery)

BONE DEVIL

BONE DEVILS ARE RUTHLESS TASKMASTERS, vigilantly watching over lesser creatures to ensure their obedience. In the Nine Hells, they fill a mid-ranking class of overseers and monitors who report on lesser devils, but they can sometimes be found in the service of powerful mortal tyrants, watching the ranks for the smallest signs of disloyalty or incompetence.

A PRIMER TO THE NINE HELLS

The Nine Hells form a single dominion on the Astral Sea. Black smoke surrounds them, and beyond this choking veil broods a great, volcanic world whose surface is a blasted plain of ash and jagged stone. This is Avernus, the first of the Nine Hells, where embers rain down from a sunless sky and iron fortresses rise up between rivers of magma. Astral vessels approaching too closely find themselves plummeting through the skies of Avernus rather than sailing in the Astral Sea, landing in the Nine Hells with a great fiery impact. A helmsman of great skill can sometimes negotiate the passage and alight on the ashen plain safely, but the only sure way to avoid fiery disaster is to find the astral influence of the River Styx and follow it down through the basalt cliffs. The Styx cuts a jagged course across Avernus and eventually plunges down into the lower Hells—each one a tremendous continent-sized cavern within the roiling world.

Avernus, the first Hell, forms the surface of this terrible dominion. It's a volcanic domain strewn with the blood and wreckage of a million battles. Fireballs plunge from the smoke-filled sky. The archdevil Bel, a military genius, protects and rules Avernus from a towering iron citadel.

A great iron gate in a mountainside of Avernus leads to Dis, the second Hell. Dis is an iron-walled city that lies within a vast cavern, sprawling unevenly amid the cavern's jagged, mountainous floor. Dispater, the ruler of this Hell, is famous as the most cautious and calculating of the archdevils.

The cavern of Dis gradually descends and broadens into the great, low, brooding vault of Minauros, the Third Hell. A constant oily rain pelts down from the ceiling, and the black soil of Minauros is a vast series of mud flats, swamps, and mires, some heated into bubbling, stinking mud volcanoes by the heat rising from below. The serpentine and supremely boastful archdevil Mammon rules here.

Phlegethos, the fourth Hell, lies far below its predecessors. Dank steps cut into the stinking fumaroles of Minauros lead down several miles to a fiery cavern, where the air ripples with heat distortion and cascades of lava pour down from volcanic fissures in the ceiling miles overhead. The ambitious archdevil Fierna presides, with her grim father Belial as the true power behind the throne.

Stygia lies as deep as Phlegethos, but is many hundreds of miles away from its fiery neighbor—it underlies Dis, and dismal stairs of ice and iron link the two. The fifth Hell is cold and dark. Within Stygia's cavern lies a vast frozen sea dotted with towering icebergs. Faint auroras of green-blue frostfire dance far above the sea, casting long shadows. Imprisoned within one of these mighty bergs is the archdevil Levistus, trapped forever by Asmodeus for some great betrayal.

Asmodeus's daughter, the fiendishly beautiful Glasya, rules Malbolge, the sixth Hell. Long, icy canals lead hundreds of miles from frozen Stygia to this great cavern, illuminated by sinister yellow-green lamps suspended from the ceiling like tiny suns. Long ago Malbolge was a vast garden, the delight of the deity who ruled this sphere before Asmodeus, but now its superficial beauty cannot hide a feculent underbelly: autumnal trees with grasping roots, beautiful white towers with corpses impaled on their battlements, shimmering ponds with poisoned waters, and the like.

Maladomini, the seventh Hell, is a tremendous maze of winding tunnels, each miles across. These passages reach several of the lower Hells, including Malbolge, Cania, and Nessus. Within these vast tunnels lie crumbling cities, sludge-filled rivers, and vast tracts of land mined to absolute depletion. Black ichor erupts from the earth, and swarms of flies harry all. Here rules the archdevil Baalzebul, a sluglike monstrosity bereft of compassion.

The icy layer of Stygia seems like a paradise compared to Cania, the eighth Hell. This vast gulf deep within the world is another cold domain, where mile-high glaciers grind across a forbidding landscape so cold that few creatures can bear it. The wickedly handsome archdevil Mephistopheles rules Cania from a palace of ice lit with crackling hellfire.

The darkest of Cania's rifts plunge hundreds of miles further down to Nessus, the ninth and deepest of the Hells. This is home to the god-tyrant Asmodeus, father of all devils. Nessus is a vast, vertical maze of chasms so large and so deep they are rooted in the seething fires at the core of the cursed sphere. Great infernal cities and fiendish armies lie hidden within these fiery depths.

Bone Devil (Osyluth)	Level 17 Controller (Leader)
Large immortal humanoid (devil)	XP 1,600

Initiative +12   **Senses** Perception +15; darkvision
Aura of Fear (Fear) aura 5; enemies in the aura take a -2 penalty to attack rolls.
Aura of Obedience (Charm, Healing) aura 5; bone devils are immune; any bloodied devil in the aura at the start of its turn takes 10 damage but gains a +4 bonus to attack rolls and deals an extra 5 damage on melee attacks until the start of its next turn. If a devil is slain by this aura, the bone devil regains 10 hit points.
HP 165; **Bloodied** 82
AC 31; **Fortitude** 29, **Reflex** 26, **Will** 27
Resist 20 fire
Speed 8, teleport 8
⊕ **Claw** (standard; at-will)
    Reach 2; +22 vs. AC; 1d6 + 7 damage.
⊠ **Poison Sting** (standard; at-will) ✦ Poison
    Reach 2; +20 vs. Fortitude; 1d6 + 7 damage, and the target takes ongoing 10 poison damage and takes a -4 penalty to its Will defense (save ends both).
⊠ **Double Attack** (standard; at-will)
    The bone devil makes two claw attacks. If both claw attacks hit the same target, the bone devil can make a secondary attack using *poison sting* against the target.
↗ **Fiendish Focus** (minor; at-will)
    Ranged 5; +18 vs. Will; the target takes a -5 penalty to all defenses until the end of the bone devil's next turn.
Alignment Evil   **Languages** Supernal
Skills Insight +15, Intimidate +18
Str 25 (+15)   **Dex** 18 (+12)   **Wis** 15 (+10)
Con 21 (+13)   **Int** 11 (+8)   **Cha** 20 (+13)

BONE DEVIL TACTICS

The bone devil targets enemies with its *fiendish focus* at the start of battle to make them more susceptible to attacks while overwhelming them with its *aura of fear*. It tries to use *double attack* whenever possible. As its allies become bloodied, the bone devil uses its *aura of obedience* to make them fight harder.

BONE DEVIL LORE

A character knows the following information with a successful Religion check.

DC 20: Bone devils (also known as osyluths) are clever and patient creatures, rarely caught off-guard. They ensure that lesser devils obey their superiors and engage foes with the proper degree of bloodthirstiness and zeal. Fanatically loyal to their superiors, bone devils are indeed severe taskmasters.

DC 25: Bone devils are universally reviled by lesser devils because of their harsh motivational techniques. They surround themselves in an aura of fear that makes enemies reluctant to attack them, and their poisoned stingers can further break down an enemy's resolve.

ENCOUNTER GROUPS

Bone devils serve more powerful devils as overseers, keeping watch on the activities of lesser fiends. Sometimes a small group of bone devils work together as roving inquisitors, driving the hesitant into battle.

Level 16 Encounter (XP 7,600)
✦ 1 bone devil (level 17 controller)
✦ 5 bearded devils (level 13 soldier)
✦ 1 cambion hellfire magus (level 18 artillery)

CHAIN DEVIL

SADISTIC TORMENTORS OF THE HAPLESS, chain devils savor their roles as the jailors and torturers of the Nine Hells. They seek to capture their victims alive so that a defeated foe's suffering can be drawn out for days.

Chain Devil (Kyton)	Level 11 Skirmisher
Medium immortal humanoid (devil)	XP 600

Initiative +14   **Senses** Perception +7; darkvision
HP 116; **Bloodied** 58
AC 25; **Fortitude** 22, **Reflex** 24, **Will** 19
Resist 20 fire
Speed 7; see also *dance of battle*
⊕ **Spiked Chain** (standard; at-will)
    Reach 2; +16 vs. AC; 2d4 + 7 damage.
⊠ **Double Attack** (standard; at-will)
    The chain devil makes two spiked chain attacks.
⊠ **Chains of Vengeance** (free, when first bloodied; encounter)
    The chain devil makes two spiked chain attacks.
⊠ **Hellish Chains** (standard; at-will)
    +14 vs. Reflex; the target is wrapped in chains and restrained (save ends). The chain devil can use its chains to restrain only one creature at a time.
Dance of Battle (minor; at-will)
    The chain devil shifts 1 square.
Dance of Defiance (immediate interrupt, when a melee attack is made against the chain devil; recharges after the chain devil uses *chains of vengeance*)
    The chain devil shifts 1 square.
Alignment Evil   **Languages** Supernal
Skills Intimidate +11
Str 19 (+9)   **Dex** 24 (+12)   **Wis** 15 (+7)
Con 20 (+10)   **Int** 14 (+7)   **Cha** 13 (+6)

CHAIN DEVIL TACTICS

A chain devil rakes enemies with its spiked chains, using *hellish chains* to restrain a particularly troublesome enemy. If it forgoes a move action, it can shift before and after making an attack. Outside of its turn, it uses *dance of defiance* to dodge attacks and *chains of vengeance* when it is first bloodied.

CHAIN DEVIL LORE

A character knows the following information with a successful Religion check.

DC 20: Chain devils (also known as kytons) use the spiked chains that shroud them to lash and restrain foes.

DC 25: Some chain devils learn rituals that allow them to animate chains that aren't attached to their bodies, causing them to writhe like serpents.

ENCOUNTER GROUPS

Chain devils work well with other devils and creatures that allow them to indulge their desire to inflict pain.

Level 11 Encounter (XP 3,100)
✦ 2 chain devils (level 11 skirmisher)
✦ 4 legion devil hellguards (level 11 minion)
✦ 1 snaketongue celebrant (level 11 controller)
✦ 4 snaketongue zealots (level 12 minion)

ICE DEVIL

ICE DEVILS HAIL FROM THE FRIGID WASTELANDS of Cania, the eighth layer of the Nine Hells. Infernal generals and evil mortals use them as bodyguards and champions, and ice devils often lead lesser devils in battle. They are poor commanders, though, because they despise weaker devils and consider them expendable.

Ice Devil (Gelugon)	Level 20 Soldier
Large immortal humanoid (devil)	XP 2,800

Initiative +18   **Senses** Perception +13; darkvision
Cold Aura (Cold) aura 5; enemies in the aura take a -2 penalty to all attack rolls.
HP 195; **Bloodied** 97
AC 36; **Fortitude** 33, **Reflex** 31, **Will** 29
Immune cold; **Resist** 20 fire
Speed 8
(+) **Icy Longspear** (standard; at-will) ✦ **Cold, Weapon**
   Reach 3; +27 vs. AC; 1d12 + 7 cold damage, and the target is slowed (save ends).
✦ **Claw** (standard; at-will)
   Reach 2; +25 vs. AC; 1d6 + 7 damage.
⬳ **Freezing Breath** (standard; recharge ⚁⚂⚃⚄) ✦ **Cold**
   Close blast 5; +23 vs. Fortitude; 2d6 + 7 cold damage, and the target is slowed (save ends).
⬳ **Chilling Command** (minor; recharge ⚃⚄) ✦ **Cold**
   Close burst 5; +23 vs. Will; the target takes ongoing 5 cold damage and is immobilized (save ends both).
Alignment Evil   **Languages** Supernal
Skills Endurance +23
Str 25 (+17)   **Dex** 22 (+16)   **Wis** 17 (+13)
Con 27 (+18)   **Int** 15 (+12)   **Cha** 19 (+14)
Equipment longspear

ICE DEVIL TACTICS

An ice devil prefers to fight its own battles, using its powers to confound multiple enemies at once. It uses *chilling command* to immobilize frontline combatants while it attacks softer targets with the aid of its superior speed and reach. If the ice devil has a spare move action, it uses *chilling command* again during its turn. It uses the numbing cold of its longspear and *freezing breath* to slow enemies and keep them from escaping.

ICE DEVIL LORE

A character knows the following information with a successful Religion check.

DC 20: Although they are most comfortable in the frozen wastelands of Cania, ice devils are unaffected by warmer climates. Wherever they go, they take a little bit of Cania with them in the form of a cold aura that surrounds them.

DC 25: Ice devils respect power and have no tolerance for weakness or frailty, either in their allies or their enemies. When confronted by multiple enemies, an ice devil almost always attacks the weakest foe first.

ENCOUNTER GROUPS

Ice devils resent devils weaker than them and cooperate with them only grudgingly.

Level 19 Encounter (XP 13,600)
✦ 2 ice devils (level 20 soldier)
✦ 2 cambion hellfire magi (level 18 artillery)
✦ 2 nabassu gargoyles (level 18 lurker)

IMP

IMPS ACT AS SPIES AND EMISSARIES for more powerful devils. Mortals often make bargains with imps, thinking that the weak devils are easy to control. Ultimately, most imps prove their loyalties lie with the Lords of the Nine and not any mortal master.

Imps are devious and deadly mischief-makers. They take pleasure in tricking mortals into harming one another.

Imp	Level 3 Lurker
Tiny immortal humanoid (devil)	XP 150

Initiative +8   **Senses** Perception +8; darkvision
HP 40; **Bloodied** 20
AC 17; **Fortitude** 15, **Reflex** 15, **Will** 15
Resist 15 fire
Speed 4, fly 6 (hover)
(+) **Bite** (standard; at-will)
   +7 vs. AC; 1d6 + 1 damage.
✦ **Tail Sting** (standard; recharges when the imp uses *vanish*) ✦ **Poison**
   +8 vs. AC; 1d8 + 3 damage, and the imp makes a secondary attack against the same target. *Secondary Attack:* +5 vs. Fortitude; the target takes ongoing 5 poison damage and a -2 penalty to Will defense (save ends both).
Vanish (standard; at-will) ✦ **Illusion**
   The imp becomes invisible until the end of its next turn or until it attacks.
Alignment Evil   **Languages** Common, Supernal
Skills Arcana +9, Bluff +9, Stealth +9
Str 12 (+2)   **Dex** 17 (+4)   **Wis** 14 (+3)
Con 16 (+4)   **Int** 16 (+4)   **Cha** 16 (+4)

IMP TACTICS

Imps are reluctant combatants. When forced to fight, an imp uses *vanish* to turn invisible and waits for an opponent to become distracted before attacking with its *tail sting*. If the battle turns against the imp or its allies, the imp doesn't hesitate to flee.

IMP LORE

A character knows the following information with a successful Religion check.

DC 15: Imps partner with mortals who seek magical power. By helping their "masters" attain new spells or locate magic items, imps foster a madness for power that leads their masters to perform evil acts.

DC 20: Imps possess impressive knowledge about magical subjects. They gain most of their information from other devils, from past experience, or from spying efforts of their own.

ENCOUNTER GROUPS

Imps can be encountered in groups, but they are more likely to serve other evil creatures.

Level 3 Encounter (XP 750)
✦ 1 imp (level 3 lurker)
✦ 1 goblin hexer (level 3 controller)
✦ 1 goblin skullcleaver (level 3 soldier)
✦ 2 goblin warriors (level 1 skirmisher)
✦ 4 goblin cutters (level 1 minion)

(Left to right) legion devil, ice devil, and imp

LEGION DEVIL

THE ARMIES OF THE NINE HELLS are largely made up of legion devils—cruel, pitiless warriors that gather in countless numbers from the scorched plains of Avernus to the deepest chasms of Nessus. Brutally disciplined, legion devils haven't the slightest regard for their own existence and live to crush their masters' foes beneath their iron-shod heels.

Legion Devil Grunt		**Level 6 Minion**
Medium immortal humanoid (devil)		XP 63

Initiative +4　　　**Senses** Perception +4; darkvision
HP 1; a missed attack never damages a minion.
AC 22; **Fortitude** 18, **Reflex** 17, **Will** 17; see also *squad defense*
Resist 5 fire
Speed 6, teleport 3
(↓) **Longsword** (standard; at-will) ✦ **Weapon**
　　+11 vs. AC; 5 damage.
Squad Defense
　　The legion devil grunt gains a +2 bonus to its defenses when adjacent to at least one other legion devil.

Alignment Evil	**Languages** Supernal	
Str 14 (+5)	**Dex** 12 (+4)	**Wis** 12 (+4)
Con 14 (+5)	**Int** 10 (+3)	**Cha** 12 (+4)

Equipment plate armor, heavy shield, longsword

Legion Devil Hellguard		**Level 11 Minion**
Medium immortal humanoid (devil)		XP 150

Initiative +6　　　**Senses** Perception +6; darkvision
HP 1; a missed attack never damages a minion.
AC 27; **Fortitude** 23, **Reflex** 22, **Will** 22; see also *squad defense*
Resist 10 fire
Speed 6, teleport 3
(↓) **Longsword** (standard; at-will) ✦ **Weapon**
　　+16 vs. AC; 6 damage.
Squad Defense
　　The legion devil hellguard gains a +2 bonus to its defenses when adjacent to at least one other legion devil.

Alignment Evil	**Languages** Supernal	
Str 14 (+7)	**Dex** 12 (+6)	**Wis** 12 (+6)
Con 14 (+7)	**Int** 10 (+5)	**Cha** 12 (+6)

Equipment plate armor, heavy shield, longsword

Legion Devil Veteran		**Level 16 Minion**
Medium immortal humanoid (devil)		XP 350

Initiative +9　　　**Senses** Perception +9; darkvision
HP 1; a missed attack never damages a minion.
AC 32; **Fortitude** 28, **Reflex** 27, **Will** 27; see also *squad defense*
Resist 10 fire
Speed 7, teleport 3
(↓) **Longsword** (standard; at-will) ✦ **Weapon**
　　+21 vs. AC; 7 damage.
Squad Defense
　　The legion devil veteran gains a +2 bonus to its defenses when adjacent to at least one other legion devil.

Alignment Evil	**Languages** Supernal	
Str 14 (+10)	**Dex** 12 (+9)	**Wis** 12 (+9)
Con 14 (+10)	**Int** 10 (+8)	**Cha** 12 (+9)

Equipment plate armor, heavy shield, longsword

Legion Devil Legionnaire		**Level 21 Minion**
Medium immortal humanoid (devil)		XP 800

Initiative +11　　　**Senses** Perception +11; darkvision
HP 1; a missed attack never damages a minion.
AC 37; **Fortitude** 33, **Reflex** 32, **Will** 32; see also *squad defense*
Resist 15 fire
Speed 7, teleport 3
(↓) **Longsword** (standard; at-will) ✦ **Weapon**
　　+26 vs. AC; 8 damage.
Squad Defense
　　The legion devil legionnaire gains a +2 bonus to its defenses when adjacent to at least one other legion devil.

Alignment Evil	**Languages** Supernal	
Str 14 (+12)	**Dex** 12 (+11)	**Wis** 12 (+11)
Con 14 (+12)	**Int** 10 (+10)	**Cha** 12 (+11)

Equipment plate armor, heavy shield, longsword

LEGION DEVIL TACTICS

Legion devils are regimented soldiers that work together to overwhelm foes. They can teleport short distances to gain flanking or position itself adjacent to an ally in order to gain the *squad defense* benefit.

LEGION DEVIL LORE

A character knows the following information with a successful Religion check.

DC 15: Legion devils are the foot soldiers of the Nine Hells. Hundreds of them garrison the fortresses and citadels that watch over this fell dominion.

DC 20: Legion devils strictly adhere to command hierarchies and rarely exercise personal initiative. They follow their orders to the letter.

ENCOUNTER GROUPS

Battalions of legion devils can be found as guards in evil temples, troops in the service of evil overlords, or marauders laying waste to defenseless lands.

Level 6 Encounter (XP 1,350)
✦ 4 legion devil grunts (level 6 minion)
✦ 2 tiefling heretics (level 6 artillery)
✦ 2 tiefling darkblades (level 7 lurker)

Level 21 Encounter (XP 16,150)
✦ 8 legion devil legionnaires (level 21 minion)
✦ 2 ice devils (level 20 soldier)
✦ 1 war devil (level 22 brute)

PIT FIEND

NOBLES OF THE NINE HELLS, pit fiends form an elite ruling class that oversees vast numbers of lesser devils. Only the archdevils known as the Lords of the Nine stand higher than the pit fiends.

Each pit fiend is lord of a large domain within one of the layers of the Nine Hells and is vassal to the archdevil who rules that layer. A pit fiend might govern a city, command a fortress,

lead a great legion, or serve as a seneschal or counselor for an archdevil. With the exception of Asmodeus, each Lord of the Nine commands no more than a dozen or so pit fiends.

As the lords, barons, viziers, and generals of the Nine Hells, pit fiends rarely confront adventurers in person. They are the progenitors of devilish schemes, and they step in only when important plans go awry or when great plots reach fruition. In the Nine Hells proper, pit fiends command vast numbers of lesser devils. Penetrating the defenses of a pit fiend's castle and destroying the mighty devil in its own demesne is a deed of truly epic proportions.

Pit Fiend	Level 26 Elite Soldier (Leader)
Large immortal humanoid (devil)	XP 18,000

Initiative +22   **Senses** Perception +23; darkvision

Aura of Fear (Fear) aura 5; enemies in the aura take a -2 penalty to attack rolls.

Aura of Fire (Fire) aura 5; enemies that enter or start their turns in the aura take 15 fire damage.

HP 486; **Bloodied** 243

AC 44; **Fortitude** 42, **Reflex** 38, **Will** 40

Resist 30 fire, 15 poison

Saving Throws +2

Speed 12, fly 12 (clumsy), teleport 10

Action Points 1

⊕ **Flametouched Mace** (standard; at-will) ✦ **Fire, Weapon**
Reach 2; +33 vs. AC; 2d10 + 11 fire damage, and ongoing 5 fire damage (save ends).

↓ **Tail Sting** (standard; at-will) ✦ **Poison**
Reach 2; +33 vs. AC; 1d6 + 11 damage, and the pit fiend makes a secondary attack against the same target. *Secondary Attack:* +29 vs. Fortitude; the target takes ongoing 15 poison damage and is weakened (save ends both).

↓ **Pit Fiend Frenzy** (standard; at-will)
The pit fiend makes a flametouched mace attack and a tail sting attack.

↗ **Point of Terror** (minor; at-will) ✦ **Fear**
Ranged 5; +30 vs. Will; the target takes a -5 penalty to all defenses until the end of the pit fiend's next turn.

↗ **Irresistible Command** (minor 1/round; at-will) ✦ **Charm, Fire**
Ranged 10; targets one devil of a lower level than the pit fiend; the target slides 5 squares and explodes, dealing 2d10 + 5 fire damage to all creatures in a close burst 2. The exploding devil is destroyed.

Infernal Summons (standard; encounter)
The pit fiend summons a group of devil allies. Summoned devils roll initiative to determine when they act in the initiative order and gain a +4 bonus to attack rolls as long as the pit fiend is alive. They remain until they are killed, dismissed by the pit fiend (free action), or the encounter ends. PCs do not earn experience points for killing these summoned creatures. The pit fiend chooses to summon one of the following groups of devils:
✦ 8 legion devil legionnaires (level 21), or
✦ 2 war devils (level 22), or
✦ 1 war devil (level 22) and 4 legion devil legionnaires (level 21)

Tactical Teleport (standard; recharge ⚄ ⚅ ⚁) ✦ **Teleportation**
The pit fiend can teleport up to 2 allies within 10 squares of it. The targets appear in any other unoccupied squares within 10 squares of the pit fiend.

Alignment Evil   **Languages** Supernal

Skills Bluff +27, Insight +23, Intimidate +27, Religion +24

Str 32 (+24)	Dex 24 (+20)	Wis 20 (+18)
Con 27 (+21)	Int 22 (+19)	Cha 28 (+22)

Equipment flametouched mace, noble signet ring

Pit Fiend Tactics

A pit fiend fights close to its enemies, catching them in its *aura of fear* and *aura of fire*. On the first round of combat, it spends an action point to use *infernal summons*. It then uses *point of terror* against a tough-looking foe and *tactical teleport* to place two allies in flanking positions around that foe. With its remaining minor action, the pit fiend uses *irresistible command* on an ally within range.

A pit fiend alternates between *point of terror* and *irresistible command*, sometimes using both if it has a spare move action it can substitute with a minor action. Otherwise, the pit fiend uses *pit fiend frenzy*, teleporting as needed to gain a better position.

Pit Fiend Lore

A character knows the following information with a successful Religion check.

DC 25: Pit fiends are the nobles of the Nine Hells. Each pit fiend serves as a vassal to one of the nine archdevils and commands a fortress, city, or army in its master's domain.

Encounter Groups

Pit fiends are rarely encountered without a fiendish entourage comprised of weaker devils or enslaved minions.

Level 25 Encounter (XP 42,900)
✦ 1 pit fiend (level 26 elite soldier)
✦ 2 war devils (level 22 brute)
✦ 2 astral stalker abominations (level 22 lurker)
✦ 1 marut concordant (level 22 elite controller)

SPINED DEVIL

Spined devils serve as scouts and sentries in the Nine Hells. They gather in raucous, marauding bands, winging through the burning skies and viciously harrying any prey they come across. Some serve as spies and messengers to powerful devils.

Spined Devil (Spinagon)		Level 6 Skirmisher
Medium immortal humanoid (devil)		XP 250

Initiative +7   **Senses** Perception +10; darkvision
HP 70; **Bloodied** 35
AC 20; **Fortitude** 18, **Reflex** 16, **Will** 16
Resist 20 fire
Speed 5, fly 7 (hover)
⊕ **Claws** (standard; at-will)
    +11 vs. AC; 2d6 + 4 damage.
↗ **Rain of Spines** (standard; at-will) ✦ **Fire, Poison**
    The spined devil flings spines that ignite as they fly through the air. Ranged 10; +9 vs. Reflex; 1d10 damage plus 1d6 fire damage, and the spined devil makes a secondary attack against the same target. *Secondary Attack:* +9 vs. Fortitude; the target takes ongoing 5 poison damage and is slowed (save ends both).
Alignment Evil   **Languages** Supernal

Str 18 (+7)	**Dex** 15 (+5)	**Wis** 14 (+5)
Con 14 (+5)	**Int** 10 (+3)	**Cha** 11 (+3)

Spined Devil Tactics

Spined devils disdain melee and prefer to pelt their victims with wave after wave of burning, poisoned spines. Only after a victim is bloodied do they descend to tear apart the hapless soul with their wicked claws.

Spined Devil Lore

A character knows the following information with a successful Religion check.

DC 15: Spined devils are commonly summoned devils because they are relatively weak and easy to control with promises of mayhem and plunder.

DC 20: Like most devils, spined devils enjoy tormenting anything that crosses their path. They are aerial scouts and skirmishers in the armies of the Nine Hells, eagerly harrying any foes they encounter with volleys of burning, poisonous spines.

Encounter Groups

While flocks of spined devils are common in the Nine Hells, they're most often encountered in fewer numbers in the material world and often in the company of other evil creatures.

(Left to right) succubus, war devil, and spined devil

Level 6 Encounter (XP 1,250)
- ✦ 2 spined devils (level 6 skirmisher)
- ✦ 1 greenscale marsh mystic lizardfolk (level 6 controller)
- ✦ 2 blackscale bruiser lizardfolk (level 6 brute)

SUCCUBUS

SUCCUBI TEMPT MORTALS into performing evil deeds, using their shapechanging abilities to appear as attractive men and women. Although seduction and betrayal are their forte, succubi are also practiced spies and assassins.

Succubi serve more powerful devils as scouts, advisors, and even concubines. Because of their guile and shapechanging ability, they are frequently chosen to serve as infernal emissaries to important mortals.

Succubus		Level 9 Controller
Medium immortal humanoid (devil, shapechanger)		XP 400

Initiative +8   **Senses** Perception +8; darkvision
HP 90; **Bloodied** 45
AC 23; **Fortitude** 17, **Reflex** 21, **Will** 23
Resist 20 fire
Speed 6, fly 6

⊕ **Corrupting Touch** (standard; at-will)
+14 vs. AC; 1d6 + 6 damage.

↟ **Charming Kiss** (standard; at-will) ✦ **Charm**
+14 vs. AC; on a hit, the succubus makes a secondary attack against the same target. *Secondary Attack:* +12 vs. Will; the target cannot attack the succubus, and if the target is adjacent to the succubus when the succubus is targeted by a melee or a ranged attack, the target interposes itself and becomes the target of the attack instead. The effects last until the succubus or one of its allies attacks the target or until the succubus dies.

If the target is still under the effect of this power at the end of the encounter, the succubus can sustain the effect indefinitely by kissing the target once per day. The succubus can affect only one target at a time with its *charming kiss*.

↗ **Dominate** (standard; at-will) ✦ **Charm**
Ranged 5; +12 vs. Will; the target is dominated until the end of the succubus's next turn.

Change Shape (minor; at-will) ✦ **Polymorph**
The succubus can alter its physical form to take on the appearance of any Medium humanoid, including a unique individual (see Change Shape, page 280).

Alignment Evil   **Languages** Common, Supernal
Skills Bluff +15, Diplomacy +15, Insight +13
| **Str** 11 (+4) | **Dex** 18 (+8) | **Wis** 19 (+8) |
| **Con** 10 (+4) | **Int** 15 (+6) | **Cha** 22 (+10) |

SUCCUBUS TACTICS

When exposed for what it is, a succubus can be a deadly foe. It can manipulate the emotions of mortal adversaries, turning them against each other or making them slavishly loyal to it with a mere kiss.

A succubus that is confronted uses *dominate* on a worthy adversary. It then uses *charming kiss* on a dominated foe, keeping him or her nearby while it attacks other enemies with its *corrupting touch*.

Level 9 Encounter (XP 2,000)
- ✦ 1 succubus (level 9 controller)
- ✦ 2 snaketongue assassins (level 9 lurker)
- ✦ 2 crushgrip constrictors (level 9 soldier)

WAR DEVIL

CHAMPIONS OF THE NINE HELLS, war devils obey only pit fiends and archdevils. They also lead lesser devils in forays against those who stand in the way of their masters' plans. War devils brought to the mortal world sometimes arise as warmasters or generals, leading the armies of evil mortal tyrants.

War Devil (Malebranche)		Level 22 Brute (Leader)
Large immortal humanoid (devil)		XP 4,150

Initiative +17   **Senses** Perception +15; darkvision
HP 255; **Bloodied** 127
AC 35; **Fortitude** 34, **Reflex** 32, **Will** 30
Resist 30 fire
Speed 8, fly 8 (clumsy)

⊕ **Claw** (standard; at-will)
+26 vs. AC; 1d6 + 8 damage.

⊕ **Trident** (standard; recharge ⚄ ⚅ ⚅) ✦ **Weapon**
Reach 2; +26 vs. AC; 4d4 + 8 damage and ongoing 5 damage (save ends), and the target slides into any square adjacent to the war devil and is knocked prone.

↗ **Besieged Foe** (minor; at-will)
Ranged sight; automatic hit; the target is marked, and allies of the war devil gain a +2 bonus to attack rolls made against the target until the encounter ends or the war devil marks a new target.

↗ **Devilish Transposition** (move; at-will) ✦ **Teleportation**
Ranged 20; the war devil and an allied devil within range swap positions.

↗ **Fiendish Tactics** (minor; recharge ⚄ ⚅)
Ranged 10; affects up to 2 allied devils of the war devil's level or lower; each target can take a move action or make a basic attack.

Alignment Evil   **Languages** Supernal
Skills Intimidate +20
| **Str** 27 (+19) | **Dex** 23 (+17) | **Wis** 19 (+15) |
| **Con** 25 (+18) | **Int** 15 (+13) | **Cha** 18 (+15) |
Equipment trident

WAR DEVIL TACTICS

Despite their brutish appearance, war devils are outstanding tacticians and clever leaders. They use *besieged foe* and *fiendish tactics* to direct their subordinates against dangerous foes, but they eagerly leap into the fray when the time is right, using *devilish transposition* to exchange places with a lesser devil (often one with the mobility to penetrate the enemies' ranks).

WAR DEVIL LORE

A character knows the following information with a successful Religion check.

DC 25: War devils (also known as malebranches) are among the most powerful devils that are routinely summoned by mortals.

ENCOUNTER GROUPS

War devils often serve as "muscle" for pit fiends or archdevils, or they directly command contingents of lesser devils.

Level 21 Encounter (XP 19,750)
- ✦ 1 war devil (level 22 brute)
- ✦ 1 ice devil (level 20 soldier)
- ✦ 2 bone devils (level 17 controller)
- ✦ 12 legion devil legionnaires (level 21 minion)

DEVOURER

When a raving murderer dies, his soul passes into the Shadowfell. There it might gather flesh again to continue its lethal ways, becoming a devourer. Without conscience, a devourer exists only to slay and consume the living.

SPIRIT DEVOURER

This cadaverous creature traps the spirit of a living humanoid inside its ribcage. This spirit manifests as a small, emaciated effigy of the trapped creature that thrashes in agony as the spirit devourer uses it for unholy fuel.

Spirit Devourer	Level 11 Elite Soldier
Large shadow humanoid (undead)	XP 1,200

Initiative +8　　　　**Senses** Perception +10; darkvision
HP 224; **Bloodied** 112
AC 27; **Fortitude** 25, **Reflex** 21, **Will** 26; see also *spirit ward*
Immune disease, poison; **Resist** 15 necrotic; **Vulnerable** 5 radiant (whenever the devourer takes radiant damage, its trapped enemy gets a saving throw to escape)
Saving Throws +2
Speed 6
Action Points 1
(+) **Claw** (standard; at-will)
　Reach 2; +17 vs. AC; 2d6 + 5 damage.
↣ **Trap Spirit** (standard; at-will) ✦ **Necrotic**
　Ranged 5; targets a living humanoid; +15 vs. Fortitude; 1d8 + 7 necrotic damage, and the target is trapped (save ends). The trapped creature is removed from play and can take no actions. If it succeeds on a saving throw, it escapes and appears in an unoccupied space of its choice adjacent to the spirit devourer. A trapped creature escapes automatically when the spirit devourer is destroyed. Only one creature can be trapped at a time.
↢ **Spirit Rupture** (standard, usable only after the spirit devourer uses *devour spirit* and only on the same turn; at-will) ✦ **Fear, Necrotic**
　Close burst 1; +15 vs. Will; 2d8 + 7 necrotic damage, and the target is immobilized until the end of the spirit devourer's next turn. *Miss:* Half damage, and the target is not immobilized.
Devour Spirit (minor; at-will) ✦ **Healing, Necrotic**
　The spirit devourer deals 10 necrotic damage to a creature it has trapped (see *trap spirit*). The spirit devourer either regains 10 hit points or uses *spirit rupture*. A creature killed by this power can't be returned to life with a Raise Dead ritual.
Spirit Ward
　The spirit devourer gains a +2 bonus to all defenses while it has a creature trapped (see *trap spirit*).

Alignment Evil	**Languages** Common	
Skills Stealth +11		
Str 20 (+10)	**Dex** 12 (+6)	**Wis** 11 (+5)
Con 16 (+8)	**Int** 16 (+8)	**Cha** 24 (+12)

SPIRIT DEVOURER TACTICS

A spirit devourer uses *trap spirit*, then *devour spirit* to deal damage to the trapped creature, and then uses the energy it devours to heal itself or use *spirit rupture*. If at any point the trapped spirit escapes, the spirit devourer uses *trap spirit* again.

VISCERA DEVOURER

This devourer wraps its drooling intestines around nearby foes. The gnashing mouths that tip its viscera latch onto flesh, allowing the creature to drain the life from its captives. Once its victims are dead, the creature hungrily devours their innards.

Viscera Devourer	Level 12 Controller
Medium shadow humanoid (undead)	XP 700

Initiative +8　　　　**Senses** Perception +10; darkvision
HP 124; **Bloodied** 63
AC 28; **Fortitude** 26, **Reflex** 23, **Will** 24; see also *visceral ward*
Immune disease, poison; **Resist** 15 necrotic; **Vulnerable** 5 radiant
Speed 6
(+) **Claw** (standard; at-will)
　+16 vs. AC; 1d10 + 4 damage.
‡ **Hungry Viscera** (minor; at-will)
　+16 vs. AC; the creature wraps a viscera tendril around the target; 1d4 + 5 damage, and the target is grabbed (until escape). A viscera devourer has four tendrils and can grab up to four creatures, or multiple tendrils can grab a single target (the target takes a -2 penalty to escape checks per additional tendril grabbing it).
Devour Viscera (minor 1/round; at-will) ✦ **Healing, Necrotic**
　The viscera devourer draws life energy from every living target it has grabbed. A grabbed target takes 5 necrotic damage per viscera tendril grabbing it, and the viscera devourer regains the same amount of hit points.
Visceral Ward
　The viscera devourer gains a +2 bonus to all defenses while it is grabbing one or more creatures.

Alignment Evil	**Languages** Common	
Skills Stealth +13		
Str 18 (+10)	**Dex** 15 (+8)	**Wis** 9 (+5)
Con 20 (+11)	**Int** 12 (+7)	**Cha** 17 (+9)

VISCERA DEVOURER TACTICS

This creature trades standard actions and move actions for minor actions, using *hungry viscera* up to three times in a round. If it has only one opponent in reach, it tries to wrap all four of its viscera tendrils around the one target. If it has multiple targets, it tries to grab as many of them as possible. When the creature is bloodied, it uses *devour viscera* to regain hit points.

SOULSPIKE DEVOURER

When a soulspike devourer slays a creature, the victim's body vanishes, and its apparition appears impaled on one of the devourer's spikes. The soulspike devourer feeds on these spirits, which howl in agony and disappear in a flash when finally consumed.

SOULSPIKED SURVIVORS

A soulspike devourer begins play with at least one spirit already impaled on its soulspikes. If this spirit escapes the devourer somehow, its body appears in a space adjacent to the creature. As the DM, you can use this soulspiked spirit as a story device: Perhaps the body belongs to an individual whom the PCs are searching for, or maybe it carries something of value. If healed or raised from the dead, this individual might stick around long enough to speak to the PCs, accompany them, or even betray them (as appropriate).

Soulspike Devourer — Level 20 Elite Soldier (Leader)

Huge shadow humanoid (undead) — XP 5,600

Initiative +11 **Senses** Perception +15; darkvision

Soulspike Ward aura 10; the soulspike devourer and all allies in the aura gain a bonus to all defenses equal to one-half the number of soulspiked spirits impaled on the creature.

HP 376; **Bloodied** 188

AC 38; **Fortitude** 37, **Reflex** 29, **Will** 34; see also *soulspike ward* above

Immune disease, poison; **Resist** 20 necrotic; **Vulnerable** 10 radiant (when the soulspike devourer takes radiant damage, its newest soulspiked spirit gets a saving throw to escape)

Saving Throws +2

Speed 6

Action Points 1

⊕ **Claw** (standard; at-will)
Reach 3; +26 vs. AC; 2d8 + 9 damage. If the attack reduces a humanoid living target to 0 hit points or fewer, the target disappears and becomes a soulspiked spirit impaled on the devourer (see *soulspiked spirit*).

⟐ **Soul Shatter** (standard; recharges when the soulspike devourer uses *devour spirit*) ✦ **Necrotic**
Close burst 3; +24 vs. Will; 5d8 + 8 necrotic damage, and the target is stunned until the end of the soulspike devourer's next turn. *Aftereffect:* The target is weakened (save ends).

Devour Spirit (standard; at-will) ✦ **Healing**
The soulspike devourer instantly kills its oldest soulspiked spirit and regains 75 hit points. A creature's dead body appears in a space adjacent to the devourer.

Soulspiked Spirit
The soulspike devourer begins the encounter with one soulspiked spirit and can impale up to four soulspiked spirits. A soulspiked spirit can take no actions and escapes when the devourer is destroyed. When a creature's spirit escapes, its body appears in an unoccupied space adjacent to the devourer, in the same state it was in when it disappeared.

Alignment Evil	**Languages** Common	
Str 29 (+19)	**Dex** 8 (+9)	**Wis** 11 (+10)
Con 20 (+15)	**Int** 20 (+15)	**Cha** 26 (+18)

Soulspike Devourer Tactics

This collector of souls wades into battle, concentrating its attacks on one foe at a time to create more soulspiked spirits. When bloodied, the devourer uses *devour spirit* to heal itself, and then spends its action point to use *soul shatter*.

Devourer Lore

A character knows the following information with a successful Religion check.

DC 20: Devourers are created from the souls of murderers lost in the Shadowfell. They feed on living humanoids and use their life energy to heal.

Encounter Groups

Although a devourer possesses a consuming hunger for the living, it knows the value of wicked alliances.

Level 11 Encounter (XP 3,025)
✦ 1 spirit devourer (level 11 elite soldier)
✦ 1 vampire lord (level 11 elite lurker)
✦ 5 vampire spawn bloodhunters (level 10 minion)

Level 13 Encounter (XP 4,000)
✦ 2 viscera devourers (level 12 controller)
✦ 1 drow arachnomancer (level 13 artillery)
✦ 3 drow warriors (level 11 lurker)

(Top to bottom) soulspike devourer, spirit devourer, and viscera devourer

DAVE ALLSOP

DISPLACER BEAST

A DISPLACER BEAST IS VEILED BY AN ILLUSION that makes pinpointing its true location difficult. Although they are native to the Feywild, displacer beasts also reside in the tangled forests and dark caverns of the natural world.

Displacer Beast		Level 9 Skirmisher
Large fey magical beast		XP 400

Initiative +11   **Senses** Perception +12; low-light vision
HP 97; **Bloodied** 48
AC 23; **Fortitude** 21, **Reflex** 22, **Will** 20; see also *displacement*
Speed 12

(+) **Tentacle** (standard; at-will)
    Reach 2; +13 vs. AC; 1d6 + 4 damage.

✦ **Bite** (standard; at-will)
    +13 vs. AC; 1d10 + 4 damage.

✦ **Beast's Fury** (standard; at-will)
    Requires combat advantage; the displacer beast makes two tentacle attacks and a bite attack against a single target.

Displacement ✦ Illusion
    All melee and ranged attacks have a 50% chance to miss the displacer beast. The effect ends when the displacer beast is hit by an attack, but it recharges as soon as the displacer beast moves 2 or more squares on its turn. Critical hits ignore displacement. (See also *shifting tactics*.)

Shifting Tactics (free, when an attack misses the displacer beast because of its displacement; at-will)
    The displacer beast shifts 1 square.

Threatening Reach
    The displacer beast can make opportunity attacks against all enemies within its reach (2 squares).

Alignment Unaligned	**Languages** –	
Skills Stealth +14		
Str 18 (+8)	**Dex** 20 (+9)	**Wis** 17 (+7)
Con 17 (+7)	**Int** 4 (+1)	**Cha** 10 (+4)

DISPLACER BEAST TACTICS

A displacer beast shows great cunning in battle, darting past defenders to attack easier targets and gaining combat advantage by flanking with an ally. If its *displacement* is negated, it moves to recharge it, risking opportunity attacks if necessary.

Displacer Beast Packlord	Level 13 Elite Skirmisher
Huge fey magical beast	XP 1,600

Initiative +14   **Senses** Perception +15; low-light vision
HP 258; **Bloodied** 124
AC 27; **Fortitude** 28, **Reflex** 26, **Will** 24; see also *displacement*
Saving Throws +2
Speed 12; see also *nimble stride*
Action Points 1

(+) **Tentacle** (standard; at-will)
    Reach 3; +18 vs. AC; 2d6 + 7 damage.

✦ **Bite** (standard; at-will)
    +18 vs. AC; 3d6 + 7 damage.

✦ **Beast's Fury** (standard; at-will)
    Requires combat advantage; the displacer beast packlord makes two tentacle attacks and a bite attack against a single target.

Displacement ✦ Illusion
    All melee and ranged attacks have a 50% chance to miss the displacer beast packlord. The effect ends when the displacer beast is hit by an attack, but it recharges as soon as the packlord moves 2 or more squares on its turn. Critical hits ignore displacement. (See also *superior shifting tactics*.)

Nimble Stride
    The displacer beast packlord ignores difficult terrain and speed penalties for squeezing.

Superior Shifting Tactics (free, when an attack misses the displacer beast packlord because of its displacement; at-will)
    The packlord makes a melee basic attack and shifts 1 square.

Threatening Reach
    The displacer beast packlord can make opportunity attacks against all enemies within its reach (3 squares).

Alignment Unaligned	**Languages** –	
Skills Stealth +17		
Str 24 (+13)	**Dex** 23 (+12)	**Wis** 18 (+10)
Con 17 (+9)	**Int** 10 (+6)	**Cha** 12 (+7)

PACKLORD TACTICS

A packlord ambushes prey in difficult terrain, where it can use *nimble stride* and benefit from its reach. It relies on speed and *displacement* to maneuver safely on the battlefield.

DISPLACER BEAST LORE

A character knows the following information with a successful Arcana check.

    DC 15: Displacer beasts can be trained as attack beasts or guard animals, but they're prone to turning against their trainers.

ENCOUNTER GROUPS

Humanoids, particularly evil fey and onis, sometimes keep displacer beasts as pets.

Level 13 Encounter (XP 4,000)
✦ 1 displacer beast packlord (level 13 elite skirmisher)
✦ 2 displacer beasts (level 9 skirmisher)
✦ 1 briar witch dryad (level 13 elite controller)

DOPPELGANGER

THE CONSUMMATE SHAPECHANGER, a doppelganger can bring entire kingdoms to ruin through duplicity and subterfuge without ever drawing a sword.

Doppelgangers are much like humans in their behavior, and as such, an individual doppelganger might have any disposition imaginable.

Doppelganger Sneak	Level 3 Skirmisher
Medium natural humanoid (shapechanger)	XP 150

Initiative +6   **Senses** Perception +2
HP 45; **Bloodied** 22
AC 18; **Fortitude** 14, **Reflex** 16, **Will** 16
Speed 6
⊕ **Short Sword** (standard; at-will) ✦ **Weapon**
  +8 vs. AC; 1d6 + 3 damage.
† **Shapeshifter Feint** (minor; at-will)
  +6 vs. Reflex; the doppelganger gains combat advantage against the target until the end of the doppelganger's next turn.
Combat Advantage
  The doppelganger sneak deals an extra 1d6 damage against any target it has combat advantage against.
Change Shape (minor; at-will) ✦ **Polymorph**
  A doppelganger can alter its physical form to take on the appearance of any Medium humanoid, including a unique individual (see Change Shape, page 280).
Alignment Unaligned   **Languages** Common
Skills Bluff +10, Insight +9, Stealth +9
Str 11 (+1)   **Dex** 16 (+4)   **Wis** 12 (+2)
Con 13 (+2)   **Int** 10 (+1)   **Cha** 15 (+3)
Equipment short sword

EVA WIDERMANN

DOPPELGANGER SNEAK TACTICS

Once its disguise is thwarted, a doppelganger sneak uses *shapeshifter feint* to gain combat advantage and deal additional damage before shifting away. It has no reservations about fleeing if the battle turns ill, using *change shape* at the earliest opportunity to lose itself in a crowd.

Doppelganger Assassin	Level 8 Lurker
Medium natural humanoid (shapechanger)	XP 350

Initiative +13   **Senses** Perception +10
HP 69; **Bloodied** 34
AC 23; **Fortitude** 18, **Reflex** 21, **Will** 21
Speed 6
⊕ **Dagger** (standard; at-will) ✦ **Weapon**
  +13 vs. AC; 1d4 + 5 damage.
† **Shapeshifter Feint** (minor; at-will)
  +11 vs. Reflex; the doppelganger assassin gains combat advantage against the target until the end of the doppelganger assassin's next turn.
↞ **Cloud Mind** (standard; sustain minor; encounter) ✦ **Charm**
  Close burst 5; +11 vs. Will; the doppelganger assassin is invisible to the target. Affected targets are unable to see the doppelganger for as long as it sustains the effect, until the doppelganger attacks, or until it is hit by an attack.
Combat Advantage
  The doppelganger assassin deals an extra 2d6 damage against any target it has combat advantage against.
Change Shape (minor; at-will) ✦ **Polymorph**
  A doppelganger can alter its physical form to take on the appearance of any Medium humanoid, including a unique individual (see Change Shape, page 280).
Alignment Evil   **Languages** Common
Skills Bluff +15, Insight +12, Stealth +14
Str 12 (+5)   **Dex** 21 (+9)   **Wis** 12 (+5)
Con 15 (+6)   **Int** 13 (+5)   **Cha** 19 (+8)
Equipment dagger

DOPPELGANGER ASSASSIN TACTICS

A doppelganger assassin might trail the party, waiting to lure a single victim away from the others, murder him, and take his place. It might also pose as a potential ally or someone in need. Once revealed for what it is, the doppelganger uses *shapeshifter feint* to gain combat advantage and *cloud mind* to escape if the battle turns against it.

DOPPELGANGER LORE

A character knows the following information with a successful Nature check.

DC 15: A doppelganger might look like an eladrin wizard, a dwarf fighter, or even a dragonborn paladin. It can't duplicate a person's apparel or carried items, so it must dress and equip itself for the part. For this reason, it keeps several changes of clothing in its lair.

ENCOUNTER GROUPS

Doppelgangers can insinuate themselves into all sorts of groups. They also form alliances with intelligent creatures that realize the benefits of having shapechangers on their side.

Level 3 Encounter (XP 775)
✦ 1 doppelganger sneak (level 3 skirmisher)
✦ 3 human guards (level 3 soldier)
✦ 1 human mage (level 4 artillery)

When a powerful dragon forsakes life and undergoes an evil ritual to become undead, the result is a dracolich. Dracoliches are selfish, greedy, and interested only in amassing more power and treasure.

DRACOLICH LORE

A character knows the following information with a successful Religion check.

DC 20: Dracoliches are unnatural creatures created by an evil ritual that requires a still-living dragon to serve as the ritual's focus. When the ritual is complete, the dragon is transformed into a skeletal thing of pure malevolence. Some evil dragons willingly undergo this ritual.

DC 25: A handful of evil cults possess a ritual for turning a dragon into a dracolich against its will. These cults do what they must to keep knowledge of that ritual from others. When a dragon is transformed into a dracolich with such a ritual, a linkage between the cult and the dragon is formed, and the cult gains influence over the dragon's behavior.

DC 30: A cult that transforms a dragon into a dracolich maintains its control over the creature through possession of the dracolich's phylactery, a vessel that imprisons the creature's soul. Most dracoliches do not have phylacteries and are not associated with a cult. Those that have phylacteries seek to destroy them so the cult that created it loses its ability to command the dracolich forever.

DC 35: Once a dracolich's physical body is demolished, its phylactery is also shattered and the beast is gone for good.

ENCOUNTER GROUPS

Dracoliches are usually encountered as lone threats; however, sometimes one might be encountered with a scattering of cultists who direct its actions.

Level 20 Encounter (XP 14,400)
- ✦ 1 dracolich (level 18 solo controller)
- ✦ 2 yuan-ti malison incanters
  (level 15 artillery)
- ✦ 2 yuan-ti abominations
  (level 14 soldier)

Dracolich	Level 18 Solo Controller
Huge natural magical beast (dragon, undead)	XP 10,000

Initiative +15   **Senses** Perception +18; darkvision
HP 885; **Bloodied** 442; see also *bloodied breath*
AC 34; **Fortitude** 34, **Reflex** 32, **Will** 30
Immune disease, fear, poison; **Resist** 30 necrotic; **Vulnerable** 10 radiant
Saving Throws +5
Speed 8, fly 10 (clumsy)
Action Points 2

⚔ **Bite** (standard; at-will) ✦ **Necrotic**
     Reach 3; +23 vs. AC; 2d8 + 8 damage. Against a stunned target, this attack deals an extra 2d8 necrotic damage.

↩ **Mesmerizing Glare** (immediate interrupt, when an enemy makes a melee attack against the dracolich; at-will) ✦ **Fear**
     Close blast 3; +20 vs. Will; the target is stunned until the end of the dracolich's next turn. *Miss:* The target takes a -2 penalty to attack rolls against the dracolich until the end of the dracolich's next turn. Using this power does not provoke opportunity attacks.

↩ **Breath Weapon** (standard; recharge ⚄ ⚅) ✦ **Necrotic**
     The dracolich breathes a coruscating blast of necrotic energy. Close blast 9; +21 vs. Reflex; 2d8 + 7 necrotic damage, and the target is stunned until the end of the dracolich's next turn. *Miss:* Half damage, and the target is not stunned. *Hit or Miss:* The target loses any necrotic resistance it has (save ends).

↩ **Bloodied Breath** (free, when first bloodied; encounter)
     The dracolich's breath weapon recharges, and the dracolich uses it immediately.

↩ **Frightful Presence** (standard; encounter) ✦ **Fear**
     Close burst 10; targets enemies; +20 vs. Will; the target is stunned until the end of the dracolich's next turn. *Aftereffect:* The target takes a -2 penalty to attack rolls until the end of the encounter.

Alignment Evil   **Languages** Draconic
Skills Arcana +17, Endurance +21, History +17, Insight +18, Intimidate +17, Religion +17

Str 26 (+17)	Dex 22 (+15)	Wis 18 (+13)
Con 25 (+16)	Int 17 (+12)	Cha 16 (+12)

FRED HOOPER

Dracolich Tactics

A dracolich blasts enemies with its breath weapon, preferably from the air or other safe position. It then enters melee, spending an action point to use *frightful presence* and then using its bite. The dracolich relies on *mesmerizing glare* to incapacitate those who attack it.

A dracolich often reserves its last action point for a tactical retreat. If incited, however, the creature might take advantage of a stunned opponent, using its bite twice on the same turn.

Blackfire Dracolich — **Level 23 Solo Controller**
Gargantuan natural magical beast (dragon, undead) — XP 25,500

Initiative +18 **Senses** Perception +21; darkvision
HP 1,095; **Bloodied** 547; see also *bloodied breath*
AC 39; **Fortitude** 40, **Reflex** 38, **Will** 36
Immune disease, fear, poison; **Resist** 35 necrotic; **Vulnerable** 10 radiant
Saving Throws +5
Speed 8, fly 10 (clumsy)
Action Points 2

Bite (standard; at-will) ✦ **Necrotic**
Reach 4; +28 vs. AC; 2d10 + 9 damage. Against a stunned target, this attack deals an extra 3d8 necrotic damage.

Mesmerizing Glare (immediate interrupt, when an enemy makes a melee attack against the dracolich; at-will) ✦ **Fear**
Close blast 3; +26 vs. Will; the target is stunned until the end of the blackfire dracolich's next turn. *Miss:* The target takes a -2 penalty to attack rolls against the blackfire dracolich until the end of the blackfire dracolich's next turn.

Blackfire (standard; recharge ⚃ ⚄ ⚅) ✦ **Fire, Necrotic**
Close blast 5; automatic hit; 2d8 + 8 necrotic damage, and ongoing 10 fire damage (save ends).

Breath Weapon (standard; recharge ⚄ ⚅) ✦ **Necrotic**
The blackfire dracolich breathes a coruscating blast of necrotic energy. Close blast 9; +26 vs. Reflex; 2d12 + 8 necrotic damage, and the target is stunned until the end of the blackfire dracolich's next turn. *Miss:* Half damage, and the target is not stunned. *Hit or Miss:* The target loses any necrotic resistance it has (save ends).

Bloodied Breath (free, when first bloodied; encounter)
The blackfire dracolich's breath weapon recharges, and the blackfire dracolich uses it immediately.

Frightful Presence (standard; encounter) ✦ **Fear**
Close burst 20; targets enemies; +26 vs. Will; the target is stunned until the end of the blackfire dracolich's next turn. *Aftereffect:* The target takes a -2 penalty to attack rolls until the end of the encounter.

Alignment Evil **Languages** Draconic
Skills Arcana +20, Endurance +24, History +20, Insight +21, Intimidate +19, Religion +20

Str 29 (+20)	**Dex** 25 (+18)	**Wis** 20 (+16)
Con 27 (+19)	**Int** 18 (+15)	**Cha** 17 (+14)

Blackfire Dracolich Tactics

A blackfire dracolich employs the same tactics as a normal dracolich, except that it uses both its *breath weapon* and its *blackfire* power on the first round (with the aid of an action point). The blackfire dracolich spends its second action point on another use of the *blackfire*, once the power recharges.
A creature of pure arrogance, it refuses to flee once the battle is joined.

Runescribed Dracolich — **Level 29 Solo Controller**
Gargantuan natural magical beast (dragon, undead) — XP 75,000

Initiative +22 **Senses** Perception +25; darkvision
HP 1,335; **Bloodied** 667; see also *bloodied breath*
AC 45; **Fortitude** 45, **Reflex** 43, **Will** 41
Immune disease, fear, poison; **Resist** 40 necrotic; **Vulnerable** 10 radiant
Saving Throws +5
Speed 8, fly 10 (clumsy)
Action Points 2

Bite (standard; at-will) ✦ **Necrotic**
Reach 4; +34 vs. AC; 2d10 + 10 damage. Against a stunned target, this attack deals an extra 4d8 necrotic damage.

Mesmerizing Glare (immediate interrupt, when an enemy makes a melee attack against the dracolich; at-will) ✦ **Fear**
Close blast 3; +32 vs. Will; the target is stunned until the end of the runescribed dracolich's next turn. *Miss:* The target takes a -2 penalty to attack rolls against the runescribed dracolich until the end of the runescribed dracolich's next turn.

Runescribed Retaliation (immediate interrupt, when the runescribed dracolich is targeted by a ranged attack; at-will)
The runescribed dracolich makes an attack against the attacking creature; +34 vs. Will; on a hit, the runescribed dracolich redirects the attack to a target of its choice within 5 squares of it.

Blackfire (standard; recharge ⚃ ⚄ ⚅) ✦ **Fire, Necrotic**
Close blast 5; automatic hit; 2d12 + 8 necrotic damage, and ongoing 15 fire damage (save ends).

Breath Weapon (standard; recharge ⚄ ⚅) ✦ **Necrotic**
The blackfire dracolich breathes a coruscating blast of necrotic energy. Close blast 20; +32 vs. Reflex; 3d12 + 8 necrotic damage, and the target is stunned until the end of the runescribed dracolich's next turn. *Miss:* Half damage, and the target is not stunned. *Hit or Miss:* The target loses any necrotic resistance it has (save ends).

Bloodied Breath (free, when first bloodied; encounter)
The runescribed dracolich's breath weapon recharges, and the runescribed dracolich uses it immediately.

Frightful Presence (standard; encounter) ✦ **Fear**
Close burst 20; targets enemies; +32 vs. Will; the target is stunned until the end of the runescribed dracolich's next turn. *Aftereffect:* The target takes a -2 penalty to attack rolls until the end of the encounter.

Alignment Evil **Languages** Draconic
Skills Arcana +24, Endurance +27, History +24, Insight +25, Intimidate +23, Religion +24

Str 31 (+24)	**Dex** 26 (+22)	**Wis** 22 (+20)
Con 27 (+22)	**Int** 20 (+19)	**Cha** 19 (+18)

Runescribed Dracolich Tactics

A runescribed dracolich uses the same tactics as a blackfire dracolich while relying on its *runescribed retaliation* power to redirect ranged attacks made against it.

Of all the monsters in the world, dragons are the most feared. A fledgling group of adventurers might have what it takes to best a weak dragon, but the most powerful dragons are awesome, devastating creatures that rival even the gods.

Dragons are diverse creatures, appearing in at least twenty-five varieties within five major families. All dragons share certain characteristics—notably the legged and winged shape of their reptilian bodies—but within each family there are even stronger similarities.

Chromatic dragons are the dragons detailed here. They are generally evil, greedy, and predatory, and they're inclined to worship Tiamat, whom they regard as their progenitor and patron. This family includes red, blue, green, black, and white dragons. Each variety has its own breath weapon—a blast of elemental substance, from blazing fire to frigid cold—that it can expel from its mouth.

Catastrophic dragons are mighty embodiments of primordial forces. They are destructive, but not devoted to evil. The ground warps and explodes violently in their presence. Earthquake and typhoon dragons are two types of catastrophic dragons.

Metallic dragons are in some ways the opposite of the chromatic dragons. Many of them are devoted to Bahamut and share his ideals of nobility and virtue. Many others fail to live up to those lofty ideals and succumb to a selfishness and aggression that seems common among all of dragonkind. Metallic dragons, including gold, silver, copper, iron, and adamantine dragons, often guard valuable treasures or powerful magic items, even artifacts. They have breath weapons similar to those of chromatic dragons, but their effects are as much defensive as offensive.

Planar dragons are dragons infused with the nature of other planes of existence. Shadow dragons, Abyssal dragons, and fey dragons are all planar dragons.

Scourge dragons, sometimes called linnorms, embody the afflictions that plague living creatures, much as catastrophic dragons embody natural disasters. They are almost universally evil, even more so than the chromatics, and they revel in the raw physicality of melee combat. Because they lack wings and rear legs, some scholars insist that they're not true dragons, but more closely related to drakes.

CHROMATIC DRAGON LORE

Chromatic dragons figure prominently in tales told to children and romantic epics sung by lantern light, and much of what the legends say about them is false.

A character knows the following information with a successful Nature check.

DC 20: Chromatic dragons bask in the adulation of lesser creatures, but soon grow weary of praise and worship—unless it is accompanied by gifts of precious metals, gems, and magic items.

DC 25: Chromatic dragons prefer ancient ruins, deep dungeons, and remote wilderness areas for their lairs. Each dragon type tends to inhabit certain climates and terrains: reds like hot areas and volcanoes, whites like cold, blues prefer coastal regions, greens like forests, and blacks like swamps. That said, an individual dragon lives wherever it pleases, as long as its territory doesn't impinge on another dragon's. One well-known white dragon of legend made its lair in the heart of a volcano.

DC 30: Dragons occasionally deal with other creatures as equals. Red dragons have an ancient pact with githyanki, and powerful githyanki knights sometimes ride them into battle. Powerful empires of the past enlisted entire flights of dragons to lead their armies in war.

THE DRAGON GODS

One story that is told about the creation of the universe concerns the dragon-god Io. The dragons, this legend says, were his particular creation, lovingly crafted to represent the pinnacle of mortal form. Though they were creatures of the world, the power of the Elemental Chaos flowed in their veins and spewed forth from their mouths in gouts of flame or waves of paralyzing cold. But they also possessed the keen minds and lofty spirits of the other mortal races, linking them to Io and the other gods of the Astral Sea.

Io's arrogance was his downfall. While the other gods banded together to combat the primordials, Io spurned the help of other gods. He was so confident in his own might that he faced a terrible primordial called Erek-Hus, the King of Terror, alone. With a rough-hewn axe of adamantine, the King of Terror split Io from head to tail, cleaving the dragon-god into two equal halves.

Erek-Hus did not have the chance to celebrate his victory, however. No sooner did Io's sundered corpse fall to the ground than each half rose up as a new god—Bahamut from the left and Tiamat from the right. Together the two gods fought and killed the King of Terror.

The legend continues to explain that Io's qualities were split between the two gods who rose from his death. His hubris, arrogance, and covetous nature were embodied in Tiamat, who is revered as a goddess of greed and envy. But Io's desire to protect creation and his sense of fairness took root in Bahamut, now worshiped as god of justice, honor, and protection.

The two dragon gods both shared one of Io's worse qualities, however—

his preference for working alone. After they defeated Erek-Hus, they locked in battle with each other, ignoring the pressing threat of the primordials. Only when Tiamat fled the battle did the two gods turn their attention back to the larger war, and each still preferred to work alone.

Of course, in these more enlightened days, any paladin of Bahamut will tell you that "the Platinum Dragon" is an honorific title, not a literal description, and that Bahamut is no more a dragon than Moradin is a dwarf. These are gods, not mere monsters.

Even so, many are the chromatic dragons that serve Tiamat, whose monstrous form is that of a colossal dragon with five heads—one head resembling each of the five main chromatic dragons.

CHROMATIC DRAGON ENCOUNTERS

Heirs of Io's hubris, chromatic dragons prefer to work and fight alone. All dragons are solo monsters, so they make fine encounters of their level all on their own. However, many dragons' lairs are surrounded by the dragon's minions, servants, or worshipers. A quest to slay a chromatic dragon can involve preliminary encounters with these servitors or allied creatures, possibly including dragonspawn or dragonborn as well as creatures native to the dragon's environment.

If an adventuring party includes more than five characters, additional creatures of the party's level can help balance the encounter. These might be trusted allies who are allowed to enter the dragon's lair, or opportunistic lurkers trying to steal some bits of the dragon's food by picking off isolated characters. Sometimes a dragon emerges from its lair to help its minions defend its sanctum, so you could build an encounter that includes the dragon along with its servitors even before the characters reach the dragon's hoard.

BLACK DRAGON

BLACK DRAGONS ARE MALICIOUS BEASTS that disgorge acid. They primarily lurk in fell swamps but are also drawn to places with strong ties to the Shadowfell.

Young Black Dragon	Level 4 Solo Lurker
Large natural magical beast (aquatic, dragon)	XP 875

Initiative +11   **Senses** Perception +9; darkvision
HP 224; **Bloodied** 112; see also *bloodied breath*
AC 22; **Fortitude** 18, **Reflex** 20, **Will** 17
Resist 15 acid
Saving Throws +5
Speed 7, fly 7 (clumsy), overland flight 10, swim 7
Action Points 2

⊕ **Bite** (standard; at-will) ✦ **Acid**
  Reach 2; +10 vs. AC; 1d6 + 3 damage, and ongoing 5 acid damage (save ends).

⊕ **Claw** (standard; at-will)
  Reach 2; +8 vs. AC; 1d4 + 3 damage.

↟ **Double Attack** (standard; at-will)
  The dragon makes two claw attacks.

↟ **Tail Slash** (immediate reaction, when a melee attack misses the dragon; at-will)
  The dragon uses its tail to attack the enemy that missed it: reach 2; +8 vs. AC; 1d6 + 4 damage, and the target is pushed 1 square.

↞ **Breath Weapon** (standard; recharge ⚅ ⚃) ✦ **Acid**
  Close blast 5; +7 vs. Reflex; 1d12 + 3 acid damage, and the target takes ongoing 5 acid damage and takes a -4 penalty to AC (save ends both).

↞ **Bloodied Breath** (free, when first bloodied; encounter) ✦ **Acid**
  The dragon's breath weapon recharges, and the dragon uses it immediately.

↞ **Cloud of Darkness** (standard; sustain minor; recharge ⚄ ⚅ ⚃)
  ✦ **Zone**
  Close burst 2; this power creates a zone of darkness that remains in place until the end of the dragon's next turn. The zone blocks line of sight for all creatures except the dragon. Any creature entirely within the area (except the dragon) is blinded.

↞ **Frightful Presence** (standard; encounter) ✦ **Fear**
  Close burst 5; targets enemies; +5 vs. Will; the target is stunned until the end of the dragon's next turn. *Aftereffect:* The target takes a -2 penalty to attack rolls (save ends).

Alignment Evil	**Languages** Common, Draconic

Skills Nature +9, Stealth +17
Str 16 (+5)   **Dex** 20 (+7)   **Wis** 15 (+4)
Con 16 (+5)   **Int** 12 (+3)   **Cha** 10 (+2)

Adult Black Dragon	Level 11 Solo Lurker
Large natural magical beast (aquatic, dragon)	XP 3,000

Initiative +15   **Senses** Perception +13; darkvision
HP 560; **Bloodied** 280; see also *bloodied breath*
AC 28; **Fortitude** 24, **Reflex** 26, **Will** 23
Resist 20 acid
Saving Throws +5
Speed 8, fly 8 (hover), overland flight 10, swim 8
Action Points 2

⊕ **Bite** (standard; at-will) ✦ **Acid**
  Reach 2; +16 vs. AC; 1d8 + 4 damage, and ongoing 5 acid damage (save ends).

⊕ **Claw** (standard; at-will)
  Reach 2; +16 vs. AC; 1d6 + 4 damage.

↟ **Double Attack** (standard; at-will)
  The dragon makes two claw attacks.

↟ **Tail Slash** (immediate reaction, when a melee attack misses the dragon; at-will)
  The dragon attacks the enemy that missed it: reach 2; +16 vs. AC; 1d8 + 6 damage, and the target is pushed 1 square.

↞ **Breath Weapon** (standard; recharge ⚅ ⚃) ✦ **Acid**
  Close blast 5; +13 vs. Reflex; 2d8 + 3 acid damage, and the target takes ongoing 5 acid damage and takes a -4 penalty to AC (save ends both).

↞ **Bloodied Breath** (free, when first bloodied; encounter) ✦ **Acid**
  The dragon's breath weapon recharges, and the dragon uses it immediately.

↞ **Cloud of Darkness** (standard; sustain minor; recharge ⚄ ⚅ ⚃)
  ✦ **Zone**
  Close burst 2; this power creates a zone of darkness that remains in place until the end of the dragon's next turn. The zone blocks line of sight for all creatures except the dragon. Any creature entirely within the area (except the dragon) is blinded.

↞ **Frightful Presence** (standard; encounter) ✦ **Fear**
  Close burst 5; targets enemies; +13 vs. Will; the target is stunned until the end of the dragon's next turn. *Aftereffect:* The target takes a -2 penalty to attack rolls (save ends).

Alignment Evil	**Languages** Common, Draconic

Skills Nature +13, Stealth +21
Str 18 (+9)   **Dex** 22 (+11)   **Wis** 16 (+8)
Con 16 (+8)   **Int** 14 (+7)   **Cha** 12 (+6)

Elder Black Dragon — Level 18 Solo Lurker

Elder Black Dragon	Level 18 Solo Lurker
Huge natural magical beast (aquatic, dragon)	XP 10,000

Initiative +21   **Senses** Perception +17; darkvision
HP 860; **Bloodied** 430; see also *bloodied breath*
AC 35; **Fortitude** 31, **Reflex** 33, **Will** 28
Resist 25 acid
Saving Throws +5
Speed 9, fly 9 (hover), overland flight 12, swim 9
Action Points 2

⊕ **Bite** (standard; at-will) ✦ **Acid**
  Reach 3; +24 vs. AC; 1d10 + 6 damage, and ongoing 10 acid damage (save ends).

⊕ **Claw** (standard; at-will)
  Reach 3; +24 vs. AC; 1d8 + 6 damage.

‡ **Double Attack** (standard; at-will)
  The dragon makes two claw attacks.

‡ **Tail Slash** (immediate reaction, when a melee attack misses the dragon; at-will)
  The dragon attacks the enemy that missed it: reach 3; +24 vs. AC; 1d10 + 8 damage, and the target is pushed 2 squares.

⟨ **Breath Weapon** (standard; recharge ⚄ ⚅) ✦ **Acid**
  Close blast 5; +22 vs. Reflex; 3d8 + 5 acid damage, and the target takes ongoing 10 acid damage and takes a -4 penalty to AC (save ends both).

⟨ **Bloodied Breath** (free, when first bloodied; encounter) ✦ **Acid**
  The dragon's breath weapon recharges, and the dragon uses it immediately.

⟨ **Cloud of Darkness** (standard; sustain minor; recharge ⚂ ⚃ ⚅) ✦ **Zone**
  Close burst 2; this power creates a zone of darkness that remains in place until the end of the dragon's next turn. The zone blocks line of sight for all creatures except the dragon. Any creature entirely within the area (except the dragon) is blinded.

⟨ **Frightful Presence** (standard; encounter) ✦ **Fear**
  Close burst 10; targets enemies; +22 vs. Will; the target is stunned until the end of the dragon's next turn. *Aftereffect:* The target takes a -2 penalty to attack rolls (save ends).

⟨ **Vitriolic Spray** (standard; encounter) ✦ **Acid**
  Close blast 5; +22 vs. Reflex; 1d10 + 5 acid damage, and the target is blinded until the end of the dragon's next turn. *Miss:* Half damage, and the target is not blinded.

Alignment Evil	**Languages** Common, Draconic

Skills Nature +17, Stealth +27

Str 22 (+15)	Dex 26 (+17)	Wis 16 (+12)
Con 20 (+14)	Int 16 (+12)	Cha 14 (+11)

Black Dragon Tactics

A black dragon attacks from hiding, either by submerging itself in water or clinging to the shadows. It uses *frightful presence* first and then spends an action point to use its *breath weapon* (or *vitriolic spray*, if elder or ancient). On its next turn, the dragon spends another action point to invoke its *cloud of darkness* power (or *acid gloom*, if ancient). It then makes a bite attack against a single foe or claw attacks against two different opponents within reach. The dragon prefers to remain in the area of its *cloud of darkness* power while making melee attacks, switching to its *breath weapon* as it recharges.

Black Dragon Lore

A character knows the following information with a successful Nature check.

DC 15: Black dragons like dismal forests and gloomy swamps, and are naturally drawn to places where the Shadowfell's influence is strong. A black dragon can surround itself with gloomy darkness, with grants it total concealment (although darkvision penetrates the darkness normally).

DC 20: A black dragon's breath weapon is a blast of caustic green acid.

Encounter Groups

A black dragon might have servitors such as lizardfolk and trolls living around its swampy lair.

Level 5 Encounter (XP 1,225)
✦ 1 young black dragon (level 4 solo lurker)
✦ 2 dark creepers (level 4 skirmisher)

Level 13 Encounter (XP 4,300)
✦ 1 adult black dragon (level 11 solo lurker)
✦ 2 trolls (level 9 brute)
✦ 1 bog hag (level 10 skirmisher)

Ancient Black Dragon — Level 26 Solo Lurker

Ancient Black Dragon	Level 26 Solo Lurker
Gargantuan natural magical beast (aquatic, dragon)	XP 45,000

Initiative +27   **Senses** Perception +22; darkvision
HP 1,190; **Bloodied** 595; see also *bloodied breath*
AC 43; **Fortitude** 39, **Reflex** 41, **Will** 35
Resist 30 acid
Saving Throws +5
Speed 10, fly 10 (hover), overland flight 15, swim 10
Action Points 2

⊕ **Bite** (standard; at-will) ✦ **Acid**
  Reach 4; +32 vs. AC; 2d8 + 8 damage, and ongoing 15 acid damage (save ends).

⊕ **Claw** (standard; at-will)
  Reach 4; +32 vs. AC; 1d10 + 8 damage.

‡ **Double Attack** (standard; at-will)
  The dragon makes two claw attacks.

‡ **Tail Slash** (immediate reaction, when a melee attack misses the dragon; at-will)
  The dragon attacks the enemy that missed it: reach 4; +32 vs. AC; 1d12 + 10 damage, and the target is pushed 3 squares.

⟨ **Acid Gloom** (standard; sustain minor; recharge ⚂ ⚄ ⚅) ✦ **Acid, Zone**
  Close burst 2; this power creates a zone of acidic darkness that remains in place until the end of the dragon's next turn. The zone blocks line of sight for all creatures except the dragon. Any creature entirely within the area (except the dragon) is blinded, and any creature that enters or starts its turn in the zone takes 15 acid damage.

⟨ **Breath Weapon** (standard; recharge ⚄ ⚅) ✦ **Acid**
  Close blast 5; +28 vs. Reflex; 4d8 + 6 acid damage, and the target takes ongoing 15 acid damage and takes a -4 penalty to AC (save ends both).

⟨ **Bloodied Breath** (free, when first bloodied; encounter) ✦ **Acid**
  The dragon's breath weapon recharges, and the dragon uses it immediately.

⟨ **Frightful Presence** (standard; encounter) ✦ **Fear**
  Close burst 10; targets enemies; +28 vs. Will; the target is stunned until the end of the dragon's next turn. *Aftereffect:* The target takes a -2 penalty to attack rolls (save ends).

⟨ **Vitriolic Spray** (standard; encounter) ✦ **Acid**
  Close blast 5; +28 vs. Reflex; 2d10 + 6 acid damage, and the target is blinded until the end of the dragon's next turn. *Miss:* Half damage, and the target is not blinded.

Alignment Evil	**Languages** Common, Draconic

Skills Nature +22, Stealth +33

Str 26 (+21)	Dex 30 (+23)	Wis 18 (+17)
Con 22 (+19)	Int 18 (+17)	Cha 16 (+16)

BLUE DRAGON

BLUE DRAGONS BREATHE BOLTS OF LIGHTNING. They can be found anywhere but prefer to lair in coastal caves, attacking and plundering ships that sail too close.

BLUE DRAGON LORE

A character knows the following information with a successful Nature check.

DC 15: Although highly adaptable, blue dragons often lair in coastal caves with entrances that aren't easily accessible by land.

DC 20: Blue dragons prefer to attack at range. A blue dragon's breath weapon is an arc of lightning that leaps from one target to another. It can also disgorge a ball of lightning that explodes on impact.

BLUE DRAGON TACTICS

A blue dragon takes to air immediately if it is not already flying. It spends an action point to use *frightful presence*, and then follows up with its *breath weapon*. Until it is forced to land, a blue dragon is content to remain airborne and switch between *lightning burst* and *breath weapon* attacks. The dragon relies on its *draconic fury* to make enemies think twice about engaging it in melee.

An elder or ancient blue dragon spends an action point to use *thunderclap* against foes that get too close. An ancient blue dragon might also swoop down on a foe, use its *wingclap* power, unleash its *draconic fury*, and spend an action point to fly back out of range.

ENCOUNTER GROUPS

Blue dragons often forge uneasy alliances with sahuagin and storm giants, demanding treasure for the protection they provide. Dragonborn are often drawn to blue dragon mounts.

Level 15 Encounter (XP 6,400)
✦ 1 adult blue dragon (level 13 solo artillery)
✦ 3 dragonborn raiders (level 13 skirmisher)

Level 24 Encounter (XP 30,600)
✦ 1 elder blue dragon (level 20 solo artillery)
✦ 2 thunderhawks (level 22 elite soldier)

THE AGES OF DRAGONS

Dragons have long natural lifespans, and they grow larger and more powerful as they age. Upon hatching, dragons are at least the size of an adult human, and they grow quickly to horse size and larger. The oldest dragons are among the most enormous creatures alive, stretching over a hundred feet long.

In game terms, dragons are grouped into four age categories: young, adult, elder, and ancient. These are all mature dragons—few adventurers ever discover hatchlings in dragon nests, and those who do must face an angry adult parent before worrying about the relatively small and weak wyrmlings.

Young and adult dragons both fall in the Large size category, although they lie at opposite ends of that range.

Young dragons are about the size of a draft horse. Adult dragons are roughly the size of a storm giant, pushing the upper limits of Large.

Elder dragons are Huge, about the size of elephants or titans. Ancient dragons are Gargantuan, almost without compare among other living creatures. There is said to be no upper limit to the size of an ancient dragon.

Young Blue Dragon — Level 6 Solo Artillery

Young Blue Dragon   **Level 6 Solo Artillery**
Large natural magical beast (dragon)   XP 1,250

Initiative +5   **Senses** Perception +10; darkvision
HP 296; **Bloodied** 148; see also *bloodied breath*
AC 23; **Fortitude** 24, **Reflex** 21, **Will** 21
Resist 15 lightning
Saving Throws +5
Speed 8, fly 10 (hover), overland flight 15
Action Points 2

(+) **Gore** (standard; at-will) ✦ **Lightning**
Reach 2; +11 vs. AC; 1d6 + 5 plus 1d6 lightning damage.

(+) **Claw** (standard; at-will)
Reach 2; +9 vs. AC; 1d4 + 5 damage.

✝ **Draconic Fury** (standard; at-will)
The dragon makes a gore attack and two claw attacks.

↗ **Breath Weapon** (standard; recharge ⚃ ⚅) ✦ **Lightning**
The dragon targets up to three creatures with its lightning breath; the first target must be within 10 squares of the dragon, the second target within 10 squares of the first, and the third target within 10 squares of the second; +11 vs. Reflex; 1d12 + 5 lightning damage. *Miss:* Half damage. This attack does not provoke opportunity attacks.

↗ **Bloodied Breath** (free, when first bloodied; encounter) ✦ **Lightning**
The dragon's breath weapon recharges, and the dragon uses it immediately.

↞ **Frightful Presence** (standard; encounter) ✦ **Fear**
Close burst 5; targets enemies; +11 vs. Will; the target is stunned until the end of the dragon's next turn. *Aftereffect:* The target takes a −2 penalty to attack rolls (save ends).

✳ **Lightning Burst** (standard; at-will) ✦ **Lightning**
Area burst 2 within 20; +11 vs. Reflex; 1d6 + 4 lightning damage. *Miss:* Half damage.

Alignment Evil   **Languages** Common, Draconic
Skills Athletics +18, Insight +10, Nature +10
Str 20 (+8)   **Dex** 15 (+5)   **Wis** 14 (+5)
Con 18 (+7)   **Int** 12 (+4)   **Cha** 13 (+4)

Adult Blue Dragon — Level 13 Solo Artillery

Adult Blue Dragon   **Level 13 Solo Artillery**
Large natural magical beast (dragon)   XP 4,000

Initiative +9   **Senses** Perception +13; darkvision
HP 655; **Bloodied** 327; see also *bloodied breath*
AC 30; **Fortitude** 31, **Reflex** 28, **Will** 27
Resist 20 lightning
Saving Throws +5
Speed 8, fly 10 (hover), overland flight 15
Action Points 2

(+) **Gore** (standard; at-will) ✦ **Lightning**
Reach 2; +18 vs. AC; 1d8 + 6 plus 1d6 lightning damage, and the target is pushed 1 square and knocked prone.

(+) **Claw** (standard; at-will)
Reach 2; +16 vs. AC; 1d6 + 6 damage.

✝ **Draconic Fury** (standard; at-will)
The dragon makes a gore attack and two claw attacks.

↗ **Breath Weapon** (standard; recharge ⚃ ⚅) ✦ **Lightning**
The dragon targets up to three creatures with its lightning breath; the first target must be within 10 squares of the dragon, the second target within 10 squares of the first, and the third target within 10 squares of the second; +18 vs. Reflex; 2d12 + 10 lightning damage. *Miss:* Half damage. This attack does not provoke opportunity attacks.

↗ **Bloodied Breath** (free, when first bloodied; encounter) ✦ **Lightning**
The dragon's breath weapon recharges, and the dragon uses it immediately.

↞ **Frightful Presence** (standard; encounter) ✦ **Fear**
Close burst 5; targets enemies; +18 vs. Will; the target is stunned until the end of the dragon's next turn. *Aftereffect:* The target takes a −2 penalty to attack rolls (save ends).

✳ **Lightning Burst** (standard; at-will) ✦ **Lightning**
Area burst 3 within 20; +18 vs. Reflex; 2d6 + 4 lightning damage. *Miss:* Half damage.

Alignment Evil   **Languages** Common, Draconic
Skills Athletics +22, Insight +13, Nature +13
Str 23 (+12)   **Dex** 16 (+9)   **Wis** 14 (+8)
Con 19 (+10)   **Int** 13 (+7)   **Cha** 14 (+8)

Elder Blue Dragon — Level 20 Solo Artillery

Elder Blue Dragon	Level 20 Solo Artillery
Huge natural magical beast (dragon)	XP 14,000

Initiative +13   **Senses** Perception +18; darkvision
HP 960; **Bloodied** 480; see also *bloodied breath*
AC 36; **Fortitude** 39, **Reflex** 34, **Will** 34
Resist 25 lightning
Saving Throws +5
Speed 10, fly 12 (hover), overland flight 15
Action Points 2

⊕ **Gore** (standard; at-will) ✦ **Lightning**
Reach 3; +25 vs. AC; 2d6 + 8 plus 2d6 lightning damage, and the target is pushed 2 squares and knocked prone.

⊕ **Claw** (standard; at-will)
Reach 3; +23 vs. AC; 1d8 + 8 damage.

↯ **Draconic Fury** (standard; at-will)
The dragon makes a gore attack and two claw attacks.

➷ **Breath Weapon** (standard; recharge ⚄ ⚅) ✦ **Lightning**
The dragon targets up to three creatures with its lightning breath; the first target must be within 20 squares of the dragon, the second target within 10 squares of the first, and the third target within 10 squares of the second; +25 vs. Reflex; 3d12 + 17 lightning damage. *Miss:* Half damage. This attack does not provoke opportunity attacks.

➷ **Bloodied Breath** (free, when first bloodied; encounter) ✦ **Lightning**
The dragon's breath weapon recharges automatically, and the dragon uses it immediately.

⬅ **Frightful Presence** (standard; encounter) ✦ **Fear**
Close burst 10; targets enemies; +25 vs. Will; the target is stunned until the end of the black dragon's next turn. *Aftereffect:* The target takes a -2 penalty to attack rolls (save ends).

⬅ **Thunderclap** (standard; at-will) ✦ **Thunder**
Close burst 3; +25 vs. Fortitude; 1d10 + 7 thunder damage, and the target is stunned until the end of the blue dragon's next turn. *Critical Hit:* As above, except that the target is stunned (save ends).

✸ **Lightning Burst** (standard; at-will) ✦ **Lightning**
Area burst 3 within 20; +25 vs. Reflex; 3d6 + 7 lightning damage. *Miss:* Half damage.

Alignment Evil   **Languages** Common, Draconic
Skills Athletics +28, Insight +18, Nature +18

Str 27 (+18)	Dex 16 (+13)	Wis 17 (+13)
Con 24 (+17)	Int 15 (+12)	Cha 16 (+13)

Ancient Blue Dragon — Level 28 Solo Artillery

Ancient Blue Dragon	Level 28 Solo Artillery
Gargantuan natural magical beast (dragon)	XP 65,000

Initiative +18   **Senses** Perception +23; darkvision
HP 1,290; **Bloodied** 645; see also *bloodied breath*
AC 42; **Fortitude** 46, **Reflex** 40, **Will** 40
Resist 30 lightning
Saving Throws +5
Speed 10, fly 12 (hover), overland flight 15
Action Points 2

⊕ **Gore** (standard; at-will) ✦ **Lightning**
Reach 4; +34 vs. AC; 2d8 + 10 plus 2d6 lightning damage, and the target is pushed 3 squares and knocked prone.

⊕ **Claw** (standard; at-will)
Reach 4; +32 vs. AC; 2d6 + 10 damage.

↯ **Draconic Fury** (standard; at-will)
The dragon makes a gore attack and two claw attacks.

↯ **Wingclap** (move; recharge ⚄ ⚅) ✦ **Thunder**
The dragon flies up to 12 squares and attacks with its wings at the end of its move: reach 4; +34 vs. Fortitude; 3d10 + 8 thunder damage. This attack does not provoke opportunity attacks.

➷ **Breath Weapon** (standard; recharge ⚄ ⚅) ✦ **Lightning**
The dragon targets up to three creatures with its lightning breath; the first target must be within 20 squares of the dragon, the second target within 10 squares of the first, and the third target within 10 squares of the second; +34 vs. Reflex; 3d12 + 22 lightning damage. *Miss:* Half damage.

➷ **Bloodied Breath** (free, when first bloodied; encounter) ✦ **Lightning**
The dragon's breath weapon recharges, and the dragon uses it immediately.

⬅ **Frightful Presence** (standard; encounter) ✦ **Fear**
Close burst 10; targets enemies; +34 vs. Will; the target is stunned until the end of the dragon's next turn. *Aftereffect:* The target takes a -2 penalty to attack rolls (save ends).

⬅ **Thunderclap** (standard; at-will) ✦ **Thunder**
Close burst 3; +34 vs. Fortitude; 2d10 + 8 thunder damage, and the target is stunned until the end of the blue dragon's next turn. *Critical Hit:* As above, except that the target is stunned (save ends).

✸ **Lightning Burst** (standard; at-will) ✦ **Lightning**
Area burst 4 within 20; +34 vs. Reflex; 5d6 + 8 lightning damage. *Miss:* Half damage.

Alignment Evil   **Languages** Common, Draconic
Skills Athletics +34, Insight +23, Nature +23

Str 31 (+24)	Dex 19 (+18)	Wis 18 (+18)
Con 26 (+22)	Int 17 (+17)	Cha 17 (+17)

GREEN DRAGON

MASTERS OF NEGOTIATION AND DECEIT, green dragons primarily live in forests or other places with strong ties to the Feywild. They breathe clouds of poisonous gas.

GREEN DRAGON TACTICS

A green dragon uses *flyby attack* and its *breath weapon* to wear down enemies before landing and engaging in melee. Once per round, it uses *luring glare* to either move a target into the area of its breath weapon or put the target within reach of its melee attacks.

An adult, elder, and ancient green dragon uses its *lashing tail* to confound opponents that try to engage it in melee. The ancient green dragon uses *mind poison* as often as it can, attacking enemy defenders first.

GREEN DRAGON LORE

A character knows the following information with a successful Nature check.

DC 15: Green dragons live primarily in forests and are often drawn to locations connected to the Feywild.

DC 20: Green dragons are manipulative creatures well versed in the art of deception. They like to bargain with other creatures while manipulating the situation to gain some hidden advantage. They breathe clouds of poisonous gas and use their tails to sweep enemies off their feet.

ENCOUNTERS

Green dragons sometimes team up with fey or other woodland creatures, and occasionally travel in pairs or even packs.

Level 7 Encounter (XP 1,500)
✦ 1 young green dragon (level 5 solo skirmisher)
✦ 2 kobold slyblades (level 4 lurker)
✦ 1 kobold wyrmpriest (level 3 artillery)

Level 13 Encounter (XP 4,900)
✦ 1 adult green dragon (level 12 solo controller)
✦ 2 banshrae warriors (level 12 skirmisher)

Young Green Dragon — Level 5 Solo Skirmisher
Large natural magical beast (dragon)   XP 1,000

Initiative +7   **Senses** Perception +10; darkvision
HP 260; **Bloodied** 130; see also *bloodied breath*
AC 21; **Fortitude** 17, **Reflex** 19, **Will** 17
Resist 15 poison
Saving Throws +5
Speed 8, fly 10 (hover), overland flight 15; see also *flyby attack*
Action Points 2

ⓣ **Bite** (standard; at-will) ✦ **Poison**
     Reach 2; +10 vs. AC; 1d8 + 5 damage, and ongoing 5 poison damage (save ends).

ⓣ **Claw** (standard; at-will)
     Reach 2; +10 vs. AC; 1d6 + 5 damage.

⫟ **Double Attack** (standard; at-will)
     The dragon makes two claw attacks.

⫟ **Flyby Attack** (standard; recharge ▣ ▦)
     The dragon flies up to 10 squares and makes a bite attack at any point during the move without provoking an opportunity attack from the target.

⫟ **Tail Sweep** (immediate reaction, if an adjacent enemy does not move on its turn; at-will)
     +8 vs. Reflex; 1d8 + 5 damage, and the target is knocked prone.

⌖ **Luring Glare** (minor 1/round; at-will) ✦ **Charm, Gaze**
     Ranged 10; +8 vs. Will; the target slides 2 squares.

⬿ **Breath Weapon** (standard; recharge ▣ ▦) ✦ **Poison**
     Close blast 5; +8 vs. Fortitude; 1d10 + 3 poison damage, and the target takes ongoing 5 poison damage and is slowed (save ends both). *Aftereffect:* The target is slowed (save ends).

⬿ **Bloodied Breath** (free, when first bloodied; encounter) ✦ **Poison**
     The dragon's breath weapon recharges, and the dragon uses it immediately.

⬿ **Frightful Presence** (standard; encounter) ✦ **Fear**
     Close burst 5; targets enemies; +8 vs. Will; the target is stunned until the end of the dragon's next turn. *Aftereffect:* The target takes a -2 penalty to attack rolls (save ends).

Alignment Evil   **Languages** Common, Draconic
Skills Bluff +15, Diplomacy +10, Insight +15, Intimidate +10

Str 15 (+4)	Dex 20 (+7)	Wis 16 (+5)
Con 17 (+5)	Int 15 (+4)	Cha 17 (+5)

Adult Green Dragon — Level 12 Solo Controller
Large natural magical beast (dragon)   XP 3,500

Initiative +12   **Senses** Perception +14; darkvision
Lashing Tail aura 1; all creatures other than the dragon treat the area within the aura as difficult terrain. The dragon loses this aura while airborne.
HP 620; **Bloodied** 310; see also *bloodied breath*
AC 28; **Fortitude** 25, **Reflex** 26, **Will** 25
Resist 20 poison
Saving Throws +5
Speed 8, fly 12 (hover), overland flight 15; see also *flyby attack*
Action Points 2

ⓣ **Bite** (standard; at-will) ✦ **Poison**
     Reach 2; +17 vs. AC; 1d10 + 6 damage, and ongoing 5 poison damage (save ends).

ⓣ **Claw** (standard; at-will)
     Reach 2; +17 vs. AC; 1d8 + 6 damage.

⫟ **Double Attack** (standard; at-will)
     The dragon makes two claw attacks.

⫟ **Flyby Attack** (standard; recharge ▣ ▦)
     The dragon flies up to 12 squares and makes a bite attack at any point during the move without provoking an opportunity attack from the target.

⫟ **Tail Sweep** (immediate reaction, if an adjacent enemy does not move on its turn; at-will)
     +15 vs. Reflex; 1d8 + 6 damage, and the target is knocked prone.

⌖ **Luring Glare** (minor 1/round; at-will) ✦ **Charm, Gaze**
     Ranged 10; +15 vs. Will; the target slides 2 squares.

⬿ **Breath Weapon** (standard; recharge ▣ ▦) ✦ **Poison**
     Close blast 5; +15 vs. Fortitude; 1d10 + 5 poison damage, and the target takes ongoing 5 poison damage and is slowed (save ends both). *Aftereffect:* The target is slowed (save ends).

⬿ **Bloodied Breath** (free, when first bloodied; encounter) ✦ **Poison**
     The dragon's breath weapon recharges, and the dragon uses it immediately.

⬿ **Frightful Presence** (standard; encounter) ✦ **Fear**
     Close burst 5; targets enemies; +15 vs. Will; the target is stunned until the end of the dragon's next turn. *Aftereffect:* The target takes a -2 penalty to attack rolls (save ends).

Alignment Evil   **Languages** Common, Draconic
Skills Bluff +21, Diplomacy +16, Insight +19, Intimidate +16

Str 16 (+9)	Dex 22 (+12)	Wis 17 (+9)
Con 20 (+11)	Int 16 (+9)	Cha 20 (+11)

Elder Green Dragon — Level 19 Solo Controller
Huge natural magical beast (dragon)   XP 12,000

Initiative +17   **Senses** Perception +17; darkvision
Lashing Tail aura 1; all creatures other than the dragon treat the area within the aura as difficult terrain. The dragon loses this aura while airborne.
HP 910; **Bloodied** 455; see also *bloodied breath*
AC 35; **Fortitude** 31, **Reflex** 33, **Will** 31
Resist 25 poison
Saving Throws +5
Speed 10, fly 14 (hover), overland flight 18; see also *flyby attack*
Action Points 2

ⓣ **Bite** (standard; at-will) ✦ **Poison**
     Reach 3; +24 vs. AC; 1d10 + 8 damage, and ongoing 10 poison damage (save ends).

ⓣ **Claw** (standard; at-will)
     Reach 3; +24 vs. AC; 1d8 + 8 damage.

⫟ **Double Attack** (standard; at-will)
     The dragon makes two claw attacks.

⫟ **Flyby Attack** (standard; recharge ▣ ▦)
     The dragon flies up to 14 squares and makes a bite attack at any point during the move without provoking an opportunity attack from the target.

⫟ **Tail Sweep** (immediate reaction, if an adjacent enemy does not move on its turn; at-will)
     +24 vs. Reflex; 2d10 + 8 damage, and the target is knocked prone.

⌖ **Luring Glare** (minor 1/round; at-will) ✦ **Charm, Gaze**
     Ranged 10; +22 vs. Will; the target slides 3 squares.

⬿ **Breath Weapon** (standard; recharge ▣ ▦) ✦ **Poison**
     Close blast 5; +22 vs. Fortitude; 2d10 + 6 poison damage, and the target takes ongoing 10 poison damage and is slowed (save ends both). *Aftereffect:* The target is slowed (save ends).

⬿ **Bloodied Breath** (free, when first bloodied; encounter) ✦ **Poison**
     The dragon's breath weapon recharges, and the dragon uses it immediately.

⬿ **Frightful Presence** (standard; encounter) ✦ **Fear**
     Close burst 10; targets enemies; +22 vs. Will; the target is stunned until the end of the dragon's next turn. *Aftereffect:* The target takes a -2 penalty to attack rolls (save ends).

Alignment Evil   **Languages** Common, Draconic
Skills Bluff +25, Diplomacy +20, Insight +22, Intimidate +20

Str 18 (+13)	Dex 26 (+17)	Wis 17 (+12)
Con 22 (+15)	Int 17 (+12)	Cha 22 (+15)

(Top, left to right) spiretop drake, guard drake, and needlefang drakes

PSEUDODRAGON

A PSEUDODRAGON IS A FICKLE DRAKE with a poisonous sting. It can be arrogant, demanding, and less than helpful at times. It can also be affectionate and playful when treated well. It is willing to serve–provided it is fed and receives lots of attention. Although it can't speak, it can vocalize animal noises, such as a purr (pleasure), a hiss (unpleasant surprise), a chirp (desire), or a growl (anger).

Pseudodragon		Level 3 Lurker
Tiny natural beast (reptile)		XP 150

Initiative +9   **Senses** Perception +8
HP 40; **Bloodied** 20
AC 17; **Fortitude** 14, **Reflex** 15, **Will** 14
Speed 4, fly 8 (hover); see also *flyby attack*
(＋) **Bite** (standard; at-will)
     +8 vs. AC; 1d8 + 4 damage.
(＋) **Sting** (standard; recharge ⚁ ⚂ ⚃) ✦ **Poison**
     +8 vs. AC; 1d8 + 4 damage, and ongoing 5 poison damage (save ends).
✦ **Flyby Attack** (standard; at-will)
     The pseudodragon flies up to 8 squares and makes one melee basic attack at any point during that movement. The pseudodragon doesn't provoke opportunity attacks when moving away from the target of the attack.
Invisibility (standard; recharges when the pseudodragon is damaged) ✦ **Illusion**
     As long as the pseudodragon doesn't move, it is invisible.
Alignment Unaligned   **Languages** –
Skills Insight +8, Stealth +10
Str 13 (+2)   **Dex** 18 (+5)   **Wis** 15 (+3)
Con 16 (+4)   **Int** 6 (-1)   **Cha** 17 (+4)

PSEUDODRAGON TACTICS

A pseudodragon prefers to use its *sting* in combat, relying on *flyby attack* to fly close to an enemy, strike, and fly away before a foe can catch it. A pseudodragon confronted with a persistent enemy shifts and uses *invisibility*.

PSEUDODRAGON LORE

A character knows the following information with a successful Nature check.

     DC 15: Pseudodragons are among the cleverest and most playful drakes, so they're highly valued as pets. They are fierce predators in the wild, but they generally don't attack humanoids unless provoked.

SPITTING DRAKE

THIS CUNNING REPTILE SPITS ACID, hence the name. In the wild, spitting drakes attack without provocation, but they can be domesticated and trained. They instinctively focus their attacks on one target at a time, determined to take it down quickly.

Spitting Drake		Level 3 Artillery
Medium natural beast (reptile)		XP 150

Initiative +5   **Senses** Perception +3
HP 38; **Bloodied** 19
AC 17; **Fortitude** 14, **Reflex** 16, **Will** 14
Resist 10 acid
Speed 7
(＋) **Bite** (standard; at-will)
     +6 vs. AC; 1d6 + 2 damage.
↗ **Caustic Spit** (standard; at-will) ✦ **Acid**
     Ranged 10; +8 vs. Reflex; 1d10 + 4 acid damage.
Alignment Unaligned   **Languages** –
Str 14 (+3)   **Dex** 18 (+5)   **Wis** 14 (+3)
Con 14 (+3)   **Int** 3 (-3)   **Cha** 12 (+2)

SPITTING DRAKE TACTICS

A spitting drake uses its *caustic spit* to attack enemies at range. Despite their low intelligence, multiple drakes gang up on a single target to take it down quickly.

SPITTING DRAKE LORE

A character knows the following information with a successful Nature check.

(Top, left to right) rage drake,
spitting drake,
and pseudodragon

DC 15: Spitting drakes make for messy pets, but humanoids train them as guardians nonetheless. In the wild, spitting drakes sometimes congregate with other drakes, such as guard drakes. Spitting drakes can also be found in clutches formed under a dominant rage drake that has no clutch of its own.

RAGE DRAKE

RAGE DRAKES SAVAGELY ATTACK all other creatures they encounter and become even more ferocious when bloodied. Adult rage drakes cannot be domesticated, but newly hatched rage drakes can be trained to serve as pets, guards, or mounts.

Rage Drake	Level 5 Brute
Large natural beast (mount, reptile)	XP 200

Initiative +3   **Senses** Perception +3
HP 77; **Bloodied** 38; see also *bloodied rage*
AC 17; **Fortitude** 17, **Reflex** 15, **Will** 15
Immune fear (while bloodied only)
Speed 8
⊕ **Bite** (standard; at-will)
  +9 vs. AC; 1d10 + 4 damage; see also *bloodied rage*.
✦ **Claw** (standard; at-will)
  +8 vs. AC; 1d6 + 4 damage; see also *bloodied rage*.
✦ **Raking Charge** (standard; at-will)
  When the rage drake charges, it makes two claw attacks against
  a single target.
Bloodied Rage (while bloodied)
  The rage drake gains a +2 bonus to attack rolls and deals an extra
  5 damage per attack.
Raging Mount (while bloodied and mounted by a friendly rider of
  5th level or higher; at-will) ✦ **Mount**
  The rage drake grants its rider a +2 bonus to attack rolls and
  damage rolls with melee attacks.
Alignment Unaligned   **Languages** –
Str 19 (+6)   **Dex** 13 (+3)   **Wis** 13 (+3)
Con 17 (+5)   **Int** 3 (–2)   **Cha** 12 (+3)

RAGE DRAKE TACTICS

A rage drake fights until killed. It makes a *raking charge* initially and then uses its bite attack on subsequent rounds, gaining bonuses on its attack rolls and damage once it becomes bloodied.

RAGE DRAKE LORE

A character knows the following information with a successful Nature check.

DC 15: "Tame" rage drakes can serve as mounts and guardians. Wild rage drakes are brutally efficient and highly territorial hunters.

DC 20: A clutch of rage drakes treats interlopers as prey, an intolerable threat, or both. A rage drake without a clutch of its own will often insinuate itself into a clutch of guard drakes or spitting drakes, effectively becoming the group's leader.

ENCOUNTER GROUPS

Drakes can appear alongside or in the home of almost any humanoid creature. Clutches of drakes can also be found in the wilderness, competing with other predators.

Level 2 Encounter (XP 625)
✦ 2 guard drakes (level 2 brute)
✦ 2 elf archers (level 2 artillery)
✦ 1 elf scout (level 2 skirmisher)

Level 4 Encounter (XP 875)
✦ 1 pseudodragon (level 3 lurker)
✦ 1 human mage (level 4 artillery)
✦ 2 human guards (level 3 soldier)
✦ 2 human bandits (level 2 skirmisher)

Level 5 Encounter (XP 1,000)
✦ 1 rage drake (level 5 brute)
✦ 1 greenscale marsh mystic lizardfolk (level 6 controller)
✦ 1 greenscale darter lizardfolk (level 5 lurker)
✦ 2 greenscale hunter lizardfolk (level 4 skirmisher)

DRIDER

BLOODTHIRSTY CREATURES THAT LURK IN THE DEPTHS of the world, driders are servants of Lolth gifted with a semblance of their god's grotesque form.

Drider Fanglord — **Level 14 Brute**
Large fey humanoid (spider) — XP 1,000

Initiative +12 **Senses** Perception +15; darkvision
HP 172; **Bloodied** 86
AC 26; **Fortitude** 27, **Reflex** 25, **Will** 23
Speed 8, climb 8 (spider climb)

Greatsword (standard; at-will) ✦ **Weapon**
+19 vs. AC; 1d12 + 7 damage.

Quick Bite (minor; at-will) ✦ **Poison**
Requires combat advantage; +16 vs. Fortitude; 1d4 damage, and ongoing 10 poison damage (save ends).

Darkfire (minor; encounter)
Ranged 10; +16 vs. Reflex; until the end of the drider's next turn, the target grants combat advantage to all attackers, and the target cannot benefit from invisibility or concealment.

Web (standard; recharge ⚃ ⚄ ⚅)
Ranged 5; +15 vs. Reflex; the target is restrained (until escape). Escaping from the web requires a successful DC 25 Acrobatics check or DC 27 Athletics check.

Alignment Evil **Languages** Elven
Skills Dungeoneering +15, Stealth +17

Str 24 (+14)	**Dex** 21 (+12)	**Wis** 16 (+10)
Con 22 (+13)	**Int** 13 (+8)	**Cha** 9 (+6)

Equipment leather armor, greatsword

DRIDER FANGLORD TACTICS

The fanglord tries to snare a foe in its *web* and rushes up to administer a *quick bite* if the foe is successfully restrained. Otherwise, the drider uses its greatsword.

DRIDER LORE

A character knows the following information with a successful Arcana check.

DC 20: In drow society, the strongest and bravest can take the Test of Lolth. Those who succeed become driders, members of a privileged caste. Those who fail usually die.

ENCOUNTER GROUPS

Driders are common among drow, and advantaged as they are, they're still subservient to Lolth's priests. Important drow operations might involve one or more driders and other spider creatures.

Level 12 Encounter (XP 3,600)
- ✦ 1 drider fanglord (level 14 brute)
- ✦ 1 drow arachnomancer (level 13 artillery)
- ✦ 3 drow warriors (level 11 lurker)

Level 14 Encounter (XP 5,000)
- ✦ 2 drider fanglords (level 14 brute)
- ✦ 1 drider shadowspinner (level 14 skirmisher)
- ✦ 1 demonweb terror spider (level 14 elite controller)

Drider Shadowspinner — **Level 14 Skirmisher**
Large fey humanoid (spider) — XP 1,000

Initiative +12 **Senses** Perception +14; darkvision
HP 134; **Bloodied** 67
AC 28; **Fortitude** 25, **Reflex** 26, **Will** 26; see also *shifting shadows*
Speed 8, climb 8 (spider climb)

Short Sword (standard; at-will) ✦ **Necrotic, Weapon**
+19 vs. AC; 1d8 + 3 plus 2d6 necrotic damage; see also *melee agility*.

Slashing Darkness (standard; at-will) ✦ **Necrotic**
Ranged 5; +17 vs. Reflex; 3d8 + 3 necrotic damage.

Web (standard; recharge ⚃ ⚄ ⚅)
Ranged 5; +17 vs. Reflex; the target is restrained (until escape). Escaping from the web requires a successful DC 26 Acrobatics check or DC 25 Athletics check.

Cloud of Darkness (minor; encounter)
Close burst 1; this power creates a cloud of darkness that remains in place until the end of the drider shadowspinner's next turn. The cloud blocks line of sight for all creatures except the shadowspinner. Any creature entirely within the cloud (except the shadowspinner) is blinded until it exits.

Combat Advantage
The drider shadowspinner deals an extra 2d6 necrotic damage on melee and ranged attacks against any target it has combat advantage against.

Melee Agility (free, when the drider shadowspinner hits with a melee attack; at-will)
The drider shadowspinner shifts 1 square.

Shifting Shadows
If a drider shadowspinner moves at least 3 squares on its turn and ends its move 3 squares away from its previous position, it gains concealment until the end of its next turn.

Alignment Evil **Languages** Elven
Skills Dungeoneering +14, Stealth +15

Str 13 (+8)	**Dex** 17 (+10)	**Wis** 14 (+9)
Con 14 (+9)	**Int** 12 (+8)	**Cha** 17 (+10)

Equipment leather armor, short sword

DRIDER SHADOWSPINNER TACTICS

After restraining a creature with its *web*, the shadowspinner uses *slashing darkness* against that foe until the victim escapes or dies, or until the drider is forced to turn its attention toward another enemy. If it can move without provoking opportunity attacks, it does so to gain the benefit of *shifting shadows*.

ANNE STOKES

ARROGANT AND PERVERSE, the drow conspire to subjugate all who don't revere their Spider Queen, the god Lolth.

Like their kin, the elves, drow were once creatures of the Feywild. However, they followed Lolth down a sinister path and now reside in the Underdark of the world. There they gather in settlements of macabre splendor, lit by luminescent flora and magic, and crawling with spiders.

DROW LORE

A character knows the following information with a successful Arcana check.

DC 20: Drow raid the surface as well as other Underdark societies for plunder and slaves. They conquer the weak and form tenuous alliances with creatures powerful enough to stand against them.

DC 25: Drow live in a matriarchal theocracy with rules and customs strictly enforced by the priests of Lolth. Male drow can't serve as clergy and are often treated as second-class citizens, but even they exercise power based on their station and the opportunities handed to them.

Drow Warrior	Level 11 Lurker
Medium fey humanoid	XP 600

Initiative +13   **Senses** Perception +11; darkvision
HP 83; **Bloodied** 41
AC 24; **Fortitude** 20, **Reflex** 22, **Will** 19
Speed 6
ⴲ **Rapier** (standard; at-will) ✦ **Poison, Weapon**
+14 vs. AC; 1d8 + 4 damage (×2)
➷ **Hand Crossbow** (standard; at-will) ✦ **Poison, Weapon**
Ranged 10/20; +14 vs. AC; 1d6 + 4 damage, and the drow warrior makes a secondary attack against the same target.
Secondary Attack: +13 vs. Fortitude; see *drow poison* for the effect.
➷ **Darkfire** (minor; encounter)
Ranged 10; +12 vs. Reflex; until the end of the drow warrior's next turn, the target grants combat advantage to all attackers, and the target cannot benefit from invisibility or concealment.
Combat Advantage
The drow warrior deals an extra 2d6 damage on melee and ranged attacks against any target it has combat advantage against.
Drow Poison ✦ **Poison**
A creature hit by a weapon coated in *drow poison* takes a -2 penalty to attack rolls (save ends). *First Failed Save:* The target is also weakened (save ends). *Second Failed Save:* The target falls unconscious until the end of the encounter.
Alignment Evil   **Languages** Common, Elven
Skills Dungeoneering +11, Intimidate +8, Stealth +15
Str 14 (+7)	**Dex** 19 (+9)	**Wis** 13 (+6)
Con 11 (+5)	**Int** 13 (+6)	**Cha** 12 (+6)
Equipment chainmail, rapier*, hand crossbow, 20 bolts*
These weapons are coated in drow poison.

DROW WARRIOR TACTICS

A drow warrior casts *darkfire* on an enemy, and then attacks the same target with its hand crossbow. It continues to assail foes with crossbow bolts or moves into a flanking position and attacks with its rapier.

Drow Arachnomancer	Level 13 Artillery (Leader)
Medium fey humanoid	XP 800

Initiative +8   **Senses** Perception +13; darkvision
HP 94; **Bloodied** 47
AC 26; **Fortitude** 22, **Reflex** 24, **Will** 24
Speed 7
ⴲ **Spider Rod** (standard; at-will)
+16 vs. AC; 1d6 damage, and the target is immobilized (save ends); see also *Lolth's judgment.*
➷ **Venom Ray** (standard; at-will) ✦ **Poison**
Ranged 10; +18 vs. Reflex; 2d8 + 3 poison damage, and ongoing 5 poison damage (save ends); see also *Lolth's judgment.*
✵ **Lolth's Grasp** (standard; encounter) ✦ **Necrotic, Zone**
Area burst 4 within 10; webs full of spectral spiders cover the zone (drow and spiders are immune); +16 vs. Reflex; the target is restrained (save ends). The zone is difficult terrain until the end of the encounter. Any creature that starts its turn in the zone takes 10 necrotic damage.
➷ **Spider Curse** (standard; encounter) ✦ **Necrotic**
Spectral spiders swarm over and bite the target: ranged 20; +16 vs. Will; 1d6 + 7 necrotic damage, and the target takes ongoing 5 necrotic damage and is weakened (save ends both); see also *Lolth's judgment.*
⬳ **Venom Blast** (standard; encounter) ✦ **Poison**
Close blast 5; +14 vs. Fortitude; 2d6 + 10 poison damage. *Miss:* Half damage.
⬳ **Cloud of Darkness** (minor; encounter)
Close burst 1; this power creates a cloud of darkness that remains in place until the end of the drow arachnomancer's next turn. The cloud blocks line of sight for all creatures except the drow arachnomancer. Any creature entirely within the cloud (except the drow arachnomancer) is blinded until it exits.
Lolth's Judgment (free, when the arachnomancer hits a target with a melee or a ranged attack; at-will)
All spider allies within 20 squares of the arachnomancer gain a +2 bonus to attack rolls against the target until the end of the arachnomancer's next turn.
Alignment Evil   **Languages** Common, Elven
Skills Arcana +14, Dungeoneering +13, Intimidate +8, Stealth +10
Str 10 (+6)	**Dex** 15 (+8)	**Wis** 14 (+8)
Con 10 (+6)	**Int** 16 (+9)	**Cha** 11 (+6)
Equipment robes, spider rod

DROW ARACHNOMANCER TACTICS

The arachnomancer stays behind its allies and targets enemies with ranged attacks. It places a *spider curse* on an enemy defender, fires *venom rays* at enemy blasters, and tries to catch enemy strikers with *Lolth's grasp*. It uses *cloud of darkness* to protect it against melee attackers.

Drow Blademaster	Level 13 Elite Skirmisher
Medium fey humanoid	XP 1,600

Initiative +13   **Senses** Perception +12; darkvision
HP 248; **Bloodied** 124
AC 30; **Fortitude** 25, **Reflex** 28, **Will** 24
Saving Throws +2
Speed 6
Action Points 1
ⴲ **Longsword** (standard; at-will) ✦ **Weapon**
+19 vs. AC; 1d8 + 5 damage.
ⴲ **Short Sword** (standard; at-will) ✦ **Weapon**
+19 vs. AC; 1d6 + 5 damage.
⸸ **Blade Mastery** (standard; at-will) ✦ **Weapon**
The drow blademaster makes one longsword attack and one short sword attack.

‡ **Excruciating Stab** (standard; recharge ⚄ ⚅) ✦ **Weapon**

Requires longsword; +19 vs. AC; 3d8 + 5 damage, and the target is stunned (save ends).

‡ **Whirling Riposte** (free, when the blademaster's movement draws an opportunity attack; at-will) ✦ **Weapon**

The drow blademaster makes a longsword attack against the triggering attacker.

↤ **Cloud of Darkness** (minor; encounter)

Close burst 1; this power creates a cloud of darkness that remains in place until the end of the drow blademaster's next turn. The cloud blocks line of sight for all creatures except the drow blademaster. Any creature entirely within the cloud (except the drow blademaster) is blinded until it exits.

↤ **Whirlwind Attack** (standard; recharge ⚁ ⚄ ⚅) ✦ **Weapon**

Close burst 1; the drow blademaster makes a longsword attack against each adjacent enemy. He can make a secondary attack using his short sword against any enemy he hits.

Alignment Evil   **Languages** Common, Elven
Skills Acrobatics +16, Dungeoneering +12, Intimidate +14, Stealth +18

Str 15 (+8)	**Dex** 21 (+11)	**Wis** 13 (+7)
Con 12 (+7)	**Int** 12 (+7)	**Cha** 12 (+7)

Equipment scale armor, longsword, short sword

DROW BLADEMASTER TACTICS

This drow faces its enemies head on, using *cloud of darkness* to thwart attacks. In melee, a drow blademaster spends an action point to use *excruciating stab* and then *blade mastery* against the same target. It uses *whirlwind attack* when two or more opponents are adjacent to it and relies on *whirling riposte* to punish an enemy bold enough to take an opportunity attack against it.

TODD LOCKWOOD

Drow Priest	**Level 15 Controller (Leader)**
Medium fey humanoid	XP 1,200

Initiative +9   **Senses** Perception +12; darkvision
Lolth's Authority aura sight; drow and spider allies in the aura gain a +1 bonus to attack rolls and a +2 bonus to damage rolls.
HP 139; **Bloodied** 69; see also *spider link*
AC 28; **Fortitude** 24, **Reflex** 26, **Will** 28
Speed 7

⊕ **Mace** (standard; at-will) ✦ **Weapon**

+18 vs. AC; 1d8 + 1 damage.

⊕ **Bite of the Spider** (standard, usable only while bloodied; at-will)

+17 vs. AC; 2d6 + 6 damage.

⟫ **Pain Web** (standard; at-will) ✦ **Necrotic**

Ranged 5; +18 vs. Reflex; 1d6 + 5 necrotic damage, and the target is immobilized and weakened (save ends both).

⟫ **Darkfire** (minor; encounter)

Ranged 10; +18 vs. Reflex; until the end of the drow priest's next turn, the target grants combat advantage to all attacks, and the target cannot benefit from invisibility or concealment.

❊ **Lolth's Wrath** (standard; recharge ⚅) ✦ **Necrotic**

Area burst 5 centered on a bloodied and willing drow ally; the ally explodes, releasing a burst of spectral spiders that bite all enemies in range; +20 vs. Reflex; 4d8 + 5 necrotic damage. The drow targeted by this power is slain.

Spider Link (minor; at-will) ✦ **Healing**

The drow priest can transfer up to 22 points of damage she has taken to a spider or a drow within 5 squares of her. She cannot transfer more hit points than the creature has remaining.

Alignment Evil   **Languages** Abyssal, Common, Elven
Skills Bluff +17, Insight +17, Intimidate +19, Religion +15, Stealth +10

Str 12 (+8)	**Dex** 15 (+9)	**Wis** 21 (+12)
Con 11 (+7)	**Int** 16 (+10)	**Cha** 20 (+12)

Equipment chainmail, mace

DROW PRIEST TACTICS

The drow priest imparts the benefits of her *Lolth's authority* aura while remaining within 5 squares of her drow and spider allies. She uses *pain web* against ranged foes and her mace in melee, and she uses *spider link* every round to transfer damage she has taken to a nearby ally. If one of her drow allies is bloodied, she uses *Lolth's wrath*.

ENCOUNTER GROUPS

Drow patrols often include one or more trained spiders. Drow expeditions, raiding parties, and armies have large numbers of enslaved nondrow among them, as servants and soldiers. Drow also form alliances with devils and demons.

Level 13 Encounter (XP 4,850)
✦ 1 drow arachnomancer (level 13 artillery)
✦ 2 drow warriors (level 11 lurker)
✦ 1 mezzodemon (level 11 soldier)
✦ 5 grimlock minions (level 14 minion)
✦ 2 blade spiders (level 10 brute)

Level 15 Encounter (XP 6,000)
✦ 1 drow priest (level 15 controller)
✦ 1 drow blademaster (level 13 elite skirmisher)
✦ 1 umber hulk (level 12 elite soldier)
✦ 3 drow warriors (level 11 lurker)

DRYAD

Dryads are wild, mysterious creatures found deep in secluded woodlands. Fierce protectors of the forest, they brook no insolence from interlopers.

Dryad	Level 9 Skirmisher
Medium fey humanoid (plant)	XP 400

Initiative +9   **Senses** Perception +12
HP 92; **Bloodied** 46
AC 23; **Fortitude** 22, **Reflex** 21, **Will** 21
Speed 8 (forest walk)
✛ **Claws** (standard; at-will)
    +14 vs. AC; 1d8 + 4 damage, or 1d8 + 9 damage if the target is the only enemy adjacent to the dryad.
Deceptive Veil (minor; at-will) ✦ **Illusion**
    The dryad can disguise itself to appear as any Medium humanoid, usually a beautiful elf or eladrin. A successful Insight check (opposed by the dryad's Bluff check) pierces the disguise.
Treestride (move; at-will) ✦ **Teleportation**
    The dryad can teleport 8 squares if it begins and ends adjacent to a tree, a treant, or a plant of Large size or bigger.
Alignment Unaligned   **Languages** Elven
Skills Bluff +10, Insight +12, Stealth +12
Str 19 (+8)	**Dex** 17 (+7)	**Wis** 17 (+7)
Con 12 (+5)	**Int** 10 (+4)	**Cha** 13 (+5)

DRYAD TACTICS

Dryads fiercely defend their forest glades and other woodland life. They use their *deceptive veil* ability to lure intruders into traps. In combat, they use a combination of speed and *treestride* to flank foes.

Briar Witch Dryad	Level 13 Elite Controller
Medium fey humanoid (plant)	XP 1,600

Initiative +8   **Senses** Perception +13
Curse of Thorns aura 3; enemies without forest walk take 2 damage each time they move—or are pulled, pushed, or slid—into a square within the aura. Creatures do not take damage when a briar witch dryad moves closer to them.
Thorn Boon aura 6; allied plants in the aura deal an extra 5 damage with each melee attack.
HP 262; **Bloodied** 131
AC 29; **Fortitude** 27, **Reflex** 25, **Will** 27
Saving Throws +2
Speed 8 (forest walk)
Action Points 1
✛ **Claws** (standard; at-will)
    +18 vs. AC; 1d8 + 3 damage.
⤳ **Briar Cage** (standard; at-will)
    Ranged 10; the target is encased in sharp briars; +16 vs. Reflex; 1d6 + 4 damage, and the target takes ongoing 5 damage and is restrained (save ends both). A creature in a briar cage has cover. A briar cage can be destroyed (25 hit points; resist 10 to all damage).
Deceptive Veil (minor; at-will) ✦ **Illusion**
    The briar witch dryad can disguise itself to appear as any Medium humanoid, usually a beautiful elf or eladrin. A successful Insight check (opposed by the dryad's Bluff check) pierces the disguise.
Thorny Body
    Any creature that grabs the briar witch dryad takes 5 damage at the start of its turn.
Treestride (move; at-will) ✦ **Teleportation**
    The briar witch dryad can teleport 8 squares if it begins and ends adjacent to a tree, a treant, or a plant of Large size or bigger.
Alignment Unaligned   **Languages** Elven
Skills Bluff +15, Insight +13, Stealth +13
Str 16 (+9)	**Dex** 14 (+8)	**Wis** 14 (+8)
Con 19 (+10)	**Int** 11 (+6)	**Cha** 19 (+10)

BRIAR WITCH DRYAD TACTICS

A briar witch dryad is a capricious creature that uses its *deceptive veil* to lure trespassers into deadly traps. The creature relies on its auras to harm foes and aid allies and uses *briar cage* to restrain enemies.

DRYAD LORE

A character knows the following information with a successful Arcana check.

DC 15: Dryads are shy forest dwellers that use their powers to frighten away trespassers or lure them into traps. They have the ability to teleport short distances within the confines of their forests.

ENCOUNTER GROUPS

Dryads are usually encountered with other plant creatures and forest-dwelling animals.

Level 9 Encounter (XP 1,950)
✦ 1 dryad (level 9 skirmisher)
✦ 1 eladrin twilight incanter (level 8 controller)
✦ 4 eladrin fey knights (level 7 soldier)

DWARF

DWARVES ARE CREATURES OF THE EARTH, as steadfast and hardy as stone. Industrious and inventive, dwarves live in the mountains of the world. They build remarkable fortress-cities among the peaks, under which they delve into the earth for riches and raw materials.

DWARF LORE

A character knows the following information with a successful Nature check.

DC 15: Dwarves acknowledge Moradin as their creator, but they revere other gods as well. Dwarf clans live together in heavily defended mountainside strongholds, clashing with orcs and goblins over territory and mining rights.

ENCOUNTER GROUPS

Although most dwarves are decent folk, an individual dwarf is as likely to throw in with villainous sorts as any individual of another race.

Level 4 Encounter (XP 925)
✦ 2 dwarf hammerers (level 5 soldier)
✦ 2 dwarf bolters (level 4 artillery)
✦ 1 cavern choker (level 4 lurker)

WILLIAM O'CONNOR

Dwarf Bolter	Level 4 Artillery
Medium natural humanoid	XP 175

Initiative +5   **Senses** Perception +8; low-light vision
HP 46; **Bloodied** 23
AC 17; **Fortitude** 16, **Reflex** 16, **Will** 14
Saving Throws +5 against poison effects
Speed 5

⊕ **Warhammer** (standard; at-will) ✦ **Weapon**
 +8 vs. AC; 1d10 + 2 damage.
➷ **Crossbow** (standard; at-will) ✦ **Weapon**
 Ranged 15/30; +10 vs. AC; 1d8 + 3 damage.
Aimed Shot
 The dwarf bolter gains a +2 bonus to attack rolls and deals an extra 1d6 damage with ranged attacks against creatures that don't have cover.
Stand Your Ground
 When an effect forces a dwarf to move—through a pull, a push, or a slide—the dwarf moves 1 square less than the effect specifies. When an attack would knock the dwarf prone, the dwarf can roll a saving throw to avoid falling prone.

Alignment Unaligned   **Languages** Common, Dwarven
Skills Dungeoneering +10, Endurance +7
| **Str** 14 (+4) | **Dex** 16 (+5) | **Wis** 12 (+3) |
| **Con** 16 (+5) | **Int** 11 (+2) | **Cha** 10 (+2) |
Equipment chainmail, warhammer, crossbow with 20 bolts

DWARF BOLTER TACTICS

Dwarf bolters take up positions in large halls or wide corridors where enemies can gain no cover and must face a barrage of *aimed shot* crossbow bolts as they approach.

Dwarf Hammerer	Level 5 Soldier
Medium natural humanoid	XP 200

Initiative +4   **Senses** Perception +4; low-light vision
HP 64; **Bloodied** 32
AC 23; **Fortitude** 18, **Reflex** 15, **Will** 17
Saving Throws +5 against poison effects
Speed 5

⊕ **Warhammer** (standard; at-will) ✦ **Weapon**
 +11 vs. AC; 1d10 + 3 damage.
↯ **Shield Bash** (minor; recharge ⚃ ⚄)
 +9 vs. Fortitude; 2d6 + 3 damage, and the target is knocked prone or pushed 1 square (dwarf hammerer's choice).
➷ **Throwing Hammer** (standard; at-will) ✦ **Weapon**
 Ranged 5/10; +10 vs. AC; 1d6 + 3 damage.
Stubborn (immediate interrupt, when an enemy tries to push the dwarf hammerer or knock it prone; at-will)
 The hammerer makes a melee basic attack against the enemy.
Stand Your Ground
 When an effect forces a dwarf to move—through a pull, a push, or a slide—the dwarf moves 1 square less than the effect specifies. When an attack would knock the dwarf prone, the dwarf can roll a saving throw to avoid falling prone.

Alignment Any   **Languages** Common, Dwarven
Skills Dungeoneering +11, Endurance +5
| **Str** 17 (+5) | **Dex** 10 (+2) | **Wis** 14 (+4) |
| **Con** 16 (+5) | **Int** 11 (+2) | **Cha** 12 (+3) |
Equipment plate armor, heavy shield, warhammer, 3 throwing hammers

DWARF HAMMERER TACTICS

A dwarf hammerer uses *shield bash* whenever possible, pushing allies back or knocking them prone so that nearby allies gain combat advantage.

EFREET

Efreets are crafty conjurers of fire native to the Elemental Chaos. Sometimes referred to as a fire genie, an efreet resembles a giant devil, its body equal parts flame and flesh.

Efreets are infamous for their hatred of servitude, their arrogance, and their cruel nature. Their primary home is the fabled City of Brass in the Elemental Chaos, where they live like kings. However, they are often called to the world to perform favors for mortals, and these favors always come with a high price.

Efreet Fireblade		Level 22 Soldier
Large elemental humanoid (fire)		XP 4,150

Initiative +18   **Senses** Perception +17
HP 206; **Bloodied** 153
AC 38; **Fortitude** 37, **Reflex** 36, **Will** 34
Immune fire
Speed 6, fly 8 (hover)
⊕ **Scimitar** (standard; at-will) ✦ **Weapon**
  Reach 2; +27 vs. AC; 2d10 + 7 damage (crit 6d10 + 27), and the target is marked until the end of the efreet fireblade's next turn.
↗ **Hurl Scimitar** (standard; recharge ⚄ ⚅) ✦ **Weapon**
  The efreet fireblade hurls its scimitar at two targets; the first target must be within 10 squares of the efreet fireblade, and the second target within 5 squares of the first target; +25 vs. AC; 2d10 + 7 damage (crit 6d10 + 27), and the target is marked until the end of the efreet fireblade's next turn. The scimitar returns to the fireblade's hand after the attacks are made.
↺ **Whirling Firesteel Strike** (standard; recharge ⚄ ⚅) ✦ **Fire, Weapon**
  Requires scimitar; close burst 2; +25 vs. AC; 2d10 + 7 damage (crit 6d10 + 27), and the target is pushed 1 square and takes ongoing 10 fire damage (save ends).
Alignment Evil   **Languages** Primordial
Skills Bluff +20, Insight +17, Intimidate +20
Str 24 (+17)   **Dex** 22 (+16)   **Wis** 15 (+12)
Con 22 (+16)   **Int** 18 (+14)   **Cha** 18 (+15)
Equipment scimitar

EFREET FIREBLADE TACTICS

The efreet fireblade uses *hurl scimitar* every chance it gets, saving its *whirling firesteel strike* power for when it has three or more enemies within melee striking range.

Efreet Cinderlord		Level 23 Artillery
Large elemental humanoid (fire)		XP 5,100

Initiative +19   **Senses** Perception +15
Blazing Soul (Fire) aura 1; any creature in the aura taking ongoing fire damage takes 5 extra ongoing fire damage.
HP 169; **Bloodied** 84; see also *curse of the efreet*
AC 36; **Fortitude** 33, **Reflex** 34, **Will** 32; see also *fiery shield*
Immune fire
Speed 6, fly 8 (hover)
⊕ **Scimitar** (standard; at-will) ✦ **Fire, Weapon**
  Reach 2; +25 vs. AC; 2d10 + 7 damage (crit 6d10 + 27), and ongoing 5 fire damage (save ends).
↗ **Fire Bolt** (standard; at-will) ✦ **Fire, Weapon**
  Ranged 10; +28 vs. AC; 2d6 + 8 fire damage, and ongoing 5 fire damage (save ends).
↗ **Curse of the Efreet** (standard; recharges when first bloodied) ✦ **Fire**
  Ranged 10; +28 vs. AC; 1d6 + 8 fire damage, and ongoing 10 fire damage (save ends), and the target's resistance to fire is negated until the end of the encounter (no save).
↗ **Fan the Flames** (standard; at-will) ✦ **Fire**
  Ranged 20; affects only a target taking ongoing fire damage; automatic hit; the target takes 3d6 fire damage, and the efreet makes a secondary attack against all creatures adjacent to the target. *Secondary Attack:* Area burst 2 centered on target; +17 vs. Reflex; 2d6 fire damage. *Miss:* Half damage.
Fiery Shield (immediate interrupt, when the efreet cinderlord is damaged by a ranged attack; at-will) ✦ **Fire**
  A fiery shield springs into being, halving the damage of the attack.
Alignment Evil   **Languages** Primordial
Skills Bluff +22, Insight +20, Intimidate +22
Str 24 (+18)   **Dex** 27 (+19)   **Wis** 18 (+15)
Con 25 (+18)   **Int** 16 (+14)   **Cha** 22 (+17)
Equipment scimitar

EFREET CINDERLORD TACTICS

A cinderlord flies beyond its enemies' reach while bombarding them with *fire bolts*. It uses *curse of the efreet*, and if it succeeds and the target continues to take ongoing fire damage, the efreet uses *fan the flames* against the same target on the following round. The cinderlord uses *curse of the efreet* again when blooded but otherwise hurls *fire bolts*.

(Left to right) efreet pyresinger, efreet fireblade, and efreet cinderlord

Efreet Flamestrider		Level 23 Skirmisher
Large elemental humanoid (fire)		XP 5,100

Initiative +20 **Senses** Perception +15
Blazing Soul (Fire) aura 1; any creature in the aura taking ongoing fire damage takes 5 extra ongoing fire damage.
HP 217; **Bloodied** 108
AC 37; **Fortitude** 36, **Reflex** 35, **Will** 34
Immune fire
Speed 6, fly 8 (hover); see also *fiery teleport*

⊕ **Scimitar** (standard; at-will) ✦ **Fire, Weapon**
Reach 2; +28 vs. AC; 2d10 + 8 damage (crit 6d10 + 28), and ongoing 5 fire damage (save ends).

↗ **Fiery Grasp** (standard; at-will) ✦ **Fire**
Ranged 20; a fiery hand appears and grabs the target; +25 vs. Reflex; 1d6 + 8 fire damage, and the target takes ongoing 10 fire damage and is immobilized (save ends both).

Fiery Teleport (move; at-will) ✦ **Teleportation**
The flamestrider can teleport 20 squares, reappearing in a puff of smoke; its destination must be adjacent to a fire creature or a fire.

Alignment Evil **Languages** Primordial
Skills Bluff +22, Insight +20, Intimidate +22
| **Str** 27 (+19) | **Dex** 24 (+18) | **Wis** 18 (+15) |
| **Con** 25 (+18) | **Int** 16 (+14) | **Cha** 22 (+17) |
Equipment scimitar

EFREET FLAMESTRIDER TACTICS

An efreet flamestrider uses *fiery teleport* to move around the battlefield and its *fiery grasp* power to immobilize and burn foes. It attacks immobilized targets with its scimitar, taking advantage of its reach.

Efreet Pyresinger		Level 25 Controller
Large elemental humanoid (fire)		XP 7,000

Initiative +20 **Senses** Perception +16
Fiery Soul (Fire) aura 1; a creature that enters or begins its turn in the aura takes 10 fire damage; any creature in the aura taking ongoing fire damage takes 5 extra ongoing fire damage.
HP 233; **Bloodied** 116
AC 40; **Fortitude** 37, **Reflex** 36, **Will** 36
Immune fire
Speed 6, fly 8 (hover)

⊕ **Scimitar** (standard; at-will) ✦ **Fire, Weapon**
Reach 2; +30 vs. AC; 2d10 + 9 damage (crit 6d10 + 29), and ongoing 5 fire damage (save ends).

↗ **Fire Bolt** (standard; at-will) ✦ **Fire, Weapon**
Ranged 10; +31 vs. AC; 3d6 + 8 fire damage, and ongoing 5 fire damage (save ends).

↗ **Fiery Chains** (standard; recharge ⚄ ⚅) ✦ **Fire**
Ranged 10; +28 vs. Reflex; 2d8 + 7 fire damage, and the target takes ongoing 20 fire damage and is restrained (save ends both). As a move action, the efreet pyresinger can slide a target wrapped in *fiery chains* 1 square.

❊ **Sheets of Flame** (standard; recharge ⚄ ⚅) ✦ **Fire**
Area burst 3 within 20; the pyresinger fills the area with 20-foot-high sheets of roaring flame. Any creature that enters or begins its turn in the area or adjacent to it takes 10 fire damage. The sheets of flame block line of sight.

Alignment Evil **Languages** Primordial
Skills Arcana +22, Bluff +25, Diplomacy +25, Insight +21, Intimidate +25
| **Str** 29 (+21) | **Dex** 26 (+20) | **Wis** 18 (+16) |
| **Con** 25 (+19) | **Int** 20 (+17) | **Cha** 26 (+20) |
Equipment scimitar, scepter

EFREET PYRESINGER TACTICS

A pyresinger remains outside of melee range and uses *fiery chains* as often as it can to restrain enemies, allowing its allies to pound on them with impunity. On the rounds in which it can't invoke fiery chains, the pyresinger hurls *fiery bolts*. The creature uses *sheets of flame* to divide the field of battle and control the flow of enemies.

Efreet Karadjin	Level 28 Soldier (Leader)
Large elemental humanoid (fire)	XP 13,000

Initiative +23   **Senses** Perception +23
HP 260; **Bloodied** 130
AC 44; **Fortitude** 45, **Reflex** 42, **Will** 42
Immune fire
Speed 6, fly 8 (hover)

ⓕ **Scimitar of Horrendous Flame** (standard; at-will) ✦ **Fire, Weapon**
  Reach 2; +27 vs. AC; 2d10 + 9 damage (crit 6d10 + 29) plus 1d10 fire damage, and the target takes ongoing 15 fire damage and is immobilized (save ends both). *Aftereffect:* Ongoing 15 fire damage (save ends). Saving throws against this power take a -2 penalty.

✝ **Fiery Vendetta** (immediate reaction, when an enemy within reach attacks one of the efreet karadjin's allies; at-will) ✦ **Fire, Weapon**
  The efreet karadjin makes a melee basic attack against the triggering enemy.

Elemental Command (minor; at-will)
  One allied elemental creature within 10 squares of the efreet karadjin (and within its line of sight) shifts.

Alignment Evil   **Languages** Primordial
Skills Arcana +25, Bluff +26, Insight +23, Intimidate +26
Str 28 (+23)   **Dex** 25 (+21)   **Wis** 18 (+18)
Con 30 (+24)   **Int** 22 (+20)   **Cha** 25 (+21)
Equipment scimitar

EFREET KARADJIN TACTICS

The mighty efreet karadjin wades into battle, uses *elemental command* up to two times every round, and swings its scimitar with maniacal glee. Whenever an enemy within reach tries to attack one of the karadjin's allies, the karadjin unleashes its *fiery vendetta*.

EFREET LORE

A character knows the following information with a successful Arcana check.

DC 20: Efreets are the self-proclaimed fiery princes of the Elemental Chaos, the strongest force of order on that tumultuous plane. Though few in number, they rule over vast armies and households of elemental slaves. The City of Brass is their greatest achievement—a permanent city-fortress in the roiling chaos, unchanging and eternal.

DC 25: There is no such thing as an "efreet commoner." Every efreet is a member of a noble house. These houses plot and scheme against each other (much as drow houses do in the Underdark), and from time to time they muster enormous armies against each other. An efreet house might contain only a small number of related efreet, but through power and intimidation they lord it over vast hosts of other elementals. Their control is by no means limited to fire creatures, and smart efreets have creatures formed of various elements serving them. On rare occasions they bind demons to servitude, although they place little trust in them and keep them at arm's length at all times.

DC 30: Efreets have no power to grant wishes, despite stories to that effect. As princes of the Elemental Chaos, however, they have power, influence, and widespread connections, and they are not averse to bargaining with weaker mortals. Thus it might be that an efreet released from servitude will grant its liberator a "wish," within reason.

As creatures of nobility and great self-importance, all efreets fear and loathe servitude to others. Sometimes when two efreet houses clash, the losing side is forced to give up a junior member of the house into a specified period of servitude to the victor. This is far more humiliating and punishing than any cost in goods or slaves. When an efreet is magically bound to serve a mortal, it considers that service the worst possible form of humiliation, and burns with resentment against its erstwhile master.

DC 35: An efreet house will sometimes sponsor a noble hunt where a few nobles of the house venture out of the Elemental Chaos into the world, the Feywild, the Shadowfell, and even into the Astral Sea, hunting particularly dangerous creatures (such as dragons) merely for the sport of doing so, as well as for a fantastic trophy to grace their house mansion.

ENCOUNTER GROUPS

Efreets are usually grouped with other efreets and elemental creatures close to their level.

Level 22 Encounter (XP 23,600)
✦ 2 efreet fireblades (level 22 soldier)
✦ 1 efreet flamestrider (level 23 skirmisher)
✦ 1 glabrezu demon (level 23 elite brute)

Level 23 Encounter (XP 26,800)
✦ 1 efreet cinderlord (level 23 artillery)
✦ 3 blood fiend abominations (level 23 soldier)
✦ 1 fire titan (level 21 elite soldier)

Level 25 Encounter (XP 37,950)
✦ 1 efreet pyresinger (level 25 controller)
✦ 1 great flameskull (level 24 artillery)
✦ 1 marilith demon (level 24 elite skirmisher)
✦ 2 fire titans (level 21 elite soldier)

Level 27 Encounter (XP 60,300)
✦ 1 efreet karadjin (level 28 soldier)
✦ 1 efreet pyresinger (level 25 controller)
✦ 1 glabrezu demon (level 23 elite brute)
✦ 2 dragonborn champions (level 26 soldier)
✦ 2 great flameskulls (level 24 artillery)

EIDOLON

ANIMATED THROUGH A DIVINE RITUAL, this intelligent construct serves as a symbol of its creators' devotion to their deity. Sometimes the divine spark that animates an eidolon becomes corrupted, causing the creature to turn against its creators. This "rogue" eidolon, believing itself to be a god, searches for new followers to worship it.

Eidolon	Level 13 Controller (Leader)
Large natural animate (construct)	XP 800

Initiative +8   **Senses** Perception +9
Fearless Followers aura 5; allies in the aura are immune to fear.
HP 132; **Bloodied** 66
AC 28; **Fortitude** 26, **Reflex** 22, **Will** 23
Immune disease, fear, sleep
Speed 5

⊕ **Slam** (standard; at-will)
    Reach 2; +19 vs. AC; 2d8 + 6 damage.

↷ **Divine Retribution** (immediate reaction, when an enemy attacks the eidolon while *hallowed stance* is active; at-will) ✦ **Radiant**
    Divine radiance strikes the creature that attacked the eidolon: ranged 20; +17 vs. Reflex; 2d8 + 5 radiant damage. *Miss:* Half damage. This attack does not provoke opportunity attacks.

↷ **Vengeful Flames** (immediate reaction, when an enemy kills one of the eidolon's allies in the eidolon's line of sight; at-will) ✦ **Fire**
    Divine fire engulfs the enemy: ranged 20; +17 vs. Reflex; 1d8 + 5 fire damage, and ongoing 5 fire (save ends). This attack does not provoke opportunity attacks.

Hallowed Stance (standard; at-will) ✦ **Radiant**
    The eidolon assumes a meditative stance. Until the end of its next turn, the eidolon gains resist 20 to all damage, and all allies in its line of sight deal an extra 1d8 radiant damage on their melee attacks. If the eidolon moves, the effect ends.

Alignment Unaligned	**Languages** –	
Str 22 (+12)	**Dex** 14 (+8)	**Wis** 16 (+9)
Con 20 (+11)	**Int** 7 (+4)	**Cha** 11 (+6)

EIDOLON TACTICS

An eidolon moves little in battle, relying on its allies, its *hallowed stance*, and its *divine retribution* power to protect it. When one of its allies falls in battle, the eidolon uses *vengeful flames*. Once all of its allies are slain, the eidolon makes slam attacks against enemies within reach, fighting until destroyed.

EIDOLON LORE

A character knows the following information with a successful Nature check.

DC 20: An eidolon is created by means of a divine ritual, the key component of which is a crystal shard containing a tiny spark of divinity. The shard is embedded deep in the eidolon and is lost when the eidolon is destroyed.

DC 25: Sometimes an eidolon is corrupted by the divine spark trapped inside it. When this happens, the eidolon suffers delusions of godhood. It kills its creators and either takes over the cult or destroys the cult and seeks out new followers to worship it.

ENCOUNTER GROUPS

Eidolons are usually encountered with a group of humanoid worshipers.

Level 11 Encounter (XP 3,200)
✦ 1 eidolon (level 13 controller)
✦ 4 githzerai cenobites (level 11 soldier)

Level 13 Encounter (XP 4,000)
✦ 1 eidolon (level 13 controller)
✦ 2 grimlock berserkers (level 13 brute)
✦ 1 medusa warrior (level 13 elite soldier)

ELADRIN

Eladrin are graceful warriors and wizards at home in the eldritch twilight of the Feywild and the dark forests of the world. Although most eladrin reside in the Feywild, a few have interests or dealings in the natural world, and it's not uncommon to find eladrin living among humans, elves, dwarfs, dragonborn, and halflings.

Eladrin Fey Knight	Level 7 Soldier (Leader)
Medium fey humanoid	XP 300

Initiative +11   **Senses** Perception +4; low-light vision
Feywild Tactics aura 10; fey creatures in the aura score a critical hit on a roll of 19 or 20 (a roll of 19 is not an automatic hit, however).
HP 77; **Bloodied** 38
AC 23; **Fortitude** 17, **Reflex** 19, **Will** 17
Saving Throws +5 against charm effects
Speed 5; see also *fey step*
🟡 **Longsword** (standard; at-will) ✦ **Weapon**
+12 vs. AC; 1d8 + 4 damage.
🗡 **Stab of the Entangling Wild** (standard or opportunity attack; recharge ⚃ ⚅) ✦ **Weapon**
Requires longsword; +12 vs. AC; 3d8 + 4 damage, and the target is restrained until the end of the eladrin fey knight's next turn. The eladrin fey knight cannot attack with its longsword while the target is restrained.
🏹 **Feywild Challenge** (standard; encounter)
Ranged 10; the target is marked until the end of the encounter or until the eladrin fey knight dies, taking 4 damage each round it does not attack the eladrin fey knight.
Fey Step (move; encounter) ✦ **Teleportation**
The eladrin fey knight can teleport 5 squares.
Harvest's Sorrow (immediate reaction, when an ally within 5 squares of the eladrin fey knight is damaged; at-will)
Half the attack's damage is negated, and the eladrin fey knight takes the other half.
Alignment Any   **Languages** Common, Elven
Skills Athletics +12, Arcana +7, History +7, Nature +9
Str 18 (+7)	**Dex** 22 (+9)	**Wis** 13 (+4)
Con 13 (+4)	**Int** 14 (+5)	**Cha** 16 (+6)
Equipment chainmail, light shield, longsword

ELADRIN FEY KNIGHT TACTICS

The eladrin fey knight issues a *Feywild challenge*. Thereafter, he uses *stab of the entangling wild* whenever that power is available and otherwise makes melee basic attacks. The fey knight tries to stay within 5 squares of his allies so that he can use *harvest's sorrow*.

Eladrin Twilight Incanter	Level 8 Controller
Medium fey humanoid	XP 350

Initiative +7   **Senses** Perception +5; low-light vision
HP 82; **Bloodied** 41
AC 22; **Fortitude** 19, **Reflex** 21, **Will** 21
Saving Throws +5 against charm effects
Speed 6; see also *fey step*
🟡 **Spear** (standard; at-will) ✦ **Weapon**
+10 vs. AC; 1d8 + 1 damage, and the target is slowed until the end of the eladrin twilight incanter's next turn.
🏹 **Binding Bolt** (standard; at-will)
Ranged 10; +12 vs. Reflex; 1d8 + 3 damage, and the target is immobilized until the end of the eladrin twilight incanter's next turn.

🏹 **Teleporting Bolt** (standard; at-will) ✦ **Teleportation**
Ranged 10; +12 vs. Reflex; 1d8 + 2 damage, and the target is teleported up to 3 squares. The target cannot be teleported into an unsafe space.
↩ **Dazzling Blast** (standard; recharge ⚄ ⚅) ✦ **Radiant**
Close blast 3; +9 vs. Will; 2d6 + 3 radiant damage, and the target is blinded until the end of the eladrin twilight incanter's next turn.
Fey Step (move; encounter) ✦ **Teleportation**
The eladrin twilight incanter can teleport 5 squares.
Alignment Any   **Languages** Common, Elven
Skills Arcana +16, History +16, Nature +10
Str 12 (+5)	**Dex** 16 (+7)	**Wis** 12 (+5)
Con 10 (+4)	**Int** 20 (+9)	**Cha** 16 (+7)
Equipment robes, spear

ELADRIN TWILIGHT INCANTER TACTICS

The eladrin twilight incanter assails enemies with *binding bolts* and *teleporting bolts*, holding them in place or moving them around so that her allies can secure the tactical advantage. If enemies get too close, the twilight incanter uses *dazzling blast* to blind them.

Bralani of Autumn Winds	Level 19 Controller
Medium fey humanoid, eladrin	XP 2,400

Initiative +17   **Senses** Perception +13; low-light vision
Cloak of Autumn Gusts aura 5; creatures other than eladrin (including flying creatures) treat the area within the aura as difficult terrain.
HP 180; **Bloodied** 90
AC 33; **Fortitude** 28, **Reflex** 31, **Will** 32
Resist 20 radiant; **Vulnerable** necrotic (slowed until the end of the bralani's next turn)
Saving Throws +5 against charm effects
Speed 6, fly 9 (hover); see also *fey step*
🟡 **Longsword** (standard; at-will) ✦ **Weapon**
+23 vs. AC; 1d8 + 8 damage.
🏹 **Autumn Chill** (standard; encounter)
Ranged 5; +22 vs. Will; the target is weakened until the end of the encounter.
↩ **Whirlwind Blast** (standard; at-will)
Close blast 5; +22 vs. Fortitude; 2d8 + 9 damage, and the target is pushed 2 squares (pushed 3 squares and knocked prone on a critical hit). *Miss:* Half damage, and the target is not pushed.
Fey Step (move; encounter) ✦ **Teleportation**
The bralani of autumn winds can teleport 5 squares.
Alignment Any   **Languages** Common, Elven
Skills Arcana +14, History +14, Intimidate +22, Nature +18
Str 15 (+11)	**Dex** 26 (+17)	**Wis** 19 (+13)
Con 20 (+14)	**Int** 16 (+12)	**Cha** 27 (+17)
Equipment leather armor, longsword

BRALANI OF AUTUMN WINDS TACTICS

A bralani uses *autumn chill* on the greatest perceived threat and then uses *whirlwind blast* to damage and push back opponents. If it can't use *whirlwind blast* because allies are in the way, it rushes into melee and makes longsword attacks.

Ghaele of Winter	Level 21 Artillery
Medium fey humanoid, eladrin	XP 3,200

Initiative +19 **Senses** Perception +16; low-light vision
HP 134; **Bloodied** 77
AC 33; **Fortitude** 30, **Reflex** 33, **Will** 33
Resist 25 cold, 25 radiant; **Vulnerable** necrotic (slowed until the end of the ghaele's next turn)
Saving Throws +5 against charm effects
Speed 6, fly 8 (hover); see also *fey step*

ⓐ **Winter's Touch** (standard; at-will) ✦ **Cold**
+25 vs. AC; 2d8 + 9 cold damage.

➹ **Freezing Ray** (standard; at-will) ✦ **Cold**
Ranged 12; +25 vs. Reflex; 2d8 + 9 cold damage, and the target is slowed (save ends).

⬳ **Chilling Defiance** (standard; at-will) ✦ **Cold, Healing**
Close burst 3; targets enemies; automatic hit; the target takes 10 cold damage and is slowed until the end of the ghaele's next turn. The ghaele of winter regains 2 hit points for each enemy who takes damage from this power.

⬳ **Imperious Wrath** (minor; recharges when the ghaele of winter regains at least 4 hit points with *chilling defiance*)
Close burst 3; +23 vs. Will; the target is dazed until the end of the encounter.

Fey Step (move; encounter) ✦ **Teleportation**
The ghaele of winter can teleport 5 squares.

Alignment Any **Languages** Common, Elven
Skills Arcana +15, Diplomacy +24, History +15, Insight +21, Intimidate +24, Nature +21
| **Str** 17 (+13) | **Dex** 28 (+19) | **Wis** 22 (+16) |
| **Con** 22 (+16) | **Int** 17 (+13) | **Cha** 29 (+19) |
Equipment robes

GHAELE OF WINTER TACTICS

A ghaele of winter uses flight and *fey step* to find ideal positions from which to safely make ranged attacks. If the ghaele gets multiple foes within 3 squares of it, it uses *chilling defiance* and *imperious wrath* in the same round, then follows up with *winter's touch* or *freezing ray*. The ghaele takes advantage of slowed enemies, retreating to a safe distance and using *freezing ray*.

ELADRIN LORE

A character knows the following information with a successful Arcana check.

DC 15: Creatures of magic with strong ties to nature, eladrin hail from shining cities in the Feywild. Their cities lie close enough to the natural world that they sometimes "cross over," appearing briefly in beautiful mountain valleys or deep forest glades before fading into the Feywild again.

Eladrin are sometimes referred to as high elves, sun elves, moon elves, or star elves. They revere Corellon as their patron deity, although they freely worship other gods as well.

ENCOUNTER GROUPS

Eladrin are typically encountered with other eladrin and fey creatures.

Level 21 Encounter (XP 16,000)
✦ 1 ghaele of winter (level 21 artillery)
✦ 4 wild hunt hounds (level 21 skirmisher)

(Left to right) ghaele of winter, eladrin fey knight, and bralani of autumn winds

BEYOND THE WORLD LIES A CHURNING MAELSTROM known as the Elemental Chaos, where air, earth, fire, water, and energy crash together in an unending cycle of creation and destruction. Creatures of all descriptions live within this primordial realm, but none typify the nature of the plane as much as elementals.

ELEMENTAL LORE

A character knows the following information with a successful Arcana check.

DC 20: Elementals are among the most common denizens of the Elemental Chaos. They come in many forms and sizes. Some elementals embody a single element, while others are combinations of two or more elements or energy types.

DC 25: Elemental creatures don't necessarily band together by element type. The most powerful denizens of the Elemental Chaos, including primordials, titans, and efreets, often assemble hosts of elemental creatures (sometimes of dissimilar element type) to march at their command. Small bands of elementals, though, are more likely to group with others of their element.

FIRELASHER

AIR AND FIRE COMBINE to create a raging creature that swirls across the blasted landscapes of the Elemental Chaos in search of things to destroy.

Firelasher	Level 11 Skirmisher
Large elemental magical beast (air, fire)	XP 600

Initiative +12   Senses Perception +5
HP 108; **Bloodied** 54
AC 25; **Fortitude** 21, **Reflex** 25, **Will** 20
Immune disease, poison; **Resist** 25 fire
Speed fly 8 (hover)
⚀ **Fire Lash** (standard; at-will) ✦ **Fire**
    Reach 2; +14 vs. Reflex; 2d8 + 5 fire damage.
⚔ **Wildfire Cyclone** (standard; recharge ⚄ ⚁) ✦ **Fire**
    Close burst 2; +14 vs. Reflex; 2d6 + 5 fire damage, and the target is pushed 1 square and knocked prone. *Miss:* Half damage, and the target is neither pushed nor knocked prone.
Whirlwind Dash (standard; recharge ⚁) ✦ **Fire**
    The firelasher can move up to twice its speed. It can move through spaces occupied by other creatures without provoking opportunity attacks. It must end its move in an unoccupied space. Any creature whose space the firelasher enters takes 10 fire damage.
Mutable Shape
    The firelasher can squeeze through spaces as though it were a Medium creature.

Alignment Unaligned	**Languages** Primordial	
Str 11 (+5)	Dex 21 (+10)	Wis 11 (+5)
Con 12 (+6)	Int 7 (+3)	Cha 8 (+4)

FIRELASHER TACTICS

The firelasher uses *whirlwind dash*, burning as many enemies as possible. If it can, it ends its dash within 2 squares of multiple foes so that it can use its *wildfire cyclone* power on the following round. Until these powers recharge and it can use them again, the firelasher makes *fire lash* attacks.

ROCKFIRE DREADNOUGHT

A FUSION OF BRIMSTONE AND FIRE, the rockfire dreadnought eagerly serves creatures smarter than itself, provided its appetite for destruction is sated.

Rockfire Dreadnought	Level 18 Soldier
Large elemental magical beast (earth, fire)	XP 2,000

Initiative +17   Senses Perception +12
Waves of Flame (Fire) aura 1; any creature that enters or starts its turn in the aura takes 10 fire damage.
HP 170; **Bloodied** 85
AC 34; **Fortitude** 34, **Reflex** 32, **Will** 29
Immune disease, petrification, poison; **Resist** 25 fire
Speed 8
⚀ **Fist of Flame** (standard; at-will) ✦ **Fire**
    Reach 2; +21 vs. Reflex; 2d8 + 8 fire damage.
⚹ **Brimstone Rock** (standard; at-will) ✦ **Fire**
    The rockfire dreadnought hurls a flaming chunk of brimstone at the target. Ranged 10/20; +23 vs. AC; 2d6 + 6 damage plus 5 fire damage.

Alignment Unaligned	**Languages** Primordial	
Str 27 (+17)	Dex 22 (+15)	Wis 16 (+12)
Con 18 (+13)	Int 8 (+8)	Cha 7 (+7)

ROCKFIRE DREADNOUGHT TACTICS

A rockfire dreadnought pummels enemies with its fiery fists while burning those caught within its aura. It hurls brimstone rocks only when its enemies are out of reach, pulling the brimstone from its own body.

EARTHWIND RAVAGER

A MAD COMBINATION OF AIR AND EARTH, the earthwind ravager can disguise itself to look like an innocuous pile of rocks until it stirs, takes form, and attacks.

Earthwind Ravager	Level 23 Controller
Large elemental magical beast (air, earth)	XP 5,100

Initiative +21   Senses Perception +14
HP 219; **Bloodied** 109
AC 37; **Fortitude** 34, **Reflex** 36, **Will** 29
Immune disease, petrification, poison
Speed fly 8 (hover)
⚀ **Slam** (standard; at-will)
    Reach 2; +26 vs. Fortitude; 2d8 + 10 damage.
⚹ **Wind Devil** (standard; sustain minor; at-will)
    The earthwind ravager causes swirling wind to rise up around the target. Ranged 5; +26 vs. Fortitude; 4d8 damage, and the target is immobilized until the end of the ravager's next turn. The creature can sustain the effect as a minor action, dealing 2d8 damage to the target (no attack roll required) and keeping it immobilized until the end of the ravager's next turn.
⚔ **Whirlwind** (standard; at-will)
    Close burst 1; +24 vs. Fortitude; 1d8 + 10 damage, and the target is pushed 2 squares.
⚔ **Buffeting Blast** (standard; recharge ⚄ ⚁)
    Close blast 3; +24 vs. Fortitude; 4d8 + 8 damage, and the target is stunned until the end of the earthwind ravager's next turn.

Alignment Unaligned	**Languages** Primordial	
Skills Stealth +26		
Str 24 (+18)	Dex 30 (+21)	Wis 17 (+14)
Con 27 (+19)	Int 6 (+9)	Cha 16 (+14)

(Left to right) earthwind ravager, thunderblast cyclone, firelasher, and rockfire dreadnought

EARTHWIND RAVAGER TACTICS

An earthwind ravager disguises itself to resemble a pile of rocks, hoping to catch enemies by surprise. When it rises, it gathers all of the rocks up into its swirling form, puts some distance between it and its prey, and uses *wind devil* repeatedly until it immobilizes an enemy. Once it succeeds, it sustains the effect with a minor action every round. It uses *buffeting blast* to stun the immobilized creature and other nearby enemies. The ravager then closes in and makes slam attacks against its immobilized prey or uses *whirlwind* to push away other enemies.

THUNDERBLAST CYCLONE

WHEN AIR AND WATER COLLIDE in the Elemental Chaos, the fusion sometimes gives rise to a vehement creature called the thunderblast cyclone.

Thunderblast Cyclone	Level 26 Elite Artillery
Huge elemental magical beast (air, water)	XP 18,000

Initiative +24   **Senses** Perception +16
HP 382; **Bloodied** 191
AC 42; **Fortitude** 40, **Reflex** 42, **Will** 35
Immune disease, poison; **Resist** 30 lightning, 30 thunder
Saving Throws +2
Speed fly 10 (hover)
Action Points 1

⊕ **Lightning Arc** (standard; at-will) ✦ **Lightning**
   Reach 3; +29 vs. Reflex; 2d8 + 11 lightning damage.

⊙ **Lightning Bolt** (standard; at-will) ✦ **Lightning**
   Ranged 10; +29 vs. Reflex; 2d8 + 11 lightning damage.

↞ **Thunderclap** (standard; at-will) ✦ **Thunder**
   Close burst 2; +28 vs. Fortitude; 2d10 + 9 thunder damage.

↞ **Charged Mist** (standard; recharge ⚄ ⚅) ✦ **Lightning**
   Close burst 3; automatic hit; 1d10 + 9 lightning damage, and the thunderblast cyclone becomes insubstantial until the end of its next turn.

✴ **Lightning Storm** (standard; begins uncharged; recharges when the thunderblast cyclone uses *charged mist*) ✦ **Lightning, Thunder**
   Area burst 3 within 20; +29 vs. Reflex; 6d8 + 9 lightning and thunder damage. *Miss:* Half damage.

Alignment Unaligned	**Languages** Primordial	
Str 25 (+20)	**Dex** 32 (+24)	**Wis** 17 (+16)
Con 29 (+22)	**Int** 8 (+12)	**Cha** 15 (+15)

THUNDERBLAST CYCLONE TACTICS

The thunderblast cyclone makes *lightning bolt* attacks until enemies come within range of its *charged mist*. One the same round it uses *charged mist*, it spends an action point to unleash *lightning storm*. It then alternates between *lightning arc* and *thunderclap*, switching out the latter for *charged mist* as soon as the power recharges.

ENCOUNTER GROUPS

Elementals are found throughout the Elemental Chaos, often in the service of more intelligent elemental beings such as titans and efreets. Mortals also invoke rituals to summon elementals to the natural world.

Level 11 Encounter (XP 3,500)
✦ 1 firelasher elemental (level 11 skirmisher)
✦ 1 snaketongue celebrant (level 11 controller)
✦ 4 snaketongue zealots (level 12 minion)
✦ 2 snaketongue assassins (level 9 lurker)
✦ 2 flame snakes (level 9 artillery)

Level 18 Encounter (XP 10,000)
✦ 1 rockfire dreadnought elemental (level 18 soldier)
✦ 2 fire giants (level 18 soldier)
✦ 1 mind flayer mastermind (level 18 elite controller)

ELF

SLENDER AND AGILE, ELVES REVERE NATURE and roam the wilderness, hunting creatures that threaten their lands. Although they trace their origins to the Feywild, most elves consider the natural world their home.

Elf Archer	Level 2 Artillery
Medium fey humanoid	XP 125

Initiative +5　　**Senses** Perception +11; low-light vision
Group Awareness aura 5; non-elf allies in the aura gain a +1 racial bonus to Perception checks.
HP 32; **Bloodied** 16
AC 15; **Fortitude** 11, **Reflex** 13, **Will** 12
Speed 7; see also *wild step*
(+) **Short Sword** (standard; at-will) ✦ **Weapon**
　　+5 vs. AC; 1d6 + 4 damage.
(↗) **Longbow** (standard; at-will) ✦ **Weapon**
　　Ranged 20/40; +7 vs. AC; 1d10 + 4 damage; see also *archer's mobility*.
Archer's Mobility
　　If the elf archer moves at least 4 squares from its original position, it gains a +2 bonus to ranged attack rolls until the start of its next turn.

Elven Accuracy (free; encounter)
　　The elf can reroll an attack roll. It must use the second roll, even if it's lower.
Not So Close (immediate reaction, when an enemy makes a melee attack against the elf archer; encounter)
　　The elf archer shifts 1 square and makes a ranged attack against the enemy.
Wild Step
　　The elf ignores difficult terrain when it shifts.
Alignment Any　　**Languages** Common, Elven
Skills Nature +11, Stealth +10
Str 13 (+2)	**Dex** 18 (+5)	**Wis** 16 (+4)
Con 14 (+3)	**Int** 12 (+2)	**Cha** 11 (+1)
Equipment leather armor, short sword, longbow, quiver of 30 arrows

ELF ARCHER TACTICS

An elf archer attacks with his longbow and uses *archer's mobility* between attacks. If an enemy engages the elf archer in melee, he uses *not so close* and moves away on his next turn.

Elf Scout	Level 2 Skirmisher
Medium fey humanoid	XP 125

Initiative +7　　**Senses** Perception +10; low-light vision
Group Awareness aura 5; non-elf allies in the aura gain a +1 racial bonus to Perception checks.
HP 39; **Bloodied** 19
AC 16; **Fortitude** 13, **Reflex** 15, **Will** 13
Speed 6; see also *wild step*
(+) **Longsword** (standard; at-will) ✦ **Weapon**
　　+7 vs. AC; 1d8 + 4 damage.
(+) **Short Sword** (standard; at-will) ✦ **Weapon**
　　+7 vs. AC; 1d6 + 4 damage.
(†) **Two-Weapon Rend** (standard; encounter) ✦ **Weapon**
　　The elf scout makes a longsword attack and a short sword attack against the same target. If both attacks hit, the elf scout deals an additional 4 damage.
Elven Accuracy (free; encounter)
　　The elf can reroll an attack roll. It must use the second roll, even if it's lower.
Combat Advantage
　　An elf scout that has combat advantage deals an extra 1d6 damage on it attacks.
Wild Step
　　The elf ignores difficult terrain when it shifts.
Alignment Any　　**Languages** Common, Elven
Skills Nature +10, Stealth +9
Str 12 (+2)	**Dex** 18 (+5)	**Wis** 14 (+3)
Con 15 (+3)	**Int** 10 (+1)	**Cha** 12 (+2)
Equipment chainmail, longsword, short sword

ELF SCOUT TACTICS

An elf scout often tries to fight an opponent in difficult terrain where she can shift but an enemy cannot. She tries to flank opponents to gain combat advantage.

ENCOUNTER GROUPS

Elves are typically encountered with other elves and creatures of the wild.

Level 2 Encounter (XP 625)
✦ 2 elf archers (level 2 artillery)
✦ 1 elf scout (level 2 skirmisher)
✦ 2 gray wolves (level 2 skirmisher)

ETTERCAP

PRIMITIVE AND INSTINCTUAL HUNTERS, ettercaps use webs to snare their prey and have few scruples about killing and eating sentient creatures.

ETTERCAP LORE

A character knows the following information with a successful Nature check.

DC 15: A spiritual kinship with arachnids allows ettercaps to live among and communicate with spiders and scorpions, and to keep such creatures as pets. An ettercap uses such beasts as a human hunter uses dogs or drakes.

ENCOUNTER GROUPS

Ettercaps are often encountered with spiders and can also be found in the service of other humanoids.

Level 4 Encounter (XP 900)
✦ 1 ettercap webspinner (level 5 controller)
✦ 2 ettercap fang guards (level 4 soldier)
✦ 2 deathjump spiders (level 4 skirmisher)

Ettercap Fang Guard	Level 4 Soldier
Medium natural humanoid (spider)	XP 175

Initiative +6   **Senses** Perception +3
HP 56; **Bloodied** 28
AC 20; **Fortitude** 17, **Reflex** 16, **Will** 15
Resist 10 poison
Speed 5, climb 5 (spider climb); see also *web walker*
⊕ **Greataxe** (standard; at-will) ✦ **Weapon**
  +9 vs. AC; 1d12 + 5 damage (crit 1d12 + 17).
↯ **Spider Bite** (standard; at-will) ✦ **Poison**
  Requires combat advantage; +9 vs. AC; 1d6 + 4 damage. If the attack hits, the ettercap makes a secondary attack against the same target. *Secondary Attack:* +7 vs. Fortitude; the target is stunned until the end of the ettercap's next turn and takes ongoing 5 poison damage (save ends).
↯ **Web Tangle** (standard; at-will)
  +7 vs. Reflex; the target is immobilized (save ends).
Web Reaper
  The ettercap fang guard gains a +2 bonus to attack rolls and deals an extra 2 damage against restrained and immobilized creatures.
Web Walker
  An ettercap ignores the movement effects of spider webs and difficult terrain related to spider swarms.
Alignment Unaligned   **Languages** –
Skills Stealth +9
Str 16 (+5)   **Dex** 14 (+4)   **Wis** 13 (+3)
Con 16 (+5)   **Int** 5 (-1)   **Cha** 11 (+2)
Equipment leather armor, greataxe

ETTERCAP FANG GUARD TACTICS

This creature uses *web tangle* to immobilize a foe, flanks with allies to gain combat advantage, and uses its *spider bite*. If the ettercap is unable to gain combat advantage, it alternates between *web tangle* and greataxe attacks, hoping to gain the benefits of its *web reaper* power.

Ettercap Webspinner	Level 5 Controller
Medium natural humanoid (spider)	XP 200

Initiative +4   **Senses** Perception +9
HP 64; **Bloodied** 32
AC 18; **Fortitude** 17, **Reflex** 16, **Will** 16
Resist 10 poison
Speed 5, climb 5 (spider climb); see also *web walker*
⊕ **Longspear** (standard; at-will) ✦ **Weapon**
  Reach 2, +10 vs. AC; 1d10 + 3 damage.
↯ **Spider Bite** (standard; at-will) ✦ **Poison**
  Requires combat advantage; +10 vs. AC; 1d6 + 3 damage, and the ettercap makes a secondary attack against the same target. *Secondary Attack:* +8 vs. Fortitude; ongoing 5 poison damage (save ends).
↣ **Web Net** (minor 1/round; at-will)
  Ranged 5; +9 vs. Reflex; the target is restrained (save ends).
❋ **Webbed Terrain** (standard; recharge ⚅) ✦ **Zone**
  Area burst 2 within 10; +9 vs. Reflex; the target is immobilized (save ends). The zone is filled with spider webs and is considered difficult terrain until the end of the encounter.
Web Walker
  An ettercap ignores the movement effects of spider webs and difficult terrain related to spider swarms.
Alignment Unaligned   **Languages** –
Skills Stealth +9
Str 16 (+5)   **Dex** 14 (+4)   **Wis** 15 (+4)
Con 16 (+5)   **Int** 5 (-1)   **Cha** 13 (+3)
Equipment leather armor, longspear

ETTERCAP WEBSPINNER TACTICS

An ettercap webspinner uses stealth to shadow its prey, waiting for an opportune moment to strike. It uses *webbed terrain* to immobilize opponents and hinder their movement. It then uses *web net* to restrain the closest target and uses its longspear to strike from a safe distance.

ETTIN

ETTINS ARE RAVENOUS TWO-HEADED GIANTS that prowl wild borderlands, forested mountains, and dark caves.

Ettin Marauder	Level 10 Elite Soldier
Large natural humanoid (giant)	XP 1,000

Initiative +8; see also *double actions* — **Senses** Perception +12
HP 222; **Bloodied** 111
AC 28; **Fortitude** 26, **Reflex** 18, **Will** 19
Saving Throws +2
Speed 6
Action Points 1

⊕ **Club** (standard; at-will) ✦ **Weapon**
　Reach 2; +15 vs. AC; 1d8 + 9 damage, and the target is pushed 1 square.

↯ **Swat** (immediate reaction, when an enemy moves into a position that flanks the ettin; at-will)
　The ettin targets one creature flanking it: +13 vs. Fortitude; the target is pushed 3 squares.

Double Actions
　An ettin rolls initiative twice, gets two turns during a round, and has a full set of actions (standard, move, minor) on each turn. Each set of actions corresponds to a different head. The ettin's ability to take immediate actions refreshes on each of its turns.

Dual Brain
　At the end of its turn, the ettin automatically saves against the dazed and stunned conditions and against charm effects that a save can end.

Alignment Chaotic evil		**Languages** Giant
Str 28 (+14)	**Dex** 12 (+6)	**Wis** 15 (+7)
Con 23 (+11)	**Int** 8 (+4)	**Cha** 9 (+4)

Equipment hide armor, 2 clubs

ETTIN MARAUDER TACTICS

An ettin marauder engages foes in melee combat, spending an action point if necessary to reach a lightly armored adversary. It uses *swat* against an enemy that tries to flank it.

Ettin Spirit-Talker	Level 12 Elite Controller
Large natural humanoid (giant)	XP 1,400

Initiative +6; see also *double actions* — **Senses** Perception +17
HP 252; **Bloodied** 126
AC 28; **Fortitude** 27, **Reflex** 21, **Will** 26
Saving Throws +2
Speed 6
Action Points 1

⊕ **Club** (standard; at-will) ✦ **Weapon**
　Reach 2; +17 vs. AC; 1d8 + 7 damage, and the target is pushed 1 square.

↗ **Curse of Shattered Bone** (standard; at-will)
　Ranged 10; +15 vs. Will; the next time the spirit talker successfully hits the target with a melee attack, the attack is treated as a critical hit and deals an extra 1d12 damage. The curse lasts until the end of the ettin spirit talker's next turn.

⤺ **Spirit Call** (standard; recharge ⚄ ⚅) ✦ **Necrotic**
　The ettin spirit-talker initiates a howling chant to demonic spirits, filling the area with swirling spectral forms: close burst 5; +15 vs. Fortitude; 2d6 + 6 necrotic damage, and the target slides 3 squares.

Double Actions
　An ettin rolls initiative twice, gets two turns during a round, and has a full set of actions (standard, move, minor) on each turn. Each set of actions corresponds to a different head. The ettin's ability to take immediate actions refreshes on each of its turns.

Dual Brain
　At the end of its turn, the ettin automatically saves against the dazed and stunned conditions and against charm effects that a save can end.

Alignment Chaotic evil		**Languages** Giant
Skills Religion +12		
Str 25 (+13)	**Dex** 10 (+6)	**Wis** 23 (+12)
Con 22 (+12)	**Int** 13 (+7)	**Cha** 15 (+8)

Equipment hide armor, 2 clubs

ETTIN SPIRIT-TALKER TACTICS

Round after round, the ettin spirit-talker uses its first turn to invoke a *curse of shattered bone*, and then uses its second turn to club the cursed target. The creature uses *spirit call* on foes that try to surround and flank it.

ETTIN LORE

A character knows the following information with a successful Nature check.

DC 15: Wandering in small bands through remote borderlands and mountain valleys, ettins feed themselves by hunting creatures of every sort, including other intelligent creatures up to and including rival ettin bands.

ENCOUNTER GROUPS

Ettins are typically encountered with other ettins and wild creatures. Sometimes ettins and demons are encountered together.

Level 10 Encounter (XP 2,550)
✦ 1 ettin marauder (level 10 elite soldier)
✦ 1 venom-eye basilisk (level 10 artillery)
✦ 3 barlgura demons (level 8 brute)

ERIC VEDDER & ADAM VEHIGE

(Left to right) foulspawn seer, grue, berserker, hulk, and mangler

Foulspawn Seer	Level 11 Artillery (Leader)
Medium aberrant humanoid	XP 600

Initiative +7   **Senses** Perception +9; low-light vision
Foul Insight aura 10; allies in the aura that can hear the foulspawn seer gain a +2 power bonus to one attack roll, skill check, ability check, or saving throw on their turn.
AC 24; **Fortitude** 19, **Reflex** 23, **Will** 21
HP 86; **Bloodied** 43
Speed 6, teleport 3
⊕ **Twisted Staff** (standard; at-will) ✦ **Weapon**
    +14 vs. AC; 1d8 + 6 damage, and the target is pushed 1 square.
⌁ **Warp Orb** (standard; at-will)
    Ranged 10; +16 vs. Reflex; 1d8 + 6 damage, and the target is dazed (save ends).
⬳ **Distortion Blast** (standard; daily)
    Close blast 5; +12 vs. Fortitude; 2d8 + 6 damage, and the target is dazed (save ends). Aberrant creatures take half damage.
Bend Space (immediate interrupt, when the foulspawn seer would be hit by an attack; recharge ⚄ ⚅) ✦ **Teleportation**
    The foulspawn seer teleports 3 squares.

Alignment Evil	**Languages** Deep Speech, telepathy 10	
Str 10 (+5)	**Dex** 14 (+7)	**Wis** 8 (+4)
Con 14 (+7)	**Int** 22 (+11)	**Cha** 18 (+9)

Equipment staff

Foulspawn Hulk	Level 12 Brute
Large aberrant humanoid	XP 700

Initiative +8   **Senses** Perception +9; low-light vision
HP 150; **Bloodied** 75
AC 24; **Fortitude** 27 (29 while bloodied), **Reflex** 22, **Will** 22
Immune fear
Speed 8
⊕ **Slam** (standard; at-will)
    Reach 2; +15 vs. AC (+17 while bloodied); 2d8 + 7 damage, or 3d8 + 9 damage while bloodied.

Alignment Evil	**Languages** Deep Speech, telepathy 10	
Str 24 (+13)	**Dex** 14 (+8)	**Wis** 7 (+4)
Con 20 (+11)	**Int** 7 (+4)	**Cha** 14 (+8)

FOULSPAWN HULK TACTICS

This fearless foulspawn attacks with its bloodsoaked fists. It fights to the death.

FOULSPAWN SEER TACTICS

The foulspawn seer uses *foul insight* to benefit allies while using its teleport ability and *bend space* power to stay out of harm's way. It hurls *warp orbs* until it can harm multiple foes with its *distortion blast*, not caring whether or not allies are caught in the effect.

GALEB DUHR

REMORSELESS CREATURES OF LIVING STONE, galeb duhrs often serve hill giants or earth titans, and their nature is similarly harsh and unrelenting.

Galeb Duhr Earthbreaker	**Level 8 Artillery**
Medium elemental humanoid (earth)	XP 350

Initiative +4 **Senses** Perception +12; tremorsense 10
HP 73; **Bloodied** 36
AC 22; **Fortitude** 23, **Reflex** 18, **Will** 20
Immune petrification, poison
Speed 4 (earth walk), burrow 6
Slam (standard; at-will)
+13 vs. AC; 1d8 + 6 damage.
Hurl Stones (standard; at-will)
Area burst 1 within 10; +13 vs. AC; 1d10 + 6 damage. All squares in the area become difficult terrain. The earthbreaker can create stones to throw when none are present.
Shock Wave (standard; recharge 5 6)
Close burst 2; +12 vs. Fortitude; 1d6 + 6 damage, and the target is pushed 1 square and knocked prone.
Alignment Unaligned **Languages** Dwarven, Giant
Skills Stealth +9

Str 23 (+10)	**Dex** 10 (+4)	**Wis** 16 (+7)
Con 19 (+8)	**Int** 12 (+5)	**Cha** 12 (+5)

Galeb Duhr Earthbreaker Tactics

A galeb duhr earthbreaker disguises itself as a boulder until it attacks. It begins combat by using its *hurl stones* power to launch rocks into a group of foes. It targets the front of the group, slowing their movement with the resulting difficult terrain. The earthbreaker continues hurling stones until opponents get too close, at which point it unleashes its *shock wave*.

Galeb Duhr Rockcaller	**Level 11 Controller**
Medium elemental humanoid (earth)	XP 600

Initiative +5 **Senses** Perception +12; tremorsense 10
HP 118; **Bloodied** 59
AC 25; **Fortitude** 26, **Reflex** 21, **Will** 22
Immune petrification, poison
Speed 4 (earth walk), burrow 6
Slam (standard; at-will)
+16 vs. AC; 2d8 + 4 damage.
Rolling Attack (standard; at-will)
The galeb duhr rockcaller moves up to 4 squares and then attacks an adjacent target; +14 vs. Fortitude; 2d8 + 6 damage, and the target is pushed 1 square and knocked prone.
Earthen Grasp (standard; at-will)
An earthen fist rises up to restrain a target. Ranged 10; +14 vs. Fortitude; the target is restrained (save ends). The target must be in direct contact with the ground or the attack fails. The rockcaller can use *earthen grasp* against only one creature at a time.
Rocky Terrain (minor; at-will)
Ranged 10; up to 4 squares within range become difficult terrain. The squares need not be contiguous, but the affected terrain must consist of earth or stone.
Alignment Unaligned **Languages** Dwarven, Giant
Skills Stealth +10

Str 19 (+9)	**Dex** 10 (+5)	**Wis** 15 (+7)
Con 22 (+11)	**Int** 13 (+6)	**Cha** 13 (+6)

Galeb Duhr Rockcaller Tactics

Like the earthbreaker, the rockcaller disguises itself as a boulder until it attacks. It uses *rocky terrain* each turn to limit its enemies' ability to shift or escape. At the same time, it uses *earthen grasp* to restrain a foe or *rolling attack* to knock an enemy prone.

Galeb Duhr Lore

A character knows the following information with a successful Arcana check.

DC 15: Long ago, all dwarves were slaves to the giants and titans. More than one variety of dwarf failed to escape during the initial revolution, including the galeb duhrs. However, unlike the azers that continue to serve their masters in the Elemental Chaos, many galeb duhrs have slipped away from their brutish masters into the world. On the other hand, some still serve their hill giant and earth titan overlords, both in the Elemental Chaos and in the natural world.

Encounter Groups

Galeb duhrs are typically encountered with others of their kind, and sometimes with gargoyles and other creatures of elemental earth.

Level 11 Encounter (XP 3,000)
- 1 galeb duhr rockcaller (level 11 controller)
- 4 gargoyles (level 9 lurker)
- 1 bulette (level 9 elite skirmisher)

FRANCIS TSAI

GARGOYLE

RESEMBLING A GROTESQUE STONE STATUE, a gargoyle is a vicious flying predator that enjoys torturing creatures weaker than itself. Gargoyles came to the world long ago from the Elemental Chaos in search of prey and make their lairs atop stone buildings and cave ledges.

GARGOYLE LORE

A character knows the following information with a successful Arcana check.

DC 15: Gargoyles prefer to nest on high rocky outcroppings and the rooftops of tall stone buildings; however, they can also be found in caverns deep below the earth. Rituals can summon gargoyles to serve as guardians of locations or prisons, or to hunt down people or items.

ENCOUNTER GROUPS

Gargoyles hunt in packs, though they also ally with other creatures tied to elemental earth as well as evil summoners and demon cultists.

Level 9 Encounter (XP 2,400)
✦ 3 gargoyles (level 9 lurker)
✦ 1 gibbering mouther (level 10 controller)
✦ 2 galeb duhr earthbreakers (level 8 artillery)

Gargoyle		Level 9 Lurker
Medium elemental humanoid (earth)		XP 400

Initiative +11   **Senses** Perception +12; darkvision
HP 77; **Bloodied** 38
AC 25; **Fortitude** 21, **Reflex** 19, **Will** 19
Immune petrification
Speed 6, fly 8; see also *flyby attack*
⊕ **Claw** (standard; at-will)
   +14 vs. AC; 2d6 + 5 damage.
↭ **Flyby Attack** (standard; recharges after using *stone form*)
   The gargoyle flies up to 8 squares and makes a melee basic attack at any point during the move without provoking an opportunity attack from the target. If the attack hits, the target is knocked prone.
Stone Form (standard; at-will)
   The gargoyle becomes a statue and gains resist 25 to all damage, regeneration 3, and tremorsense 10. It loses all other senses and can take no actions in stone form other than revert to its normal form (as a minor action).

Alignment Evil	**Languages** Primordial	
Skills Stealth +12		
Str 21 (+9)	**Dex** 17 (+7)	**Wis** 17 (+7)
Con 17 (+7)	**Int** 5 (+1)	**Cha** 17 (+7)

GARGOYLE TACTICS

Gargoyles often appear as statues until they detect intruders using their tremorsense. When prey comes within 10 squares, a gargoyle reverts to normal form and makes *flyby attacks* against targets in range. Eventually its impatience gets the better of it, and it lands to engage foes in melee. Faced with difficult opponents, a gargoyle flees and finds a safe place to roost while it reverts to *stone form* and regenerates.

Nabassu Gargoyle		Level 18 Lurker
Medium elemental humanoid (earth)		XP 2,000

Initiative +20   **Senses** Perception +17; darkvision
Bloodfire Gaze (Fire) aura 2; any creature taking ongoing damage that enters or starts its turn in the aura takes 5 fire damage and is weakened (the effect ends when the creature leaves the aura). This aura is not active while the nabassu gargoyle is in *stone form*.
HP 136; **Bloodied** 68
AC 32; **Fortitude** 30, **Reflex** 30, **Will** 28
Immune petrification
Speed 6, fly 8
⊕ **Claw** (standard; at-will)
   +23 vs. AC; 2d8 + 7 damage, and ongoing 5 damage (save ends).
↭ **Savage Bite** (standard; recharge ⚅ ⚄) ✦ **Healing**
   +23 vs. AC; 2d6 + 7 damage, or 2d10 + 7 damage against a bloodied or weakened target. In addition, the gargoyle regains a number of hit points equal to the amount of damage dealt.
Stone Form (standard; at-will)
   The gargoyle becomes a statue and gains resist 30 to all damage, regeneration 5, and tremorsense 10. It loses all other senses and can take no actions in stone form other than revert to its normal form (as a minor action).

Alignment Evil	**Languages** Primordial	
Skills Stealth +21		
Str 25 (+16)	**Dex** 24 (+16)	**Wis** 17 (+12)
Con 22 (+15)	**Int** 5 (+6)	**Cha** 20 (+14)

NABASSU GARGOYLE TACTICS

A nabassu gargoyle disguises itself as a stone statue until opponents draw near, at which point it reverts to normal form and makes claw attacks, hoping to affect wounded enemies with its *bloodfire gaze*. It uses its *savage bite* against the first enemy that succumbs to its aura, and uses it again once the power recharges.

GHOSTS HAUNT FORLORN PLACES, bound to their fate until they are finally put to rest. Sometimes they exist for a purpose, and other times they defy death through sheer will.

A ghost is the spirit of a dead creature, often a Medium humanoid killed in some traumatic fashion. Its form resembles the body it had in life, but its appearance might be altered by the nature of its demise. Some ghosts look angelic, while some appear twisted or disfigured. Others can change their appearance to suit their current disposition.

Phantom Warrior		Level 4 Soldier
Medium shadow humanoid (undead)		XP 175

Initiative +8   **Senses** Perception +13; darkvision
HP 40; **Bloodied** 20
AC 18; **Fortitude** 16, **Reflex** 15, **Will** 16
Immune disease, poison; **Resist** insubstantial
Speed 6, fly 6 (hover); phasing

(✦) **Phantom Sword** (standard; at-will) ✦ **Necrotic**
+9 vs. Reflex; 1d8 + 2 necrotic damage, and the target is marked until the end of the phantom warrior's next turn.

Phantom Tactics
A phantom warrior has combat advantage against any target that has another phantom warrior adjacent to it.

Alignment Any	**Languages** Common	
Str 14 (+4)	**Dex** 12 (+3)	**Wis** 11 (+2)
Con 12 (+3)	**Int** 10 (+2)	**Cha** 14 (+4)

PHANTOM WARRIOR TACTICS

A phantom warrior patrols the location where it died, attacking anything it perceives as an enemy.

Trap Haunt		Level 8 Lurker
Medium shadow humanoid (undead)		XP 350

Initiative +12   **Senses** Perception +9; darkvision
HP 52; **Bloodied** 26
AC 20; **Fortitude** 16, **Reflex** 18, **Will** 17
Immune disease, poison; **Resist** insubstantial
Speed fly 6 (hover); phasing

(✦) **Grave Touch** (standard; at-will) ✦ **Necrotic**
+12 vs. Fortitude; 2d6 necrotic damage.

✦ **Ghostly Possession** (standard; recharge ⚅ ⚅) ✦ **Charm**
Target must be a living humanoid; +12 vs. Will; the trap haunt enters the target's space and is removed from play, and the target is dominated (save ends). The trap haunt can use this power against only one creature at a time. When the target is no longer dominated, or when the trap haunt chooses to end its *ghostly possession* (a free action), the trap haunt reappears in a square of its choice adjacent to the target.

Trapbound
A trap haunt cannot voluntarily move more than 20 squares from the place where it died. If it is forced beyond this range, it is weakened and unable to use its *ghostly possession* power until it moves back within range.

Alignment Any	**Languages** Common	
Str 10 (+4)	**Dex** 18 (+8)	**Wis** 11 (+4)
Con 14 (+6)	**Int** 11 (+4)	**Cha** 16 (+7)

TRAP HAUNT TACTICS

A trap haunt believes that the only way to free itself from eternal torment is to lead other creatures into the same trap that killed it. It uses *ghostly possession* to accomplish its goal.

ANNE STOKES

Gibbering Orb	Level 27 Solo Controller
Huge aberrant magical beast	XP 55,000

Initiative +22 **Senses** Perception +20; all-around vision, darkvision

Merciless Eyes aura 5; at the start of each enemy's turn, if that creature is within the aura and in the gibbering orb's line of sight, the gibbering orb uses one random *eye ray* power against that creature.

HP 1,230; **Bloodied** 615

AC 41; **Fortitude** 33, **Reflex** 39, **Will** 40

Saving Throws +5

Speed fly 8 (hover)

Action Points 2

(↓) **Bite** (standard; at-will)

+30 vs. AC; 4d6 + 10 damage, and the mouth detaches from the gibbering orb and makes a new bite attack against the target each round at the start of the gibbering orb's turn. When the mouth misses, it drops off and turns into useless, dead gray flesh.

(↤) **Gibbering** (free, once on the gibbering orb's turn before it takes other actions; at-will) ✦ **Psychic**

Close burst 10; deafened creatures are immune; +29 vs. Will; the target is dazed until the end of the gibbering orb's next turn.

(↗) **Eye Rays** (standard; at-will) ✦ see text

The gibbering orb can use two different *eye ray* powers (chosen from the list below or rolled randomly). Each power must target a different creature. Using eye rays does not provoke opportunity attacks.

1—Mindcarving Ray (Psychic): Ranged 10; +30 vs. Will; 2d8 + 12 psychic damage, and the target is dazed (save ends).

2—Flesheating Ray (Necrotic): Ranged 10; +30 vs. Fortitude; 2d8 + 12 necrotic damage, and ongoing 10 necrotic damage (save ends).

3—Bonewarping Ray: Ranged 10; +30 vs. Fortitude; 2d8 + 12 damage, the target is weakened (save ends).

4—Bloodfeasting Ray: Ranged 10; +30 vs. Reflex; 2d8 + 12 damage, and ongoing 10 damage (save ends).

5—Farsending Ray (Psychic, Teleportation): Ranged 10; +30 vs. Reflex; the target is briefly transported to the Far Realm, reappearing in the same space (or the nearest unoccupied space if that space is occupied) at the end of the gibbering orb's next turn. Upon its return, the target takes 2d8 + 12 psychic damage and takes a –5 penalty to saving throws until the end of the encounter.

6—Souleating Ray (Necrotic): Ranged 10; +30 vs. Will; the target is slowed (save ends). *First Failed Save:* The target is immobilized instead of slowed (save ends). *Second Failed Save:* The target dies.

Alignment Unaligned	**Languages** —	
Str 27 (+21)	**Dex** 28 (+22)	**Wis** 15 (+15)
Con 22 (+19)	**Int** 17 (+16)	**Cha** 31 (+23)

GIBBERING ORB TACTICS

A gibbering orb keeps its distance, attacking enemies with its *eye rays* while gibbering each round as a free action. It uses its action points to make additional *eye ray* attacks. If forced into melee combat, it makes bit attacks, detaching its mouths and retreating as they continue biting foes.

GIBBERING BEAST LORE

A character knows the following information with a successful Dungeoneering check.

DC 15: Gibbering beasts spontaneously arise when creatures, especially sentient ones, die in a place touched by the Far Realm.

DC 20: For the most part, gibbering beasts speak nonsense. Occasionally, a gibbering beast speaks an intelligible word or phrase, usually mingled with its mad gibbering. The word or phrase could be a clue or warning, or it could just be something of no importance whatsoever.

DC 25: Gibbering orbs are denizens of the Far Realm that wander the planes and the places between, consuming living creatures. Although they appear insane, gibbering orbs are perversely rational, and they pursue secret objectives all their own.

ENCOUNTER GROUPS

Lesser gibbering beasts live among other aberrant creatures. They are clever enough to associate with nonaberrant creatures when it's to their advantage. The gibbering orb travels alone, though strange events and creatures might serve as omens to its coming.

Level 10 Encounter (XP 2,900)
✦ 2 gibbering mouthers (level 10 controller)
✦ 1 foulspawn seer (level 11 artillery)
✦ 2 foulspawn berserkers (level 9 soldier)
✦ 1 chuul (level 10 soldier)

Level 18 Encounter (XP 10,050)
✦ 1 gibbering abomination (level 18 controller)
✦ 2 nabassu gargoyles (level 18 lurker)
✦ 1 aboleth lasher (level 17 brute)
✦ 7 kuo-toa guards (level 16 minion)

GITHYANKI

Born out of slavery, the githyanki are fierce psychic warriors that ply the Astral Sea and fight with silver swords.

The githyanki and the githzerai were once a single race—the gith—enslaved by mind flayers, but they split into two races after winning their freedom. Whereas the githzerai fled to the Elemental Chaos and became introspective and monastic, the githyanki fled to the Astral Sea and became xenophobic and militaristic. They built citadels and armies, and from there they set out to conquer everything in their path.

Githyanki Warrior	Level 12 Soldier
Medium natural humanoid	XP 700

Initiative +13   **Senses** Perception +12
HP 118; **Bloodied** 59
AC 28; **Fortitude** 25, **Reflex** 23, **Will** 22
Saving Throws +2 against charm effects
Speed 5; see also *telekinetic leap*
(+) **Silver Greatsword** (standard; at-will) ✦ **Psychic, Weapon**
   +17 vs. AC; 1d10 + 5 plus 1d6 psychic damage, plus an extra 3d6 psychic damage if the target is immobilized.
↗ **Telekinetic Grasp** (standard; sustain minor; encounter)
   Ranged 5; Medium or smaller target; +15 vs. Fortitude; the target is immobilized (save ends).
↗ **Telekinetic Leap** (move; encounter)
   Ranged 10; the githyanki warrior or an ally within range can fly up to 5 squares.
Alignment Evil   **Languages** Common, Deep Speech
Skills History +9, Insight +12
Str 21 (+11)   **Dex** 17 (+9)   **Wis** 12 (+7)
Con 14 (+8)   **Int** 12 (+7)   **Cha** 13 (+7)
Equipment plate armor, silver greatsword

GITHYANKI WARRIOR TACTICS

Although this githyanki favors melee, it generally begins battle by using its *telekinetic grasp* to immobilize an opponent. It then attacks the immobilized target with its silver greatsword, dealing additional psychic damage on a hit.

Githyanki Mindslicer	Level 13 Artillery
Medium natural humanoid	XP 800

Initiative +11   **Senses** Perception +12
HP 98; **Bloodied** 49
AC 27; **Fortitude** 24, **Reflex** 25, **Will** 24
Saving Throws +2 against charm effects
Speed 6; see also *telekinetic leap*
(+) **Silver Longsword** (standard; at-will) ✦ **Psychic, Weapon**
   +18 vs. AC; 1d8 + 2 plus 1d8 psychic damage.
↗ **Mindslice** (standard; at-will) ✦ **Psychic**
   Ranged 10; +16 vs. Will; 2d8 + 3 psychic damage.
↗ **Telekinetic Leap** (move; encounter)
   Ranged 10; the githyanki mindslicer or an ally within range can fly up to 5 squares.
⋇ **Psychic Barrage** (standard; recharge ⚄⚅) ✦ **Psychic**
   Area burst 1 within 20; +16 vs. Will; 1d6 + 3 psychic damage, and ongoing 5 psychic damage (save ends), and the target can't use daily or encounter powers (save ends).
Alignment Evil   **Languages** Common, Deep Speech
Skills History +11, Insight +12
Str 14 (+8)   **Dex** 16 (+9)   **Wis** 12 (+7)
Con 14 (+8)   **Int** 17 (+9)   **Cha** 11 (+6)
Equipment robes, overcoat, silver longsword

GITHYANKI MINDSLICER TACTICS

A mindslicer begins combat by unleashing a *psychic barrage* against multiple enemies. It stays at the periphery of the battlefield, assailing foes with its *mindslice* power until it can recharge and unleash *psychic barrage* again.

Githyanki Gish	Level 15 Elite Skirmisher
Medium natural humanoid	XP 2,400

Initiative +13   **Senses** Perception +14
HP 226; **Bloodied** 113
AC 31; **Fortitude** 28, **Reflex** 29, **Will** 29
Saving Throws +2 (+4 against charm effects)
Speed 5; see also *astral stride*
Action Points 1
(+) **Silver Longsword** (standard; at-will) ✦ **Psychic, Weapon**
   +20 vs. AC; 1d8 + 3 plus 1d8 psychic damage.
╫ **Double Attack** (standard; at-will) ✦ **Psychic, Weapon**
   The githyanki gish makes two silver longsword attacks.
↗ **Force Bolt** (standard; recharge ⚄⚅) ✦ **Force**
   Ranged 10; +18 vs. Reflex; 3d6 + 4 force damage.
↗ **Storm of Stars** (standard; encounter) ✦ **Fire**
   The githyanki gish makes four attacks, no more than two of them against a single target: ranged 5; +20 vs. AC; 2d8 + 4 fire damage.
↗ **Astral Stride** (move; at-will) ✦ **Teleportation**
   The githyanki gish teleports 6 squares and gains the insubstantial and phasing qualities until the start of its next turn.
Alignment Evil   **Languages** Common, Deep Speech, Draconic
Skills Arcana +16, History +13, Insight +14
Str 16 (+10)   **Dex** 14 (+9)   **Wis** 14 (+9)
Con 17 (+10)   **Int** 19 (+11)   **Cha** 17 (+10)
Equipment chainmail, silver longsword

GITHYANKI GISH TACTICS

A githyanki gish uses ranged attacks (*force bolt* and *storm of stars*) to soften up foes before engaging in melee combat, using *astral stride* to gain a flanking position when possible and making a *double attack* at every opportunity. If the battle turns against the gish and its allies, it uses *astral stride* to escape.

GITHYANKI LORE

A character knows the following information with a successful Nature check.

DC 20: The ancient gith escaped from their mind flayer overlords long ago, only to fall prey to internecine strife that created the rival githyanki and githzerai races. In time, the githyanki established a tyranny almost as bloodthirsty as the illithids that once enslaved them. Githyanki attack mind flayers on sight, and they are equally cruel toward their githzerai kin.

Githyanki speak Common. They also learned Deep Speech from their mind flayer overlords.

DC 25: Githyanki cities and citadels in the Astral Sea are built upon nameless and forgotten dead entities. The githyanki sail the Astral Sea in astral ships, looking for debris of dead gods and shattered realms to add to their own fortresses and hoards. Occasionally they set their sights on other worlds, intent on plundering them as well.

DC 30: Githyanki don't have families; from birth they belong to military training groups called cadres. A githyanki views her cadre as singularly important and typically does not know the name of her parents or siblings. Even more important than a githyanki's cadre is her weapon. A githyanki lavishes more care on her weapon than her fellows.

DC 35: Tu'narath is the largest githyanki city. It is built atop the body of a dead god adrift in the Astral Sea and ruled by Vlaakith, the githyanki lich queen, who has ruled supreme for over a thousand years. The githyanki revere the lich-queen as the stepmother of their race. To them, her word is truth. She has the reputation for slaying any who challenge her policy or power, devouring their life essences.

Githyanki have a pact with red dragons, which sometimes agree to allow githyanki to ride upon them.

ENCOUNTER GROUPS

Githyanki rarely associate with other races, but they have a forged pact with red dragons and occasionally take beasts as pets.

Level 12 Encounter (XP 3,500)
✦ 3 githyanki warriors (level 12 soldier)
✦ 2 redspawn firebelcher dragonspawn (level 12 artillery)

Level 13 Encounter (XP 4,400)
✦ 4 githyanki warriors (level 12 soldier)
✦ 2 githyanki mindslicers (level 13 artillery)

Level 15 Encounter (XP 6,100)
✦ 3 githyanki warriors (level 12 soldier)
✦ 1 githyanki mindslicer (level 13 artillery)
✦ 1 githyanki gish (level 15 elite skirmisher)
✦ 1 nightmare (level 13 skirmisher)

(Left to right) githyanki mindslicer, githyanki warrior, and githyanki gish

GITHZERAI

GITHZERAI ARE SECRETIVE BEINGS with an ascetic and disciplined culture. They congregate in hidden monastic settlements across the Elemental Chaos and in remote corners of the world.

The githzerai and githyanki were once a single race enslaved by the mind flayers until they won their freedom, at which point a schism formed and the free gith turned on each other. After much bloodshed, the githyanki retreated to the Astral Sea and the githzerai withdrew to the Elemental Chaos.

Deep within the Elemental Chaos, the githzerai study chaos, disciplining their minds and bodies to better counter it. They are formidable psychic warriors when provoked and maintain a deep-seeded hatred for mind flayers and their evil githyanki kin.

Githzerai Cenobite		Level 11 Soldier
Medium natural humanoid		XP 600

Initiative +12 **Senses** Perception +13
HP 108; **Bloodied** 54
AC 27; **Fortitude** 22, **Reflex** 23, **Will** 23; see also *iron mind*
Speed 7; see also *inescapable fate*

(↓) **Unarmed Strike** (standard; at-will)
+17 vs. AC; 2d8 + 3 damage.

✝ **Stunning Strike** (standard; at-will)
+14 vs. Fortitude; 1d8 + 3 damage, and the target is stunned until the end of the githzerai cenobite's next turn.

Inescapable Fate (immediate reaction, when an adjacent enemy shifts away from the githzerai cenobite; at-will)
The cenobite shifts to remain adjacent to the enemy. The cenobite cannot use this power if the enemy shifts using a movement mode the cenobite does not possess.

Iron Mind (immediate interrupt, when the githzerai cenobite would be hit by an attack; encounter)
The githzerai cenobite gains a +2 bonus to all defenses until the end of its next turn.

Trace Chance (standard; recharge ⚅)
Ranged 5; no attack roll required; the next melee attack made against the target gains a +5 power bonus to the attack roll and, if it hits, it is automatically a critical hit.

Alignment Unaligned   **Languages** Common, Deep Speech
Skills Acrobatics +15, Athletics +9, Insight +13
Str 15 (+7)	**Dex** 17 (+8)	**Wis** 16 (+8)
Con 12 (+6)	**Int** 10 (+5)	**Cha** 11 (+5)

GITHZERAI CENOBITE TACTICS

A githzerai cenobite uses its *trace chance* power to ensure that its first hit is a good one. It then makes a *stunning strike* against its foe. It alternates between *unarmed strikes* and *stunning strikes* on subsequent rounds, using *inescapable fate* to stay within striking distance of its opponent.

Githzerai Zerth		Level 13 Elite Controller
Medium natural humanoid		XP 1,600

Initiative +12   **Senses** Perception +15
HP 248; **Bloodied** 124
AC 29; **Fortitude** 26, **Reflex** 28, **Will** 28; see also *iron mind*
Saving Throws +2
Speed 7
Action Points 1

(↓) **Unarmed Strike** (standard; at-will)
+18 vs. AC; 2d8 + 4 damage.

➶ **Inner Spark** (standard; at-will) ✦ **Lightning, Teleportation**
Ranged 5; +16 vs. Reflex; 1d8 + 4 lightning damage, and the target teleports 5 squares, to an unoccupied space of the zerth's choosing.

⬱ **Psychic Fists** (standard; encounter) ✦ **Psychic**
Close burst 5; targets enemies; +17 vs. Will; 1d8 + 4 psychic damage.

➶ **Reorder Chaos** (standard; recharge ⚄ ⚅) ✦ **Teleportation**
Ranged sight; up to 4 Medium or smaller targets; +17 vs. Fortitude; the targets teleport to swap spaces as the zerth chooses.

Avenging Wind (immediate interrupt, when targeted by a ranged attack; encounter) ✦ **Teleportation**
The attack targets another creature within 5 squares of the zerth, and the zerth teleports 10 squares into a square adjacent to the attacker.

Iron Mind (immediate interrupt, when the githzerai zerth would be hit by an attack; encounter)
The githzerai zerth gains a +2 bonus to all defenses until the end of its next turn.

Trace Chance (standard; recharge ⚅)
Ranged 5; no attack roll required; the next melee attack made against the target gains a +5 power bonus to the attack roll and, if it hits, it is automatically a critical hit.

Alignment Unaligned   **Languages** Common, Deep Speech
Skills Acrobatics +17, Athletics +10, Insight +15
Str 15 (+8)	**Dex** 19 (+10)	**Wis** 19 (+10)
Con 12 (+7)	**Int** 14 (+8)	**Cha** 13 (+7)

GITHZERAI ZERTH TACTICS

A githzerai zerth spends its action point to use *trace chance*, then attacks the same foe with *inner spark*, teleporting it to a space where it can be isolated and attacked. The zerth then closes in on its enemies, pounding them with *psychic fists* and using *avenging wind* to deflect a ranged attack and teleport next to its attacker. Between *unarmed strikes* and *inner spark* attacks, the zerth uses *reorder chaos* to alter the complexion of the battlefield, swapping allies and enemies to its advantage.

Githzerai Mindmage — Level 14 Artillery
Medium natural humanoid — XP 1,000

Initiative +13 — **Senses** Perception +16
HP 105; **Bloodied** 52
AC 28; **Fortitude** 24, **Reflex** 26, **Will** 26; see also *iron mind*
Speed 7

⊕ **Unarmed Strike** (standard; at-will)
+19 vs. AC; 2d8 + 4 damage.

↗ **Mindstrike** (standard; at-will) ✦ **Psychic**
Ranged 20; +17 vs. Reflex; 2d8 + 4 psychic damage, and the target is dazed (save ends); see also *accurate mind*.

↗ **Elemental Bolts** (standard; daily) ✦ see text
Ranged 10; the githzerai mindmage makes up to 3 attacks, each against a different target; +17 vs. Reflex; 4d8 acid, cold, fire, or lightning damage (the mindmage chooses the damage type for each attack); see also *accurate mind*.

✷ **Concussion Orb** (standard; encounter)
Area burst 2 within 10; +17 vs. Fortitude; 1d10 + 4 damage, and the target is knocked prone.

Accurate Mind
The githzerai mindmage's ranged attacks ignore cover and concealment (but not total cover or total concealment).

Iron Mind (immediate interrupt, when the githzerai mindmage would be hit by an attack; encounter)
The githzerai mindmage gains a +2 bonus to all defenses until the end of its next turn.

Alignment Unaligned — **Languages** Common, Deep Speech
Skills Acrobatics +18, Arcana +13, Athletics +10, Insight +16
Str 13 (+8) — **Dex** 19 (+11) — **Wis** 19 (+11)
Con 15 (+9) — **Int** 13 (+8) — **Cha** 10 (+7)

Githzerai Mindmage Tactics

This githzerai relies on ranged attacks, using its *accurate mind* power to ignore cover and concealment.

Githzerai Lore

A character knows the following information with a successful Nature check.

DC 20: Slaves in a long lost illithid empire, the githzerai were once one people with the githyanki. Philosophical differences split the freed people. The githzerai chose an introspective path, building monasteries in which they learn to harness the power of the mind and soul. Many of these monasteries are sequestered in the Elemental Chaos, although some githzerai sects maintain hidden refuges in the natural world.

DC 25: Most githzerai have martial arts training, enabling them to better protect their settlements. A few mix more arcane teachings with martial prowess, becoming multitalented githzerai called zerths.

DC 30: Githzerai warriors form parties to hunt the enemies of their people, particularly mind flayers. Githzerai are also encouraged to pursue their individual goals, some benign and others less so. Githzerai are as capable of evildoing as any sentient race, although particularly wicked githzerai tend to live outside of githzerai society.

DC 35: Zerthadlun, an austere walled settlement with many open fields and markets, is the greatest and most widely known githzerai city—an oasis of calm in the otherwise tumultuous Elemental Chaos. There, the githzerai contemplate order, destiny, entropy, and destruction. They perfect their bodies and minds, testing themselves against the dangers of the Elemental Chaos.

Encounter Groups

A githzerai can work with almost any creature, provided the alliance serves its needs.

Level 12 Encounter (XP 3,900)
✦ 3 githzerai cenobites (level 11 soldier)
✦ 1 guardian naga (level 12 elite artillery)
✦ 1 firelasher elemental (level 11 skirmisher)

Level 14 Encounter (XP 5,000)
✦ 1 githzerai mindmage (level 14 artillery)
✦ 1 githzerai zerth (level 13 elite controller)
✦ 4 githzerai cenobites (level 11 soldier)

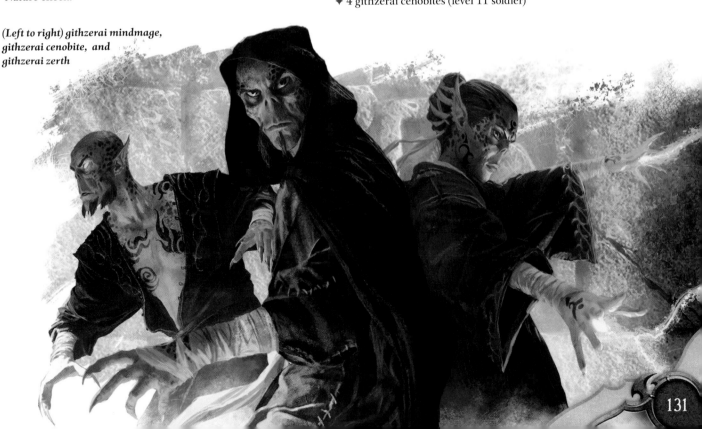

(Left to right) githzerai mindmage, githzerai cenobite, and githzerai zerth

Gnolls are feral, demon-worshiping marauders that kill, pillage, and destroy. They attack communities along the borderlands without warning and slaughter without mercy, all in the name of the demon lord Yeenoghu.

Gnoll Huntmaster		Level 5 Artillery
Medium natural humanoid		XP 200

Initiative +6   **Senses** Perception +11; low-light vision
HP 50; **Bloodied** 25
AC 19; **Fortitude** 16, **Reflex** 17, **Will** 14
Speed 7

(+) **Handaxe** (standard; at-will) ✦ **Weapon**
+9 vs. AC; 1d6 + 3 damage, or 1d6 + 5 damage while bloodied; see also *pack attack*.

↗ **Longbow** (standard; at-will) ✦ **Weapon**
Ranged 20/40; +10 vs. AC; 1d10 + 4 damage, or 1d10 + 6 damage while bloodied; see also *pack attack*.

Pack Attack
The gnoll huntmaster deals an extra 5 damage on melee and ranged attacks against an enemy that has two or more of the huntmaster's allies adjacent to it.

Alignment Chaotic evil   **Languages** Abyssal, Common
Skills Intimidate +7, Stealth +11

Str 16 (+5)	Dex 19 (+6)	Wis 14 (+4)
Con 14 (+4)	Int 8 (+1)	Cha 7 (+0)

Equipment leather armor, handaxe, longbow, quiver of 30 arrows

GNOLL HUNTMASTER TACTICS

A gnoll huntmaster often delays its initial turn, waiting until its allies move in and attack. The creature stays at the edge of its range, attacking with its longbow and using *pack attack* to deal extra damage.

Gnoll Claw Fighter		Level 6 Skirmisher
Medium natural humanoid		XP 250

Initiative +7   **Senses** Perception +6; low-light vision
HP 70; **Bloodied** 35
AC 20; **Fortitude** 18, **Reflex** 16, **Will** 15
Speed 8; see also *mobile melee attack*

(+) **Claw** (standard; at-will)
+11 vs. AC; 1d6 + 4 damage, or 1d6 + 6 while bloodied; see also *pack attack* below.

↓ **Clawing Charge** (standard; at-will)
The gnoll claw fighter charges and makes two claw attacks against a single target instead of one melee basic attack.

↓ **Mobile Melee Attack** (standard; at-will)
The gnoll claw fighter can move up to 4 squares and make one melee basic attack at any point during that movement. The gnoll doesn't provoke opportunity attacks when moving away from the target of its attack.

Pack Attack
The gnoll claw fighter deals an extra 5 damage on melee attacks against an enemy that has two or more of the gnoll claw fighter's allies adjacent to it.

Alignment Chaotic evil   **Languages** Abyssal, Common
Skills Intimidate +8

Str 19 (+7)	Dex 15 (+5)	Wis 12 (+4)
Con 14 (+5)	Int 9 (+2)	Cha 7 (+1)

Equipment leather armor

GNOLL CLAW FIGHTER TACTICS

This gnoll makes a *clawing charge* and then uses *mobile melee attack* to make claw attacks, positioning itself to reap the benefit of its *pack attack* power.

Gnoll Marauder		Level 6 Brute
Medium natural humanoid		XP 250

Initiative +5   **Senses** Perception +7; low-light vision
HP 84; **Bloodied** 42
AC 18; **Fortitude** 18, **Reflex** 15, **Will** 15
Speed 7

(+) **Spear** (standard; at-will) ✦ **Weapon**
+10 vs. AC; 1d8 + 6 damage, or 1d8 + 8 while bloodied; see also *quick bite* and *pack attack*.

↓ **Quick Bite** (free, when the gnoll marauder hits a bloodied enemy with a melee attack; at-will)
The gnoll marauder makes a bite attack against the same target: +7 vs. AC; 1d6 + 2 damage, or 1d6 + 4 damage while bloodied.

Pack Attack
The gnoll marauder deals an extra 5 damage on melee attacks against an enemy that has two or more of the marauder's allies adjacent to it.

Alignment Chaotic evil   **Languages** Abyssal, Common
Skills Intimidate +8, Stealth +10

Str 20 (+8)	Dex 14 (+5)	Wis 14 (+5)
Con 14 (+5)	Int 9 (+2)	Cha 7 (+1)

Equipment leather armor, light shield, spear

GNOLL MARAUDER TACTICS

Gnoll marauders gang up on a single target to gain the benefit of their *pack attack* power. It uses its *quick bite* against bloodied foes whenever possible.

Gnoll Demonic Scourge		Level 8 Brute (Leader)
Medium natural humanoid		XP 350

Initiative +6   **Senses** Perception +7; low-light vision
Leader of the Pack aura 5; allies in the aura gain a +1 bonus to attack rolls. While this creature is bloodied, the bonus increases to +2.
HP 106; **Bloodied** 53
AC 20; **Fortitude** 21, **Reflex** 18, **Will** 18
Speed 5

(+) **Heavy Flail** (standard; at-will) ✦ **Weapon**
+13 vs. AC; 2d6 + 5 damage, or 2d6 + 7 while bloodied; against a bloodied enemy, this attack also knocks the target prone; see also *pack attack*.

Bloodthirst
If the gnoll demonic scourge bloodies an enemy with a melee attack, an ally adjacent to the enemy can make a melee attack against that enemy as an immediate reaction.

Overwhelming Attack (free; encounter)
The gnoll demonic scourge applies its *bloodthirst* power to two allies instead of one.

Pack Attack
The gnoll demonic scourge deals an extra 5 damage on melee attacks against an enemy that has two or more of the demonic scourge's allies adjacent to it.

Alignment Chaotic evil   **Languages** Abyssal, Common
Skills Insight +10, Intimidate +13, Religion +10

Str 20 (+9)	Dex 14 (+6)	Wis 12 (+5)
Con 16 (+7)	Int 13 (+5)	Cha 15 (+6)

Equipment hide armor, heavy flail

GNOLL DEMONIC SCOURGE TACTICS

This gnoll leads weaker gnolls into battle, imparting the benefits of its *leader of the pack* aura while commanding nearby allies to concentrate their attacks on one target at a time. Like other gnolls, the demonic scourge attempts to shift into a position where it can gain the *pack attack* bonus. The first time it bloodies a foe and the opportunity to use *bloodthirst* arises, the demonic scourge uses *overwhelming attack*.

GNOLL LORE

A character knows the following information with a successful Nature check.

DC 15: Gnolls are nomadic and rarely stay in one place for long. When gnolls attack and pillage a settlement, they leave nothing behind except razed buildings and gnawed corpses. Gnolls often decorate their armor and encampments with the bones of their victims. Impatient and unskilled artisans, they wear patchwork armor and wield weapons stolen from their victims.

DC 20: Gnolls don't bargain or parley, and they can't be bribed or reasoned with. Gnolls are often encountered with hyenas, which they keep as pets and hunting animals. They also work with demons.

DC 25: Gnolls detest physical labor and often use slaves to perform menial chores. The life of a slave in a gnoll camp is brutal and short. That said, slaves who show strength and savagery might be indoctrinated into the gnoll vanguard. Such creatures are usually broken in mind and spirit, having become as cruel and ruthless as their captors.

DC 30: As the mortal instruments of the demon lord Yeenoghu, who is called the Beast of Butchery and Ruler of Ruin, gnolls constantly perform atrocities. When not scouring the land in Yeenoghu's name, gnolls fight among themselves and participate in rituals that involve acts of depravity and self-mutilation.

ENCOUNTER GROUPS

Gnolls raid and war in rapacious packs, their numbers supplemented by demons (especially evistros and barlguras), raving slaves, and beasts driven to madness and cruelty.

Powerful humanoids sometimes manage to take gnolls as slaves or even to raise gnoll pups as servants. Such gnolls serve their masters as fierce warriors.

Level 4 Encounter (XP 950)
✦ 1 gnoll huntmaster (level 5 artillery)
✦ 6 hyenas (level 2 skirmisher)

Level 6 Encounter (XP 1,250)
✦ 3 gnoll marauders (level 6 brute)
✦ 2 evistro demons (level 6 brute)

Level 7 Encounter (XP 1,550)
✦ 1 gnoll demonic scourge (level 8 brute)
✦ 2 gnoll claw fighters (level 6 skirmisher)
✦ 2 gnoll huntmasters (level 5 artillery)
✦ 1 cacklefiend hyena (level 7 brute)

(Left to right) gnoll marauder, gnoll demonic scourge, gnoll clawfighter, and gnoll huntmaster

GNOME

Gnomes are sly tricksters who excel at avoiding notice as they move between the Feywild and the world, driven by curiosity and wanderlust. When they are noticed, they tend to use humor to deflect attention and hide their true thoughts.

Gnome Skulk	Level 2 Lurker
Small fey humanoid	XP 125

Initiative +8   **Senses** Perception +2; low-light vision
HP 34; **Bloodied** 17
AC 16; **Fortitude** 14, **Reflex** 14, **Will** 12
Speed 5
(+) **War Pick** (standard; at-will) ✦ **Weapon**
    +7 vs. AC; 1d8 + 3 damage (crit 1d8 + 11).
➶ **Hand Crossbow** (standard; at-will) ✦ **Weapon**
    Ranged 10/20; +7 vs. AC; 1d6 + 3 damage.
Combat Advantage
    The gnome skulk deals an extra 1d6 damage on melee and ranged attacks against any target it has combat advantage against.
Fade Away (immediate reaction, when the gnome skulk takes damage; encounter) ✦ **Illusion**
    The gnome skulk turns invisible until it attacks or until the end of its next turn.
Reactive Stealth
    If a gnome has cover or concealment when it makes an initiative check at the start of an encounter, it can make a Stealth check to escape notice.
Shadow Skulk
    When a gnome skulk makes a melee or a ranged attack from hiding and misses, it is still considered to be hiding.

Alignment Unaligned   **Languages** Common, Elven
Skills Arcana +10, Stealth +11, Thievery +9
Str 8 (+0)   **Dex** 17 (+4)   **Wis** 12 (+2)
Con 16 (+4)   **Int** 14 (+3)   **Cha** 13 (+2)
Equipment leather armor, war pick, hand crossbow with 20 bolts

Gnome Skulk Tactics

A gnome skulk tries to gain combat advantage by surprising or flanking enemies, or by attacking dazed foes.

Gnome Arcanist	Level 3 Controller (Leader)
Small fey humanoid	XP 150

Initiative +1   **Senses** Perception +1; low-light vision
Aura of Illusion (Illusion) aura 5; the gnome arcanist and all allies in the aura gain concealment and can hide in the aura.
HP 46; **Bloodied** 23
AC 16; **Fortitude** 13, **Reflex** 15, **Will** 13
Speed 5; see also *fey step*
(+) **Dagger** (standard; at-will) ✦ **Weapon**
    +6 vs. AC; 1d4 damage.
➶ **Scintillating Bolt** (standard; at-will) ✦ **Radiant**
    Ranged 10; +6 vs. Fortitude; 1d6 + 4 radiant damage, and the target is dazed (save ends).
➶ **Startling Glamor** (minor; at-will) ✦ **Fear, Illusion**
    Ranged 10; +7 vs. Will; the target slides 1 square.
⟲ **Illusory Terrain** (standard; recharge ⚁ ⚂ ⚃) ✦ **Illusion**
    Close burst 5; targets enemies; +7 vs. Will; the target is slowed (save ends).
Fade Away (immediate reaction, when the gnome arcanist takes damage; encounter) ✦ **Illusion**
    The gnome arcanist turns invisible until it attacks or until the end of its next turn.
Fey Step (move; encounter) ✦ **Teleportation**
    The gnome arcanist teleports 5 squares.
Reactive Stealth
    If a gnome has cover or concealment when it makes an initiative check at the start of an encounter, it can make a Stealth check to escape notice.

Alignment Unaligned   **Languages** Common, Elven
Skills Arcana +12, Bluff +8, Insight +6, Stealth +8
Str 10 (+1)   **Dex** 10 (+1)   **Wis** 11 (+1)
Con 14 (+3)   **Int** 18 (+5)   **Cha** 15 (+3)
Equipment robes, dagger

Gnome Arcanist Tactics

This gnome hides within its *aura of illusion* until it's ready to attack. It uses *scintillating bolt* and *startling glamor* each round, dazing enemies and sliding them into positions where they can be flanked by the gnome arcanist's allies. When enemies get within 5 squares, it uses *illusory terrain* to further hinder them.

Gnome Lore

A character knows the following information with a successful Arcana check.

DC 15: Gnomes dwell in homes burrowed under the roots of trees. Their homes are easily overlooked by untrained eyes.

DC 20: When they feel threatened, gnomes use illusions to steer foes away from their homes or lure them into traps or ambushes.

Encounter Groups

Gnomes are commonly encountered with other fey. In the natural world, they often travel with elves, eladrin, or dwarves.

Level 3 Encounter (XP 750)
✦ 2 gnome arcanists (level 3 controller)
✦ 2 iron defenders (level 3 soldier)
✦ 1 pseudodragon (level 3 lurker)

GOBLIN

In common parlance, "goblin" refers to a specific sort of small, ill-tempered humanoid, but the word also refers to related beings of various sizes, such as bugbears and hobgoblins. Goblins are as prolific as humankind, but as a people, they're less creative and more prone to warlike behavior.

Most goblins live in the wild places of the world, often underground, but they stay close enough to other humanoid settlements to prey on trade caravans and unwary travelers. Goblins form tribes, each ruled by a chieftain. The chieftain is usually the strongest member of the tribe, though some chieftains rely on guile more than martial strength.

Hobgoblins rule the most civilized goblin tribes, sometimes building small settlements and fortresses that rival those of human construction. Goblins and bugbears, left to their own devices, are more barbaric and less industrious than hobgoblins. Bugbears are dominant in a few mixed tribes, but hobgoblins tend to rise above their more brutish cousins unless severely outnumbered.

A member of the goblin species has skin of yellow, orange, or red, often shading to brown. Its eyes have the same color variance; its hair is always dark. Big, pointed ears stick out from the sides of the head, and prominent sharp teeth sometimes jut from the mouth. Males have coarse body hair and might grow facial hair.

LORE

The following information about goblins can be obtained with a successful Nature check.

DC 15: Goblins' bellicose nature can be traced, in part, to their reverence for the god Bane, whom they see as the mightiest hobgoblin warchief in the cosmos. Some of Bane's exarchs are goblins. Maglubiyet, the Battle Lord, and Hruggek, the Master of Ambush, are most prominent among these.

DC 20: Hobgoblins once had an empire in which bugbears and goblins were their servants. This empire fell to internal strife and interference from otherworldly forces—perhaps the fey, whom many goblins hate.

DC 25: Hobgoblins developed mundane and magical methods for taming and breeding beasts as guards, laborers, and soldiers. They have a knack for working with wolves and worgs, and some drake breeds owe their existence directly to hobgoblin meddling. All goblins carry on this tradition of domesticating beasts.

DC 30: Given their brutal magical traditions, hobgoblins might have created their cousins in ancient times: Bugbears served as elite warriors, and goblins worked as scouts and infiltrators. The disintegration of hobgoblin power led to widespread and diverse sorts of goblin tribes.

THE GOBLIN FAMILY

There are goblins, and then there are *goblins*. The word "goblin" refers to both the goblin creature as well as to a family of creatures that include bugbears, hobgoblins, and regular goblins.

BUGBEAR

Big, tough goblins that love to fight, bugbears are the champions, picked guards, and muscle for more clever goblins.

Bugbears take whatever they want and bully others into doing their work. They hunt for food, eating any creature they can kill—including other goblins.

Bugbear Warrior		Level 5 Brute
Medium natural humanoid		XP 200

Initiative +5   **Senses** Perception +4; low-light vision
HP 76; **Bloodied** 38
AC 18; **Fortitude** 17, **Reflex** 15, **Will** 14
Speed 6
⊕ **Morningstar** (standard; at-will) ✦ **Weapon**
   +7 vs. AC; 1d12 + 6 damage.
⊢ **Skullthumper** (standard; encounter) ✦ **Weapon**
   Requires morningstar and combat advantage; +5 vs. Fortitude; 1d12 + 6 damage, and the target is knocked prone and dazed (save ends).
Predatory Eye (minor; encounter)
   The bugbear warrior deals an extra 1d6 damage on the next attack it makes with combat advantage. It must apply this bonus before the end of its next turn.
Alignment Evil   **Languages** Common, Goblin
Skills Intimidate +9, Stealth +11
Str 20 (+7)   **Dex** 16 (+5)   **Wis** 14 (+4)
Con 16 (+5)   **Int** 10 (+2)   **Cha** 10 (+2)
Equipment hide armor, morningstar

BUGBEAR WARRIOR TACTICS

Bugbear warriors are surprisingly sneaky for their size. They sometimes send out their smaller kin to lead overeager adventurers into a trap. If they can't achieve surprise, bugbear warriors look for chances to flank their foes.

STEVE PRESCOTT

Bugbear Strangler	Level 6 Lurker
Medium natural humanoid	XP 250

Initiative +11   **Senses** Perception +5; low-light vision
HP 82; **Bloodied** 46
AC 21; **Fortitude** 18, **Reflex** 18, **Will** 16; see also *body shield*
Speed 7

⊕ **Morningstar** (standard; at-will) ✦ **Weapon**
+10 vs. AC; 1d12 + 4 damage.

† **Strangle** (standard; sustain standard; at-will)
Requires combat advantage; +9 vs. Reflex; 1d10 + 4 damage, and the target is grabbed (until escape). A target trying to escape the grab takes a -4 penalty to the check. The bugbear strangler can sustain the power as a standard action, dealing 1d10 + 4 damage and maintaining the grab.

Body Shield (immediate interrupt, when targeted by a melee or a ranged attack against AC or Reflex; recharge ⚅ ⚅ ⚅)
The bugbear strangler makes its grabbed victim the target instead. The bugbear strangler can't use this power to redirect attacks made by a creature it is currently grabbing.

Predatory Eye (minor; encounter)
The bugbear strangler deals an extra 1d6 damage on the next attack it makes with combat advantage. It must apply this bonus before the end of its next turn.

Alignment Evil   **Languages** Common, Goblin
Skills Intimidate +10, Stealth +14
| **Str** 18 (+7) | **Dex** 18 (+7) | **Wis** 14 (+5) |
| **Con** 16 (+6) | **Int** 10 (+3) | **Cha** 10 (+3) |
Equipment leather armor, morningstar, rope garrote

BUGBEAR STRANGLER TACTICS

A bugbear strangler uses tactics similar to the bugbear warrior but likes to stay hidden for a round or two at the beginning of a fight. Only after most of its enemies are busy does the strangler attack, singling out a target that doesn't have much help nearby.

BUGBEAR LORE

A character knows the following information with a successful Nature check.

DC 15: A bugbear has little tolerance for talk and resorts to conversation only if the advantage of doing so is apparent. The most common situation is when foes are too strong to challenge openly.

DC 20: Bugbears often decapitate their foes to honor their greatest hero, Hruggek, who is known to decapitate his enemies.

GOBLIN

GOBLINS ARE WICKED, TREACHEROUS CREATURES that love plunder and cruelty. They're not very big or strong, but they're dangerous when they gang up.

Goblins breed quickly and can live most anywhere, from caves to ruins to a city's sewers. They survive by raiding and robbery, taking every usable item they can carry from their victims.

Goblin Cutter	Level 1 Minion
Small natural humanoid	XP 25

Initiative +3   **Senses** Perception +1; low-light vision
HP 1; a missed attack never damages a minion.
AC 16; **Fortitude** 12, **Reflex** 14, **Will** 11
Speed 6; see also *goblin tactics*

⊕ **Short Sword** (standard; at-will) ✦ **Weapon**
+5 vs. AC; 4 damage (5 damage if the goblin cutter has combat advantage against the target).

Goblin Tactics (immediate reaction, when missed by a melee attack; at-will)
The goblin shifts 1 square.

Alignment Evil   **Languages** Common, Goblin
Skills Stealth +5, Thievery +5
| **Str** 14 (+2) | **Dex** 17 (+3) | **Wis** 12 (+1) |
| **Con** 13 (+1) | **Int** 8 (-1) | **Cha** 8 (-1) |
Equipment leather armor, short sword

GOBLIN CUTTER TACTICS

Goblin cutters—like all goblins—don't fight fair. They gang up on a single enemy and quickly take advantage of *goblin tactics* to achieve flanking positions. If it dawns on them that they're losing the battle, they flee, hoping to live to fight another day.

Goblin Blackblade	Level 1 Lurker
Small natural humanoid	XP 100

Initiative +7   **Senses** Perception +1; low-light vision
HP 25; **Bloodied** 12
AC 16; **Fortitude** 12, **Reflex** 14, **Will** 11
Speed 6; see also *goblin tactics*

⊕ **Short Sword** (standard; at-will) ✦ **Weapon**
+5 vs. AC; 1d6 + 2 damage.

Combat Advantage
The goblin blackblade deals an extra 1d6 damage against any target it has combat advantage against.

Goblin Tactics (immediate reaction, when missed by a melee attack; at-will)
The goblin shifts 1 square.

Sneaky
When shifting, a goblin blackblade can move into a space occupied by an ally of its level or lower. The ally shifts into the blackblade's previous space as a free action.

Alignment Evil   **Languages** Common, Goblin
Skills Stealth +10, Thievery +10
| **Str** 14 (+2) | **Dex** 17 (+3) | **Wis** 12 (+1) |
| **Con** 13 (+1) | **Int** 8 (-1) | **Cha** 8 (-1) |
Equipment leather armor, short sword

GOBLIN BLACKBLADE TACTICS

Goblin blackblades have more stomach for melee than most goblins, preferring to flank a single enemy to gain combat advantage. When bloodied, they use their *sneaky* power to trade places with fresher goblins.

Goblin Warrior — Level 1 Skirmisher
Small natural humanoid · XP 100

Initiative +5 · **Senses** Perception +1; low-light vision
HP 29; **Bloodied** 14
AC 17; **Fortitude** 13, **Reflex** 15, **Will** 12
Speed 6; see also *mobile ranged attack* and *goblin tactics*

(+) **Spear** (standard; at-will) ✦ **Weapon**
+6 vs. AC; 1d8 + 2 damage.

(↗) **Javelin** (standard; at-will) ✦ **Weapon**
Ranged 10/20; +6 vs. AC; 1d6 + 2 damage.

(↗) **Mobile Ranged Attack** (standard; at-will)
The goblin warrior can move up to half its speed; at any point during that movement, it makes one ranged attack without provoking an opportunity attack.

Great Position
If, on its turn, the goblin warrior ends its move at least 4 squares away from its starting point, it deals an extra 1d6 damage on its ranged attacks until the start of its next turn.

Goblin Tactics (immediate reaction, when missed by a melee attack; at-will)
The goblin shifts 1 square.

Alignment Evil · **Languages** Common, Goblin
Skills Stealth +10, Thievery +10
Str 14 (+2) · **Dex** 17 (+3) · **Wis** 12 (+1)
Con 13 (+1) · **Int** 8 (–1) · **Cha** 8 (–1)
Equipment leather armor, spear, 5 javelins in sheaf

GOBLIN WARRIOR TACTICS

Goblin warriors would rather fight at range, using *great position* to deal more damage with their javelins. In melee combat, they use *goblin tactics* to maneuver into flanking positions. Once bloodied (or once they've seen several of their comrades cut down), warriors tend to flee and leave allies to fend for themselves.

Goblin Sharpshooter — Level 2 Artillery
Small natural humanoid · XP 125

Initiative +5 · **Senses** Perception +2; low-light vision
HP 31; **Bloodied** 15
AC 16; **Fortitude** 12, **Reflex** 14, **Will** 11
Speed 6; see also *goblin tactics*

(+) **Short Sword** (standard; at-will) ✦ **Weapon**
+6 vs. AC; 1d6 + 2 damage.

(↗) **Hand Crossbow** (standard; at-will) ✦ **Weapon**
Ranged 10/20; +9 vs. AC; 1d6 + 4 damage.

Sniper
When a goblin sharpshooter makes a ranged attack from hiding and misses, it is still considered to be hiding.

Combat Advantage
The goblin sharpshooter deals an extra 1d6 damage against any target it has combat advantage against.

Goblin Tactics (immediate reaction, when missed by a melee attack; at-will)
The goblin shifts 1 square.

Alignment Evil · **Languages** Common, Goblin
Skills Stealth +12, Thievery +12
Str 14 (+3) · **Dex** 18 (+5) · **Wis** 13 (+2)
Con 13 (+2) · **Int** 8 (+0) · **Cha** 8 (+0)
Equipment leather armor, short sword, hand crossbow with 20 bolts

GOBLIN SHARPSHOOTER TACTICS

Sharpshooters prefer hit-and-run tactics—if an enemy swings at a goblin and misses, the goblin usually skitters away to start its next turn at a safe distance.

Goblin Hexer — Level 3 Controller (Leader)
Small natural humanoid · XP 150

Initiative +3 · **Senses** Perception +2; low-light vision
HP 46; **Bloodied** 23
AC 17; **Fortitude** 14, **Reflex** 15, **Will** 16; see also *lead from the rear*
Speed 6; see also *goblin tactics*

(+) **Hexer Rod** (standard; at-will) ✦ **Weapon**
+7 vs. AC; 1d6 + 1 damage.

(↗) **Blinding Hex** (standard; at-will)
Ranged 10; +7 vs. Fortitude; 2d6 + 1 damage, and the target is blinded (save ends).

(↗) **Stinging Hex** (standard; recharge ⚄ ⚅)
Ranged 10; +7 vs. Will; the target takes 3d6 + 1 damage if it moves during its turn (save ends).

(✳) **Vexing Cloud** (standard; sustain minor; encounter) ✦ **Zone**
Area burst 3 within 10; automatic hit; all enemies within the zone take a –2 penalty to attack rolls. The zone grants concealment to the goblin hexer and its allies. The goblin hexer can sustain the zone as a minor action, moving it up to 5 squares.

(↗) **Incite Bravery** (immediate reaction, when an ally uses *goblin tactics*; at-will)
Ranged 10; the targeted ally can shift 2 more squares and make an attack.

Goblin Tactics (immediate reaction, when missed by a melee attack; at-will)
The goblin shifts 1 square.

Lead from the Rear (immediate interrupt, when targeted by a ranged attack; at-will)
The goblin hexer can change the attack's target to an adjacent ally of its level or lower.

Alignment Evil · **Languages** Common, Goblin
Skills Stealth +10, Thievery +10
Str 10 (+1) · **Dex** 15 (+3) · **Wis** 13 (+2)
Con 14 (+3) · **Int** 9 (+0) · **Cha** 18 (+5)
Equipment leather robes, hexer rod

GOBLIN HEXER TACTICS

The goblin hexer uses *lead from the rear* to turn nearby allies into meat shields while it casts *vexing cloud* around itself and its closest allies and enemies. It then targets an enemy defender with *stinging hex* and uses its *blinding hex* on foes making ranged attacks. When another goblin within 10 squares uses *goblin tactics*, the goblin hexer uses *incite bravery* to allow that goblin to make a free attack.

Goblin Skullcleaver — Level 3 Brute
Small natural humanoid · XP 150

Initiative +3 · **Senses** Perception +2; low-light vision
HP 53; **Bloodied** 26; see also *bloodied rage*
AC 16; **Fortitude** 15, **Reflex** 14, **Will** 12
Speed 5; see also *goblin tactics*

(+) **Battleaxe** (standard; at-will) ✦ **Weapon**
+6 vs. AC; 1d10 + 5 damage, or 2d10 + 5 while bloodied.

Bloodied Rage (while bloodied)
The goblin skullcleaver loses the ability to use *goblin tactics* and can do nothing but attack the nearest enemy, charging when possible.

Goblin Tactics (immediate reaction, when missed by a melee attack; at-will)
The goblin shifts 1 square.

Alignment Evil · **Languages** Common, Goblin
Skills Stealth +9, Thievery +9
Str 18 (+5) · **Dex** 14 (+3) · **Wis** 13 (+2)
Con 13 (+2) · **Int** 8 (+0) · **Cha** 8 (+0)
Equipment chainmail, battleaxe

GOBLIN SKULLCLEAVER TACTICS

Uncharacteristically brave, goblin skullcleavers charge boldly (perhaps foolishly) into melee and use *goblin tactics* to move into flanking positions. When bloodied, they fly into a savage rage, attacking without concern for their own wellbeing.

Goblin Underboss	Level 4 Elite Controller (Leader)
Small natural humanoid	XP 350

Initiative +4   **Senses** Perception +8; low-light vision
HP 110; **Bloodied** 55
AC 18; **Fortitude** 17, **Reflex** 15, **Will** 16; see also *survival instinct*
Speed 5; see also *superior goblin* tactics
(+) **Short Sword** (standard; at-will) ✦ **Weapon**
   +9 vs. AC; 1d6 + 4 damage. Miss: An adjacent ally makes a free basic attack.
Superior Goblin Tactics (immediate reaction, when missed by a melee attack; at-will)
   The goblin underboss and up to two allies within its line of sight shift 1 square.
Survival Instinct
   The goblin underboss gains a +3 bonus to defenses while bloodied.
Alignment Evil   **Languages** Common, Goblin
Skills Stealth +10, Thievery +10
Str 18 (+6)	**Dex** 14 (+4)	**Wis** 13 (+3)
Con 15 (+4)	**Int** 11 (+2)	**Cha** 16 (+5)

Equipment chainmail, short sword

GOBLIN UNDERBOSS TACTICS

The goblin underboss tries to stay adjacent to one or more allies and uses *superior goblin tactics* to move its allies into advantageous positions.

GOBLIN LORE

A character knows the following information with a successful Nature check.

DC 15: Goblins are cowardly and tend to retreat or surrender when outmatched. They are fond of taking slaves and often become slaves themselves.

DC 20: Goblins sleep, eat, and spend leisure time in shared living areas. Only a leader has private chambers. A goblin lair is stinking and soiled, though easily defensible and often riddled with simple traps designed to snare or kill intruders.

HOBGOBLIN

HOBGOBLINS LIVE FOR WAR AND BLOODSHED, killing or enslaving creatures weaker than themselves. More aggressive and organized than their goblin and bugbear cousins, they see all other creatures as lesser beings to be subjugated, and they reserve a special loathing for all fey, especially elves and eladrin.

Hobgoblins prize their possessions and make their own weapons and armor. Compared to their more brutish kin, they wear decent clothing and armor, and they maintain their personal armaments with care. Hobgoblins prefer bold colors, especially crimson and black.

Hobgoblin Grunt	Level 3 Minion
Medium natural humanoid	XP 38

Initiative +4   **Senses** Perception +1; low-light vision
HP 1: a missed attack never damages a minion.
AC 17 (19 with *phalanx soldier*); **Fortitude** 15, **Reflex** 13, **Will** 12
Speed 6
(+) **Longsword** (standard; at-will) ✦ **Weapon**
   +6 vs. AC; 5 damage.
Hobgoblin Resilience (immediate reaction, when the hobgoblin grunt suffers an effect that a save can end; encounter)
   The hobgoblin grunt makes a saving throw against the triggering effect.
Phalanx Soldier
   The hobgoblin grunt gains a +2 bonus to AC while at least one hobgoblin ally is adjacent to it.
Alignment Evil   **Languages** Common, Goblin
Skills Athletics +6, History +2
Str 18 (+4)	**Dex** 14 (+2)	**Wis** 13 (+1)
Con 15 (+2)	**Int** 10 (+0)	**Cha** 9 (-1)

Equipment leather armor, light shield, longsword

HOBGOBLIN GRUNT TACTICS

Hobgoblin grunts work so closely together that their maneuvers seem instinctual. They form strong lines so that they gain the benefit of *phalanx soldier* while preventing enemies from gaining flanking positions.

Hobgoblin Warrior	Level 8 Minion
Medium natural humanoid	XP 88

Initiative +7   **Senses** Perception +5; low-light vision
HP 1: a missed attack never damages a minion.
AC 22 (24 with *phalanx soldier*); **Fortitude** 20, **Reflex** 18, **Will** 18
Speed 6
(+) **Longsword** (standard; at-will) ✦ **Weapon**
   +10 vs. AC; 6 damage.
Hobgoblin Resilience (immediate reaction, when the hobgoblin warrior suffers an effect that a save can end; encounter)
   The hobgoblin warrior makes a saving throw against the triggering effect.
Phalanx Soldier
   The hobgoblin warrior gains a +2 bonus to AC while at least one hobgoblin ally is adjacent to it.
Alignment Evil   **Languages** Common, Goblin
Skills Athletics +9, History +5
Str 19 (+7)	**Dex** 14 (+5)	**Wis** 14 (+5)
Con 15 (+5)	**Int** 11 (+3)	**Cha** 10 (+3)

Equipment scale armor, light shield, longsword

HOBGOBLIN WARRIOR TACTICS

Hobgoblin warriors use the same tactics as hobgoblin grunts (see above), although they are more disciplined and fight to the last.

GUARDIAN

CONSTRUCTS CREATED BY SPELLCASTERS to serve as body-guards, guardians protect their masters with unswerving diligence.

Shield Guardian		Level 14 Soldier
Large natural animate (construct)		XP 1,000

Initiative +9   **Senses** Perception +15; darkvision
Shield Other aura 2; as long as its master is within the aura, the shield guardian grants its master a +2 bonus to all defenses and takes half of its master's damage until it is destroyed.
HP 138; **Bloodied** 69
AC 30; **Fortitude** 29, **Reflex** 22, **Will** 27
Immune charm, disease, fear, poison, sleep
Speed 4
(+) **Slam** (standard; at-will)
    Reach 2; +20 vs. AC; 2d6 + 7 damage.

Alignment Unaligned	**Languages** —	
Str 24 (+14)	**Dex** 10 (+7)	**Wis** 16 (+10)
Con 18 (+11)	**Int** 7 (+5)	**Cha** 9 (+6)

SHIELD GUARDIAN TACTICS

A shield guardian stays within 2 squares of its master and attacks whichever enemy poses the most immediate threat.

Battle Guardian		Level 17 Controller
Large natural animate (construct)		XP 1,600

Initiative +8   **Senses** Perception +15; darkvision
HP 163; **Bloodied** 81
AC 32; **Fortitude** 32, **Reflex** 26, **Will** 29
Immune charm, disease, fear, poison, sleep
Speed 8
(+) **Slam** (standard; at-will)
    Reach 2; +19 vs. AC; 3d6 + 7 damage, and the target is immobilized (save ends).
+ **Block Charge** (immediate interrupt, when an enemy ends the movement portion of a charge within 8 squares of the battle guardian; at-will)
    The battle guardian charges the enemy and makes a slam attack. The target is knocked prone on a hit.
Cover Retreat
    An ally adjacent to a battle guardian does not provoke opportunity attacks when moving, as long as that ally remains adjacent.

Alignment Unaligned	**Languages** —	
Str 24 (+14)	**Dex** 11 (+8)	**Wis** 14 (+10)
Con 19 (+12)	**Int** 7 (+6)	**Cha** 11 (+8)

BATTLE GUARDIAN TACTICS

When tasked with guard duty, a battle guardian uses its *block charge* and slam attacks to immobilize enemies while covering its master's retreat.

GUARDIAN LORE

A character knows the following information with a successful Arcana check.

DC 20: A guardian is created by means of a ritual, the main component of which is an amulet to which the guardian is keyed.

DC 25: A guardian obeys its master's verbal commands to the best of its ability, although it is not good for much beyond combat and simple manual labor. It can also be instructed to perform specific tasks at specific times or when certain conditions are met.

DC 30: If a guardian's master dies, the guardian carries out the last command it was given until its control amulet falls into the hands of a new owner and new orders are given.

ENCOUNTER GROUPS

Guardians are almost always encountered in the company of their creators.

Level 14 Encounter (XP 5,200)
✦ 1 shield guardian (level 14 soldier)
✦ 1 githzerai mindmage (level 14 artillery)
✦ 4 gray slaads (level 13 skirmisher)

WISE IN THE WAYS OF DARK MAGIC AND CURSES, hags sometimes choose to serve more powerful evil beings as advisors and soothsayers. Cruel and dangerous fey, hags haunt the Feywild and the lonely places of the world. Most hags are petty tyrants who prefer to bully weaker monsters and foment wicked schemes against mortals unfortunate enough to live close by.

HAG LORE

A character knows the following information with a successful Arcana check.

DC 15: Hags often know dark rituals that allow them to scry distant places, see into the future, manipulate the weather, or place curses on those who anger them. They gather in small groups called covens, thereby combining their ritual knowledge.

DC 20: Hags are living manifestations of nature's ugliness, much as eladrin and elves embody nature's beauty. Miserable and conniving, they seek to destroy those who are content in life. They like to collect treasure and will often impart knowledge or free captives in exchange for valuable items.

ENCOUNTER GROUPS

Any hag might be found bossing around dumb creatures such as trolls or ogres, or advising more powerful creatures such as giants.

Level 9 Encounter (XP 2,000)
✦ 2 howling hags (level 7 controller)
✦ 2 gnoll demonic scourges (level 8 brute)
✦ 2 barlgura demons (level 8 brute)

Level 10 Encounter (XP 2,600)
✦ 1 bog hag (level 10 skirmisher)
✦ 1 venom-eye basilisk (level 10 artillery)
✦ 2 shambling mounds (level 9 brute)
✦ 2 trolls (level 9 brute)

Bog hag

Howling Hag	Level 7 Controller
Medium fey humanoid	XP 300

Initiative +7   **Senses** Perception +10; low-light vision
Baleful Whispers (Psychic) aura 5; an enemy that ends its turn in the aura takes 1d6 psychic damage.
HP 83; **Bloodied** 41; see also *shriek of pain*
AC 21; **Fortitude** 20, **Reflex** 19, **Will** 18
Resist 10 thunder
Speed 6; see also *fey step*
⊕ **Quarterstaff** (standard; at-will) ✦ **Weapon**
+9 vs. AC; 1d8 + 4 damage.
↢ **Howl** (standard; at-will) ✦ **Thunder**
Close blast 5; +10 vs. Fortitude; 1d6 + 4 thunder damage, and the target is pushed 3 squares.
↢ **Shriek of Pain** (standard; recharges when first bloodied) ✦ **Thunder**
Close blast 5; +8 vs. Fortitude; 3d6 + 4 thunder damage, or 3d6 + 9 thunder damage if the howling hag is bloodied. *Miss:* Half damage.
Change Shape (minor; at-will) ✦ **Polymorph**
A howling hag can alter its physical form to appear as an old crone of any Medium humanoid race (see Change Shape, page 280).
Fey Step (move; encounter) ✦ **Teleportation**
The howling hag can teleport 10 squares.
Alignment Evil	**Languages** Common, Elven

Skills Bluff +11, Insight +10, Intimidate +11, Nature +10

Str 18 (+7)	**Dex** 18 (+7)	**Wis** 15 (+5)
Con 19 (+7)	**Int** 12 (+4)	**Cha** 16 (+6)

Equipment quarterstaff

HOWLING HAG TACTICS

A howling hag prefers to remain at range, attacking first with its *shriek of pain* and then using *howl*. When cornered, the hag uses *fey step* to escape.

Bog Hag	Level 10 Skirmisher
Medium fey humanoid (aquatic)	XP 500

Initiative +11   **Senses** Perception +7; low-light vision
Unwholesome Presence aura 3; enemies in the aura gain only half the normal hit points from spending healing surges.
HP 107; **Bloodied** 53; see also *rending claws*
AC 24; **Fortitude** 23, **Reflex** 21, **Will** 19
Speed 8 (swamp walk), swim 8
⊕ **Claw** (standard; at-will)
+15 vs. AC; 1d8 + 6 damage.
✦ **Rending Claws** (standard; recharges when first bloodied)
The bog hag makes two claw attacks against the same target; if both claws hit, the hag deals an extra 5 damage to the target.
Change Shape (minor; at-will) ✦ **Polymorph**
A bog hag can alter its physical form to appear as a beautiful young female elf, half-elf, eladrin, or human (see Change Shape, page 280).
Evasive Charge
The bog hag shifts 2 squares after charging.
Alignment Evil	**Languages** Common, Elven

Skills Intimidate +12, Nature +12, Stealth +14

Str 22 (+11)	**Dex** 18 (+9)	**Wis** 15 (+7)
Con 19 (+9)	**Int** 12 (+6)	**Cha** 14 (+7)

BOG HAG TACTICS

A bog hag rends its victims to pieces with its claws in a series of hit-and-run attacks, using *evasive charge* to move past enemies.

Death hag

NIGHT HAG TACTICS

A night hag uses its *change shape* power to assume a benign disguise, luring enemies within range of its *wave of sleep*. It then steps into the dreams of an unconscious victim to destroy its mind with nightmares, usually while the hag's minions or allies keep others from interfering.

Death Hag	Level 18 Soldier
Medium fey humanoid	XP 2,000

Initiative +15   **Senses** Perception +12; low-light vision
HP 171; **Bloodied** 85; see also *life drain*
AC 34; **Fortitude** 34, **Reflex** 31, **Will** 32
Resist 10 necrotic
Speed 6

⊕ **Claw** (standard; at-will) ✦ **Necrotic**
+24 vs. AC; 1d8 + 7 necrotic damage, and the target is marked and cannot spend healing surges or regain hit points until the end of the death hag's next turn.

↢ **Life Drain** (standard; recharge ⚁ ⚄ ⚅) ✦ **Healing, Necrotic**
Close blast 3; +22 vs. Fortitude; 1d8 + 4 necrotic damage, and the death hag regains 5 hit points for each creature damaged by this attack.

Change Shape (minor; at-will) ✦ **Polymorph**
A death hag can alter its physical form to appear as female of any Medium humanoid race (see Change Shape, page 280).

Alignment Evil   **Languages** Common, Elven
Skills Bluff +19, Insight +17, Intimidate +19, Nature +17

Str 25 (+16)	**Dex** 18 (+13)	**Wis** 17 (+12)
Con 19 (+13)	**Int** 16 (+12)	**Cha** 20 (+14)

DEATH HAG TACTICS

The death hag relishes melee combat and uses *life drain* as often as it can.

Night Hag	Level 14 Lurker
Medium fey humanoid	XP 1,000

Initiative +15   **Senses** Perception +10; darkvision
Shroud of Night aura 5; bright light in the aura is reduced to dim light, and dim light becomes darkness.
HP 109; **Bloodied** 54
AC 27; **Fortitude** 28, **Reflex** 26, **Will** 26
Speed 8

⊕ **Claw** (standard; at-will)
+19 vs. AC; 1d6 + 6 damage. If the night hag has combat advantage against the target, the target is also stunned (save ends).

⊹ **Dream Haunting** (standard; at-will) ✦ **Psychic**
The night hag moves into a stunned or unconscious creature's space and makes an attack against it; +18 vs. Will; 3d6 + 4 psychic damage, and the night hag disappears into the target's mind. While in this state, the night hag is removed from play and does nothing on subsequent turns except deal 3d6 + 4 psychic damage to the target (no attack roll required). As long as the target remains stunned or unconscious, the night hag can't be attacked. When the target is no longer stunned or unconscious, or when the target dies, the hag reappears adjacent to the target and is insubstantial until the start of its next turn.

↢ **Wave of Sleep** (standard; recharge ⚅) ✦ **Psychic, Sleep**
Close blast 5; +17 vs. Will; 1d8 + 3 psychic damage, and the target is dazed (save ends). *First Failed Save:* The target falls unconscious (no save).

Change Shape (minor; at-will) ✦ **Polymorph**
A night hag can alter its physical form to appear as an old crone of any Medium humanoid race (see Change Shape, page 280).

Alignment Evil   **Languages** Common, Elven
Skills Arcana +14, Bluff +16, Intimidate +16, Stealth +16

Str 22 (+13)	**Dex** 18 (+11)	**Wis** 17 (+10)
Con 19 (+11)	**Int** 14 (+9)	**Cha** 18 (+11)

Night hag

HALFLING

Halflings are a civilized race of plucky, clever riverfolk welcome in many lands. Small in size, halflings are tougher than they look and fearless in the face of danger.

Halflings live among other civilized races. They also band together in small riverside communities, fishing for food and using the rivers for travel.

Halfling Lore

A character knows the following information with a successful Nature check.

DC 15: Halflings are resourceful rovers who use the rivers of the world as roads. They're friendly and inclusive among strangers, and protective of their own kind. A reputation for hospitality but also minor larceny follows them.

Halfling Slinger		Level 1 Artillery
Small natural humanoid		XP 100

Initiative +4   **Senses** Perception +5
HP 22; **Bloodied** 11
AC 15; **Fortitude** 12, **Reflex** 15, **Will** 13; see also *nimble reaction*
Saving Throws +5 against fear effects
Speed 6
(✦) **Dagger** (standard; at-will) ✦ **Weapon**
     +4 vs. AC; 1d4 + 4 damage.
(➤) **Sling** (standard; at-will) ✦ **Weapon**
     Ranged 10/20; +6 vs. AC; 1d6 + 4 damage.
➤ **Stone Rain** (standard; recharge ⚃ ⚅) ✦ **Weapon**
     The halfling slinger makes three sling attacks, each with a –2 penalty to the attack roll.
Combat Advantage
     The halfling slinger deals an extra 1d6 damage on ranged attacks against any target it has combat advantage against.
Nimble Reaction
     Halflings gain a +2 racial bonus to AC against opportunity attacks.
Second Chance (immediate interrupt, when the halfling would be hit by an attack; encounter)
     The halfling slinger forces the attacker to reroll the attack and take the new result.
Sniper
     A hidden halfling slinger that misses with a ranged attack remains hidden.
Alignment Any   **Languages** Common, one other
Skills Acrobatics +6, Stealth +9, Thievery +11

Str 12 (+1)	**Dex** 18 (+4)	**Wis** 11 (+0)
Con 10 (+0)	**Int** 10 (+0)	**Cha** 14 (+2)

Equipment leather armor, dagger, sling with 20 bullets

Halfling Slinger Tactics

Halfling slingers like to set ambushes, using the Stealth skill to gain combat advantage and their *sniper* power to remain hidden. Once revealed, halfling slingers take cover and bombard enemies with sling stones from a safe distance.

Halfling Stout		Level 2 Minion
Small natural humanoid		XP 31

Initiative +3   **Senses** Perception +5
HP 1; a missed attack never damages a minion.
AC 16; **Fortitude** 12, **Reflex** 14, **Will** 14; see also *nimble reaction*
Saving Throws +5 against fear effects
Speed 6
(✦) **Short Sword** (standard; at-will) ✦ **Weapon**
     +7 vs. AC; 4 damage.
(➤) **Sling** (standard; at-will) ✦ **Weapon**
     Ranged 10/20; +7 vs. AC; 4 damage.
Nimble Reaction
     Halflings gain a +2 racial bonus to AC against opportunity attacks.
Second Chance (immediate interrupt, when the halfling would be hit by an attack; encounter)
     The halfling stout forces the attacker to reroll the attack and take the new result.
Alignment Any   **Languages** Common, one other
Skills Acrobatics +10, Thievery +10

Str 11 (+1)	**Dex** 15 (+3)	**Wis** 9 (+0)
Con 10 (+1)	**Int** 10 (+1)	**Cha** 14 (+3)

Equipment leather armor, short sword, sling with 20 bullets

Halfling Stout Tactics

Halfling stouts don't scare easily and therefore make reliable guards. They use *second chance* when hit by a damage-dealing attack.

Halfling Thief		Level 2 Skirmisher
Small natural humanoid		XP 125

Initiative +6   **Senses** Perception +1
HP 34; **Bloodied** 17
AC 16; **Fortitude** 13, **Reflex** 15, **Will** 14; see also *nimble reaction*
Saving Throws +5 against fear effects
Speed 6; see also *mobile melee attack*
(✦) **Dagger** (standard; at-will) ✦ **Weapon**
     +7 vs. AC; 1d4 + 3 damage.
(➤) **Dagger** (standard; at-will) ✦ **Weapon**
     Ranged 5/10; +7 vs. AC; 1d4 + 3 damage.
✦ **Mobile Melee Attack** (standard; at-will)
     The halfling thief can move up to 3 squares and make one melee basic attack at any point during that movement. The halfling thief doesn't provoke opportunity attacks when moving away from the target of its attack.
Combat Advantage
     The halfling thief deals an extra 1d6 damage on melee attacks against any target it has combat advantage against.
Nimble Reaction
     Halflings gain a +2 racial bonus to AC against opportunity attacks.
Second Chance (immediate interrupt, when the halfling would be hit by an attack; encounter)
     The halfling thief forces the attacker to reroll the attack and take the new result.
Alignment Any   **Languages** Common, one other
Skills Acrobatics +11, Stealth +9, Thievery +11

Str 12 (+2)	**Dex** 16 (+4)	**Wis** 11 (+1)
Con 10 (+1)	**Int** 10 (+1)	**Cha** 14 (+3)

Equipment leather armor, 4 daggers, thieves' tools

HALFLING THIEF TACTICS

Halfling thieves rely on their Stealth skill to gain surprise and combat advantage. If they can't surprise enemies, halfling thieves resort to hit-and-run tactics, looking for ways to flank foes and avoid retaliation.

Halfling Prowler	Level 6 Lurker
Small natural humanoid	XP 250

Initiative +11   **Senses** Perception +8
HP 52; **Bloodied** 26
AC 18; **Fortitude** 14, **Reflex** 17, **Will** 15; see also *crowd shield* and *nimble reaction*
Saving Throws +5 against fear effects
Speed 6
⊕ **Short Sword** (standard; at-will) ✦ **Poison, Weapon**
+10 vs. AC; 1d6 + 4 damage, and the halfling prowler makes a secondary attack. *Secondary Attack:* +8 vs. Fortitude; the target takes ongoing 3 poison damage and is slowed (save ends both).
⊕ **Hand Crossbow** (standard; at-will) ✦ **Poison, Weapon**
Ranged 10/20; +10 vs. AC; 1d6 + 4 damage, and the halfling prowler makes a secondary attack. *Secondary Attack:* +8 vs. Fortitude; the target takes ongoing 3 poison damage and is slowed (save ends both).
Catfall
If the halfling prowler falls, reduce the distance it falls by 20 feet when determining how much damage it takes.
Crowd Shield
The halfling prowler gains a +2 bonus to its AC and Reflex defense if it has one creature adjacent to it, or a +4 bonus if two or more creatures are adjacent to it.
Nimble Reaction
Halflings gain a +2 racial bonus to AC against opportunity attacks.
Second Chance (immediate interrupt, when the halfling would be hit by an attack; encounter)
The halfling prowler forces the attacker to reroll the attack and take the new result.
Alignment Any   **Languages** Common, one other
Skills Acrobatics +14, Athletics +9, Stealth +12, Streetwise +10, Thievery +14
Str 12 (+4)   **Dex** 18 (+7)   **Wis** 10 (+3)
Con 10 (+3)   **Int** 10 (+3)   **Cha** 15 (+5)
Equipment leather armor, poisoned short sword, hand crossbow with 10 poisoned bolts, thieves' tools

HALFLING PROWLER TACTICS

Halfling prowlers haunt both urban and wilderness settings, preying on treasure-laden passersby. They look for high vantage points to make crossbow attacks before leaping down and attacking with their short swords. They stay close to their allies and enemies, reaping the benefit of *crowd shield*. They typically flee when bloodied, easily outrunning their poisoned foes.

ENCOUNTER GROUPS

Halflings are most often found in homogenous clans or small criminal gangs. They also tame beasts, which they keep as pets and guardians.

Level 2 Encounter (XP 625)
✦ 4 halfling stouts (level 2 minion)
✦ 1 halfling thief (level 2 skirmisher)
✦ 2 guard drakes (level 2 brute)
✦ 1 needlefang drake swarm (level 2 soldier)

Level 2 Encounter (XP 700)
✦ 2 halfling slingers (level 1 artillery)
✦ 2 halfling thieves (level 2 skirmisher)
✦ 2 guard drakes (level 2 brute)

Level 6 Encounter (XP 1,350)
✦ 4 halfling prowlers (level 6 lurker)
✦ 2 human berserkers (level 4 brute)

HARPY

HARPIES USE THEIR SWEET SONGS to pacify victims before tearing them to pieces with their claws. They favor dismal, wild settings such as swamps, badlands, and scrubland. However, they also haunt rocky coasts, ruins, and caves.

Harpy		Level 6 Controller
Medium fey humanoid		XP 250

Initiative +5   **Senses** Perception +5
HP 71; **Bloodied** 35
AC 20; **Fortitude** 17, **Reflex** 17, **Will** 19
Resist 10 thunder
Speed 6, fly 8 (clumsy)
(+) **Claw** (standard; at-will)
+11 vs. AC; 1d8 + 2 damage.
(←) **Alluring Song** (standard; sustain minor; at-will) ✦ **Charm**
Close burst 10; deafened creatures are immune; +12 vs. Will; the target is pulled 3 squares and immobilized (save ends). When the harpy sustains the power, any target that has not yet saved against the effect is pulled 3 squares and immobilized (save ends).
(←) **Deadly Screech** (standard; recharge [5][6]) ✦ **Thunder**
Close burst 4; +12 vs. Fortitude; 1d6 + 4 thunder damage, and the target is dazed (save ends).
Alignment Evil   **Languages** Common
Skills Stealth +10
Str 15 (+5)   **Dex** 15 (+5)   **Wis** 14 (+5)
Con 15 (+5)   **Int** 10 (+3)   **Cha** 19 (+7)

HARPY TACTICS

A harpy uses its *alluring song* to draw enemies toward it. A clumsy flier, it lands and makes claw attacks against the most isolated target. It uses *deadly screech* against other enemies that get too close and takes to the air when confronted by multiple adversaries.

Bloodfire Harpy		Level 9 Soldier
Medium fey humanoid		XP 400

Initiative +10   **Senses** Perception +11
Burning Song (Fire) aura 20; enemies within the aura at the start of their turns take 5 fire damage (deafened creatures are immune).
HP 100; **Bloodied** 50
AC 25; **Fortitude** 23, **Reflex** 22, **Will** 23
Resist 10 fire
Speed 6, fly 8 (clumsy)
(+) **Claw** (standard; at-will) ✦ **Fire**
+14 vs. AC; 1d8 + 2 damage plus 1d8 fire damage.
(←) **Cloud of Ash** (standard; recharge [4][5][6]) ✦ **Fire**
The bloodfire harpy disgorges a cloud of burning ash. Close blast 3; +12 vs. Fortitude; 1d10 + 5 fire damage, and the target is blinded (save ends).
Alignment Evil   **Languages** Common
Str 15 (+6)   **Dex** 18 (+8)   **Wis** 14 (+6)
Con 20 (+9)   **Int** 12 (+5)   **Cha** 21 (+9)

BLOODFIRE HARPY TACTICS

The bloodfire harpy uses its *burning song* to boil the blood of its enemies while using *cloud of ash* to blind foes that get too close for comfort.

HARPY LORE

A character knows the following information with a successful Arcana check.

DC 15: Harpies can be either male or female. A male harpy and female harpy will share a nest just long enough to propagate, but once the eggs have been laid, the male abandons the nest and leaves the female to rear the hatchlings. For this reason, harpies are seldom encountered in mixed-gender groups.

DC 20: According to legend, harpies are descended from an evil elf witch-queen who often took the form of a golden eagle to spy on her subjects. A mighty hero drove her into exile long ago, breaking the magic tiara that allowed her to change shape. The elf-queen and her unscrupulous children were cursed with half-bird forms for the rest of their days. The alluring song of the harpy is a legacy of the sinister enchantments wielded by the long-lost elf-queen against her people.

ENCOUNTER GROUPS

Harpies are cruel, malicious, and domineering. They do not cooperate well with other creatures. However, they sometimes agree to serve powerful monsters or villains as scouts, spies, or assassins.

Level 6 Encounter (XP 1,250)
✦ 3 harpies (level 6 controller)
✦ 2 spined devils (level 6 skirmisher)

Level 8 Encounter (XP 1,750)
✦ 1 bloodfire harpy (level 9 soldier)
✦ 3 gnoll marauders (level 6 brute)
✦ 2 cacklefiend hyenas (level 7 brute)

Level 8 Encounter (XP 1,850)
✦ 2 harpies (level 6 controller)
✦ 1 sahuagin priest (level 8 artillery)
✦ 3 sahuagin raiders (level 6 soldier)

HELMED HORROR

An elemental spirit infuses a helmed horror, granting it intelligence and a cruel will. That will is usually bent to remorselessly carrying out the wishes of the helmed horror's creator.

Helmed Horror		Level 13 Soldier
Medium elemental animate (construct)		XP 800

Initiative +11   **Senses** Perception +15; darkvision, truesight 10
HP 131; **Bloodied** 65
Regeneration 5
AC 29; **Fortitude** 28, **Reflex** 23, **Will** 24
Immune charm, disease, fear, poison, sleep
Speed 6, fly 6 (clumsy)
⊕ **Elemental Greatsword** (standard; at-will) ✦ **Weapon; Cold, Fire, Lightning, or Thunder**
    +20 vs. AC; 1d10 + 7 damage plus 1d10 cold, fire, lightning, or thunder damage (helmed horror's choice).
† **Blade Sweep** (standard; encounter) ✦ **Weapon; Cold, Fire, Lightning, or Thunder**
    The helmed horror makes an elemental greatsword attack against two different targets within reach.
Tactical Step (free, when the helmed horror hits with an opportunity attack; at-will)
    The helmed horror shifts 2 squares.
Alignment Unaligned   **Languages** Common, Primordial
Skills Insight +15
Str 24 (+13)   **Dex** 16 (+9)   **Wis** 18 (+10)
Con 19 (+10)   **Int** 10 (+6)   **Cha** 14 (+8)
Equipment greatsword

Greater Helmed Horror		Level 18 Elite Soldier
Medium elemental animate (construct)		XP 4,000

Initiative +16   **Senses** Perception +20; darkvision, truesight 10
HP 348; **Bloodied** 174
Regeneration 10
AC 35; **Fortitude** 33, **Reflex** 30, **Will** 31
Immune charm, disease, fear, poison, sleep
Saving Throws +2
Speed 8, fly 8 (clumsy)
Action Points 1
⊕ **Elemental Greatsword** (standard; at-will) ✦ **Weapon; Cold, Fire, Lightning, or Thunder**
    +24 vs. AC; 1d10 + 8 damage plus 1d10 cold, fire, lightning, or thunder damage (helmed horror's choice).
† **Blade Sweep** (standard; encounter) ✦ **Weapon; Cold, Fire, Lightning, or Thunder**
    The greater helmed horror makes an elemental greatsword attack against two different targets within reach.
↞ **Elemental Burst** (standard; recharge ⚃ ⚅) ✦ **Cold, Fire, Lightning, or Thunder**
    Close burst 5; +20 vs. Reflex; 2d6 + 6 cold, fire, lightning, or thunder damage (greater helmed horror's choice).
Tactical Step (free, when the helmed horror hits with an opportunity attack; at-will)
    The greater helmed horror shifts 3 squares.
Alignment Unaligned   **Languages** Common, Primordial
Skills Insight +20
Str 26 (+17)   **Dex** 21 (+14)   **Wis** 22 (+15)
Con 22 (+15)   **Int** 12 (+10)   **Cha** 18 (+13)
Equipment greatsword

HELMED HORROR TACTICS

A helmed horror hovers toward enemies but lands to fight. It opens with *blade sweep* if it can, but it might also use that power to punish foes who dare flank it. After making an opportunity attack, it uses *tactical step* to maneuver around its foes to reach a soft target.

HELMED HORROR LORE

A character knows the following information with a successful Arcana check.

DC 20: Helmed horrors are created by means of an ancient ritual. A helmed horror has truesight and regeneration, and it can channel different kinds of energy through its greatsword.

ENCOUNTER GROUPS

A helmed horror can be found with any creature capable of creating it. Many serve as guardians.

Level 14 Encounter (XP 5,000)
✦ 2 helmed horrors (level 13 soldier)
✦ 1 mummy lord (level 13 elite controller)
✦ 3 firelasher elementals (level 11 skirmisher)

HOMUNCULUS

HOMUNCULI ARE MINOR CONSTRUCTS created to guard specific places, objects, or beings. They require no food or sleep, and they can maintain their watch indefinitely.

Homunculi can understand fairly complex orders, and they follow instructions with no thought of self-preservation (unless, of course, they are ordered to avoid taking damage).

GUARD

A homunculus can be attuned to a specific area, creature, or object, guarding it with its life. Attuning the homunculus to the desired area, creature, or object takes 1 minute and can be done only by the homunculus's creator or its new owner (as designated by its creator). The homunculus gains certain powers and benefits in this guard role (as noted in its statistics).

Guarded Area: A specific area up to 5 squares on a side.

Guarded Creature: A specific creature, typically (but not always) the homunculus's creator.

Guarded Object: A specific item of any size weighing up to 50 pounds.

Clay Scout	Level 2 Lurker
Small natural animate (construct, homunculus)	XP 125

Initiative +7 **Senses** Perception +6; darkvision
HP 31; **Bloodied** 15
AC 16; **Fortitude** 13, **Reflex** 14, **Will** 15
Immune disease, poison
Speed 6, fly 3 (clumsy)

ⓐ **Bite** (standard; at-will) ✦ **Poison**
+3 vs. AC; 1d6 damage, and the homunculus makes a secondary attack against the same target. *Secondary Attack:* +2 vs. Fortitude; the target is slowed (save ends). See also *guard object*.

⇺ **Mind Touch** (standard; at-will) ✦ **Psychic**
Ranged 10; +5 vs. Reflex; 1d6 + 3 psychic damage, and the target is dazed (save ends); see also *guard object*.

Guard Object
The clay scout gains a +4 bonus to attack rolls against targets adjacent to or carrying its guarded object (see the "Guard" sidebar).

Limited Invisibility ✦ **Illusion**
The clay scout is invisible to dazed creatures.

Redirect (immediate interrupt, when targeted by a melee or a ranged attack; at-will)
The clay scout makes an attack against the attacker: +4 vs. Will; the triggering attack targets a creature adjacent to the clay scout instead (as chosen by the clay scout).

Alignment Unaligned   **Languages** —
Skills Stealth +8
Str 10 (+1)   **Dex** 15 (+3)   **Wis** 10 (+1)
Con 13 (+2)   **Int** 10 (+1)   **Cha** 16 (+4)

CLAY SCOUT TACTICS

A clay scout is often tasked with guarding an object. It tries to remain unseen until it attacks, preferring to use *mind touch* to daze enemies (thus becoming invisible to them). It then tries to bite creatures that can't see it while using *redirect* to protect itself.

Iron Defender	Level 3 Soldier
Medium natural animate (construct, homunculus)	XP 150

Initiative +5   **Senses** Perception +6; darkvision
HP 47; **Bloodied** 23
AC 18; **Fortitude** 16, **Reflex** 15, **Will** 13
Immune disease, poison
Speed 6

ⓐ **Bite** (standard; at-will)
+8 vs. AC; 1d8 + 3 damage.

✝ **Guard Creature** (immediate reaction, when an adjacent enemy attacks the creature guarded by the iron defender; at-will)
The iron defender makes a bite attack against the enemy (see the "Guard" sidebar).

Pursue and Attack
When the iron defender makes an opportunity attack, it shifts 1 square before or after the attack.

Alignment Unaligned   **Languages** —
Str 16 (+4)   **Dex** 15 (+3)   **Wis** 11 (+1)
Con 15 (+3)   **Int** 5 (-2)   **Cha** 8 (+0)

IRON DEFENDER TACTICS

An iron defender is often tasked with guarding another creature, usually its creator. It uses *pursue and attack* to stay close to its charge.

HOMUNCULUS LORE

A character knows the following information with a successful Arcana check.

DC 15: A homunculus obeys its creator until he or she specifies a new owner, at which point the homunculus bonds with its new master. A homunculus is often tasked with guarding a specific creature, object, or location and gains powers that better enable it to perform this task.

ENCOUNTER GROUPS

Homunculi can be ordered to obey new masters, so a number of these constructs eventually pass out of the control of the wizards who create them and wind up serving others.

Level 9 Encounter (XP 1,950)
- ✦ 2 iron cobras (level 6 skirmisher)
- ✦ 2 snaketongue warriors (level 8 brute)
- ✦ 1 snaketongue assassin (level 9 lurker)

Iron Cobra	Level 6 Skirmisher
Medium natural animate (construct, homunculus)	XP 250

Initiative +7   **Senses** Perception +9; darkvision
HP 75; **Bloodied** 37
AC 20; **Fortitude** 20, **Reflex** 18, **Will** 17
Immune disease, poison
Speed 7; see also *slithering shift*

ⓟ **Bite** (standard; at-will) ✦ **Poison**
   +11 vs. AC; 1d8 + 3 damage, and ongoing 5 poison damage (save ends).

↗ **Poison the Mind** (standard; recharge ▪ ▪▪ ▪▪ ▪▪) ✦ **Psychic**
   Ranged 10; affects only creatures taking ongoing poison damage; +8 vs. Will; the target is dazed and slowed (save ends both); see also *guard area*.

Guard Area
   An iron cobra can use its *poison the mind* power against any creature in its guarded area (see the "Guard" sidebar), even if the power hasn't recharged and even if the target isn't taking ongoing poison damage.

Slithering Shift (move; at-will)
   The iron cobra shifts 3 squares as a move action.

Alignment Unaligned	**Languages** –	

Skills Stealth +10

Str 17 (+6)	**Dex** 15 (+5)	**Wis** 13 (+4)
Con 19 (+7)	**Int** 5 (+0)	**Cha** 12 (+4)

IRON COBRA TACTICS

An iron cobra is often tasked with guarding an area. It attacks with its poisonous bite first and uses *poison the mind* against the envenomed creature before moving on to the next target using *slithering shift*.

HOOK HORROR

Hook horrors drag victims to their deaths using their powerful hooked arms. These pack omnivores scour the Underdark in search of live prey, foraging when necessary.

Hook horrors communicate with one another using a complex series of clicking noises they make with their mouths and carapace. The eerie clicks echo in the Underdark, warning prey that death is near.

Hook Horror	Level 13 Soldier
Large natural beast	XP 800

Initiative +12   **Senses** Perception +9; blindsight 10
HP 137; **Bloodied** 68
AC 28; **Fortitude** 27, **Reflex** 24, **Will** 24
Speed 4, climb 4
(+) **Hook** (standard; at-will)
    Reach 2; +20 vs. AC; 1d12 + 7 damage, and the target is pulled 1 square.
† **Rending Hooks** (standard; at-will)
    The hook horror makes two hook attacks, each at a -2 penalty. If both hooks hit the same target, the hook horror deals an extra 1d12 damage and the target is grabbed (until escape).
† **Bite** (minor 1/round; at-will)
    Grabbed target only; +20 vs. AC; 1d8 + 7 damage.
† **Fling** (standard; recharge ⚅)
    +19 vs. Fortitude; 2d12 + 7 damage, and the target slides 3 squares and is knocked prone.
Alignment Unaligned   **Languages** –
Skills Athletics +18
Str 24 (+13)   **Dex** 19 (+10)   **Wis** 16 (+9)
Con 25 (+13)   **Int** 3 (+2)   **Cha** 12 (+7)

HOOK HORROR LORE

A character knows the following information with a successful Nature check.

DC 20: Hook horrors live in total darkness. They can see in lit environments, but in the dark of the deep earth they navigate using echolocation. They also make clicking noises to communicate with one another. An Underdark explorer might become aware of nearby hook horrors by these noises.

DC 25: Although they hunt in small packs, hook horrors also gather in larger groups called clans. A particular clan, ruled by its strongest egg-laying female, ranges over a wide area in the Underdark. Its members defend clan territory fiercely from any intruder, including unrelated hook horrors.

DC 30: Hook horrors are omnivorous but prefer meat to plants. Rumor has it that they prefer the flesh of drow over any other. Not surprisingly, drow slay wild hook horrors and take young and eggs to raise as slaves.

ENCOUNTER GROUPS

Humanoids sometimes capture and train hook horrors as guardian beasts and shock troops.

Level 13 Encounter (XP 4,000)
✦ 3 hook horrors (level 13 soldier)
✦ 1 balhannoth (level 13 elite lurker)

Level 13 Encounter (XP 4,000)
✦ 1 hook horror (level 13 soldier)
✦ 2 grimlock berserkers (level 13 brute)
✦ 1 beholder eye of flame (level 13 elite artillery)

HOOK HORROR TACTICS

Hook horrors are so good at climbing and jumping that they often attack from an unexpected direction. A hook horror prefers to get close enough to use *rending hooks*, followed by a *bite*. It uses its melee basic attack to drag prey closer.

A hook horror sometimes flings a tasty victim at the feet of its packmates, but it more typically uses its *fling* power to toss aside prey that has proven too difficult to kill.

HORSE

Horses are widely used as riding mounts and beasts of burden. Wild horses are also common sights in the valleys and plains of the world, as well as the Feywild.

Celestial chargers are a special breed infused with divine energy and bred to serve the noblest warriors. They are much smarter than normal horses. Although it does not speak, a celestial charger dimly understands its rider's language.

Encounter Groups

Herds of wild horses roam the world's plains and valleys, but an encounter with a horse almost always involves dealing with a mount and its rider.

Level 4 Encounter (XP 900)
✦ 3 warhorses (level 3 brute)
✦ 3 human guards (level 3 soldier)

Riding Horse		Level 1 Brute
Large natural beast		XP 100
Initiative +1	**Senses** Perception +5; low-light vision	
HP 36; **Bloodied** 18		
AC 14; **Fortitude** 15, **Reflex** 13, **Will** 10		
Speed 10		
⊕ **Kick** (standard; at-will)		
+4 vs. AC; 1d6 + 4 damage.		
Alignment Unaligned	**Languages** —	
Str 19 (+4)	**Dex** 13 (+1)	**Wis** 11 (+0)
Con 16 (+3)	**Int** 2 (−4)	**Cha** 9 (−1)

Riding Horse Tactics

Riding horses usually panic and bolt when faced with danger, striking out with their hooves only when trapped or startled.

Warhorse		Level 3 Brute
Large natural beast (mount)		XP 150
Initiative +3	**Senses** Perception +8; low-light vision	
HP 58; **Bloodied** 29		
AC 17; **Fortitude** 16, **Reflex** 14, **Will** 14		
Speed 8		
⊕ **Kick** (standard; at-will)		
+6 vs. AC; 1d6 + 5 damage.		
↟ **Trample** (standard; at-will)		
The warhorse can move up to its speed and enter enemies' spaces. This movement provokes opportunity attacks, and the warhorse must end its move in an unoccupied space. When it enters an enemy's space, the warhorse makes a trample attack: +4 vs. Reflex; 1d6 + 6 damage, and the target is knocked prone.		
Charger (while mounted by a friendly rider of 3rd level or higher; at-will) ✦ **Mount**		
The warhorse grants its rider a +5 bonus to damage rolls on charge attacks.		
Alignment Unaligned	**Languages** —	
Str 21 (+6)	**Dex** 14 (+3)	**Wis** 14 (+3)
Con 18 (+5)	**Int** 2 (−3)	**Cha** 10 (+1)

Warhorse Tactics

Unlike riding horses, warhorses are trained for battle. When ridden aggressively, they lash out with their hooves or trample foes underfoot.

Celestial Charger		Level 10 Soldier
Large immortal beast (mount)		XP 500
Initiative +10	**Senses** Perception +12; low-light vision	
HP 111; **Bloodied** 55		
AC 26; **Fortitude** 24, **Reflex** 22, **Will** 21		
Saving Throws +5 against fear effects		
Speed 8; see also *zephyr footing*		
⊕ **Kick** (standard; at-will)		
+16 vs. AC; 1d8 + 6 damage.		
↟ **Trample** (standard; at-will)		
The celestial charger can move up to its speed and enter enemies' spaces. This movement provokes opportunity attacks, and the celestial charger must end its move in an unoccupied space. When it enters an enemy's space, the charger makes a trample attack: +14 vs. Reflex; 1d8 + 6 damage, and the target is knocked prone.		
Celestial Charge (while mounted by a friendly rider of 10th level or higher; at-will) ✦ **Mount, Radiant**		
On charge attacks, a celestial charger's rider deals an extra 2d6 radiant damage.		
Zephyr Footing		
The celestial charger ignores difficult terrain and can move across any solid or liquid surface.		
Alignment Lawful good	**Languages** —	
Skills Endurance +16		
Str 23 (+11)	**Dex** 17 (+8)	**Wis** 15 (+7)
Con 23 (+11)	**Int** 3 (+1)	**Cha** 15 (+7)

Celestial Charger Tactics

These noble steeds charge fearlessly into battle, trampling enemies while ignoring difficult terrain.

HOUND

Hounds are ferocious beasts that serve as loyal companions to a wide variety of creatures, often assisting their masters in hunting, tracking, and killing prey.

HELL HOUND

Hell hounds breathe fire and gather in fearsome packs that live in barren mountains, deserts, and fiery caverns.

Hell Hound Tactics

Hell hounds bound into the midst of their enemies and use their *fiery breath* with abandon, not hesitating to include other hell hounds in its area.

Firebred hell hounds use tactics similar to hell hounds, saving their *fiery burst* power for when they're flanked or otherwise surrounded.

Hell Hound Lore

A character knows the following information with a successful Arcana check.

DC 15: Primordials created hell hounds when the world was young. Even though the beasts did not originate in the Nine Hells, they are so named because of their fiery and terrifying aspect.

DC 20: Fire giants bred captive populations of hell hounds thousands of years ago, selecting them for size and prowess, until they crafted the firebred hell hound. Firebred hell hounds possess an instinctive loyalty to their age-old masters.

Hell Hound		Level 7 Brute
Medium elemental beast (fire)		XP 300

Initiative +5   **Senses** Perception +11
Fire Shield (Fire) aura 1; any creature that enters or begins its turn in the aura takes 1d6 fire damage.
HP 96; **Bloodied** 48
AC 20; **Fortitude** 18, **Reflex** 17, **Will** 18
Resist 20 fire
Speed 7
⊕ **Bite** (standard; at-will) ✦ **Fire**
  +10 vs. AC; 1d8 + 2 plus 1d8 fire damage.
↤ **Fiery Breath** (standard; recharge ⚄ ⚅ ⚀) ✦ **Fire**
  Close blast 3; +9 vs. Reflex; 2d6 + 3 fire damage.

Alignment Unaligned	**Languages** –	
Str 14 (+5)	**Dex** 14 (+5)	**Wis** 17 (+6)
Con 16 (+6)	**Int** 2 (–1)	**Cha** 10 (+3)

Firebred Hell Hound		Level 17 Brute
Medium elemental beast (fire)		XP 1,600

Initiative +10   **Senses** Perception +17
Fire Shield (Fire) aura 1; any creature that enters or begins its turn in the aura takes 1d10 fire damage.
HP 205; **Bloodied** 102
AC 30; **Fortitude** 30, **Reflex** 28, **Will** 29
Resist 40 fire
Speed 8
⊕ **Bite** (standard; at-will) ✦ **Fire**
  +20 vs. AC; 1d10 + 6 plus 1d10 fire damage.
↤ **Fiery Breath** (standard; recharge ⚄ ⚅ ⚀) ✦ **Fire**
  Close blast 3; +18 vs. Reflex; 4d6 + 7 fire damage.
↤ **Fiery Burst** (standard; recharge ⚀) ✦ **Fire**
  Close burst 3; +18 vs. Reflex; 4d10 + 7 fire damage.

Alignment Unaligned	**Languages** –	
Str 22 (+14)	**Dex** 14 (+10)	**Wis** 19 (+12)
Con 25 (+15)	**Int** 2 (+4)	**Cha** 12 (+9)

Encounter Groups

Hell hounds serve as faithful pets to many different creatures, including fire giants and azers.

Level 17 Encounter (XP 8,000)
✦ 2 firebred hell hounds (level 17 brute)
✦ 2 azer beastlords (level 17 soldier)
✦ 1 azer taskmaster (level 17 controller)

SHADOW HOUND

Monsters of the Shadowfell use these feared hunters to harry the daylit lands, kill hapless travelers, or track impudent heroes. Shadow hounds sometimes slip into the natural world on their own, roving in packs, predating on villages, and foreshadowing death with their baying howls.

Shadow Hound		Level 6 Skirmisher
Medium shadow magical beast		XP 250

Initiative +7   **Senses** Perception +9; darkvision
Shroud of Night aura 5; bright light in the aura is reduced to dim light, and dim light becomes darkness.
HP 70; **Bloodied** 35
AC 19; **Fortitude** 20, **Reflex** 18, **Will** 17
Vulnerable 5 radiant
Speed 7, teleport 7
⊕ **Bite** (standard; at-will)
  +11 vs. AC; 1d8 + 4 damage; see also *shadow ambush*.
↤ **Baying** (minor; recharge ⚄ ⚀) ✦ **Fear**
  Close burst 5; deafened creatures are immune; +8 vs. Will; the target takes a –2 penalty to all defenses until the end of the shadow hound's next turn.
Shadow Ambush
  When the shadow hound teleports adjacent to an enemy, it gains combat advantage and deals an extra 1d6 damage on the next attack it makes against that enemy this turn.

Alignment Unaligned	**Languages** –	
Skills Endurance +10, Stealth +10		
Str 19 (+7)	**Dex** 15 (+5)	**Wis** 13 (+4)
Con 14 (+5)	**Int** 6 (+1)	**Cha** 16 (+6)

Shadow Hound Tactics

Shadow hounds trail their quarry until they find a place where the shadows are deep and dark—a lonely forest road, a deserted alley, a campsite after dusk. They use their *baying* at the start of the encounter to terrify their quarry, and then use *shadow ambush* to teleport next to victims.

SHADOW HOUND LORE

A character knows the following information with a successful Arcana check.

DC 15: When a shadow hound catches the scent of its prey, nothing can discourage it from making the kill. When it eventually finds its prey, it sounds its whispery, hunting bay.

ENCOUNTER GROUPS

Some shadow hounds are tamed by shadar-kai, vampires, and other creatures of the night.

Level 6 Encounter (XP 1,300)
✦ 2 shadow hounds (level 6 skirmisher)
✦ 2 shadar-kai gloomblades (level 6 lurker)
✦ 1 shadar-kai witch (level 7 controller)

WILD HUNT HOUND

GREAT LORDS OF THE FEYWILD BREED THESE MASTIFFS as hunting hounds. They are savage and dangerous, eager to pull down whatever quarry they are set on.

WILD HUNT HOUND TACTICS

Wild hunt hounds growl constantly, filling the hearts of nearby mortals with bonechilling terror. In battle they begin with a few rounds of hit-and-run attacks to harry and separate their quarry from its fellows.

WILD HUNT HOUND LORE

A character knows the following information with a successful Arcana check.

DC 25: Allowed to drink from the pure heart springs of the Feywild, wild hunt hounds are infused with a vigor unmatched by lesser dogs. They tirelessly guard the manors of eladrin nobles and accompany them on great hunts.

Wild Hunt Hound	**Level 21 Skirmisher**
Medium fey magical beast	XP 3,200

Initiative +21   **Senses** Perception +23; low-light vision
Menacing Growl (Fear) aura 10; enemies within the aura take a -2 penalty to all defenses.
HP 205; **Bloodied** 102
AC 35 (37 against opportunity attacks); **Fortitude** 34, **Reflex** 33, **Will** 32
Speed 10, fly 10 (clumsy); see also *mobile melee attack*
⚔ **Bite** (standard; at-will)
     +26 vs. AC; 1d8 + 10 damage (1d8 + 20 against an immobilized enemy), and the target cannot teleport and is slowed (save ends both). If the target is already slowed, it is immobilized instead.
⚔ **Mobile Melee Attack** (standard; at-will)
     The wild hunt hound can move up to 5 squares and make one bite attack at any point during that movement. The hound doesn't provoke opportunity attacks when moving away from the target of its attack.
Combat Advantage
     The wild hunt hound deals an extra 1d8 damage on melee attacks against any target it has combat advantage against.
Alignment Unaligned   **Languages** —
Skills Endurance +24, Stealth +24
| **Str** 30 (+20) | **Dex** 28 (+19) | **Wis** 27 (+18) |
| **Con** 29 (+19) | **Int** 6 (+8) | **Cha** 9 (+9) |

ENCOUNTER GROUPS

Wild hunt hounds can be encountered as a pack, or as part of a group led by a powerful fey creature.

Level 20 Encounter (XP 15,200)
✦ 4 wild hunt hounds (level 21 skirmisher)
✦ 1 bralani of autumn winds (level 19 controller)

HUMAN

Humans are the most diverse humanoid race in appearance, habits, outlook, motivations, and talents. Human settlements are found in every terrain and climate, from the depths of tropical jungles to the frozen polar wastes.

If humans have a failing, it's their corruptibility. Although they are capable of great achievements and tremendously noble acts, they are also easily overcome by greed and the promise of power.

Human Rabble		Level 2 Minion
Medium natural humanoid		XP 31

Initiative +0   **Senses** Perception +0
HP 1; a missed attack never damages a minion.
AC 15; **Fortitude** 13, **Reflex** 11, **Will** 11; see also *mob rule*
Speed 6
  ⊕ **Club** (standard; at-will) ✦ **Weapon**
    +6 vs. AC; 4 damage.
Mob Rule
    The human rabble gains a +2 power bonus to all defenses while at least two other human rabble are within 5 squares of it.

Alignment Any	**Languages** Common	
Str 14 (+2)	**Dex** 10 (+0)	**Wis** 10 (+0)
Con 12 (+1)	**Int** 9 (-1)	**Cha** 11 (+0)

Equipment club

HUMAN RABBLE TACTICS
Human rabble don't really have tactics, other than to gang up on the nearest target. They are rarely inclined to fight to the death.

Human Lackey		Level 7 Minion
Medium natural humanoid		XP 75

Initiative +3   **Senses** Perception +4
HP 1; a missed attack never damages a minion.
AC 19; **Fortitude** 17, **Reflex** 14, **Will** 15; see also *mob rule*
Speed 6
  ⊕ **Club** (standard; at-will) ✦ **Weapon**
    +12 vs. AC; 6 damage.
Mob Rule
    The human lackey gains a +2 power bonus to all defenses while at least two other human lackeys are within 5 squares of it.

Alignment Any	**Languages** Common	
Str 16 (+6)	**Dex** 11 (+3)	**Wis** 12 (+4)
Con 14 (+5)	**Int** 10 (+3)	**Cha** 13 (+4)

Equipment leather armor, club

HUMAN LACKEY TACTICS
Lackeys are a cut above rabble, and can be fiercely loyal to a powerful or charismatic leader. They are likely to break and run if their leader is defeated.

Human Bandit		Level 2 Skirmisher
Medium natural humanoid		XP 125

Initiative +6   **Senses** Perception +1
HP 37; **Bloodied** 18
AC 16; **Fortitude** 12, **Reflex** 14, **Will** 12
Speed 6
  ⊕ **Mace** (standard; at-will) ✦ **Weapon**
    +4 vs. AC; 1d8 + 1 damage, and the human bandit shifts 1 square.
  ⊗ **Dagger** (standard; at-will) ✦ **Weapon**
    Ranged 5/10; +6 vs. AC; 1d4 + 3 damage.
  ✦ **Dazing Strike** (standard; encounter) ✦ **Weapon**
    Requires mace; +4 vs. AC; 1d8 + 1 damage, the target is dazed until the end of the human bandit's next turn, and the human bandit shifts 1 square.
Combat Advantage
    The human bandit deals an extra 1d6 damage on melee and ranged attacks against any target it has combat advantage against.

Alignment Any	**Languages** Common	
Skills Stealth +9, Streetwise +7, Thievery +9		
Str 12 (+2)	**Dex** 17 (+4)	**Wis** 11 (+1)
Con 13 (+2)	**Int** 10 (+1)	**Cha** 12 (+2)

Equipment leather armor, mace, 4 daggers

HUMAN BANDIT TACTICS
Bandits prefer ambushes, making good use of available cover to lie in wait. If they can't surprise their targets, they try to flank as many as possible, using *dazing strike* to help them maneuver into position. They are usually cowardly and look to retreat once bloodied.

Human Guard		Level 3 Soldier
Medium natural humanoid		XP 150

Initiative +5   **Senses** Perception +6
HP 47; **Bloodied** 23
AC 18; **Fortitude** 16, **Reflex** 15, **Will** 14
Speed 5
  ⊕ **Halberd** (standard; at-will) ✦ **Weapon**
    Reach 2; +10 vs. AC; 1d10 + 3 damage, and the target is marked until the end of the human guard's next turn.
  ✦ **Powerful Strike** (standard; recharge ⚄ ⚅) ✦ **Weapon**
    Requires halberd; reach 2; +10 vs. AC; 1d10 + 7 damage, and the target is knocked prone.
  ⊗ **Crossbow** (standard; at-will) ✦ **Weapon**
    Ranged 15/30; +9 vs. AC; 1d8 + 2 damage.

Alignment Any	**Languages** Common	
Skills Streetwise +7		
Str 16 (+4)	**Dex** 14 (+3)	**Wis** 11 (+1)
Con 15 (+3)	**Int** 10 (+1)	**Cha** 12 (+2)

Equipment chainmail, halberd, crossbow with 20 bolts

HUMAN GUARD TACTICS
Human guards are determined foes. They fight well together, standing close enough to protect their comrades. They use *powerful strike* against mobile enemies and use their crossbows only when foes are beyond their reach.

Human Berserker — Level 4 Brute
Medium natural humanoid — XP 175

Initiative +3 — **Senses** Perception +2
HP 66; **Bloodied** 33; see also *battle fury*
AC 15; **Fortitude** 15, **Reflex** 14, **Will** 14
Speed 7

⊕ **Greataxe** (standard; at-will) ✦ **Weapon**
+7 vs. AC; 1d12 + 4 damage (crit 1d12 + 16).

⸸ **Battle Fury** (free, when first bloodied; encounter)
The human berserker makes a melee basic attack with a +4 bonus to the attack roll and deals an extra 1d6 damage on a hit.

⟐ **Handaxe** (standard; at-will) ✦ **Weapon**
Ranged 5/10; +5 vs. AC; 1d6 + 3 damage.

Alignment Any — **Languages** Common
Skills Athletics +9, Endurance +9
Str 17 (+5) — **Dex** 12 (+3) — **Wis** 11 (+2)
Con 16 (+5) — **Int** 10 (+2) — **Cha** 12 (+3)
Equipment hide armor, greataxe, 2 handaxes

HUMAN BERSERKER TACTICS
Berserkers hurl themselves headlong into fights, eager to conquer or die. Usually begin by throwing axes, and then charge into melee. They use *battle fury* when first bloodied, hoping to overwhelm enemies with their sudden burst of rage.

Human Mage — Level 4 Artillery
Medium natural humanoid — XP 175

Initiative +4 — **Senses** Perception +5
HP 42; **Bloodied** 21
AC 17; **Fortitude** 13, **Reflex** 14, **Will** 15
Speed 6

⊕ **Quarterstaff** (standard; at-will) ✦ **Weapon**
+4 vs. AC; 1d8 damage.

⟐ **Magic Missile** (standard; at-will) ✦ **Force**
Ranged 20; +7 vs. Reflex; 2d4 + 4 force damage.

⟐ **Dancing Lightning** (standard; encounter) ✦ **Lightning**
The mage makes a separate attack against 3 different targets: ranged 10; +7 vs. Reflex; 1d6 + 4 lightning damage.

✳ **Thunder Burst** (standard; encounter) ✦ **Thunder**
Area burst 1 within 10; +7 vs. Fortitude; 1d8 + 4 thunder damage, and the target is dazed (save ends).

Alignment Any — **Languages** Common
Skills Arcana +11
Str 10 (+2) — **Dex** 14 (+4) — **Wis** 17 (+5)
Con 12 (+3) — **Int** 18 (+6) — **Cha** 12 (+3)
Equipment robes, quarterstaff, wand

HUMAN MAGE TACTICS
A human mage prefers to fight at range, picking off enemies with *magic missile*, *dancing lightning*, and *thunder burst*.

HUMAN LORE
A character knows the following information with a successful Nature check.

DC 15: Humans are a scattered and divided people. They inhabit kingdoms, fiefdoms, and isolated settlements throughout the world, expanding their influence, exploring the darkest frontiers, and making war against their rivals.

DC 20: The ruins of ancient human empires are scattered throughout the world. No present-day human kingdom matches these fallen empires in terms of scale and grandeur, but humans remain undaunted. Their culture has reasserted itself, and humans have begun to expand their influence.

ENCOUNTER GROUPS
Humans can play secondary roles in encounters featuring just about any other creature, but in these encounters, the humans take center stage.

Level 3 Encounter (XP 775)
✦ 1 human berserker (level 4 brute)
✦ 2 human guards (level 3 soldier)
✦ 2 spitting drakes (level 3 artillery)

Level 4 Encounter (XP 889)
✦ 1 human mage (level 4 artillery)
✦ 2 human bandits (level 2 skirmisher)
✦ 2 gravehound zombies (level 3 brute)
✦ 3 zombie rotters (level 3 minion)

Level 5 Encounter (XP 1,050)
✦ 2 human mages (level 4 artillery)
✦ 6 human lackeys (level 7 minion)
✦ 1 evistro demon (level 6 brute)

HYDRA

A HYDRA IS A SERPENTINE BEAST WITH MANY HEADS. It lurks in swamps, bogs, and flooded caverns, preying upon virtually anything that crosses its path.

Fen Hydra	Level 12 Solo Brute
Large natural beast (reptile)	XP 3,500

Initiative +9   **Senses** Perception +13; all-around vision
HP 620; **Bloodied** 310
AC 25; **Fortitude** 26, **Reflex** 24, **Will** 23
Saving Throws +5
Speed 5, swim 10
Action Points 2

ⓉBite (standard; at-will)
    Reach 2; +14 vs. AC; 1d8 + 5 damage.
╪Hydra Fury (standard; at-will)
    The fen hydra makes four bite attacks.
Many-Headed
    Each time the fen hydra becomes dazed or stunned, it loses one attack on its next turn instead. Multiple such effects stack.
Threatening Reach
    The fen hydra can make opportunity attacks against all enemies within its reach (2 squares).

Alignment Unaligned   **Languages** –
Skills Stealth +14
Str 20 (+11)   **Dex** 16 (+9)   **Wis** 14 (+8)
Con 20 (+11)   **Int** 2 (+2)   **Cha** 8 (+5)

FEN HYDRA TACTICS

A fen hydra lurks out of sight in a bog, hoping to surprise prey. When the time is right, it slithers out of hiding and attacks with its multiple heads, spending its action points to use *hydra fury* twice in a round.

Fen hydra

Mordant hydra

Mordant Hydra	Level 18 Solo Brute
Huge natural beast (reptile)	XP 10,000

Initiative +13   **Senses** Perception +17; all-around vision, low-light vision
HP 880; **Bloodied** 440
AC 31; **Fortitude** 33, **Reflex** 30, **Will** 29
Resist 15 acid
Saving Throws +5
Speed 6, swim 12
Action Points 2

ⓉBite (standard; at-will)
    Reach 3; +21 vs. AC; 1d8 + 6 damage.
⊗Acid Spit (standard; at-will) ✦ Acid
    Ranged 10; +18 vs. Reflex; 1d8 + 6 acid damage.
╪Hydra Fury (standard; at-will)
    The mordant hydra makes six basic attacks (any combination of bite attacks and *acid spit* attacks).
Many-Headed
    Each time the mordant hydra becomes dazed or stunned, it loses one attack on its next turn instead. Multiple such effects stack.
Threatening Reach
    The mordant hydra can make opportunity attacks against all enemies within its reach (3 squares).

Alignment Unaligned   **Languages** –
Str 22 (+15)   **Dex** 18 (+13)   **Wis** 16 (+12)
Con 24 (+16)   **Int** 2 (+5)   **Cha** 8 (+8)

MORDANT HYDRA TACTICS

A mordant hydra usually spits acid with half its heads and bites with the other half, spending its action points to use *hydra fury* twice in a round. If multiple targets are within its reach, the hydra splits its attention between the closest foe and the enemy that hurt it the most since its last turn.

Primordial Hydra	Level 25 Solo Brute
Gargantuan elemental beast (reptile)	XP 35,000

Initiative +18   **Senses** Perception +21; all-around vision, darkvision

HP 1,200; **Bloodied** 600

AC 38; **Fortitude** 40, **Reflex** 35, **Will** 33

Resist 20 acid, 20 fire

Saving Throws +5

Speed 8, swim 16

Action Points 2

⚔ **Bite** (standard; at-will)

Reach 4; +28 vs. AC (+30 with opportunity attacks); 1d10 + 8 damage, or 1d10 + 13 on a successful opportunity attack.

⟐ **Flaming Acid Spit** (standard; at-will) ✦ **Acid, Fire**

Ranged 10; +25 vs. Reflex; 1d10 + 8 acid and fire damage.

⚔ **Hydra Fury** (standard; at-will)

The primordial hydra makes eight basic attacks (any combination of bite attacks and *flaming acid spit* attacks).

Many-Headed

Each time the primordial hydra becomes dazed or stunned, it loses one attack on its next turn instead. Multiple such effects stack.

Threatening Reach

The primordial hydra can make opportunity attacks against all enemies within its reach (4 squares).

Alignment Chaotic evil	**Languages** –	
Str 26 (+20)	**Dex** 22 (+18)	**Wis** 18 (+16)
Con 32 (+23)	**Int** 4 (+9)	**Cha** 12 (+13)

PRIMORDIAL HYDRA TACTICS

A primordial hydra spits flaming acid at ranged foes and makes bite attacks against enemies within reach. It spends its action points to use *hydra fury* twice in a given round.

HYDRA LORE

A character knows the following information with a successful skill check.

Nature DC 20: Legends that speak of hydras that can regenerate severed heads have so far proven false.

Nature DC 25: Although hydras spend much of their time in water, they are not amphibious–they must surface to breathe.

Arcana DC 30: The first hydras sprang from the spilled blood of Bryakus, a terrible primordial who battled the gods in ancient times. Although the gods defeated Bryakus long ago, his monstrous progeny still thrive in the Elemental Chaos and elsewhere. Particularly powerful hydras have the ability to spit acid and other forms of energy, such as fire or lightning.

Primordial hydra

ENCOUNTER GROUPS

A hydra is the largest and most dangerous monster in the vicinity of its lair. Most of the time, no other monsters dare come near. However, creatures such as otyughs sometimes haunt the area of a hydra's lair, hoping to feed on the larger monster's leavings. More intelligent lone monsters sometimes coax hydras to lair nearby as a perimeter defense.

Level 14 Encounter (XP 5,000)
✦ 1 fen hydra (level 12 solo brute)
✦ 3 bog hags (level 10 skirmisher)

Level 19 Encounter (XP 12,000)
✦ 1 mordant hydra (level 18 solo brute)
✦ 1 gibbering abomination (level 18 controller)

Level 26 Encounter (XP 45,100)
✦ 1 primordial hydra (level 25 solo brute)
✦ 2 earthwind ravager elementals (level 23 controller)

HYENA

CLEVER SCAVENGERS THAT ROAM THE PLAINS AND DESERTS OF THE WORLD, hyenas pose a real danger to humanoids in the wild. They make good use of pack tactics to harry and pull down their prey.

Hyena		Level 2 Skirmisher
Medium natural beast		XP 125

Initiative +5   **Senses** Perception +7; low-light vision
HP 37; **Bloodied** 18
AC 16; **Fortitude** 14, **Reflex** 13, **Will** 12
Speed 8
⊕ **Bite** (standard; at-will)
    +7 vs. AC; 1d6 + 3 damage; see also *pack attack*.
Pack Attack
    A hyena deals an extra 1d6 damage against an enemy adjacent to two or more of the hyena's allies.
Harrier
    If a hyena is adjacent to an enemy, all other creatures have combat advantage against that enemy when making melee attacks.

Alignment Unaligned		**Languages** –
Str 16 (+4)	**Dex** 15 (+3)	**Wis** 12 (+2)
Con 13 (+2)	**Int** 2 (-3)	**Cha** 5 (-2)

HYENA TACTICS

The *pack attack* and *harrier* powers reward hyenas for ganging up on one target at a time, so a pack normally chooses a single foe and tries to pull it down.

Cacklefiend Hyena		Level 7 Brute
Large elemental beast		XP 300

Initiative +5   **Senses** Perception +11; low-light vision
HP 96; **Bloodied** 48; see also *acid bloodspurt*
AC 19; **Fortitude** 20, **Reflex** 17, **Will** 18
Resist 20 acid
Speed 8
⊕ **Bite** (standard; at-will) ✦ **Acid**
    +10 vs. AC; 1d6 + 5 damage, and ongoing 5 acid damage (save ends); see also *pack attack*.

↫ **Fiendish Cackle** (minor; recharge ⚄ ⚅) ✦ **Fear**
    Close burst 3; deafened creatures are immune; targets enemies; +8 vs. Will; the target takes a -2 penalty to attack rolls until the end of the cacklefiend hyena's next turn.
↫ **Acid Bloodspurt** (when first bloodied; encounter) ✦ **Acid**
    Close burst 1; automatic hit; 2d8 acid damage, and ongoing 5 acid damage (save ends).
Pack Attack
    A cacklefiend hyena deals an extra 1d6 damage against an enemy adjacent to two or more of the cacklefiend hyena's allies.
Harrier
    If a cacklefiend hyena is adjacent to an enemy, all other creatures have combat advantage against that enemy when making melee attacks.

Alignment Chaotic evil		**Languages** Abyssal, Common
Str 20 (+8)	**Dex** 14 (+5)	**Wis** 14 (+5)
Con 16 (+6)	**Int** 6 (+1)	**Cha** 10 (+3)

CACKLEFIEND HYENA TACTICS

A cacklefiend hyena uses its *fiendish cackle* to unnerve enemies before attacking, and again as soon as the power recharges. It works with its allies to take down one foe at a time, reaping the benefits of its *pack attack* and *harrier* powers.

HYENA LORE

A character knows the following information with a successful skill check.

    Nature DC 15: Hyenas are commonly regarded as cowardly, gluttonous, filthy, and destructive beasts. Gnolls often keep hyenas as pets and hunting animals.

    Arcana DC 25: Cacklefiend hyenas are native to the Abyss. Their jaws drip with acid, and their cackle is extremely unnerving. Yeenoghu, the demon god of gnolls, sends cacklefiend hyenas to serve favored gnoll chieftains.

ENCOUNTER GROUPS

Hyenas are frequently tamed by gnolls and trained to hunt alongside gnoll war parties.

Level 4 Encounter (XP 900)
✦ 4 hyenas (level 2 skirmisher)
✦ 2 gnoll huntmasters (level 5 artillery)

KOBOLD

KOBOLDS REVERE DRAGONS and tend to dwell in and around places where dragons are known to lair. They skulk in the darkness, hiding from stronger foes and swarming to overwhelm weaker ones. Kobolds are cowardly and usually flee once bloodied unless a strong leader is present.

Kobolds like to set traps and ambushes. If they can't get their enemies to walk into a trap, they try to sneak up as close as they can and then attack in a sudden rush.

Kobold Minion	Level 1 Minion
Small natural humanoid	XP 25

Initiative +3   **Senses** Perception +1; darkvision
HP 1; a missed attack never damages a minion.
AC 15; **Fortitude** 11, **Reflex** 13, **Will** 11; see also *trap sense*
Speed 6
(✦) **Javelin** (standard; at-will) ✦ **Weapon**
    +5 vs. AC; 4 damage.
(➶) **Javelin** (standard; at-will) ✦ **Weapon**
    Ranged 10/20; +5 vs. AC; 4 damage.
Shifty (minor; at-will)
    The kobold shifts 1 square.
Trap Sense
    The kobold gains a +2 bonus to all defenses against traps.
Alignment Evil   **Languages** Common, Draconic
Skills Stealth +4, Thievery +4
Str 8 (-1)	**Dex** 16 (+3)	**Wis** 12 (+1)
Con 12 (+1)	**Int** 9 (-1)	**Cha** 10 (+0)
Equipment hide armor, light shield, 3 javelins

KOBOLD MINION TACTICS

Kobold minions are fierce in packs, but cowardly when separated. They can shift as a minor action each round to achieve flanking positions.

Kobold Skirmisher	Level 1 Skirmisher
Small natural humanoid	XP 100

Initiative +5   **Senses** Perception +0; darkvision
HP 27; **Bloodied** 13
AC 15; **Fortitude** 11, **Reflex** 14, **Will** 13; see also *trap sense*
Speed 6
(✦) **Spear** (standard; at-will) ✦ **Weapon**
    +6 vs. AC; 1d8 damage; see also *mob attack*.
Combat Advantage
    The kobold skirmisher deals an extra 1d6 damage on melee and ranged attacks against any target it has combat advantage against.
Mob Attack
    The kobold skirmisher gains a +1 bonus to attack rolls per kobold ally adjacent to the target.
Shifty (minor; at-will)
    The kobold shifts 1 square.
Trap Sense
    The kobold gains a +2 bonus to all defenses against traps.
Alignment Evil   **Languages** Common, Draconic
Skills Acrobatics +7, Stealth +9, Thievery +9
Str 8 (-1)	**Dex** 16 (+3)	**Wis** 10 (+0)
Con 11 (+0)	**Int** 6 (-2)	**Cha** 15 (+2)
Equipment hide armor, spear

KOBOLD SKIRMISHER TACTICS

Kobold skirmishers gang up on a single target to gain the benefit of *mob attack*, shifting as a minor action to gain combat advantage. They retreat when the fight turns against them, leading pursuers through passages and rooms riddled with traps, if possible.

(Left to right) kobold skirmisher, kobold dragonshield, and kobold wyrmpriest

Kobold Slinger — Level 1 Artillery

Small natural humanoid · XP 100

Initiative +3 **Senses** Perception +1; darkvision
HP 24; **Bloodied** 12
AC 13; **Fortitude** 12, **Reflex** 14, **Will** 12; see also *trap sense*
Speed 6

⊕ Dagger (standard; at-will) ✦ **Weapon**
+5 vs. AC; 1d4 + 3 damage.

⊛ Sling (standard; at-will) ✦ **Weapon**
Ranged 10/20; +6 vs. AC; 1d6 + 3 damage; see also *special shot*.

Special Shot
The kobold slinger can fire special ammunition from its sling. It typically carries 3 rounds of special shot, chosen from the types listed below. A *special shot* attack that hits deals normal damage and has an additional effect depending on its type:
Stinkpot: The target takes a -2 penalty to attack rolls (save ends).
Firepot (Fire): The target takes ongoing 2 fire damage (save ends).
Gluepot: The target is immobilized (save ends).

Shifty (minor; at-will)
The kobold shifts 1 square.

Trap Sense
The kobold gains a +2 bonus to all defenses against traps.

Alignment Evil **Languages** Common, Draconic
Skills Acrobatics +8, Stealth +10, Thievery +10
Str 9 (-1) **Dex** 17 (+3) **Wis** 12 (+1)
Con 12 (+1) **Int** 9 (-1) **Cha** 10 (+0)
Equipment leather armor, dagger, sling with 20 bullets and 3 rounds of special shot (see above)

KOBOLD SLINGER TACTICS

Kobold slingers avoid melee combat. They prefer to stay behind cover and bombard foes with *special shot* and sling stones.

Kobold Dragonshield — Level 2 Soldier

Small natural humanoid · XP 125

Initiative +4 **Senses** Perception +2; darkvision
HP 36; **Bloodied** 18
AC 18; **Fortitude** 14, **Reflex** 13, **Will** 13; see also *trap sense*
Resist 5 (damage type of the dragon served)
Speed 5

⊕ Short Sword (standard; at-will) ✦ **Weapon**
+7 vs. AC; 1d6 + 3 damage, and the target is marked until the end of the kobold dragonshield's next turn.

Dragonshield Tactics (immediate reaction, when an adjacent enemy shifts away or an enemy moves adjacent; at-will)
The kobold dragonshield shifts 1 square.

Mob Attack
The kobold dragonshield gains a +1 bonus to attack rolls per kobold ally adjacent to the target.

Shifty (minor; at-will)
The kobold shifts 1 square.

Trap Sense
The kobold gains a +2 bonus to all defenses against traps.

Alignment Evil **Languages** Common, Draconic
Skills Acrobatics +5, Stealth +7, Thievery +7
Str 14 (+3) **Dex** 13 (+2) **Wis** 12 (+2)
Con 12 (+2) **Int** 9 (+0) **Cha** 10 (+1)
Equipment scale armor, heavy shield, short sword

KOBOLD DRAGONSHIELD TACTICS

Kobold dragonshields are capable frontline combatants, keeping enemies away from their weaker kobold allies with their swords and shields. They like to gang up on single targets.

A kobold dragonshield gains resist 5 against a specific damage type based on the type of dragon it serves or reveres. For example, a kobold dragonshield working for a blue dragon has resist 5 lightning.

Kobold Wyrmpriest — Level 3 Artillery (Leader)

Small natural humanoid · XP 150

Initiative +4 **Senses** Perception +4; darkvision
HP 36; **Bloodied** 18
AC 17; **Fortitude** 13, **Reflex** 15, **Will** 15; see also *trap sense*
Speed 6

⊕ Spear (standard; at-will) ✦ **Weapon**
+7 vs. AC; 1d8 damage.

⊛ Energy Orb (standard; at-will) ✦ see text
Ranged 10; +6 vs. Reflex; 1d10 + 3 damage of a chosen type (based on the dragon served).

↞ Incite Faith (minor; encounter)
Close burst 10; kobold allies in the burst gain 5 temporary hit points and shift 1 square.

↞ Dragon Breath (standard; encounter) ✦ see text
Close blast 3; +6 vs. Fortitude; 1d10 + 3 damage of a chosen type (based on the dragon served). *Miss:* Half damage.

Shifty (minor; at-will)
The kobold shifts 1 square.

Trap Sense
The kobold gains a +2 bonus to all defenses against traps.

Alignment Evil **Languages** Common, Draconic
Skills Stealth +10, Thievery +10
Str 9 (+0) **Dex** 16 (+4) **Wis** 17 (+4)
Con 12 (+2) **Int** 9 (+0) **Cha** 12 (+2)
Equipment hide armor, spear, bone mask

KOBOLD WYRMPRIEST TACTICS

A wyrmpriest keeps lots of kobold underlings between it and its enemies, using *incite faith* to embolden them. It prefers to make ranged attacks using *energy orb*, and enemies that get too close are blasted with *dragon breath*.

A wyrmpriest's *energy orb* deals damage of a specific type based on the type of dragon the wyrmpriest serves or reveres. For example, a kobold wyrmpriest working for a black dragon deals acid damage with its *energy orb* power.

Kobold Slyblade

Kobold Slyblade	Level 4 Lurker
Small natural humanoid	XP 175

Initiative +10 · **Senses** Perception +3; darkvision
HP 42; **Bloodied** 21
AC 18; **Fortitude** 12, **Reflex** 16, **Will** 14; see also *trap sense*
Speed 6

⊕ **Short Sword** (standard; at-will) ✦ **Weapon**
+9 vs. AC; 1d6 damage.

† **Twin Slash** (standard; at-will) ✦ **Weapon**
Requires combat advantage; the kobold slyblade makes 2 short sword attacks. If both attacks hit the same target, the target takes ongoing 5 damage (save ends).

Combat Advantage
The kobold slyblade deals an extra 1d6 damage on melee attacks against any target it has combat advantage against.

Sly Dodge (immediate interrupt, when targeted by a melee or a ranged attack; at-will)
The kobold slyblade redirects the attack to an adjacent kobold minion.

Shifty (minor; at-will)
The kobold shifts 1 square.

Trap Sense
The kobold gains a +2 bonus to all defenses against traps.

Alignment Evil · **Languages** Common, Draconic
Skills Acrobatics +11, Stealth +13, Thievery +13
Str 9 (+1) · **Dex** 18 (+6) · **Wis** 12 (+3)
Con 12 (+3) · **Int** 9 (+1) · **Cha** 14 (+4)
Equipment leather armor, 2 short swords

Kobold Slyblade Tactics

The kobold slyblade stays close to other kobolds, using *sly dodge* to turn them into living shields while it makes *twin slash* attacks against foes. Whenever possible, it shifts as a minor action, moves into a flanking position, and gains combat advantage.

Kobold Lore

A character knows the following information with a successful Nature check.

DC 15: Kobolds often dwell near a dragon's lair, maintaining a safe distance but bringing sacrificial offerings to their "god." Most dragons ignore kobolds, as a crocodile ignores the birds that pick its teeth clean. Once in a great while, however, a young dragon takes an interest in its kobold cult, which then becomes a real menace to the dragon's enemies.

DC 20: Kobolds are skilled at making traps, which they use to capture prey and to acquire sacrifices for their dragon lords.

Encounter Groups

Kobolds bully what few weaker creatures they can find and are bullied by everything else.

Level 1 Encounter (XP 500)
✦ 2 kobold skirmishers (level 1 skirmisher)
✦ 2 fire beetles (level 1 brute)
✦ 1 stirge (level 1 lurker)

Level 1 Encounter (XP 500)
✦ 2 kobold slingers (level 1 artillery)
✦ 8 kobold minions (level 1 minion)
✦ 1 stormclaw scorpion (level 1 soldier)

Level 2 Encounter (XP 625)
✦ 2 kobold slingers (level 1 artillery)
✦ 4 kobold minions (level 1 minion)
✦ 2 dire rats (level 1 brute)
✦ 1 rat swarm (level 2 skirmisher)

Level 3 Encounter (XP 750)
✦ 1 kobold wyrmpriest (level 3 artillery)
✦ 2 kobold dragonshields (level 2 soldier)
✦ 4 kobold minions (level 1 minion)
✦ 2 guard drakes (level 2 brute)

Level 3 Encounter (XP 750)
✦ 1 kobold wyrmpriest (level 3 artillery)
✦ 2 kobold skirmishers (level 1 skirmisher)
✦ 6 kobold minions (level 1 minion)
✦ 2 needlefang drake swarms (level 2 soldier)

Level 3 Encounter (XP 750)
✦ 1 kobold wyrmpriest (level 3 artillery)
✦ 2 kobold skirmishers (level 1 skirmisher)
✦ 1 spitting drake (level 3 artillery)
✦ 6 kobold minions (level 1 minion)
✦ 4 fire beetles (level 1 brute)

Level 4 Encounter (XP 875)
✦ 1 kobold slyblade (level 4 lurker)
✦ 4 kobold dragonshields (level 2 skirmisher)

Level 6 Encounter (XP 1,250)
✦ 3 kobold dragonshields (level 2 soldier)
✦ 1 young black dragon (level 4 solo lurker)

KRUTHIK

KRUTHIKS BURROW THROUGH THE EARTH, riddling the Underdark with tunnels. They hunt in packs and nest in sprawling subterranean warrens.

Kruthiks dig tunnels that remain intact behind them. Often the first clue to the presence of a kruthik hive is a preponderance of such tunnels in the vicinity.

Kruthiks communicate with one another through a series of hisses and chitters. A typical kruthik hive is ruled by the largest kruthik, called the hive lord.

Kruthik Hatchling		Level 2 Minion
Small natural beast (reptile)		XP 31

Initiative +3   **Senses** Perception +0; low-light vision, tremorsense 10

Gnashing Horde aura 1; an enemy that ends its turn in the aura takes 2 damage.

HP 1; a missed attack never damages a minion.

AC 15; **Fortitude** 13, **Reflex** 15, **Will** 12

Speed 8, burrow 2 (tunneling), climb 8

⊕ **Claw** (standard; at-will)
+5 vs. AC; 4 damage.

Alignment Unaligned	**Languages** –	
Str 13 (+1)	Dex 16 (+3)	Wis 10 (+0)
Con 13 (+1)	Int 4 (−3)	Cha 6 (−2)

KRUTHIK HATCHLING TACTICS

Kruthik hatchlings swarm around the nearest foe in a vicious, biting horde. They typically fight until slain.

Kruthik Young		Level 2 Brute
Small natural beast (reptile)		XP 125

Initiative +4   **Senses** Perception +1; low-light vision, tremorsense 10

Gnashing Horde aura 1; an enemy that ends its turn in the aura takes 2 damage.

HP 43; **Bloodied** 21

AC 15; **Fortitude** 13, **Reflex** 14, **Will** 11

Speed 8, burrow 2, climb 8

⊕ **Claw** (standard; at-will)
+5 vs. AC; 1d8 + 2 damage.

Alignment Unaligned	**Languages** –	
Str 15 (+3)	Dex 16 (+4)	Wis 10 (+1)
Con 13 (+2)	Int 4 (−2)	Cha 6 (−1)

KRUTHIK YOUNG TACTICS

A kruthik young joins the hatchlings in attacking a singular target, raking the hapless creature to pieces with its claws. It typically fights until slain.

Kruthik Adult		Level 4 Brute
Medium natural beast (reptile)		XP 175

Initiative +6   **Senses** Perception +4; low-light vision, tremorsense 10

Gnashing Horde aura 1; an enemy that ends its turn in the aura takes 2 damage.

HP 67; **Bloodied** 33

AC 17; **Fortitude** 14, **Reflex** 15, **Will** 13

Speed 6, burrow 3 (tunneling), climb 6

⊕ **Claw** (standard; at-will)
+8 vs. AC; 1d10 + 3 damage.

↗ **Toxic Spikes** (standard; recharge ⚄ ⚅) ✦ **Poison**
The kruthik makes 2 attacks against two different targets: ranged 5; +7 vs. AC; 1d8 + 4 damage, and the target takes ongoing 5 poison damage and is slowed (save ends both).

Alignment Unaligned	**Languages** –	
Str 17 (+5)	Dex 18 (+6)	Wis 12 (+4)
Con 17 (+5)	Int 4 (−1)	Cha 8 (+1)

KRUTHIK ADULT TACTICS

A kruthik adult uses its *toxic spikes* on tempting targets within range before closing to melee. From that point on, it tries to stay adjacent to an enemy, using its *toxic spikes* only when it can't otherwise reach a target.

Kruthik Hive Lord	Level 6 Elite Controller (Leader)
Large natural beast (reptile)	XP 500

Initiative +7   **Senses** Perception +4; low-light vision, tremorsense 10

Hive Frenzy aura 2; allied kruthiks in the aura deal double damage with basic attacks.

HP 148; **Bloodied** 74

AC 22; **Fortitude** 21, **Reflex** 20, **Will** 17

Saving Throws +2

Speed 6, burrow 3 (tunneling), climb 6

Action Points 1

⊕ **Claw** (standard; at-will)
+11 vs. AC; 1d10 + 5 damage.

◁ **Acid Blast** (standard; at-will) ✦ **Acid**
Close blast 5; targets enemies; +9 vs. Fortitude; 1d6 + 4 acid damage, and the target takes ongoing 5 acid damage and is weakened (save ends both).

Alignment Unaligned	**Languages** –	
Str 20 (+8)	Dex 18 (+7)	Wis 12 (+4)
Con 18 (+7)	Int 4 (+0)	Cha 10 (+3)

KRUTHIK HIVE LORD TACTICS

The hive lord uses its *acid blast* to weaken enemies at the start of battle. It then makes claw attacks, staying within 2 squares of as many other kruthiks as possible so that they benefit from its *hive frenzy* aura.

KRUTHIK LORE

A character knows the following information with a successful Nature check.

DC 15: Kruthiks are chitinous reptilian hunters that form small hives underground. They use their superior numbers to overwhelm and devour all other nearby creatures.

Kruthiks hunt methodically, stripping one area of prey before expanding their territory. They butcher their kills and carry treasure back to their nesting warrens. Mauled carcasses and strange tracks that look as if they were made by spikes are sure signs of a kruthik horde.

DC 20: Kruthiks communicate with one another through a complex series of insectlike chitters and reptilian hisses. These sounds can often be heard in advance of a kruthik attack.

Kruthiks hatch from eggs and undergo several metamorphoses during their life cycle. Hatchlings grow into young, but young and adults enter a hard cocoon to change into the next larger breed of kruthik.

DC 25: Kruthiks take the scent of their own dead as a warning, and they avoid areas where many other kruthiks have died. Slaying enough kruthiks in one area might drive the remaining hive elsewhere.

DC 30: The origin of the kruthik lies in the cruel history of the tiefling empire of Bael Turath. Tiefling mages infused worldly reptiles with fiendish blood, creating the kruthiks as infiltrators to weaken enemy holdings from within. Perhaps the tieflings had a way to control the kruthiks at that time, but if so, that technique was lost with the fall of the tiefling empire.

ENCOUNTER GROUPS

Kruthiks build lairs underground, slowly digging through earth and rock to form warrens. They're attracted to sites that already have open underground chambers and supernatural energies. Although kruthiks can feed on carrion, they prefer live prey, so undead are safe from kruthik predation and can even live unmolested in proximity to a kruthik hive. It is entirely possible that a sentient creature could uncover the means to control kruthiks, bringing them to bear as living weapons. The most likely candidates for such an accomplishment are tieflings, devils, and evil creatures willing to deal with devils.

Level 3 Encounter (XP 767)
+ 1 kruthik adult (level 4 brute)
+ 3 kruthik young (level 2 brute)
+ 8 kruthik hatchlings (level 2 minion)

Level 4 Encounter (XP 875)
+ 3 kruthik adults (level 4 brute)
+ 2 corruption corpse zombies (level 4 artillery)

Level 5 Encounter (XP 1,005)
+ 1 kruthik hive lord (level 6 elite controller)
+ 2 kruthik adults (level 4 brute)
+ 5 kruthik hatchlings (level 2 minion)

KUO-TOA

KUO-TOAS ARE LOATHSOME FISH-PEOPLE who live in the black seas of the Underdark, building great temples to alien gods. They regard all other races as potential slaves or sacrifices.

Kuo-toa Guard		Level 16 Minion
Medium natural humanoid (aquatic)		XP 350

Initiative +11   **Senses** Perception +12; darkvision
HP 1; a missed attack never damages a minion.
AC 29; **Fortitude** 24, **Reflex** 25, **Will** 23
Speed 6, swim 6
(+) **Spear** (standard; at-will) ✦ **Weapon**
  +21 vs. AC; 7 damage.
Slick Maneuver (move; at-will)
  A kuo-toa adjacent to an enemy shifts to any other square adjacent to that enemy.

Alignment Evil	**Languages** Deep Speech	
Str 15 (+10)	**Dex** 16 (+11)	**Wis** 9 (+7)
Con 15 (+10)	**Int** 11 (+8)	**Cha** 13 (+9)

Equipment leather armor, light shield, spear

KUO-TOA GUARD TACTICS

In the presence of a strong leader (a whip or monitor), kuo-toa guards fight with fanatical zeal. If their leader is killed, kuo-toa guards tend to flee.

Kuo-toa Marauder		Level 12 Skirmisher
Medium natural humanoid (aquatic)		XP 700

Initiative +11   **Senses** Perception +11; darkvision
HP 119; **Bloodied** 59
AC 25; **Fortitude** 22, **Reflex** 23, **Will** 21 (25 while bloodied)
Speed 6, swim 6
(+) **Skewering Spear** (standard; at-will) ✦ **Weapon**
  +17 vs. AC (+19 while bloodied); 1d8 + 4 damage, and ongoing 5 damage (save ends).
† **Sticky Shield** (immediate reaction, when missed by a melee attack; at-will)
  The kuo-toa marauder makes an attack against the attacker: +15 vs. Reflex; a weapon wielded by the target drops in the target's space.
Quick Step (minor, usable only while bloodied; at-will)
  The kuo-toa marauder shifts 1 square.
Slick Maneuver (move; at-will)
  A kuo-toa adjacent to an enemy shifts to any other square adjacent to that enemy.

Alignment Evil	**Languages** Deep Speech	
Str 15 (+8)	**Dex** 16 (+9)	**Wis** 11 (+6)
Con 15 (+8)	**Int** 11 (+6)	**Cha** 13 (+7)

Equipment leather armor, slimy light shield, spear

KUO-TOA MARAUDER TACTICS

Kuo-toa marauders are so named because they often roam the Underdark in search of slaves. Tainted by madness, they rarely flee a battle, even if hopelessly outmatched. A marauder uses *quick step* to shift before or after making an attack with its spear, and it uses *slick maneuver* to gain a flanking position.

Kuo-toa Harpooner		Level 14 Soldier
Medium natural humanoid (aquatic)		XP 1,000

Initiative +12   **Senses** Perception +13; darkvision
HP 137; **Bloodied** 68
AC 28; **Fortitude** 26, **Reflex** 26, **Will** 24
Speed 6, swim 6
(+) **Harpoon** (standard; at-will) ✦ **Weapon**
  +20 vs. AC; 1d8 + 3 damage, and the target is grabbed and takes ongoing 5 damage (until escape). While the target is grabbed, the kuo-toa harpooner cannot use the harpoon to make attacks.
(→) **Reeling Harpoon** (standard; at-will) ✦ **Weapon**
  Ranged 5/10; +20 vs. AC; 1d8 + 3 damage, and the kuo-toa harpooner makes a secondary attack against the same target. *Secondary Attack:* +18 vs. Fortitude; 1d8 + 3 damage, and the target is pulled 3 squares.
† **Sticky Shield** (immediate reaction, when missed by a melee attack; at-will)
  The kuo-toa harpooner makes an attack against the attacker: +18 vs. Reflex; a weapon wielded by the target drops in the target's space.
Slick Maneuver (move; at-will)
  A kuo-toa adjacent to an enemy shifts to any other square adjacent to that enemy.

Alignment Evil	**Languages** Deep Speech	
Str 17 (+10)	**Dex** 17 (+10)	**Wis** 13 (+8)
Con 17 (+10)	**Int** 13 (+8)	**Cha** 15 (+9)

Equipment leather armor, slimy light shield, 4 harpoons

KUO-TOA HARPOONER TACTICS

This kuo-toa attaches slimy cords to its harpoons, allowing it to reel in distant enemies. Once in melee combat with a foe, the harpooner tries to impale its enemy on a harpoon, dealing automatic damage each round the target remains impaled.

Kuo-toa Monitor		Level 16 Skirmisher
Medium natural humanoid (aquatic)		XP 1,400

Initiative +15   **Senses** Perception +15; darkvision
HP 153; **Bloodied** 76
AC 30; **Fortitude** 27, **Reflex** 28, **Will** 26
Speed 6, swim 6
(+) **Slam** (standard; at-will)
  +21 vs. AC; 2d10 + 4 damage.
(→) **Crossbow** (standard; at-will) ✦ **Weapon**
  Ranged 15/30; +21 vs. AC; 1d8 + 5 damage.
† **Leap Kick** (standard; at-will)
  The kuo-toa monitor shifts 2 squares and makes a slam attack.
† **Lightning Fist** (standard; encounter) ✦ **Lightning**
  +19 vs. Reflex; 3d8 + 4 lightning damage, and the target is stunned (save ends).
Slick Maneuver (move; at-will)
  A kuo-toa adjacent to an enemy shifts to any other square adjacent to that enemy.

Alignment Evil	**Languages** Deep Speech	
Skills Acrobatics +18, Dungeoneering +15		
Str 19 (+12)	**Dex** 20 (+13)	**Wis** 15 (+10)
Con 17 (+11)	**Int** 15 (+10)	**Cha** 16 (+11)

Equipment leather armor, crossbow with 20 bolts

KUO-TOA MONITORS TACTICS

The kuo-toa monitor hurls itself into melee combat, using *leap kick* to shift up to 2 squares before or after making a slam attack. The first time it flanks a foe, it uses *lightning fist*.

Kuo-toa Whip	Level 16 Controller (Leader)
Medium natural humanoid (aquatic)	XP 1,400

Initiative +12   **Senses** Perception +16; darkvision
HP 156; **Bloodied** 78
AC 30; **Fortitude** 28, **Reflex** 27, **Will** 27
Speed 6, swim 6
(+) **Pincer Staff** (standard; sustain standard; at-will) ✦ **Weapon**
   Reach 2; +19 vs. AC; 1d8 + 3 damage, and the target is grabbed (until escape). While the target is grabbed, the kuo-toa whip cannot make attacks with its pincer staff. When the kuo-toa whip sustains the grab, it deals 1d10 damage to the target. The kuo-toa whip can release the target as a minor action, sliding the target to any other square within its reach.
✦ **Lightning Strike** (standard; at-will) ✦ **Lightning**
   Ranged 10; +18 vs. Reflex; 2d8 + 5 lightning damage, and the target is blinded until the end of the kuo-toa whip's next turn.
✳ **Slime Vortex** (standard; encounter)
   Area burst 4 within 20; targets enemies; +18 vs. Fortitude; 1d10 + 5 damage, the target takes a -2 penalty to attack rolls (save ends), and the target slides 3 squares and is knocked prone. *Miss*: Half damage, and the target slides 1 square.
Slick Maneuver (move; at-will)
   A kuo-toa adjacent to an enemy shifts to any other square adjacent to that enemy.
Alignment Evil   **Languages** Deep Speech
Skills Dungeoneering +16, Religion +15
Str 17 (+11)   **Dex** 18 (+12)   **Wis** 17 (+11)
Con 20 (+13)   **Int** 15 (+10)   **Cha** 18 (+12)
Equipment coat, pincer staff, headdress

KUO-TOA WHIP TACTICS

The kuo-toa whip begins battle by casting *slime vortex* on the largest group of enemies, then targets them one at a time with *lightning strike*. It uses its pincer staff against enemies in melee combat, sliding them within reach of its allies.

KUO-TOA LORE

A character knows the following information with a successful Nature check.

DC 20: Kuo-toas live in the Underdark, where they worship dark gods and work toward sinister ends, seeing themselves as superior to all other humanoids. They are at home in water and on land, so they can be encountered in dry caverns as well as subterranean bodies of water.

On the edge of underground lakes or seas, kuo-toas build settlements around their shrines. Within these places, priests called whips make up the top caste of kuo-toa society. Kuo-toa monitors are the whips' agents as well as an elite warrior force that keeps lower ranking kuo-toas in line.

DC 25: Madness taints kuo-toa civilization, and it can spread through a kuo-toa settlement like a disease. The mental disciplines practiced by whips and monitors often protect them from lunacy, but kuo-toa leaders must carefully control and watch the common populace. This madness has caused some kuo-toa communities to disintegrate, leaving behind ruins populated by mad kuo-toas and wandering monsters.

ENCOUNTER GROUPS

Kuo-toas range from their settlements to acquire slaves for themselves and sacrifices for their aboleth "gods." Some kuo-toas escape their depraved society to become slaves, mercenaries, or even leaders among other Underdark races.

Level 12 Encounter (XP 3,500)
✦ 3 kuo-toa marauders (level 12 skirmisher)
✦ 1 foulspawn hulks (level 12 brute)

Level 18 Encounter (XP 11,000)
✦ 2 kuo-toa monitors (level 16 skirmisher)
✦ 4 kuo-toa guards (level 16 minion)
✦ 1 aboleth overseer (level 18 elite controller)
✦ 8 aboleth servitors (level 16 minion)

(Left to right) kuo-toa monitor, kuo-toa whip, and kuo-toa harpooner

LAMIA

Lamias lure victims to their deaths by assuming a pleasing humanoid guise. Some lamias, driven by the need to consume other sentient creatures, simply stalk humanoids wherever they can find them. Others possess a twisted thirst for knowledge, seeking to acquire arcane lore and magical power at any cost.

In its true form, a lamia is a swarm of black scarab beetles assembled into a coherent mass around the flesh-stripped bones of a powerful fey creature. This swarm shares a single intelligence and can mask itself in the guise of an attractive humanoid. It sometimes appears to be a human, elf, eladrin, or drow partly comprised of scores of beetles.

LAMIA LORE

A character knows the following information with a successful Arcana check.

DC 20: A lamia is a bizarre fey comprised of hundreds of black scarab beetles. It lures wayfarers to their deaths by assuming a pleasing humanoid guise.

DC 25: When a lamia slays a humanoid creature, it adds another beetle to its evergrowing swarm. When a lamia's swarm grows too large, it reproduces by first slaying a worthy fey creature such as a powerful eladrin. Rather than consuming the body, the lamia divides itself, filling the corpse with hundreds of its beetles. Over time, these beetles devour the corpse and arise as a new lamia. This newborn lamia gains much of the victim's memories and knowledge in the process.

Lamia	Level 12 Elite Controller (Leader)
Medium fey magical beast (shapechanger)	XP 1,400

Initiative +8   **Senses** Perception +13

Swarm's Embrace aura 1; an enemy that starts its turn in the aura takes 10 damage.

HP 244; **Bloodied** 122

AC 28; **Fortitude** 25, **Reflex** 24, **Will** 26

Resist takes half damage from melee and ranged attacks; **Vulnerable** 10 against close and area attacks.

Saving Throws +2

Speed 6, climb 6

Action Points 1

⊕ **Cursed Touch** (standard; at-will) ✦ **Healing**
+16 vs. Fortitude; 1d6 + 4 damage, and the target is dazed (save ends). In addition, the lamia regains a number of hit points equal to the amount of damage dealt.

⊥ **Devouring Swarm** (standard; sustain minor; at-will)
Reach 5; +16 vs. Fortitude; 3d6 + 4 damage. When the lamia sustains this power, the devouring swarm deals 3d6 + 4 damage to the target (no attack roll required). The target must be within this power's range for the lamia to sustain the power.

↢ **Pacifying Burst** (standard; recharge ⚄ ⚅) ✦ **Psychic**
Close burst 5; +16 vs. Will; the target is stunned (save ends).

Change Shape (minor; at-will) ✦ **Polymorph**
A lamia can alter its physical form to appear as an attractive Medium humanoid of any race or gender (see Change Shape, page 280).

Squeezing Swarm
By altering its shape, a lamia can squeeze through small openings as if it were a Tiny creature (see "Squeeze", *Player's Handbook* 292).

Alignment Evil   **Languages** Common, Elven

Skills Arcana +14, Bluff +16, Insight +13

Str 13 (+7)	**Dex** 14 (+8)	**Wis** 14 (+8)
Con 18 (+10)	**Int** 17 (+9)	**Cha** 21 (+11)

LAMIA TACTICS

The lamia uses *change shape* to assume a pleasing appearance, hoping to lure enemies within range of its *pacifying burst*. It spends its action point to use this power, and then immediately uses *devouring swarm* against a stunned foe within range. It sustains *devouring swarm* round after round as a minor action, attacking a new target only if the previous target moves out of range. The lamia heals itself by making *cursed touch* attacks and unleashes another *pacifying burst* as soon as the power recharges.

ENCOUNTER GROUPS

Lamias often enslave weaker creatures to serve as bodyguards or fodder.

Level 12 Encounter (XP 3,600)
✦ 1 lamia (level 12 elite controller)
✦ 2 mezzodemons (level 11 soldier)
✦ 4 cyclops guards (level 14 minion)

LARVA MAGE

When a powerful evil spellcaster dies, his spirit sometimes takes control of the wriggling mass of worms and maggots devouring his corpse. This mass of vermin rises as a larva mage to continue the spellcaster's dark schemes or to seek revenge against those who slew him.

Larva Mage	Level 21 Elite Artillery
Medium natural magical beast (undead)	XP 6,400

Initiative +13 **Senses** Perception +12
HP 304; **Bloodied** 152
AC 35; **Fortitude** 30, **Reflex** 33, **Will** 27
Immune disease, poison; **Resist** 10 necrotic; takes half damage from melee and ranged attacks; **Vulnerable** 10 radiant, 10 against close and area attacks.
Saving Throws +2
Speed 6
Action Points 1
⊕ **Corrupting Touch** (standard; at-will) ✦ **Necrotic**
  +24 vs. Fortitude; 2d6 + 5 necrotic damage.
⤳ **Horrific Visage** (minor; recharge ⚄ ⚅) ✦ **Fear**
  Ranged 10; +24 vs. Will; the target cannot attack the larva mage until the end of its next turn and is immobilized (save ends).
⤳ **Ray of Cold Death** (standard; at-will) ✦ **Cold, Necrotic**
  Ranged 20; +26 vs. AC; 2d8 + 8 cold and necrotic damage, or 4d8 + 8 cold and necrotic damage if the target is bloodied.
⤳ **Worm's Feast** (standard; recharge ⚅) ✦ **Illusion**
  Ranged 5; the target is tricked into believing that worms are devouring its flesh; +26 vs. Will; 4d10 + 8 damage. If this damage doesn't reduce the target to 0 or fewer hit points, the target takes no damage but is stunned until the end of its next turn.
⤌ **Withering Flame** (standard; at-will) ✦ **Fire, Necrotic**
  Area burst 1 within 20; +24 vs. Reflex; 2d6 + 8 fire and necrotic damage.
Squeezing Swarm
  By altering its shape, a larva mage can squeeze through small openings as if it were a Tiny creature (see "Squeeze", *Player's Handbook* 292).
Alignment Evil   **Languages** Common
Skills Arcana +23, History +23, Religion +23
Str 14 (+12)	**Dex** 16 (+13)	**Wis** 14 (+12)
Con 20 (+15)	**Int** 26 (+18)	**Cha** 15 (+12)

LARVA MAGE TACTICS

The larva mage uses *horrific visage* to hold off enemy defenders and melee strikers while using *ray of cold death* and *withering flame* to soften up ranged targets. The larva mage uses *worm's feast* against a bloodied foe and normally spends its action point to take a second move action when it needs to put some added distance between itself and its enemies.

LARVA MAGE LORE

A character knows the following information with a successful Religion check.

DC 25: Only the most evil spellcasters return to unlife as larva mages. When a larva mage is destroyed, the maggots and worms that comprise its physical form lose their sentience and become harmless vermin.

DC 30: Particularly powerful larva mages retain more of their previous spellcasting ability than others, and know

several wizard powers. They often carry their old spellbooks around with them.

DC 35: An elder evil being called Kyuss created the first larva mages to guard vaults of forbidden lore. These larva mages are among the most powerful of their kind and wield an impressive array of spells.

Encounter Groups

Larva mages often compel other monsters to serve them. They occasionally convene in small groups to work their dark magic or achieve some common goal.

Level 21 Encounter (XP 16,000)
✦ 1 larva mage (level 21 elite artillery)
✦ 4 slaughter wights (level 18 brute)
✦ 1 sword wraith (level 17 lurker)

Level 22 Encounter (XP 21,175)
✦ 1 larva mage (level 21 elite artillery)
✦ 3 rot harbingers (level 20 soldier)
✦ 5 abyssal ghoul myrmidons (level 23 minion)

Level 22 Encounter (XP 25,100)
✦ 2 larva magi (level 21 elite artillery)
✦ 2 rockfire dreadnought elementals (level 18 soldier)
✦ 8 grimlock followers (level 22 minion)

LICH

A LICH IS AN UNDEAD SPELLCASTER created by means of an ancient ritual. Wizards and other arcane spellcasters who choose this path to immortality escape death by becoming undead, but prolonged existence in this state often drives them mad.

Liches are cold, scheming creatures that hunger for ever greater power, long-forgotten knowledge, and the most terrible of arcane secrets.

"Lich" is a monster template that can be applied to non-player characters. See the *Dungeon Master's Guide* for rules on creating new liches using the template.

Lich (Human Wizard)	Level 14 Elite Controller
Medium natural humanoid (undead)	XP 2,000

Initiative +8   **Senses** Perception +8; darkvision
Necromantic Aura (Necrotic) aura 5; any living creature that enters or starts its turn in the aura takes 5 necrotic damage.
HP 218; **Bloodied** 109
Regeneration 10 (if the lich takes radiant damage, regeneration doesn't function on its next turn)
AC 28; **Fortitude** 24, **Reflex** 28, **Will** 26
Immune disease, poison; **Resist** 10 necrotic
Saving Throws +2
Speed 6
Action Points 1
ⓨ **Shadow Ray** (standard; at-will) ✦ **Necrotic**
    Ranged 20; +18 vs. Reflex; 2d8 + 6 necrotic damage.
❊ **Frostburn** (standard; sustain minor; recharge ▣ ▦) ✦ **Cold, Necrotic, Zone**
    Area burst 2 within 20; +18 vs. Fortitude; 3d8 + 6 cold and necrotic damage. The burst creates a zone that lasts until the end of the lich's next turn. The zone is considered difficult terrain. Any creature that starts its turn within the zone takes 10 cold and necrotic damage. The lich can sustain or dismiss the zone as a minor action.
Indestructible
    When a lich is reduced to 0 hit points, its body and possessions crumble into dust, but it is not destroyed. It reappears (along with its possessions) in 1d10 days within 1 square of its phylactery, unless the phylactery is also found and destroyed.
Second Wind (standard; encounter) ✦ **Healing**
    The lich spends a healing surge and regains 54 hit points. The lich gains a +2 bonus to all defenses until the start of its next turn.
Alignment Evil	**Languages** Abyssal, Common

Skills Arcana +18, History +18, Insight +13
Str 11 (+7)	**Dex** 12 (+8)	**Wis** 13 (+8)
Con 14 (+9)	**Int** 22 (+13)	**Cha** 18 (+11)

HUMAN LICH TACTICS
As long as its phylactery is safe, this lich doesn't show much concern for its own wellbeing. It uses *frostburn* as often as it can and spends its action point to use *second wind* when first bloodied.

Lich (Eladrin Wizard)	Level 24 Elite Controller
Medium natural humanoid (undead)	XP 12,100

Initiative +14   **Senses** Perception +14; darkvision
Necromantic Aura (Necrotic) aura 5; any living creature that enters or starts its turn in the aura takes 5 necrotic damage.
HP 362; **Bloodied** 181
Regeneration 10 (if the lich takes radiant damage, regeneration doesn't function on its next turn)
AC 38; **Fortitude** 33, **Reflex** 38, **Will** 38
Immune disease, poison; **Resist** 10 necrotic
Saving Throws +2
Speed 6
Action Points 1
ⓨ **Shadow Ray** (standard; at-will) ✦ **Necrotic**
    Ranged 20; +28 vs. Reflex; 3d8 + 7 necrotic damage.
⤳ **Necrotic Orb** (standard; recharge ▣ ▦) ✦ **Necrotic**
    Ranged 20; +28 vs. Fortitude; 3d8 + 7 necrotic damage, and the target is stunned until the end of the lich's next turn.
❊ **Entropic Pulse** (standard; recharge ▣ ▦) ✦ **Necrotic**
    Area burst 2 within 20; +28 vs. Reflex; 6d6 + 7 necrotic damage.
Indestructible
    When a lich is reduced to 0 hit points, its body and possessions crumble into dust, but it is not destroyed. It reappears (along with its possessions) in 1d10 days within 1 square of its phylactery, unless the phylactery is also found and destroyed.
Second Wind (standard; encounter) ✦ **Healing**
    The lich spends a healing surge and regains 90 hit points. The lich gains a +2 bonus to all defenses until the start of its next turn.
Alignment Evil	**Languages** Common, Elven

Skills Arcana +24, History +24, Insight +19
Str 12 (+13)	**Dex** 15 (+14)	**Wis** 15 (+14)
Con 18 (+16)	**Int** 25 (+19)	**Cha** 21 (+17)

ELADRIN LICH TACTICS
This lich uses *entropic pulse* and *necrotic orb* as often as it can. Once bloodied, it spends an action point to use *second wind*.

LICH VESTIGE
A LICH VESTIGE IS THE ARCANE REMNANT OF A DESTROYED LICH. Its frail skeletal body trails off into wisps of shadow, and it seems to glide across the ground. Unlike liches, a lich vestige does not have a phylactery. Highly unstable, it crumbles to dust when damaged.

Lich Vestige	Level 26 Minion
Medium natural humanoid (undead)	XP 2,250

Initiative +14   **Senses** Perception +19; darkvision
Necromantic Aura (Necrotic) aura 2; any living creature that enters or starts its turn in the aura takes 5 necrotic damage.
HP 1; a missed attack never damages a minion.
AC 40; **Fortitude** 36, **Reflex** 40, **Will** 38
Immune disease, poison; **Resist** 20 necrotic
Speed 6
ⓣ **Death's Touch** (standard; at-will) ✦ **Necrotic**
    +30 vs. AC; 10 necrotic damage, and the target is weakened (save ends).
ⓨ **Shadow Ray** (standard; at-will) ✦ **Necrotic**
    Ranged 20; +30 vs. Reflex; 10 necrotic damage, or 15 necrotic damage if the target is an arcane power user (such as a wizard).
❊ **Orb of Obliteration** (standard; encounter) ✦ **Fire, Necrotic**

Two, three, or four lich vestiges acting on the same initiative count can use their standard actions to hurl a single orb of black fire that detonates on impact. Make one attack roll: Area burst 5 within 10 of one of the lich vestiges; +30 vs. Reflex; 5 fire and necrotic damage per lich vestige making the attack, and ongoing fire and necrotic damage equal to 5 per lich vestige making the attack (save ends).

Alignment Evil	Languages Abyssal, Common	
Skills Arcana +24		
Str 11 (+13)	Dex 12 (+14)	Wis 13 (+14)
Con 14 (+15)	Int 22 (+19)	Cha 18 (+17)

LICH VESTIGE TACTICS

The lich vestige joins forces with other nearby lich vestiges to unleash *orb of obliteration* as soon as possible, and then zaps enemies with its *shadow ray*. It uses *death's touch* only when forced into melee combat.

LICH LORE

A character knows the following information with a successful Religion check.

DC 20: A mortal becomes a lich by performing a dark and terrible ritual. In this ritual the mortal dies, but rises again as an undead creature. Most liches are wizards or warlocks, but a few multiclassed clerics follow this dark path.

LICH TRANSFORMATION

You call upon Orcus, Demon Prince of the Undead, to transform your body into a skeletal thing, undead and immortal, and bind your life force within a specially prepared receptacle called a phylactery.

Level: 14 (caster must be humanoid)
Category: Creation
Time: 1 hour; see text
Duration: Permanent; see text
Component Cost: 100,000 gp
Market Price: 250,000 gp
Key Skill: Arcana or Religion (no check)

At the conclusion of this ritual, you die, transform into a lich, and gain the lich template (*Dungeon Master's Guide* 179).

An integral part of becoming a lich is creating a phylactery, a magical receptacle containing your life force. When you are reduced to 0 hit points or fewer, you and your possessions crumble to dust. Unless your phylactery is located and destroyed, your reappear in a space adjacent to the phylactery after 1d10 days.

You must construct your phylactery before the ritual can be performed. The phylactery, which takes 10 days to create, usually takes the form of a sealed metal box containing strips of parchment on which magical phrases have been transcribed in your blood. The box measures 6 inches on a side and has 40 hit points and resist 20 to all damage. Other kinds of phylacteries include rings and amulets, which are just as durable.

If your phylactery is destroyed, you can build a new one; the process takes 10 days and costs 50,000 gp.

DC 25: A lich's life force is bound up in a magic phylactery, which typically takes the form of a fist-sized metal box containing strips of parchment on which magical phrases have been written. If you destroy a lich, its spirit returns to its phylactery. Its body reforms in 1d10 days at the location of the phylactery unless you also destroy the phylactery. Most liches hide their phylacteries in secret (and well-guarded) vaults, sometimes on other planes.

Destroying a lich and its phylactery does not guarantee that the lich is gone forever. Powerful beings associated with undeath, including Orcus and Vecna, can reform a destroyed lich, turning it into a lich vestige.

DC 30: Some of the most fearsome villains in the long history of the world have been liches, including Acererak–master of the Tomb of Horrors–and the god Vecna himself. All liches pay homage to Orcus, and it is said that Orcus can instantly destroy the phylactery of any lich that displeases him.

ENCOUNTER GROUPS

Liches often command armies of lesser undead or have demons or devils serving them.

Level 25 Encounter (XP 35,400)
✦ 1 eladrin lich (level 24 elite controller)
✦ 2 great flameskulls (level 24 artillery)
✦ 2 soulspike devourers (level 20 elite soldier)

Level 26 Encounter (XP 49,500)
✦ 6 lich vestiges (level 26 minion)
✦ Doresain the Ghoul King (level 27 elite skirmisher)
✦ 2 dread wraiths (level 25 lurker)

LIZARDFOLK

Lizardfolk inhabit swamps and marshes, feeding on local wildlife and driving off or killing trespassers entering their territory. Some especially cruel and savage lizardfolk capture and eat other humanoid creatures, boldly launching raids against the lands of nearby humanoids to capture victims for their feasts.

Lizardfolk excel at swimming and often take to the water to stalk prey and evade pursuit. They can hold their breath for up to ten minutes without trouble.

Lizardfolk come in many varieties, including greenscale lizardfolk (the most common breed) and blackscales. Blackscales are dumb, hulking brutes that often inhabit the same swamps and marshes as their smaller kin. A blackscale tribe might be an enemy to a lizardfolk tribe, but more often the two work together or even intermingle in the same village. Blackscales rarely become leaders of mixed tribes since they are simply too dull-witted for the job, but they frequently accompany raiding parties or serve as bodyguards to the tribal chieftain or marsh mystic.

LIZARDFOLK LORE

A character knows the following information with a successful Nature check.

DC 15: Lizardfolk favor humid climates. They dwell in warm or temperate marshes, swamps, and jungles, or more rarely in flooded cavern systems.

Lizardfolk occasionally trade with humanoids they trust (usually halflings), bartering for finished goods. However, tribes that prey on other humanoids generally don't engage in any kind of trade.

DC 20: Lizardfolk hatch from eggs and grow quickly to adulthood; by 2 years of age, they are fully grown. A tribe maintains a communal incubator in which all the tribe's eggs are sealed together. Young lizardfolk are raised together by the whole tribe. Parental relationships do not exist among lizardfolk.

Lizardfolk have a patriarchal society in which the most powerful member rules the others as chieftain. Shamans and mystics commonly advise the chieftain.

DC 25: Lizardfolk do not worship gods, but large tribes often elevate one of their own to the status of a living deity. This figure becomes the tribe's lizard king. A lizard king usually possesses unusual strength, ferocity, and cleverness and might be tainted by primordial or demonic influences. Powerful reptilian creatures such as dragons sometimes usurp this role and command a tribe's loyalty.

ENCOUNTER GROUPS

Insular and fierce, lizardfolk rarely combine forces with other humanoids. However, they frequently tame reptilian creatures such as behemoths, crocodiles, or drakes, or serve more powerful monsters such as dragons.

Level 4 Encounter (XP 900)
- ✦ 2 greenscale hunters (level 4 skirmisher)
- ✦ 2 visejaw crocodiles (level 4 soldier)
- ✦ 1 vine horror (level 5 controller)

Level 6 Encounter (XP 1,300)
- ✦ 1 greenscale marsh mystic (level 6 controller)
- ✦ 2 blackscale bruisers (level 6 brute)
- ✦ 1 greenscale darter (level 5 lurker)
- ✦ 2 greenscale hunters (level 4 skirmisher)

Greenscale Hunter		Level 4 Skirmisher
Medium natural humanoid (reptile)		XP 175

Initiative +6   **Senses** Perception +8
HP 54; **Bloodied** 27
AC 17; **Fortitude** 15, **Reflex** 14, **Will** 13
Speed 6 (swamp walk)
⊕ **Spear** (standard; at-will) ✦ **Weapon**
  +9 vs. AC; 1d8 + 3 damage.
† **Sidestep Attack** (standard; at-will) ✦ **Weapon**
  The lizardfolk shifts and make a melee basic attack.

Alignment Unaligned	**Languages** Draconic

Skills Athletics +10, Nature +8

Str 17 (+5)	**Dex** 15 (+4)	**Wis** 12 (+3)
Con 14 (+4)	**Int** 8 (+1)	**Cha** 8 (+1)

Equipment light shield, spear

GREENSCALE HUNTER TACTICS

Greenscale hunters like to set traps and ambush prey. In combat, they use *sidestep attack* to maneuver into flanking positions.

Greenscale Darter		Level 5 Lurker
Medium natural humanoid (reptile)		XP 200

Initiative +10   **Senses** Perception +9
HP 50; **Bloodied** 25
AC 18; **Fortitude** 14, **Reflex** 17, **Will** 14
Speed 6 (swamp walk)
⊕ **Club** (standard; at-will) ✦ **Weapon**
  +10 vs. AC; 1d6 + 1 damage.
↗ **Blowgun** (standard; at-will) ✦ **Poison, Weapon**
  Loading the blowgun takes a minor action; Ranged 6/12; +10 vs. AC; 1 damage, and the greenscale darter makes a secondary attack against the same target. *Secondary Attack:* +8 vs Fortitude; the target takes ongoing 5 poison damage and is slowed (save ends both).
Sniper
  A hidden lizardfolk darter that misses with a ranged attack remains hidden.

Alignment Unaligned	**Languages** Draconic

Skills Athletics +8, Stealth +11

Str 13 (+3)	**Dex** 18 (+6)	**Wis** 15 (+4)
Con 14 (+4)	**Int** 8 (+1)	**Cha** 8 (+1)

Equipment club, blowgun with 20 poisoned darts

GREENSCALE DARTER TACTICS

Greenscale darters hide in the undergrowth, attacking with their blowguns and using their stealth and *sniper* power to remain hidden.

Greenscale Marsh Mystic — Level 6 Controller (Leader)
Medium natural humanoid (reptile) — XP 250

Initiative +4   **Senses** Perception +7
Marsh Blessing (Healing) aura 5; allies that start their turns in the aura regain 3 hit points.
HP 70; **Bloodied** 35
AC 19; **Fortitude** 15, **Reflex** 14, **Will** 19
Speed 6 (swamp walk)

(⊕) **Spear** (standard; at-will) ✦ **Weapon**
   +7 vs. AC; 1d8 + 2 damage.

✵ **Swamp's Grasp** (standard; encounter) ✦ **Zone**
   Area burst 2 within 10; +9 vs. Reflex; the target is immobilized (save ends). The zone is difficult swamp terrain until the end of the encounter.

✵ **Bog Cloud** (standard; recharge ▨ ▥) ✦ **Poison**
   Area burst 2 within 10; +9 vs. Fortitude; 2d8 + 4 poison damage, and the target is dazed until the end of the marsh mystic's next turn.

Alignment Unaligned   **Languages** Draconic
Skills Athletics +10, Nature +12

Str 15 (+5)	**Dex** 13 (+4)	**Wis** 19 (+7)
Con 14 (+5)	**Int** 10 (+3)	**Cha** 12 (+4)

Equipment spear, bone breastplate

Blackscale Bruiser — Level 6 Brute
Large natural humanoid (reptile) — XP 250

Initiative +6   **Senses** Perception +9
HP 86; **Bloodied** 43
AC 18; **Fortitude** 19, **Reflex** 16, **Will** 14
Speed 8 (swamp walk)

(⊕) **Greatclub** (standard; at-will) ✦ **Weapon**
   Reach 2; +9 vs. AC; 1d10 + 6 damage, and the target is pushed 1 square.

‡ **Tail Slap** (standard; at-will)
   +7 vs. Reflex; 1d8 + 6 damage, and the target is knocked prone.

Alignment Unaligned   **Languages** Draconic
Skills Athletics +14

Str 22 (+9)	**Dex** 16 (+6)	**Wis** 12 (+4)
Con 16 (+6)	**Int** 5 (+0)	**Cha** 6 (+1)

Equipment greatclub

BLACKSCALE BRUISER TACTICS
This blackscale bruiser pulverizes enemies with its greatclub and pushes them into reach of its allies, if possible. It uses its *tail slap* to make opportunity attacks.

GREENSCALE MARSH MYSTIC TACTICS
The marsh mystic normally begins a fight by using *swamp's grasp* to immobilize enemies and create difficult terrain through which its allies can move with impunity. It stays close to its allies so that they benefit from its *marsh blessing* aura, attacking with its spear and using *bog cloud* whenever it becomes available.

(Left to right) greenscale marsh mystic, blackscale bruiser, greenscale hunter, and greenscale darter

STEVE PRESCOTT

LYCANTHROPE

A LYCANTHROPE IS A BESTIAL SHAPECHANGER that preys on other living creatures. It often assumes animal form in the wild, hunting in packs with similar animals or others of its kind. When infiltrating civilized humanoid settlements, it assumes a benign humanoid form, blending in with the local populace.

Lycanthropes gather in clannish communities hidden in remote places, or they live secretly among other races. Although they hunt when they please, lycanthropes are most active on nights of the full moon.

A lycanthrope superficially resembles a human or other humanoid creature. It stands erect but has the head of a ravenous animal, such as a rat or wolf.

A lycanthrope can assume the form of a specific humanoid, usually a human with subtle physical traits that betray the creature's true heritage (long hair, long fingernails, or pointed teeth, for instance). A lycanthrope assumes humanoid form only when it needs to disguise itself as something nonthreatening.

In animal form, a lycanthrope resembles a powerful version of the normal animal, although its eyes betray a spark of unnatural intelligence. A lycanthrope typically assumes animal form when it hunts, and sometimes when it needs to flee.

LYCANTHROPE LORE
A character knows the following information with a successful Nature check.

DC 15: Lycanthropy is hereditary, and lycanthropes mate with those of a similar species to produce lycanthrope offspring. Some lycanthropes can also mate with similarly sized humanoids, sometimes producing lycanthrope children. However, the blood is diluted in this way, and many such children never change or instead become shifters.

ENCOUNTER GROUPS
Lycanthropes mix with other humanoids. They also form bands that include likeminded lycanthropes. Fey and lycanthropes often get along, as do shifters and lycanthropes.

Level 4 Encounter (XP 886)
✦ 2 wererats (level 3 skirmisher)
✦ 4 dire rats (level 1 brute)
✦ 6 human rabble (level 2 minion)

Level 9 Encounter (XP 2,200)
✦ 4 werewolves (level 8 brute)
✦ 4 dire wolves (level 5 skirmisher)

Wererat		Level 3 Skirmisher
Medium natural humanoid (shapechanger)		XP 150

Initiative +7   **Senses** Perception +7; low-light vision
HP 48; **Bloodied** 24
Regeneration 5 (if the wererat takes damage from a silver weapon, its regeneration doesn't function on its next turn)
AC 17; **Fortitude** 15, **Reflex** 16, **Will** 13
Immune filth fever (see below)
Speed 6, climb 4 (not in human form)
ⓐ **Short Sword** (standard; at-will) ✦ **Weapon**
+8 vs. AC; 1d6 + 4 damage.
ⓐ **Bite** (standard; at-will) ✦ **Disease**
+8 vs. AC; 1d4 + 2 damage, and the target takes ongoing 2 damage (save ends) and contracts filth fever (see below).
Change Shape (minor; at-will) ✦ **Polymorph**
A wererat can alter its physical form to appear as a dire rat or a unique human (see Change Shape, page 280). It loses its bite attack in human form.
Combat Advantage
The wererat deals an extra 1d6 damage on melee attacks against any target it has combat advantage against.
Alignment Evil   **Languages** Common
Skills Bluff +6, Stealth +10, Streetwise +6, Thievery +10
| **Str** 10 (+1) | **Dex** 18 (+5) | **Wis** 12 (+2) |
| **Con** 16 (+4) | **Int** 10 (+1) | **Cha** 11 (+1) |
Equipment cloak, short sword

WERERAT TACTICS
Wererats usually assume dire rat form and wait in ambush, hoping to surprise their enemies and gain combat advantage. They use *change shape* to assume their natural hybrid forms and try to flank foes. They prefer to attack with their short swords, resorting to bite attacks when disarmed.

Filth Fever	Level 3 Disease	Endurance stable DC 16, improve DC 21
The target is cured.	◀ **Initial Effect:** The target loses 1 healing surge.	◀▶ The target takes a -2 penalty to AC, Fortitude defense, and Reflex defense.	▶ **Final State:** The target takes a -2 penalty to AC, Fortitude defense, and Reflex defense. The target loses all healing surges and cannot regain hit points.

CHRIS STEVENS & JIM ZUBKAVICH

Werewolf		Level 8 Brute
Medium natural humanoid (shapechanger)		XP 350

Initiative +7 **Senses** Perception +11; low-light vision
HP 108; **Bloodied** 54
Regeneration 5 (if the werewolf takes damage from a silver weapon, its regeneration doesn't function on its next turn)
AC 20; **Fortitude** 20, **Reflex** 19, **Will** 18
Immune moon frenzy (see below)
Speed 6 (8 in wolf form)
① **Greatclub** (standard; at-will) ✦ **Weapon**
　+12 vs. AC; 2d4 + 4 damage; see also *blood rage*.
① **Bite** (standard; at-will) ✦ **Disease**
　+12 vs. AC; 1d6 + 4 damage, and the target takes ongoing 5 damage (save ends) and contracts moon frenzy (see below); see also *blood rage*.
Blood Rage
　The werewolf's melee attacks deal 4 extra damage against a bloodied target.

Change Shape (minor; at-will) ✦ **Polymorph**
　A werewolf can alter its physical form to appear as a gray wolf or a unique human (see Change Shape, page 280). It cannot use its bite attack in human form and cannot make greatclub attacks in wolf form.

Alignment Evil	**Languages** Common	
Skills Bluff +9, Insight +11, Intimidate +9, Nature +11		
Str 19 (+8)	**Dex** 16 (+7)	**Wis** 14 (+6)
Con 18 (+8)	**Int** 10 (+4)	**Cha** 11 (+4)
Equipment leather armor, greatclub		

WEREWOLF TACTICS

A lone werewolf tries to isolate and pick off victims one at a time. When bloodied, it usually flees to regenerate. In the wild, werewolves tend to hunt in packs. When a pack of werewolves attacks, half of the pack fights in true hybrid form (wielding greatclubs) and other half fights in wolf form.

Moon Frenzy	Level 8 Disease	Endurance stable DC 20, improve DC 24

◄ The target is cured. ◄▶ **Initial Effect:** The target takes a –2 penalty to Will defense. ◄▶ While bloodied, the target must make a saving throw at the end of each turn. If the saving throw fails, the target makes a melee attack on its next turn against a random target within 5 squares of it. If no targets are within 5 squares, the target does nothing but move in a randomly chosen direction. ▶ **Final State:** The target attacks the nearest creature in its line of sight. If it can't see any other creatures, it does nothing but move in a randomly chosen direction.

MAGMA BEAST

Magma beasts are fiery elementals from the depths of the Elemental Chaos. They sometimes find their way to the world through planar rifts or elemental vortices in places of intense volcanic activity.

Magma beasts can survive on various ores and clays or minor elemental creatures, but they prefer to hunt organic creatures, savoring the taste of burned flesh.

Magma Beast Lore

A character knows the following information with a successful Arcana check.

DC 15: Magma beasts are elemental beings that originate in the Elemental Chaos. Many now live in the natural world, having crossed over into volcanic regions of the surface and the Underdark.

DC 20: Magma brutes and magma hurlers are smarter than most magma beasts and can sometimes be bribed with regular gifts of food. They serve anyone who can promise them interesting meals, and they occasionally bully lesser magma beasts into fighting alongside them.

DC 25: Humanoids slain by magma beasts are usually devoured in their entirety—including their equipment. Magma beasts consume even the steel of armor and weapons, given time.

Magma Claw

This creature poses as a hunk of volcanic rock until it's ready to strike. It then rushes toward its prey and immobilizes it by disgorging sticky lava through its claws around the victim's legs. It then burns and bludgeons the trapped victim to death.

Magma Claw		Level 4 Brute
Medium elemental magical beast (earth, fire)		XP 175

Initiative +3   **Senses** Perception +7
HP 64; **Bloodied** 32
AC 16; **Fortitude** 16, **Reflex** 14, **Will** 13
Immune petrification; **Resist** 10 fire; **Vulnerable** cold (slowed until the end of the magma claw's next turn)
Speed 4 (8 while charging)
(+) **Claw** (standard; at-will) ✦ **Fire**
  +7 vs. AC; 1d6 + 4 damage plus 1d6 fire damage.
† **Spew Lava** (standard; at-will) ✦ **Fire**
  +5 vs. Reflex; the target takes ongoing 5 fire damage and is immobilized (save ends both).
Alignment Unaligned   **Languages** Primordial
Skills Endurance +9, Stealth +8
Str 18 (+6)	**Dex** 12 (+3)	**Wis** 11 (+2)
Con 14 (+4)	**Int** 2 (-2)	**Cha** 6 (+0)

Magma Claw Tactics

The magma claw uses its natural stealth to pose as an outcropping of volcanic rock until a target comes close enough for the magma claw to charge it. The magma claw then uses its *spew lava* power to trap its foe in cooling lava while it makes claw attacks.

MAGMA HURLER

This elemental hurls globs of molten magma at enemies from a distance before closing in to feast on the burned flesh.

Magma Hurler		Level 4 Artillery
Medium elemental humanoid (earth, fire)		XP 175

Initiative +8   **Senses** Perception +4
HP 41; **Bloodied** 20
AC 18; **Fortitude** 15, **Reflex** 17, **Will** 13
Immune petrification; **Resist** 10 fire; **Vulnerable** cold (slowed until the end of the magma hurler's next turn)
Speed 4
(+) **Slam** (standard; at-will)
  +8 vs. AC; 1d6 + 4 damage.
➷ **Magma Ball** (standard; at-will) ✦ **Fire**
  Ranged 15; +7 vs. Reflex; 1d6 + 6 fire damage. *Miss:* Creatures adjacent to the target take 1d6 fire damage.
Alignment Unaligned   **Languages** Primordial
Skills Endurance +7
Str 18 (+6)	**Dex** 22 (+8)	**Wis** 14 (+4)
Con 11 (+2)	**Int** 5 (-1)	**Cha** 8 (+1)

Magma Hurler Tactics

A magma hurler disgorges magma into one of its scoop-like arms and hurls it at an enemy in range. It tries to pelt enemies to death from a distance. Once an enemy gets close, the magma hurler abandons ranged combat and makes slam attacks instead.

MAGMA STRIDER

Magma striders are relentless predators that are willing to pursue victims for miles, wearing down their prey through sheer persistence.

Magma Strider		Level 10 Skirmisher
Large elemental magical beast (earth, fire)		XP 500

Initiative +12   **Senses** Perception +7
Blazing Heat (Fire) aura 2; enemies in the aura at the start of their turns take 5 fire damage.
HP 105; **Bloodied** 52
AC 24; **Fortitude** 20, **Reflex** 22, **Will** 19
Immune petrification; **Resist** 10 fire; **Vulnerable** cold (slowed until the end of the magma strider's next turn)
Speed 6, climb 6
(+) **Bite** (standard; at-will) ✦ **Fire**
  Reach 2; +15 vs. AC; 1d6 + 5 damage, and ongoing 5 fire damage (save ends).
† **Burn Across the Battlefield** (free, when the magma strider hits with its bite attack; recharge ▢ ▢ ▢ ▢)
  The magma strider can charge another target up to 6 squares away and make another bite attack.
Burning Mobility ✦ **Fire**
  Any creature that makes an opportunity attack against the magma strider takes ongoing 5 fire damage (save ends).
Alignment Unaligned   **Languages** Primordial
Skills Endurance +13
Str 16 (+8)	**Dex** 21 (+10)	**Wis** 14 (+7)
Con 17 (+8)	**Int** 2 (+1)	**Cha** 10 (+5)

(Top left, clockwise) magma strider, magma brute, magma claw, and magma hurler

R SPEARS

MAGMA STRIDER TACTICS

Magma striders dash from foe to foe, heedless of opportunity attacks (their *burning mobility* makes it dangerous to strike at them). They try to set fire to as many targets as possible by biting a different target each round and using *burn across the battlefield* as often as possible.

MAGMA BRUTE

MAGMA BRUTES ARE ILL-TEMPERED ELEMENTALS easily cajoled or intimidated into serving more powerful elemental monsters. Left to their own devices, they are solitary scavengers that wander the Elemental Chaos or fiery regions of the natural world.

Magma Brute	Level 13 Brute
Large elemental humanoid (earth, fire)	XP 800

Initiative +9   **Senses** Perception +7
HP 156; **Bloodied** 78
AC 25; **Fortitude** 26, **Reflex** 23, **Will** 21
Immune petrification; **Resist** 20 fire; **Vulnerable** cold (slowed until the end of the magma brute's next turn)
Speed 4
⊕ **Slam** (standard; at-will) ✦ **Fire**
     Reach 2; +17 vs. AC; 1d8 + 6 damage, and ongoing 5 fire damage (save ends).
Alignment Unaligned   **Languages** Primordial
Skills Endurance +14
Str 22 (+12)   **Dex** 16 (+9)   **Wis** 13 (+7)
Con 16 (+9)   **Int** 5 (+3)   **Cha** 8 (+5)

MAGMA BRUTE TACTICS

Magma brutes use their slam attacks to crush and burn anything in their path. Usually they turn on whichever enemy hurt them the most in the previous round.

ENCOUNTER GROUPS

Mixed groups of magma beasts are common, and any type of magma beast can be lured into fighting for powerful fire monsters such as salamanders, fire archons, or even fire giants.

Level 5 Encounter (XP 1,100)
✦ 2 magma claws (level 4 brute)
✦ 2 magma hurlers (level 4 artillery)
✦ 2 fire bats (level 5 skirmisher)

Level 13 Encounter (XP 4,000)
✦ 3 magma brutes (level 13 brute)
✦ 1 beholder eye of flame (level 13 elite artillery)

A MANTICORE FLINGS IRON SPIKES from its tail. Irritable and mean, it attacks without provocation and does not negotiate with prey.

Manticores often make their lairs in caves or on sheltered ledges high on rocky peaks. They hunt by picking a high spot that offers a good view and watching for something worth eating.

Manticore	Level 10 Elite Skirmisher
Large natural magical beast (mount)	XP 1,000

Initiative +12   **Senses** Perception +13
HP 210; **Bloodied** 105
AC 26; **Fortitude** 24, **Reflex** 24, **Will** 22
Saving Throws +2
Speed 6, fly 8, overland flight 10
Action Points 1

⊕ **Claw** (standard; at-will)
+15 vs. AC; 2d6 + 5 damage.

↗ **Spike** (standard; at-will)
Ranged 10; +15 vs. AC (see also *guided sniper*); 1d8 + 5 damage.
Hit or Miss: The manticore shifts 3 squares after making the attack.

⊕↗ **Manticore's Fury** (standard; at-will)
The manticore makes a claw attack and a spike attack (in any order) and shift 1 square between the two attacks.

✳ **Spike Volley** (standard; recharge ⚄ ⚅)
Area burst 1 within 10; +15 vs. AC (see also *guided sniper*); 1d8 + 5 damage.

Guided Sniper (while mounted by a friendly rider of 10th level or higher; at-will) ✦ **Mount**
A manticore with a rider gains a +2 bonus to attack rolls with its spike attack and *spike volley* power.

Alignment Chaotic evil   **Languages** Common
Skills Stealth +15
Str 21 (+10)	**Dex** 20 (+10)	**Wis** 17 (+8)
Con 17 (+8)	**Int** 4 (+2)	**Cha** 12 (+6)

MANTICORE TACTICS

A manticore prefers to begin a fight from the air. It flies overhead and bombards enemies with *spike volleys* before landing to finish them off with *manticore's fury* attacks. If faced with a dangerous foe on the ground, a manticore usually takes to the air again and harries its foe with repeated *spike volleys* as quickly as they recharge.

MANTICORE LORE

A character knows the following information with a successful Nature check.

DC 15: Manticores are wicked predators that delight in devouring intelligent creatures, especially dwarves and humans. They fling iron spikes from their tails with deadly precision.

DC 20: Manticores have three rows of teeth, which constantly grow throughout their lives. They often leave old teeth and iron spikes in the bodies of their mauled victims as sure signs of manticore attack.

Although dimwitted, manticores understand Common and can speak a few Common words and phrases. They are exceedingly impatient and tend to attack those who attempt to parley with them.

ENCOUNTER GROUPS

Manticores hunt in small prides of two or three individuals, or sometimes singly. They are brutish, violent creatures that can be brought under control only by masters too strong to be eaten. Goblins or other intelligent monsters often entice manticores to help them for a time with gifts of food or treasure. However, manticores are greedy and disloyal and rarely stay bribed for long.

Level 11 Encounter (XP 3,000)
✦ 1 manticore (level 10 elite skirmisher)
✦ 1 galeb duhr rockcaller (level 11 controller)
✦ 4 ogre savages (level 8 brute)

Level 13 Encounter (XP 4,200)
✦ 2 manticores (level 10 elite skirmisher)
✦ 2 hill giants (level 13 brute)
✦ 4 ogre thugs (level 11 minion)

MARUT

MARUTS ARE ENIGMATIC MERCENARIES that wander the Astral Sea and occasionally find their way to other planes and the natural world.

Marut Blademaster		Level 21 Soldier
Medium immortal humanoid		XP 3,200

Initiative +18 **Senses** Perception +22; truesight 10
HP 201; **Bloodied** 100
Regeneration 20
AC 37; **Fortitude** 37, **Reflex** 32, **Will** 33
Immune sleep; **Resist** 10 thunder
Speed 8, fly 4 (hover), teleport 4

ⓟ **Greatsword** (standard; at-will) ✦ **Thunder, Weapon**
  +27 vs. AC; 1d10 + 11 damage plus 1d6 thunder damage, the target is pushed 1 square, and the target is marked until the end of the marut blademaster's next turn.

† **Double Attack** (standard; recharge ⚄ ⚅) ✦ **Thunder, Weapon**
  The marut blademaster makes two greatsword attacks.

Alignment Unaligned **Languages** Supernal
Skills Endurance +22, Intimidate +17
| **Str** 32 (+21) | **Dex** 23 (+16) | **Wis** 25 (+17) |
| **Con** 25 (+17) | **Int** 14 (+12) | **Cha** 15 (+12) |
Equipment greatsword

MARUT BLADEMASTER TACTICS

The blademaster's primary objective is to form and maintain a battle line, protecting softer allies. It uses *double attack* as often as possible.

Marut Concordant		Level 22 Elite Controller
Large immortal humanoid		XP 8,300

Initiative +12 **Senses** Perception +23; truesight 10
HP 418; **Bloodied** 209
Regeneration 20
AC 38; **Fortitude** 39, **Reflex** 33, **Will** 36
Immune sleep; **Resist** 10 thunder
Saving Throws +2
Speed 8, fly 4 (hover), teleport 4
Action Points 1

ⓟ **Slam** (standard; at-will) ✦ **Thunder**
  Reach 2; +26 vs. AC; 2d6 + 10 damage plus 1d6 thunder damage.

↗ **Dictum** (minor; at-will) ✦ **Thunder**
  Ranged 10; +24 vs. Fortitude; the target is immobilized (save ends).

✳ **Fortune's Chains** (standard; recharge ⚃ ⚄ ⚅) ✦ **Psychic**
  Area burst 5 within 20; enemies in the area are struck by arcs of coruscating psychic energy; +22 vs. Will; 3d6 + 6 psychic damage, and the target is dazed (save ends).

⬅ **Thunderous Edict** (standard; recharge ⚄ ⚅) ✦ **Thunder**
  Close burst 10; targets enemies; +24 vs. Fortitude; 3d6 + 8 thunder damage, and the target is pushed 4 squares. *Miss:* Half damage, and the target is not pushed.

Alignment Unaligned **Languages** Supernal
Skills Endurance +23, Intimidate +24
| **Str** 30 (+21) | **Dex** 13 (+12) | **Wis** 25 (+18) |
| **Con** 25 (+18) | **Int** 22 (+17) | **Cha** 26 (+19) |

MARUT CONCORDANT TACTICS

A marut concordant uses *dictum* to pin down a strong foe. It then centers *fortune's chains* in an area most likely to catch multiple enemies. The concordant uses *thunderous edict* to push multiple enemies away.

MARUT LORE

A character knows the following information with a successful Religion check.

DC 25: No one knows what purpose the maruts ultimately pursue, but the price for a marut's service is always a reciprocal service; that is to say, maruts seem to be gathering favors. Maruts keep records of their verbal contracts in their fortresses on the Astral Sea.

ENCOUNTER GROUPS

Maruts work with any being that agrees to acceptable terms and keep to the spirit of a contract.

Level 23 Encounter (XP 25,250)
✦ 1 marut corcordant (level 22 elite controller)
✦ 2 marut blademasters (level 21 soldier)
✦ 1 war devil (level 22 brute)
✦ 8 legion devil legionnaires (level 21 minion)

MEDUSA

A MEDUSA IS A SCALY MONSTER WITH A HORRIFYING GAZE. Females of the species use their gaze to turn other creatures to stone, and their lairs are filled with lifelike statues. Male medusas use their gaze to poison the minds and bodies of their victims before hacking them to pieces, and their lairs are painted with the blood of fallen prey.

Medusa Archer (Female)	Level 10 Elite Controller
Medium natural humanoid	XP 1,000

Initiative +10 **Senses** Perception +13
HP 212; **Bloodied** 106
AC 26; **Fortitude** 23, **Reflex** 24, **Will** 25
Immune petrification; **Resist** 10 poison
Saving Throws +2
Speed 7
Action Points 1

⊕ **Snaky Hair** (standard; at-will) ✦ **Poison**
+15 vs. AC; 1d6 + 5 damage, and the target takes ongoing 10 poison damage and takes a -2 penalty to Fortitude defense (save ends both).

⊕ **Longbow** (standard; at-will) ✦ **Poison, Weapon**
Ranged 20/40; +15 vs. AC; 1d10 + 5 damage, and the medusa archer makes a secondary attack against the same target. *Secondary Attack:* +13 vs. Fortitude; the target takes ongoing 10 poison damage and takes a -2 penalty to Fortitude defense (save ends both).

↞ **Petrifying Gaze** (standard; at-will) ✦ **Gaze**
Close blast 5; blind creatures are immune; +14 vs. Fortitude; the target is slowed (save ends). *First Failed Save:* The target is immobilized instead of slowed (save ends). *Second Failed Save:* The target is petrified (no save).

Alignment Evil	**Languages** Common	
Skills Bluff +16, Diplomacy +16, Intimidate +16, Stealth +15		
Str 16 (+8)	**Dex** 21 (+10)	**Wis** 17 (+8)
Con 18 (+9)	**Int** 12 (+6)	**Cha** 22 (+11)

Equipment hooded cloak, longbow, quiver of 30 arrows

MEDUSA ARCHER TACTICS

The medusa archer makes longbow attacks from a safe distance, relying on its poisoned arrows to reduce the Fortitude defense of its enemies and make them more susceptible to its *petrifying gaze*. The creature is not afraid to enter melee combat, using its *snaky hair* and then targeting the same foe and other nearby enemies with its *petrifying gaze*.

Medusa Warrior (Male)	Level 13 Elite Soldier
Medium natural humanoid	XP 1,600

Initiative +13 **Senses** Perception +16
HP 272; **Bloodied** 136
AC 30; **Fortitude** 28, **Reflex** 26, **Will** 27
Immune petrification; **Resist** 20 poison
Saving Throws +2
Speed 6
Action Points 1

⊕ **Longsword** (standard; at-will) ✦ **Poison, Weapon**
+20 vs. AC; 1d8 + 8 damage, and the medusa warrior makes a secondary attack against the same target. *Secondary Attack:* +18 vs. Fortitude; the target takes ongoing 10 poison damage and is slowed (save ends both).

⊕ **Longbow** (standard; at-will) ✦ **Poison, Weapon**
Ranged 20/40; +17 vs. AC; 1d10 + 5 damage, and ongoing 10 poison damage (save ends).

⊹ **Double Attack** (standard; at-will) ✦ **Poison, Weapon**
The medusa warrior makes two longsword attacks, dealing an extra 2d8 damage on a hit against a dazed target.

↞ **Venomous Gaze** (standard; at-will) ✦ **Gaze, Poison, Psychic**
Close blast 5; blind creatures are immune; +19 vs. Will; 3d6 + 6 poison and psychic damage, and the target is dazed and weakened (save ends both).

Alignment Evil	**Languages** Common	
Skills Bluff +17, Intimidate +17, Stealth +15		
Str 26 (+14)	**Dex** 20 (+11)	**Wis** 20 (+11)
Con 24 (+13)	**Int** 16 (+9)	**Cha** 22 (+12)

Equipment chainmail, longsword, longbow, quiver of 30 arrows

MEDUSA WARRIOR TACTICS

The medusa warrior hides its true nature, hoping to lure enemies within range of its *venomous gaze*. In battle, the creature alternates between its *venomous gaze* and *double attack* powers, since its longsword attacks deal more damage against creatures affected by its gaze. The medusa warrior draws its longbow only when it has no targets it can engage in melee.

STEVE PRESCOTT

Medusa Shroud of Zehir (Female) Level 18 Skirmisher

Medium natural humanoid   XP 2,000

Initiative +18   **Senses** Perception +12
HP 172; **Bloodied** 86
AC 32; **Fortitude** 28, **Reflex** 30, **Will** 29
Immune petrification; **Resist** 10 acid, 10 poison
Speed 8

(+) **Short Sword** (standard; at-will) ✦ **Acid, Poison, Weapon**
   +15 vs. AC; 1d6 + 7 damage, and the target takes ongoing 10
   acid and poison damage (save ends).

✝ **Fangs of Death** (standard; recharge ⚃ ⚄ ⚅)
   The medusa shroud of Zehir makes two melee basic attacks and
   can shift up to 3 squares between attacks.

✝ **Snaky Hair** (minor 1/round; at-will) ✦ **Acid, Poison**
   +23 vs. AC; 1d6 + 7 damage, and the target takes ongoing 10
   acid and poison damage and takes a -2 penalty to Fortitude
   defense (save ends both).

↤ **Petrifying Gaze** (standard; at-will) ✦ **Gaze**
   Close blast 5; blind creatures are immune; +21 vs. Fortitude;
   the target is slowed (save ends). *First Failed Save:* The target is
   immobilized instead of slowed (save ends). *Second Failed Save:*
   The target is petrified (no save).

Alignment Evil   **Languages** Common
Skills Acrobatics +21, Bluff +20, Stealth +21
Str 16 (+12)   **Dex** 24 (+16)   **Wis** 17 (+12)
Con 20 (+14)   **Int** 13 (+10)   **Cha** 22 (+15)
Equipment black hooded cloak, 2 short swords

Medusa Shroud of Zehir Tactics

The medusa shroud of Zehir uses *fangs of death* to weave
through the battlefield. It follows its sword attacks with a
snaky hair attack. It uses *petrifying gaze* or makes melee basic
attacks while waiting for *fangs of death* to recharge.

Medusa Lore

A character knows the following information with a successful
Nature check.

DC 15: Medusas are known and feared for their gaze
attacks. It is possible to close one's eyes while fighting a
medusa, but fighting the creature blindly is rarely a good
choice.

DC 20: Medusas are accomplished archers and shoot
arrows poisoned with their own saliva.

Medusas prefer to live alone or in small groups, but they
desire wealth and, most important, power and influence in
the societies of other humanoids. A brood of medusas might
rule over a terrified populace as a royal family, or a single
medusa might act as the secret boss of an assassins' guild.

DC 25: Male medusas don't have the snaky hair of their
female counterparts, but their blood is even more poisonous.
The gaze of a female medusa turns creatures to stone, while
the gaze of a male medusa ravages the mind and body, leaving
its victims dazed, weak, and ripe for killing.

DC 30: The blood of a medusa can reverse petrification.
One must apply a few drops of the creature's blood to the lips
or mouth of a petrified creature and succeed on a DC 20 Heal
check. The medusa must have been killed within the past 24
hours for the blood to work.

Encounter Groups

A medusa often allies with creatures that are immune to its
gaze, such as grimlocks and gargoyles.

Medusas also enjoy gathering humanoids to serve as servants, soldiers, thieves, spies, and assassins. Even though the
medusa must purposefully use her gaze to petrify foes, the
threat of such is usually enough to keep humanoid servants
in line.

Medusas readily consort with creatures of equivalent
or greater might. They work with yuan-ti and hold them in
high regard.

Level 11 Encounter (XP 3,075)
✦ 1 medusa archer (level 10 elite controller)
✦ 1 venom-eye basilisk (level 10 artillery)
✦ 5 snaketongue zealots (level 12 minion)
✦ 2 snaketongue warriors (level 8 brute)

Level 14 Encounter (XP 5,000)
✦ 1 medusa warrior (level 13 elite soldier)
✦ 2 grimlock berserkers (level 13 brute)
✦ 4 grimlock minions (level 14 minion)
✦ 2 gargoyles (level 9 lurker)

Level 17 Encounter (XP 8,600)
✦ 2 medusa shrouds of Zehir (level 18 skirmisher)
✦ 1 yuan-ti malison disciple of Zehir (level 17 controller)
✦ 3 yuan-ti abominations (level 14 soldier)

MIND FLAYER

MIND FLAYERS USE THEIR FORMIDABLE PSYCHIC POWERS to shatter the minds of their foes. Once their enemies are knocked senseless, the mind flayers crack open the victims' skulls and devour their brains. Not all creatures that cross a mind flayer's path end up as food; some are enslaved, while others are transformed into obedient thralls.

Mind flayers, also known as illithids, came to the natural world from the Far Realm long ago. They are usually encountered in the Underdark, venturing to the surface only on special missions.

Mind Flayer Infiltrator	Level 14 Lurker
Medium aberrant humanoid	XP 1,000

Initiative +16　　**Senses** Perception +14
HP 107; **Bloodied** 53
AC 27; **Fortitude** 25, **Reflex** 27, **Will** 28
Speed 7
(⬇) **Tentacles** (standard; at-will)
　　+19 vs. AC; 2d6 + 5 damage, and the target is grabbed (until escape).
✝ **Bore into Brain** (standard; at-will)
　　Grabbed or stunned target only; +17 vs. Fortitude; 3d6 + 5 damage, and the target is dazed (save ends). If this power reduces the target to 0 hit points or fewer, the mind flayer devours its brain, killing the target instantly.
⬅ **Mind Blast** (standard; recharge ⊡⊡) ✦ **Psychic**
　　Close blast 5; mind flayers and their thralls are immune; +18 vs. Will; 2d8 + 6 psychic damage, and the target is dazed (save ends). *Miss:* Half damage, and the target is not dazed.
Stalk the Senseless
　　The mind flayer infiltrator is invisible to dazed or stunned creatures.
Alignment Evil　　**Languages** Deep Speech, telepathy 10
Skills Bluff +18, Diplomacy +18, Dungeoneering +14, Stealth +17
Str 13 (+8)　　**Dex** 20 (+12)　　**Wis** 14 (+9)
Con 17 (+10)　　**Int** 17 (+10)　　**Cha** 23 (+13)

MIND FLAYER INFILTRATOR TACTICS

This mind flayer uses its natural stealth to creep toward its enemies unseen, and then unleashes its *mind blast*. From its dazed foes, it chooses one creature to attack with its tentacles while relying on its *stalk the senseless* power to avoid attacks. If it succeeds in grabbing a victim with its tentacles, the infiltrator uses its *bore into brain* power until the victim dies or manages to free itself.

Mind Flayer Mastermind	Level 18 Elite Controller
Medium aberrant humanoid	XP 4,000

Initiative +12　　**Senses** Perception +18
Psychic Static (Psychic) aura 10; while the mind flayer mastermind is not bloodied, enemies in the aura take a –2 penalty to Will defense.
HP 324; **Bloodied** 162
AC 33; **Fortitude** 33, **Reflex** 33, **Will** 35; see also *interpose thrall*
Saving Throws +2
Speed 7
Action Points 1
(⬇) **Tentacles** (standard; at-will)
　　+21 vs. AC; 3d6 + 3 damage, and the target is grabbed (until escape).
✝ **Bore into Brain** (standard; at-will) ✦ see text
　　Grabbed or stunned target only; +21 vs. Fortitude; 4d10 + 3 damage, and the target is stunned (save ends). If this power reduces the target to 0 hit points or fewer, the mind flayer mastermind can either devour its brain or turn it into a thrall (see below):
　　Devour Brain (**Healing**): The mind flayer mastermind devours the target's brain. The target is killed instantly, and the mind flayer mastermind regains 25 hit points.
　　Create Thrall (**Charm**): The target is dominated (no save) and regains enough hit points to restore it to its bloodied value. As a thrall, the target is immune to the *mind blast* power of mind flayers and gains a +5 bonus to its Will defense while within 10 squares of the controlling mind flayer mastermind. The target is no longer dominated and no longer a thrall once the controlling mastermind dies.
⬅ **Mind Blast** (standard; recharge ⊡⊡) ✦ **Psychic**
　　Close blast 5; mind flayers and their thralls are immune; +21 vs. Will; 3d8 + 7 psychic damage, and the target is dazed (save ends). *Miss:* Half damage, and the target is not dazed.
➢ **Enslave** (standard; recharge ⊡⊡) ✦ **Charm**
　　Ranged 10; +21 vs. Will; the target is dominated (save ends). While dominated, the target is immune to the *mind blast* power of mind flayers and gains a +5 bonus to its Will defense while within 10 squares of the controlling mind flayer mastermind. The mastermind can use *enslave* on only one creature at a time.
✴ **Illusion of Pain** (standard; recharge ⊡⊡) ✦ **Illusion, Psychic**
　　Area burst 1 within 10; enemies within the burst imagine that the area is filled with writhing, barbed tentacles; +27 vs. Will; 2d10 + 5 psychic damage, and the target takes ongoing 10 psychic damage and is immobilized (save ends both).
Cradle of the Elder Brain (immediate interrupt, when attacked; recharge ⊡⊡) ✦ **Teleportation**
　　The mind flayer mastermind teleports 20 squares.
Interpose Thrall (immediate interrupt, when targeted by a melee attack; at-will)
　　The mastermind redirects the attack to an adjacent thrall.
Alignment Evil　　**Languages** Deep Speech, telepathy 10
Skills Arcana +18, Bluff +21, Insight +18, Intimidate +21
Str 11 (+9)　　**Dex** 16 (+12)　　**Wis** 18 (+13)
Con 18 (+13)　　**Int** 18 (+13)　　**Cha** 24 (+16)

MIND FLAYER MASTERMIND TACTICS

Throughout combat, the mastermind remains adjacent to at least one of its thralls, using it as a meat shield to block attacks while it targets enemies with its *mind blast*, *mind warp*, and *enslave* powers. If an opportunity presents itself, the mastermind rushes up to a stunned foe and attacks it with its tentacles, spending its action point to use *bore into brain* on the same round. It devours a brain in combat only if it needs the healing; otherwise, it creates a new thrall. If multiple enemies try to gang up on it, the illithid uses *cradle of the elder brain* to teleport to a safer location.

MIND FLAYER LORE

A character knows the following information with a successful Dungeoneering check.

DC 20: Mind flayers (or illithids, as they call themselves) bend others to their will and wield powers that shatter the minds of their foes. Mind flayers subsist on the devoured brains of intelligent creatures. They are coldly self-serving and think nothing of sacrificing companions or thralls to save themselves.

DC 25: Mind flayers communicate via telepathy, although they also understand Dark Speech. A mind flayer's thralls are completely loyal and obedient. They obey the illithid's telepathic commands in a dark, hopeless, dreamlike state, following the spirit of their instructions and not just the letter.

DC 30: Mind flayers are often solitary masterminds who manipulate hosts of weak-willed thralls to do their bidding, but sometimes they gather in small cabals of like-minded individuals. Horrible cities and kingdoms of mind flayers, organized around mighty disembodied intellects known as elder brains, lurk in the deepest portions of the Underdark.

DC 35: A mind flayer begins life as a small, tentacled, tadpolelike parasite that invades the skull of a helpless humanoid victim, devours its brain, and then subverts the body to its own use. Within a matter of days, it transforms the body it steals into an adult illithid, and all traces of the creature's former being are permanently extinguished.

ENCOUNTER GROUPS

Illithids are usually encountered with other illithids and with thralls. Lone mind flayers can also be found in Underdark settlements rules by the drow and other evil races.

Level 14 Encounter (XP 4,800)
✦ 1 mind flayer infiltrator (level 14 lurker)
✦ 1 drider fanglord (level 14 brute)
✦ 1 drow blademaster (level 13 elite skirmisher)
✦ 2 drow warriors (level 11 lurker)

Level 18 Encounter (XP 10,114)
✦ 1 mind flayer mastermind (level 18 elite controller)
✦ 1 mind flayer infiltrator (level 14 lurker)
✦ 3 grimlock followers (level 22 minion)
✦ 2 war trolls (level 14 soldier)

MINOTAUR

Minotaur Warrior		Level 10 Soldier
Medium natural humanoid		XP 500

Initiative +7 **Senses** Perception +14
HP 106; **Bloodied** 53; see also *ferocity*
AC 26; **Fortitude** 27, **Reflex** 21, **Will** 23
Speed 5

⊕ **Battleaxe** (standard; at-will) ✦ **Weapon**
+16 vs. AC; 1d10 + 6 damage, and the target is marked until the end of the minotaur warrior's next turn.

⥮ **Goring Charge** (standard; at-will)
The minotaur warrior makes a charge attack: +17 vs. AC; 1d6 + 6 damage, and the target is knocked prone.

Ferocity (when reduced to 0 hit points)
The minotaur warrior makes a melee basic attack.

Alignment Any **Languages** Common
Skills Dungeoneering +12, Intimidate +11, Nature +9
Str 23 (+11) **Dex** 10 (+5) **Wis** 14 (+7)
Con 18 (+9) **Int** 9 (+4) **Cha** 13 (+6)
Equipment scale armor, heavy shield, battleaxe

MINOTAUR WARRIOR TACTICS

A minotaur warrior normally begins with a *goring charge*, and then fights with its battleaxe. Given a chance, it will charge again.

Minotaur Cabalist	Level 13 Controller (Leader)
Medium natural humanoid	XP 800

Initiative +7 **Senses** Perception +16
Baphomet's Boon aura 10; allies who start their turns in the aura gain a +2 bonus to attack rolls when charging.
HP 129; **Bloodied** 63; see also *ferocity*
AC 27; **Fortitude** 29, **Reflex** 24, **Will** 26
Speed 6

⊕ **Great Cursed Mace** (standard; at-will) ✦ **Necrotic, Weapon**
+15 vs. AC; 1d10 + 6 damage plus 1d6 necrotic damage.

⥮ **Goring Charge** (standard; at-will)
The minotaur cabalist makes a charge attack: +16 vs. AC; 2d6 + 6 damage, and the target is knocked prone.

⤳ **Call Out the Beast** (standard; at-will)
Ranged 10; one bloodied ally in range makes a melee attack against one enemy within its reach.

⤳ **Horns of Force** (standard; at-will) ✦ **Force**
Ranged 5; +18 vs. AC; 1d8 + 3 force damage, and the target is pushed 2 squares.

Ferocity (when reduced to 0 hit points)
The minotaur cabalist makes a melee basic attack.

Alignment Chaotic evil **Languages** Abyssal, Common
Skills Dungeoneering +14, Intimidate +14, Nature +16, Religion +12
Str 22 (+12) **Dex** 12 (+7) **Wis** 17 (+9)
Con 17 (+9) **Int** 13 (+7) **Cha** 16 (+9)
Equipment robes, mace

MINOTAUR CABALIST TACTICS

A cabalist calls out to Baphomet for strength while striking foes with its mace. It uses *horns of force* to knock an enemy out of a flanking position or into a more dangerous situation. Once bloodied, the cabalist tries to extricate itself from combat while using *call out the beast* to grant one of its allies a melee attack as a free action.

MINOTAURS ARE FIERCE, BULL-HEADED MONSTERS that worship demons and enslave and plunder weaker creatures. All minotaurs have a liking for mazes and often seek out buried labyrinths or sprawling dungeons as lairs.

Most adult minotaurs are warriors. Minotaurs of the warrior caste are fiercely loyal once they have given their allegiance. In evil minotaur lands, they serve minotaur cabalists as bodyguards, slave-drivers, and raiders. While they are not particularly clever, they possess a certain bestial cunning and have uncannily sharp senses.

The most intelligent and strong-willed of the evil minotaurs are cabalists—the leaders of the cults of Baphomet, a demon lord often referred to as the Horned King. They form a priestly caste that plots the subjugation of neighboring peoples. Like the warriors, the minotaur cabalists are strong and fierce enemies, but they also command several mystical powers that make them even more dangerous in battle.

Savage minotaurs are hulking, dimwitted, temperamental brutes infused with demonic blood. Bloodthirsty predators and rapacious robbers, they haunt lonely and wild places, killing and eating any who cross their paths.

Savage Minotaur	Level 16 Brute
Large natural humanoid	XP 1,400

Initiative +9　　　**Senses** Perception +19
HP 190; **Bloodied** 95; see also *ferocity*
AC 28; **Fortitude** 32, **Reflex** 26, **Will** 29
Speed 8

⊕ **Greataxe** (standard; at-will) ✦ **Weapon**
　Reach 2; +19 vs. AC; 2d8 + 7 damage (crit 4d8 + 23), and the
　target is pushed 1 square.

↯ **Goring Charge** (standard; at-will)
　The savage minotaur makes a charge attack: +20 vs. AC; 2d6 + 7
　damage, and the target is knocked prone.

↯ **Thrashing Horns** (standard, usable only when charging; at-will)
　+19 vs. AC; 2d6 + 7 damage, and the target slides 2 squares.

Ferocity (when reduced to 0 hit points)
　The savage minotaur makes a melee basic attack.

Alignment Chaotic evil　　　**Languages** Common
Skills Dungeoneering +14, Intimidate +14, Nature +14
Str 24 (+15)　　**Dex** 12 (+9)　　**Wis** 19 (+12)
Con 20 (+13)　　**Int** 5 (+5)　　**Cha** 12 (+9)
Equipment greataxe

SAVAGE MINOTAUR TACTICS

A savage minotaur enters battle with a *goring charge*, and then swings its greataxe at any foe within reach. If there's something dangerous in the environment nearby, such as a pit or roaring fire, it uses *thrashing horns* to throw enemies in when it gets the chance.

MINOTAUR LORE

A character knows the following information with a successful Nature check.

DC 15: The archetypical minotaur is a savage, dungeon-dwelling brute that kills for pleasure. However, many minotaurs are civilized and cultured. These minotaurs are smaller than their savage kin, and they gather in settlements of all sizes.

DC 20: The cult of Baphomet, the demon lord also known as the Horned King, is a widespread substrate within minotaur society dedicated to embracing the beast within.

Some minotaur city-states or temple strongholds are entirely populated with devotees of the demon prince and ruled by cabalists in a malevolent theocracy. In other minotaur societies, Baphomet's cult is a hidden, subversive force of evil.

Minotaur realms are hidden in the most remote and forbidding places of the world, in secret mountain citadels, snow-covered temple-states, and buried fortresses. Evil minotaurs are slave takers and plunderers that seek to weaken their targets before launching surprise attacks that leave no foe behind. Their more benign kin are contemplative warriors who remain mostly secluded, shrouding themselves and their society in secrecy.

Good or evil, minotaurs are guided by their religious leaders. Cabalists devoted to Baphomet lead both evil temple-states and hidden cults in other cities. In settlements where the Horned King's cult has not seized control, priests of Bahamut, Erathis, Moradin, or Pelor hold sway.

DC 25: Minotaurs like mazes. They employ twisting designs on their clothing, armor, and weapons, and lay out simple or exceedingly complex labyrinths in their temples and gardens. Among benign minotaurs, these labyrinths are places of quiet contemplation. Evil minotaurs throw prisoners in labyrinths and allow their savage kin or summoned demons to hunt the hapless captives through the twisting corridors.

ENCOUNTER GROUPS

Minotaurs prefer the company of their own kind, but they employ a wide variety of other creatures when necessary. Minotaur devotees of Baphomet are often accompanied by gnoll or demon allies.

Level 13 Encounter (XP 3,900)
✦ 1 minotaur cabalist (level 13 controller)
✦ 3 minotaur warriors (level 10 soldier)
✦ 2 vrock demons (level 13 skirmisher)

Level 18 Encounter (XP 10,000)
✦ 2 savage minotaurs (level 16 brute)
✦ 1 rakshasa noble (level 19 controller)
✦ 3 rakshasa assassins (level 17 skirmisher)

MUMMY

Mummies defend tombs and other sacred places against intrusion, striking down foes with a deadly rotting disease.

Soulless beings animated by necromantic magic, mummy guardians are not very intelligent and retain none of the powers or knowledge they had in life. More powerful mummies known as mummy lords retain much of their power and intelligence, attacking the living out of sheer hate.

"Mummy lord" is a monster template that can be applied to nonplayer characters. See the *Dungeon Master's Guide* for rules on creating new mummies using the template.

Mummy Guardian	Level 8 Brute
Medium natural humanoid (undead)	XP 350

Initiative +6   **Senses** Perception +10; darkvision
Despair (Fear) aura 5; enemies within the aura take a -2 penalty to attack rolls against the mummy guardian.
HP 108; **Bloodied** 54
Regeneration 10 (if the mummy guardian takes radiant damage, regeneration doesn't function on its next turn)
AC 20; **Fortitude** 18, **Reflex** 16, **Will** 17; see also *despair* above
Immune disease, poison; **Resist** 5 necrotic; **Vulnerable** 5 fire
Speed 5
(+) **Rotting Slam** (standard; at-will) ✦ **Disease, Necrotic**
    +11 vs. AC; 2d8 + 3 necrotic damage, and the target contracts level 8 mummy rot (see below).

Alignment Unaligned	**Languages** Common	
Str 16 (+7)	**Dex** 14 (+6)	**Wis** 12 (+5)
Con 18 (+8)	**Int** 6 (+2)	**Cha** 16 (+7)

Mummy Guardian Tactics

A mummy guardian is a straightforward combatant that makes *rotting slam* attacks round after round. It specifically targets enemies that deal fire or radiant damage with their attacks.

Mummy Lord (Human Cleric)	Level 13 Elite Controller
Medium natural humanoid (undead)	XP 1,600

Initiative +7   **Senses** Perception +10; darkvision
Despair (Fear) aura 5; enemies within the aura take a -2 penalty to attack rolls against the mummy lord.
HP 205; **Bloodied** 102
Regeneration 10 (if the mummy lord takes radiant damage, regeneration doesn't function on its next turn)
AC 27 (see also *shielding mace*); **Fortitude** 25, **Reflex** 23, **Will** 27
Immune disease, poison; **Resist** 10 necrotic; **Vulnerable** 5 fire
Saving Throws +2
Speed 5
Action Points 1
(+) **Shielding Mace** (standard; at-will) ✦ **Weapon**
    +15 vs. AC; 1d8 + 9 damage, and the mummy lord and one adjacent ally gain a +1 power bonus to AC until the end of the mummy lord's next turn.
† **Awe Strike** (standard; encounter) ✦ **Fear, Weapon**
    Requires mace; +15 vs. Will; 1d8 + 9 damage, and the target is immobilized (save ends).
↗ **Plague of Doom** (standard; encounter) ✦ **Necrotic**
    Ranged 10; +15 vs. Fortitude; 3d8 + 9 necrotic damage, and the target takes a -2 penalty to all defenses until the end of the mummy lord's next turn.
↞ **Mummy's Curse** (when reduced to 0 hit points) ✦ **Disease**
    Close burst 10; targets enemies; +15 vs. Will; the target contracts level 13 mummy rot (see below).
Unholy Aid (immediate interrupt, when the mummy lord suffers an effect that a save can end; recharge ⚃)
    The mummy lord automatically saves against the triggering effect.
Second Wind (standard; encounter) ✦ **Healing**
    The mummy lord spends a healing surge and regains 51 hit points. The mummy lord gains a +2 bonus to all defenses until the start of its next turn.

Alignment Unaligned	**Languages** Common	
Skills History +13, Insight +15, Intimidate +13, Religion +13		
Str 18 (+10)	**Dex** 12 (+7)	**Wis** 18 (+10)
Con 15 (+8)	**Int** 14 (+8)	**Cha** 15 (+8)
Equipment chainmail, mace		

Mummy Rot (Mummy Guardian)	Level 8 Disease	Endurance stable DC 20, improve DC 24

◄ The target is cured. | **Initial Effect:** The target regains only half the normal number of hit points from healing effects. | ◄► The target regains only half the normal number of hit points from healing effects. In addition, the target takes 10 necrotic damage, which cannot be healed until the target is cured of the disease. | ► The target dies.

Mummy Rot (Mummy Lord)	Level 13 Disease	Endurance stable DC 22, improve DC 26

◄ The target is cured. | **Initial Effect:** The target regains only half the normal number of hit points from healing effects. | ◄► The target regains only half the normal number of hit points from healing effects. In addition, the target takes 10 necrotic damage, which cannot be healed until the target is cured of the disease. | ► The target dies.

Mummy Rot (Giant Mummy)	Level 21 Disease	Endurance stable DC 33, improve DC 37

◄ The target is cured. | **Initial Effect:** The target regains only half the normal number of hit points from healing effects. | ◄► The target regains only half the normal number of hit points from healing effects. In addition, the target takes 10 necrotic damage, which cannot be healed until the target is cured of the disease. | ► The target dies.

MUMMY LORD TACTICS

A mummy lord uses *plague of doom* against a foe before entering melee combat. It stays close to an ally while making *shielding mace* attacks, focusing on enemies that target it with fire or radiant attacks. It uses *awe strike* to immobilize a slippery foe and *unholy aid* to remove a particularly debilitating condition (such as blinded or stunned). Once bloodied, the mummy lord spends its action point to use *second wind*.

Giant Mummy	Level 21 Brute
Large natural humanoid (undead)	XP 3,200

Initiative +12   **Senses** Perception +16; darkvision
Despair (Fear) aura 5; enemies within the aura take a -2 penalty to attack rolls against the giant mummy.
HP 240; **Bloodied** 120; see also *dust of death*
Regeneration 10 (if the giant mummy takes radiant damage, regeneration doesn't function on its next turn)
AC 33; **Fortitude** 34, **Reflex** 30, **Will** 31; see also *despair* above
Immune disease, poison; **Resist** 10 necrotic; **Vulnerable** 10 fire
Speed 6
⊕ **Rotting Slam** (standard; at-will) ✦ **Disease, Necrotic**
   +24 vs. AC; 3d8 + 6 necrotic damage, and the target contracts level 21 mummy rot (see below).
↢ **Dust of Blinding Death** (when first bloodied and again when reduced to 0 hit points) ✦ **Acid**
   The giant mummy releases a cloud of corrosive dust: close burst 2; +22 vs. Fortitude; 1d8 + 7 acid damage, and the target takes ongoing 10 acid damage and is blinded (save ends both).
Alignment Unaligned   **Languages** Giant
Str 22 (+16)   **Dex** 14 (+12)   **Wis** 12 (+11)
Con 24 (+17)   **Int** 6 (+8)   **Cha** 16 (+13)

GIANT MUMMY TACTICS

The giant mummy pounds enemies to death with its fists, focusing its rage on those making fire or radiant attacks.

MUMMY LORE

A character knows the following information with a successful Religion check.

DC 15: Mummy guardians are created to protect important tombs against robbers. A mummy guardian either wanders its tomb, attacking all who enter, or it lies in its sarcophagus, rising to attack when the sarcophagus is opened.

DC 20: A mummy lord is usually created from the remains of an important evil cleric or priest. A mummy lord might guard an important tomb or lead a cult. Yuan-ti often create mummy lords to guard temples of Zehir.

ENCOUNTER GROUPS

A tomb is the mummy guardian's natural habitat, and it's most often found in the company of other creatures that haunt such places.

Mummy lords are often found in the company of undead servitors or living devotees.

Level 8 Encounter (XP 1,750)
✦ 2 mummy guardians (level 8 brute)
✦ 2 rot scarab swarms (level 8 soldier)
✦ 1 flameskull (level 8 artillery)

Level 15 Encounter (XP 6,050)
✦ 1 mummy lord (level 13 elite controller)
✦ 3 yuan-ti malison sharp-eye (level 13 artillery)
✦ 1 yuan-ti abomination (level 14 soldier)
✦ 6 snaketongue zealots (level 12 minion)

Level 17 Encounter (XP 8,400)
✦ 2 mummy lords (level 13 elite controller)
✦ 2 rakshasa warriors (level 15 soldier)
✦ 1 sphinx (level 16 elite soldier)

Level 21 Encounter (XP 16,000)
✦ 3 giant mummies (level 21 brute)
✦ 1 dark naga (level 21 elite controller)

NAGA

SERPENTINE CREATURES WITH HUMANLIKE FACES, nagas are guardians of secret places or magical lore. Some nagas choose to subjugate nearby creatures and rule over them. Others ruthlessly destroy trespassers with powerful enchantments and deadly poison.

Nagas often work closely with yuan-ti, guarding their vaults and temples. A lone naga sometimes rules a primitive tribe of kobolds, lizardfolk, or troglodytes who regard it as a god.

Nagas can survive without food or water indefinitely. They are fond of treasure, however, and fill their lairs with trinkets seized from interlopers.

Guardian Naga		Level 12 Elite Artillery
Large immortal magical beast (reptile)		XP 1,400

Initiative +10　　**Senses** Perception +13; darkvision
HP 186; **Bloodied** 93
AC 25; **Fortitude** 23, **Reflex** 24, **Will** 22
Saving Throws +2
Speed 6
Action Points 1
⊕ **Tail Slap** (standard; at-will)
　Reach 2; +16 vs. AC; 1d8 + 3 damage, and the target is pushed 2 squares.
↠ **Word of Pain** (standard; at-will) ✦ Psychic
　Ranged 20; +17 vs. Will; 2d8 + 4 psychic damage, and the target is immobilized (save ends).
↞ **Spit Poison** (standard; recharge ⚄ ⚅) ✦ Poison
　Close blast 3; +15 vs. Fortitude; 1d8 + 2 poison damage, and the target takes ongoing 5 poison damage, a -2 penalty to Fortitude defense, and a -2 penalty to saving throws (save ends all).
❊ **Thunderstrike** (standard; recharge ⚄ ⚅) ✦ Thunder
　Area burst 1 within 20; +16 vs. Fortitude; 2d10 + 4 thunder damage, and the target is dazed (save ends). *Miss:* Half damage, and the target is not dazed.
Alignment Any　　**Languages** Common, Draconic, Supernal
Skills Arcana +15, History +15, Insight +13
| **Str** 16 (+9) | **Dex** 18 (+10) | **Wis** 14 (+8) |
| **Con** 15 (+8) | **Int** 18 (+10) | **Cha** 12 (+7) |

GUARDIAN NAGA TACTICS

A guardian naga favors ranged combat and tries to catch multiple foes with *thunderstrike* before spending its action point to immobilize an enemy defender or striker with *word of pain*. It continues to use *word of pain* on subsequent rounds until enemies come within range of its *spit poison* attack.

Bone Naga		Level 16 Elite Controller
Large immortal magical beast (undead)		XP 2,800

Initiative +11　　**Senses** Perception +13; darkvision
Death Rattle (Necrotic) aura 2; enemies that start their turns in the aura are dazed.
HP 328; **Bloodied** 164
AC 32; **Fortitude** 32, **Reflex** 28, **Will** 29
Immune disease, poison; **Resist** 20 necrotic; **Vulnerable** 10 radiant
Saving Throws +2
Speed 7
Action Points 1
⊕ **Bite** (standard; at-will) ✦ Necrotic
　Reach 2; +20 vs. AC; 2d4 + 6 damage, and ongoing 5 necrotic damage (save ends). *Aftereffect:* The target is weakened (save ends).
↞ **Death Sway** (standard; at-will) ✦ Necrotic
　Close burst 3; blind creatures are immune; +21 vs. Will; the target is dazed (save ends). If the target is already dazed, it takes 2d6 + 6 necrotic damage instead.
Alignment Unaligned　　**Languages** Common, Draconic, Supernal
Skills Arcana +18, History +18, Insight +18, Religion +18
| **Str** 22 (+14) | **Dex** 16 (+11) | **Wis** 20 (+13) |
| **Con** 28 (+17) | **Int** 20 (+13) | **Cha** 22 (+14) |

BONE NAGA TACTICS

A bone naga alerts other creatures to its presence with its *death rattle* aura. If one or more enemies succumb to the aura's effect, it uses *death sway* to damage them. The first time is uses this power, it spends an action point to use it again in the same round.

Dark Naga		Level 21 Elite Controller
Large immortal magical beast (reptile)		XP 6,400

Initiative +14　　**Senses** Perception +21; darkvision
HP 404; **Bloodied** 202
AC 36; **Fortitude** 34, **Reflex** 33, **Will** 36
Saving Throws +2
Speed 8
Action Points 1
⊕ **Tail Sting** (standard; at-will) ✦ Poison
　Reach 2; +24 vs. AC; 2d6 + 8 poison damage (3d6 + 8 damage against a dazed target), and the target is slowed (save ends).
↞ **Lure** (minor; at-will) ✦ Charm
　Close burst 5; targets enemies; +25 vs. Will; the target is pulled 1 square and dazed (save ends).
↞ **Psychic Miasma** (standard; recharge ⚄ ⚅) ✦ Psychic
　Close burst 3; +26 vs. Will; 3d6 + 10 psychic damage, and the target is dazed (save ends). *First Failed Save:* The target is stunned (save ends).
Alignment Evil　　**Languages** Common, Draconic, Supernal
Skills History +22, Insight +21, Stealth +19
| **Str** 26 (+18) | **Dex** 18 (+14) | **Wis** 22 (+16) |
| **Con** 26 (+18) | **Int** 24 (+17) | **Cha** 30 (+20) |

DARK NAGA TACTICS

The dark naga uses *lure* every round to pull enemies within reach of its tail. If it gets two enemies within striking distance, it spends its action point to make two *tail sting* attacks in one round. It uses *psychic miasma* at the earliest opportunity.

(Left to right) orc raider, orc bloodrager, orc eye of Gruumsh, and orc warrior

ORC LORE

A character knows the following information with a successful Nature check.

DC 15: Orcs favor hills and mountains, places pocked by caverns easily turned into defensible lairs. Bloodthirsty marauders and cannibals, orcs venerate Gruumsh and thereby delight in slaughter and destruction.

Orcs don't build settlements of their own, instead improving existing shelters with crude fortifications. They prefer to settle in natural caves or structures abandoned by other, more skillful races. Orcs can manage simple ironwork and stonework, but they are lazy and grasping, preferring to take by force the tools, weapons, and goods other folk make.

DC 20: Orcs band together into loose tribal associations. The strongest individual in a tribe leads as a despotic chieftain. Individual bands within a tribe might wander far from their native lands, but they still recognize orcs from the same tribe as kin.

DC 25: Orcs often demonstrate their faith in Gruumsh by gouging out one of their eyes and offering it as a sacrifice to their one-eyed god.

According to myth, Corellon shot out Gruumsh's eye with an arrow. For this reason, orcs hold a special hatred for elves and eladrin.

ENCOUNTER GROUPS

Orc tribes use ogres and trolls as muscle for war and labor. They sometimes keep boars, drakes, and other beasts as pets.

Level 4 Encounter (XP 900)
+ 2 orc raiders (level 3 skirmisher)
+ 2 orc berserkers (level 4 brute)
+ 1 dire boar (level 6 brute)

Level 6 Encounter (XP 1,350)
+ 1 orc eye of Gruumsh (level 5 controller)
+ 2 orc berserkers (level 4 brute)
+ 4 orc warriors (level 9 minion)
+ 2 dire wolves (level 5 skirmisher)

Level 9 Encounter (XP 2,150)
+ 1 orc chieftain (level 8 elite brute)
+ 5 orc warriors (level 9 minion)
+ 1 dire boar (level 6 brute)
+ 2 ogre skirmishers (level 8 skirmisher)

Level 10 Encounter (XP 2,650)
+ 2 orc bloodragers (level 7 elite brute)
+ 1 bloodspike behemoth (level 9 brute)
+ 1 ogre skirmisher (level 8 skirmisher)
+ 1 oni night haunter (level 8 elite controller)

ORCUS

Orcus, Demon Prince of the Undead, is one of the most powerful demons in the Abyss–powerful enough to threaten gods. He commands legions of followers, living and dead, and cults dedicated to him are terrifyingly widespread in the natural world.

Orcus finds amusement in the suffering and anguish of the living and satisfaction only when he drinks their blood. Most living things enrage him by their mere presence, and Orcus permits only undead to be near him; even his demon servitors are undead. He has destroyed hundreds of mighty heroes and laid waste to countless kingdoms.

Orcus is a foul and corpulent humanoid creature who has powerful goat legs and a desiccated head similar to that of a ram. His great black wings stir up a reeking cloud of diseased air. He seems somewhere between life and undeath–his sore-ridden body suggests diseased life, but his head and glowing red eyes suggest undeath. His thick, spiny tail is in constant motion.

Orcus carries a heavy mace tipped with an enormous skull. Known as the *Wand of Orcus*, this weapon transforms those it slays into undead horrors. Its haft is smooth obsidian studded with blood rubies.

Dead creatures respond to the presence of Orcus, even without his command. Skeletal arms claw up from the ground where he walks and grab at the feet of his foes. Spirits fill the air with a ghostly chorus of piteous moans, tugging at his foes and hindering their movement.

ORCUS LORE

A character knows the following information with a successful Arcana check.

DC 15: Orcus is known as the Demon Lord of Undeath, the Demon Prince of the Undead, and the Blood Lord. He is worshiped by undead and living creatures that do not fear undeath.

DC 20: Orcus desires destruction like all demons, but he has set his sights higher, aiming at the gods themselves. In particular, Orcus hungers for the death of the Raven Queen and to usurp her control over death and the souls of the dead.

DC 25: Orcus rules one of the many layers of the Abyss. His realm, Thanatos, is a dark landscape of death shrouded by gray clouds and often obscured by fog. Light filters weakly through the clouds and mists, illuminating the realm like a moonlit night. Dead forests filled with twisted black trees and barren moors dominate. Bleak mountains rise feebly into the black sky, and cities and villages in ruins crouch in hidden places as though fearful. Strewn all over the realm are tombs, mausoleums, gravestones, and sarcophagi. They stand on rooftops and building eaves like gargoyles, they litter forests like boulders left by a glacier, and they jut from moors like the masts of sinking ships. Undead abound within the realm, and no living thing survives long there.

DC 30: At the heart of Thanatos stands a vast obsidian palace with embedded bones barely visible through the semitransparent black stone. This palace, Everlost, straddles a yawning chasm whose sheer slopes hold hundreds of tombs and burial sites, creating a tiered necropolis below the palace.

DC 35: Orcus wields an artifact called the *Wand of Orcus*. Legends say that the skull atop the wand once belonged to a god of virtue and chivalry who dared challenge Orcus in battle. Other legends identify it as the skull of a human hero, but if that is true, it has been magically enlarged to its current size. In any event, the powerful good that once resided in the skull is warped and perverted into the most monstrous evil.

Orcus	Level 33 Solo Brute (Leader)
Gargantuan elemental humanoid (demon)	XP 155,000

Initiative +22   **Senses** Perception +28; darkvision, low-light vision

Aura of Death (Necrotic) aura 20; enemies that enter or start their turns in the aura take 10 necrotic damage (20 necrotic damage while Orcus is bloodied).

The Dead Rise aura 6; enemies (including flying ones) treat the area within the aura as difficult terrain, and any dead creature within the aura at the start of Orcus's turn (except those killed by the *Wand of Orcus*) rises as an abyssal ghoul myrmidon (page 119) to fight at Orcus's command.

HP 1,525; **Bloodied** 762

AC 48; **Fortitude** 51, **Reflex** 46, **Will** 49

Immune disease, poison, necrotic; **Resist** 10 variable (3/encounter; see glossary)

Saving Throws +5

Speed 6, fly 10 (clumsy), teleport 6

Action Points 2

⊕ **Wand of Orcus** (standard; at-will) ✦ **Necrotic, Weapon**
Reach 4; +37 vs. AC; 2d12 + 12 damage plus 1d12 necrotic damage, and the target is weakened (save ends); see also *master of undeath*.

↯ **Touch of Death** (standard; recharge ⚅) ✦ **Necrotic**
Reach 4; +33 vs. Fortitude; the target is reduced to 0 hit points (resistance or immunity to necrotic damage does not apply). *Miss:* The target takes necrotic damage equal to its bloodied value.

↯ **Tail Lash** (immediate reaction, when an enemy moves or shifts into a square adjacent to Orcus; at-will)
+36 vs. AC; 2d8 + 12 damage, and the target is stunned until the end of Orcus's next turn and is knocked prone.

⬳ **Necrotic Burst** (standard; recharge ⚅) ✦ **Healing, Necrotic**
Close burst 10; +38 vs. Fortitude; 2d12 + 12 necrotic damage, and all undead in the burst regain 20 hit points.

Master of Undeath
At the start of Orcus's turn, any creature killed by the *Wand of Orcus* that is still dead rises as a dread wraith (page 267) under Orcus's command.

Alignment Chaotic evil		**Languages** Abyssal, Common
Skills Arcana +28, History +28, Intimidate +31, Religion +28		
Str 35 (+28)	**Dex** 22 (+22)	**Wis** 25 (+23)
Con 33 (+27)	**Int** 25 (+23)	**Cha** 30 (+26)
Equipment *Wand of Orcus*		

ORCUS'S TACTICS

Those unfortunate enough to meet Orcus rarely survive the experience. The demon lord surrounds himself with undead guards and minions, and eagerly meets any challenge to battle. He likes to crush foes with the *Wand of Orcus* and uses *master of undeath* to make dread wraiths out of those he slays. Against a particularly troublesome foe, he uses *touch of death*. When an enemy moves into an adjacent square, the demon lord strikes with his spined tail. When surrounded by numerous foes, he spends an action point to use *necrotic burst*.

ASPECT OF ORCUS

AN ASPECT OF ORCUS IS CONJURED BY MEANS OF A RITUAL
known only to Orcus's most devout deathpriests. It is, in
essence, a weaker version of the demon lord that heeds the
commands of its summoner.

Orcus has no link to his aspect. He can't see through its
eyes, speak through the aspect, command it remotely, or
even sense when it's been destroyed. However, it thinks and
behaves very much like the demon lord and usually disappears once its assigned task is completed.

Aspect of Orcus	Level 24 Elite Brute
Large elemental humanoid (demon)	XP 12,100

Initiative +15 **Senses** Perception +21; low-light vision, darkvision

Lesser Aura of Death (Necrotic) aura 10; enemies that enter or start their turns in the aura take 5 necrotic damage (10 necrotic damage while the aspect of Orcus is bloodied).

HP 560; **Bloodied** 280

AC 37; **Fortitude** 39, **Reflex** 35, **Will** 36

Immune disease, poison; **Resist** 20 necrotic, 10 variable (3/ encounter; see glossary)

Saving Throws +2

Speed 6, fly 8 (clumsy)

Action Points 1

(+) **Skull Mace** (standard; at-will) ✦ **Necrotic, Weapon**
Reach 2; +27 vs. AC; 1d10 + 10 damage, and the target is weakened (save ends).

‡ **Tail Lash** (immediate reaction, when an enemy moves or shifts into a square adjacent to the aspect of Orcus; at-will)
+27 vs. AC; 2d6 + 10 damage, and the target is knocked prone.

Alignment Chaotic evil **Languages** Abyssal, Common

Skills Arcana +23, History +23, Intimidate +24, Religion +23

Str 30 (+22)	**Dex** 17 (+15)	**Wis** 19 (+16)
Con 30 (+22)	**Int** 22 (+18)	**Cha** 25 (+19)

Equipment skull mace

ASPECT OF ORCUS TACTICS

Aspects of Orcus are usually called to fight, and do so effectively. An aspect prefers to focus on one foe at a time rather
than spreading out its attacks. It doesn't wait to spend its
action point, doing so at the start of combat to make an additional attack.

ASPECT OF ORCUS LORE

A character knows the following information with a successful
Arcana check.

DC 25: Powerful deathpriests of Orcus can summon an
aspect of the demon lord by means of a ritual.

DC 30: An aspect is sentient, though its mind is no more
privy to the secret thoughts of the demon lord than his
worshipers' minds are. An aspect is capable of independent
thought, but it obeys the commands of its creator unless they
clearly contradict Orcus's ethos or goals.

DORESAIN, EXARCH OF ORCUS

THE MIGHTIEST OF ORCUS'S SERVANTS are his exarchs, undead
demons imbued with shards of his semidivine power. Doresain, the Ghoul King, is foremost among these servitors.

Doresain appears as a ghoul, though he stands upright
rather than adopting the hunched posture of his subjects. His
eyes blaze with a sickly green light. He wears an elegant coat
of supple human flesh and a suit of pale leather armor studded with skulls. A crown of bones rests on his bald head, and
he wields a staff called *Toothlust*, formed of the rigid spinal
column of some past victim. The staff is topped by a skull, in
homage to his lord, Orcus.

Doresain, the Ghoul King	Level 27 Elite Skirmisher
Medium natural humanoid (undead)	XP 22,000

Initiative +25 **Senses** Perception +24; darkvision

HP 508; **Bloodied** 254

AC 43; **Fortitude** 41, **Reflex** 41, **Will** 38

Immune disease, poison; **Resist** 20 necrotic; **Vulnerable** 10 radiant

Saving Throws +2

Speed 8; see also *ravenous frenzy* and *teleport*

Action Points 1

(+) **Toothlust** (standard; at-will) ✦ **Weapon**
+32 vs. AC; 1d6 + 9 damage, and ongoing 10 damage (save ends).

‡ **Cloak of Mouths** (standard; at-will)
+30 vs. AC; 1d8 + 10 damage, and the target is slowed (save ends).

‡ **Ravenous Frenzy** (standard; recharge ⚅)
Doresain can move up to 8 squares without provoking opportunity attacks and makes a *cloak of mouths* attack against each creature he moves adjacent to during the move.

‡ **Teleport** (move; recharge ⚄ ⚅) ✦ **Teleportation**
Doresain can teleport 12 squares.

Alignment Chaotic evil **Languages** Abyssal, Common

Skills Bluff +25, Insight +24, Religion +23

Str 29 (+22)	**Dex** 30 (+23)	**Wis** 23 (+19)
Con 30 (+23)	**Int** 20 (+18)	**Cha** 25 (+20)

Equipment *Toothlust* (staff), *Cloak of Mouths*

DORESAIN'S TACTICS

The Ghoul King begins combat by spending his action point to
use *ravenous frenzy*, ending his move adjacent to a target so that
he can also make a melee basic attack. Until he can use *ravenous frenzy* again, Doresain alternates between making attacks
with Toothlust and the Cloak of Mouths.

DORESAIN LORE

A character knows the following information with a successful
Religion check.

DC 25: Doresain, the Ghoul King, serves Orcus as an
exarch of cannibalism and murder. Doresain's strength flows
from his insatiable hunger. He is never seen without his bone
staff and his undead cloak made of stitched flesh and biting
mouths.

DC 30: Doresain has a domain in Thanatos known as the
White Kingdom, primarily inhabited by ghouls and other
flesheating undead. Its name comes from the bones that make
up every building—walking through its streets kicks up clouds
of bone-white dust to create a fog that coats the city in white.

DEATHPRIEST HIEROPHANT

CULTISTS OF ORCUS ARE DEMENTED INDIVIDUALS, and this deathpriest has risen to their highest ranks. He is not a cleric, since Orcus lives in the Abyss and cannot grant divine magic to his priests. Nevertheless, he is blessed with great power from his demonic master, and himself teeters on the edge between life and undeath.

Deathpriest Hierophant	Level 21 Elite Controller
Medium natural humanoid, human	XP 6,400

Initiative +11   **Senses** Perception +14

Aura of Decay (Necrotic) aura 5; living enemies in the aura take a -2 penalty to all defenses.

HP 382; **Bloodied** 191

AC 35; **Fortitude** 35, **Reflex** 32, **Will** 37

Resist 10 necrotic

Saving Throws +2

Speed 5

Action Points 1

⊕ **Mace** (standard; at-will) ✦ **Necrotic, Weapon**
+24 vs. AC; 1d8 + 5 damage, and ongoing 10 necrotic damage (save ends).

⟿ **Vision of Death** (standard; recharge ⚃ ⚄ ⚅) ✦ **Psychic**
Ranged 10; +24 vs. Will; 2d6 + 7 psychic damage, and the target is dazed (save ends).

⟻ **Word of Orcus** (standard; recharge ⚅) ✦ **Healing, Necrotic**
Close burst 5; targets enemies; +24 vs. Fortitude; 2d6 + 7 necrotic damage, and the target is stunned (save ends). Undead in the burst regain 15 hit points.

Alignment Chaotic evil		**Languages** Abyssal, Common
Skills Religion +17		
Str 20 (+15)	**Dex** 13 (+11)	**Wis** 18 (+14)
Con 15 (+12)	**Int** 14 (+12)	**Cha** 24 (+17)
Equipment plate armor, mace, censer		

DEATHPRIEST HIEROPHANT TACTICS

The deathpriest hierophant uses *vision of death* to keep a foe off-balance while confronting other enemies. Most of his attacks are basic attacks with his mace, but he invokes *word of Orcus* as often as he can.

DEATHPRIEST HIEROPHANT LORE

A character knows the following information with a successful Nature check.

DC 25: Deathpriest hierophants are among Orcus's most powerful worshipers. A few of them know the ritual to summon an aspect of Orcus.

DC 30: A deathpriest hierophant usually leads a cult of several hundred members, spread out over a large area. He appoints lesser deathpriests to lead smaller groups within the cult, and each group is usually tasked with a specific goal, such as desecrating a temple, stealing bones from a king's tomb, or poisoning a village's water supply.

CULTS OF ORCUS

CULTS DEDICATED TO THE BLOOD LORD operate in secret except among the most corrupt of barbarian hordes and undead legions. Orcus's cultists gather in hidden spots associated with death: graveyards, mausoleums, tombs, and ancient necropoli.

The cults of Orcus have no symbol in common; each cult invents its own iconography to remind them of Orcus's awful power. These symbols typically incorporate skulls and bones, ram's horns, or blasphemous runes. Black and blood red are favored colors among his devotees.

Orcus enjoys the suffering of the living, and disease is an excellent way to spread suffering. His followers foul wells with corpses, block sewers, and commit all manner of criminal acts to ensure that disease is an ever-present threat.

Orcus's worshipers do not see undead as holy, but rather as a means to accomplish their goals and Orcus's ambition to extinguish life. They therefore create as many terrible undead as they can. Powerful cultists might treat a vampire or a mummy as an equal and a participant in the cult, whereas a zombie or a skeleton is nothing more than an expendable servant. Ultimately, every worshiper hopes to throw off the shackles of mortality and become a powerful, intelligent undead creature such as a lich, a death knight, a mummy, or a vampire, and thereby gain control over lesser undead. In practice, very few accomplish this goal, but Orcus's worshipers consider undeath a great service to Orcus and a means of escaping punishment in the afterlife, so they welcome even transformation into a zombie or a skeleton.

The point of a sacrifice to Orcus is not simply the death of the victim but also the collection and distribution of the victim's blood. Religious leaders fill a skull with blood and drink it, then fill it again for Orcus and pour it out over his idol. This rite takes place once a month, and if the worshipers can find no sentient creature for sacrifice, they must fill the cup with blood from one of their own, a consequence that cults desperately seek to avoid. His cultists see the drinking of blood as a sign of true dedication to Orcus, and they say that Orcus tastes the blood his worshipers drink.

Deathpriest of Orcus	Level 9 Controller (Leader)
Medium natural humanoid, human	XP 400

Initiative +4   Senses Perception +12
Death's Embrace (Necrotic) aura 10; enemies in the aura take a -2 penalty to death saves.
HP 96; **Bloodied** 48
AC 23; **Fortitude** 21, **Reflex** 19, **Will** 21; see also *dark blessing*
Speed 5
⊕ **Mace** (standard; at-will) ✦ **Necrotic**
   +12 vs. AC; 1d8 + 1 damage plus 1d8 necrotic damage.
↗ **Ray of Black Fire** (standard; at-will) ✦ **Fire, Necrotic**
   Ranged 10; +10 vs. Reflex; 1d8 + 3 fire and necrotic damage, and one ally in the deathpriest's line of sight gains a +2 power bonus to its next attack roll against the target.
↩ **Dark Blessing** (standard; encounter) ✦ **Necrotic**
   Close burst 2; +10 vs. Fortitude; 2d8 + 3 necrotic damage, and the target is pushed 1 square. *Hit or Miss:* The deathpriest and all allies in the burst gain a +2 power bonus to AC until the end of the encounter.
Alignment Evil   **Languages** Abyssal, Common
Skills Arcana +10, Religion +10
Str 13 (+5)   Dex 10 (+4)   Wis 16 (+7)
Con 16 (+7)   Int 12 (+5)   Cha 15 (+6)
Equipment chainmail, skull-headed mace

DEATHPRIEST OF ORCUS TACTICS

The deathpriest stays close to its allies, waiting for the best moment to invoke its *dark blessing*. Until then, it attacks enemies with its mace or *ray of black fire*.

Crimson Acolyte	Level 7 Skirmisher
Medium natural humanoid, human	XP 300

Initiative +4   Senses Perception +9
HP 76; **Bloodied** 38
AC 21; **Fortitude** 18, **Reflex** 19, **Will** 18
Speed 6
⊕ **Scythe** (standard; at-will) ✦ **Necrotic**
   +12 vs. AC (+14 against a bloodied enemy); 2d4 + 2 damage plus 5 necrotic damage.
Crimson Path (minor; at-will)
   The crimson acolyte shifts 1 square (2 squares while bloodied).
Alignment Evil   **Languages** Abyssal, Common
Skills Acrobatics +11, Religion +8
Str 14 (+5)   Dex 16 (+6)   Wis 13 (+4)
Con 12 (+4)   Int 10 (+3)   Cha 15 (+5)
Equipment leather armor, scythe

CRIMSON ACOLYTE TACTICS

The crimson acolyte uses *crimson path* to weave through its enemies' defenses while striking with its bloodstained scythe.

ENCOUNTER GROUPS

Orcus is one of the most powerful creatures that adventurers can ever hope to defeat. Unfortunately for them, he is rarely encountered alone.

Orcus's living worshipers often strike up alliances with demons and undead.

Level 9 Encounter (XP 2,400)
✦ 1 deathpriest of Orcus (level 9 controller)
✦ 4 crimson acolytes (level 7 skirmisher)
✦ 2 battle wights (level 9 soldier)

Level 22 Encounter (XP 22,525)
✦ 1 deathpriest hierophant (level 21 elite controller)
✦ 5 abyssal ghoul myrmidons (level 23 minion)
✦ 2 rot harbingers (level 20 soldier)
✦ 1 rot slinger (level 22 artillery)

Level 24 Encounter (XP 33,800)
✦ 1 deathpriest hierophant (level 21 elite controller)
✦ 3 blood fiend abominations (level 23 soldier)
✦ 1 aspect of Orcus (level 24 elite brute)

Level 28 Encounter (XP 65,950)
✦ Doresain the Ghoul King (level 27 elite skirmisher)
✦ 1 dread wraith (level 25 lurker)
✦ 2 eladrin liches (level 24 elite controller)
✦ 10 abyssal ghoul myrmidons (level 23 minion)

Level 34 Encounter (XP 225,000)
✦ Orcus (level 33 solo brute)
✦ 2 atropal abominations (level 28 elite brute)
✦ 8 lich vestiges (level 26 minion)

OTYUGH

This tentacled scavenger feeds on carrion and lurks under mounds of filth and refuse. Careless creatures that blunder within reach of its tentacles are dragged toward its maw and quickly dispatched. The otyugh then buries the carcasses under heaps of offal and waits for them to rot before devouring them.

OTYUGH LORE

A character knows the following information with a successful Nature check.

DC 15: Some intelligent monsters capture otyughs and use them as guardians, but otyughs are best used as living garbage disposals. Otyughs often infest the sewer systems of large cities, lurking in the darkest and most stagnant portions.

DC 20: Otyughs usually attack creatures that wander too near their filthy larders, even if they're not particularly hungry. They rarely devour the carcasses of slain creatures immediately, preferring to let them rot first.

Otyugh	Level 7 Soldier
Large natural beast	XP 300

Initiative +5   **Senses** Perception +11; darkvision
Otyugh Stench aura 1; living enemies in the aura take a −2 penalty to attack rolls.
HP 82; **Bloodied** 41
AC 23; **Fortitude** 22, **Reflex** 16, **Will** 19
Immune disease
Speed 5, swim 5
  ⊕ **Tentacle** (standard; at-will)
    Reach 3; +12 vs. AC; 1d8 + 6 damage, and the target is pulled 2 squares and grabbed (until escape).
  ↓ **Diseased Bite** (standard; at-will) ✦ **Disease**
    +12 vs. AC; 1d10 + 6 damage, and the target contracts filth fever (see below).
Spying Eye
    An otyugh can hide beneath murky water or refuse, leaving only its eyestalk exposed. While doing so, it gains a +10 bonus to Stealth checks but is immobilized.
Alignment Unaligned   **Languages** —
Skills Stealth +8 (+18 while using *spying eye*)
| **Str** 22 (+9) | **Dex** 11 (+3) | **Wis** 16 (+6) |
| **Con** 18 (+7) | **Int** 1 (−2) | **Cha** 5 (+0) |

OTYUGH TACTICS

An otyugh hides until prey comes by, and then attacks with its long tentacles. It uses its melee basic attack to snag a potential meal and drag it close. If an otyugh begins its turn with a foe adjacent to it, it makes a *diseased bite* attack instead.

Groups of otyughs do not cooperate in any way, and an unfortunate adventurer caught between several otyughs is likely to be dragged from one to the other several times as the monsters fight for their prize.

ENCOUNTER GROUPS

Otyughs rarely appear with allied creatures. However, clever monsters might seek to trap adventurers between themselves and otyughs, or build pits leading to otyugh lairs. Also, carrion crawlers might naturally be encountered near otyugh lairs because they feed opportunistically and steal the otyughs' kills.

Level 7 Encounter (XP 1,450)
✦ 1 otyugh (level 7 soldier)
✦ 2 troglodyte maulers (level 6 soldier)
✦ 1 troglodyte curse chanter (level 8 controller)
✦ 1 troglodyte impaler (level 7 artillery)

Level 7 Encounter (XP 1,500)
✦ 2 otyughs (level 7 soldier)
✦ 3 carrion crawlers (level 7 controller)

Filth Fever	Level 3 Disease	Endurance stable DC 16, improve DC 21
The target is cured.	◄ **Initial Effect:** The target loses 1 healing surge. ◄► The target takes a −2 penalty to AC, Fortitude defense, and Reflex defense.	► **Final Effect:** The target takes a −2 penalty to AC, Fortitude defense, and Reflex defense. The target loses all healing surges and cannot regain hit points.

OWLBEAR

INFAMOUS FOR ITS BAD TEMPER, an owlbear attacks anything it thinks it can kill.

Owlbear	Level 8 Elite Brute
Large fey beast	XP 700

Initiative +6   **Senses** Perception +12; low-light vision
HP 212; **Bloodied** 106; see also *stunning screech*
AC 22; **Fortitude** 22, **Reflex** 19, **Will** 20
Saving Throws +2
Speed 7
Action Points 1
⊕ **Claw** (standard; at-will)
   Reach 2; +12 vs. AC; 2d6 + 5 damage.
⊹ **Double Attack** (standard; at-will)
   The owlbear makes two claw attacks. If both claws hit the same target, the target is grabbed (until escape).
⊹ **Bite** (standard; at-will)
   Grabbed target only; automatic hit; 4d8 + 5 damage.
↵ **Stunning Screech** (free, when first bloodied; encounter)
   Close burst 1; +10 vs. Fortitude; the target is stunned (save ends).
Alignment Unaligned   **Languages** —
Str 20 (+9)	**Dex** 14 (+6)	**Wis** 16 (+7)
Con 16 (+7)	**Int** 2 (+0)	**Cha** 10 (+4)

OWLBEAR TACTICS

An owlbear attacks its closest enemy, using *double attack* when it can. If an owlbear hits with both claws, it grabs its victim and bites it on the following round. When first bloodied, it uses *stunning screech* and attacks the nearest stunned target.

Winterclaw Owlbear	Level 14 Elite Controller
Huge fey beast	XP 2,000

Initiative +9   **Senses** Perception +15; low-light vision
HP 280; **Bloodied** 140; see also *frost wail*
AC 28; **Fortitude** 28, **Reflex** 23, **Will** 24
Saving Throws +2
Speed 7 (ice walk)
Action Points 1
⊕ **Winterclaw** (standard; at-will) ✦ **Cold**
   Reach 3; +18 vs. AC; 1d8 + 7 damage plus 1d8 cold damage, and the target is slowed (save ends).
⊹ **Double Attack** (standard; at-will) ✦ **Cold**
   The winterclaw owlbear makes two winterclaw attacks. If both claws hit the same target, the target is immobilized (save ends). *Aftereffect:* The target is slowed (save ends).
↵ **Frost Wail** (standard; recharges when first bloodied) ✦ **Cold**
   Close burst 3; +16 vs. Fortitude; 1d10 + 5 cold damage, and the target is immobilized (save ends).
Alignment Unaligned   **Languages** —
Str 24 (+14)	**Dex** 14 (+9)	**Wis** 16 (+10)
Con 20 (+12)	**Int** 2 (+3)	**Cha** 12 (+8)

WINTERCLAW OWLBEAR TACTICS

The winterclaw owlbear charges the nearest foe and attacks with its claws, spending its action point to use *frost wail* at the start of battle. It uses this power again when bloodied.

OWLBEAR LORE

A character knows the following information with a successful Nature check.

DC 15: Owlbears are dangerous predators of the Feywild that made their way to the natural world long ago. They typically lair in forests and shallow caves. They can be active during the day or night, depending on the habits of the available prey. Adults live in mated pairs and hunt in packs, leaving their young in the lair.

ENCOUNTER GROUPS

Some humanoids charm or tame owlbears as guard beasts. Such owlbears consider the area they guard to be their personal hunting ground, relentlessly pursuing strangers that blunder within.

Level 7 Encounter (XP 1,650)
✦ 1 owlbear (level 8 elite brute)
✦ 2 satyr rakes (level 7 skirmisher)
✦ 1 satyr piper (level 8 controller)

Level 14 Encounter (XP 5,000)
✦ 1 winterclaw owlbear (level 14 elite controller)
✦ 3 cyclops ramblers (level 14 skirmisher)

PANTHER

THE COMMON PANTHER, WHILE FEROCIOUS, tends to hunt only small game. However, some panthers are supernatural creatures touched by the magic of other planes, and they are known to stalk humanoid prey.

Fey Panther		Level 4 Skirmisher
Medium fey beast		XP 175

Initiative +8   **Senses** Perception +8; low-light vision
HP 54; **Bloodied** 27
AC 18; **Fortitude** 16, **Reflex** 18, **Will** 15
Speed 8, climb 6; see also *fey step*
⊕ **Bite** (standard; at-will)
    +9 vs. AC; 1d6 + 4 damage, and the fey panther shifts 1 square.
Charging Pounce
    When the fey panther charges, it deals an extra 1d6 damage and knocks the target prone.
Fey Step (move; encounter) ✦ **Teleportation**
    The fey panther can teleport 5 squares.
Alignment Unaligned   **Languages** —
Skills Stealth +11
Str 14 (+4)   **Dex** 18 (+6)   **Wis** 13 (+3)
Con 14 (+4)   **Int** 2 (-2)   **Cha** 11 (+2)

FEY PANTHER TACTICS

A fey panther springs from hiding and makes a *charging pounce* attack, pouncing again whenever it begins its turn with no enemies adjacent to it.

Spectral Panther		Level 9 Lurker
Medium shadow beast		XP 400

Initiative +13   **Senses** Perception +10; low-light vision
HP 76; **Bloodied** 38
AC 23; **Fortitude** 22, **Reflex** 24, **Will** 20
Speed 7
⊕ **Claws** (standard; at-will)
    +14 vs. AC; 2d6 + 5 damage.
↯ **Tail Spike** (immediate reaction, when an enemy moves or shifts into a square adjacent to the spectral panther; at-will)
    +14 vs. AC; 1d6 + 2 damage.
Combat Advantage
    The spectral panther deals an extra 2d6 damage against any target it has combat advantage against.
Invisibility (standard, usable only while in *spectral form*; at-will) ✦ **Illusion**
    The spectral panther is invisible until it makes an attack. It can end this effect on its turn as a free action.
Spectral Form (standard; at-will)
    The spectral panther becomes insubstantial. It gains a +5 power bonus to Stealth checks but deals only half damage with its attacks. It can end this effect on its turn as a free action.
Alignment Unaligned   **Languages** —
Skills Stealth +14 (+19 in *spectral form*)
Str 15 (+6)   **Dex** 21 (+9)   **Wis** 13 (+5)
Con 16 (+7)   **Int** 2 (+0)   **Cha** 12 (+5)

SPECTRAL PANTHER TACTICS

A spectral panther is invisible until it attacks, which allows it to gain combat advantage. After its initial attack, it uses *spectral form* to become insubstantial and moves away. On the following round, it turns invisible again and moves into a position to make another attack. If an enemy moves adjacent to the spectral panther, it makes a *tail spike* attack.

PANTHER LORE

Many animals touched by the magic of other planes exist in the world; the fey panther and spectral panther are just two examples. A character knows the following information with a successful Arcana check.

    DC 15: Fey panthers can move between the natural world and the Feywild at nightfall and sunrise.

    DC 20: Spectral panthers can move between the natural world and the Shadowfell at nightfall and sunrise.

ENCOUNTER GROUPS

Intelligent monsters often keep panthers as pets. Fey panthers are best suited as hunting or battle companions; spectral panthers are trackers and killers.

Level 9 Encounter (XP 2,000)
✦ 2 spectral panthers (level 9 lurker)
✦ 1 dark stalker (level 10 lurker)
✦ 2 shadar-kai warriors (level 8 soldier)

PURPLE WORM

Purple worms are enormous burrowing predators that eat anything, living or dead. They pose a real danger to adventurers exploring the deep natural caverns of the Underdark.

Purple Worm Tactics

A purple worm often burrows up through a cavern floor to attack creatures standing on the ground. Once it has grabbed a creature, it uses *clamping jaws* to deal damage round after round until it can swallow the creature.

Purple Worm Lore

A character knows the following information with a successful Dungeoneering or Nature check.

DC 20: A purple worm can burrow through solid rock, leaving tunnels in its wake. The purple worm eats anything and relies on its blindsight and tremorsense to detect prey.

Encounter Groups

Purple worms are lone hunters. However, they are occasionally drawn to the sounds and vibrations of battle, exploding out of the floor or wall to catch all other creatures by surprise.

Level 18 Encounter (XP 9,800)
✦ 1 purple worm (level 16 solo soldier)
✦ 2 savage minotaurs (level 16 brute)

Purple Worm	Level 16 Solo Soldier
Huge natural beast (blind)	XP 7,000

Initiative +13   **Senses** Perception +10; blindsight 10, tremorsense 20

HP 780; **Bloodied** 390

AC 33 (26 against swallowed creatures); **Fortitude** 34, **Reflex** 30, **Will** 29

Immune gaze, illusion

Saving Throws +5

Speed 6, burrow 3 (tunneling)

Action Points 2

⊕ **Bite** (standard; at-will)

Reach 3; +21 vs. Reflex; 2d8 + 7 damage, plus the target is grabbed (until escape). The purple worm cannot make bite attacks while grabbing a creature, but it can use *clamping jaws*.

↯ **Clamping Jaws** (standard; at-will)

If a purple worm begins its turn with a target grabbed in its jaws, it makes an attack against the grabbed creature: +21 vs. Reflex; 2d8 + 7 damage. *Miss:* Half damage.

↯ **Swallow** (standard; at-will)

The purple worm attempts to swallow a bloodied Medium or smaller creature it is grabbing: +21 vs. Fortitude; on a hit, the target is swallowed and restrained (no save) and takes 10 damage plus 10 acid damage on subsequent rounds at the start of the purple worm's turn. The swallowed creature can make melee basic attacks only, and only with one-handed or natural weapons. If the purple worm dies, any creature trapped in its gullet can escape as a move action, ending that action in a square formerly occupied by the purple worm.

Alignment Unaligned   **Languages** –

Str 24 (+15)	**Dex** 16 (+11)	**Wis** 14 (+10)
Con 20 (+13)	**Int** 2 (+4)	**Cha** 4 (+5)

Elder Purple Worm	Level 24 Solo Soldier
Gargantuan natural beast (blind)	XP 30,250

Initiative +18   **Senses** Perception +15; blindsight 10, tremorsense 20

HP 1,145; **Bloodied** 572

AC 41 (34 against swallowed creatures); **Fortitude** 41, **Reflex** 36, **Will** 35

Immune gaze, illusion

Saving Throws +5

Speed 8, burrow 4 (tunneling)

Action Points 2

⊕ **Bite** (standard; at-will)

Reach 4; +29 vs. Reflex; 2d10 + 9 damage, plus the target is grabbed (until escape). The elder purple worm cannot make bite attacks while grabbing a creature, but it can use *clamping jaws*.

↯ **Clamping Jaws** (standard; at-will)

If an elder purple worm begins its turn with a target grabbed in its jaws, it makes an attack against the grabbed creature: +29 vs. Reflex; 2d10 + 9 damage. *Miss:* Half damage.

↯ **Swallow** (standard; at-will)

The elder purple worm attempts to swallow a bloodied Large or smaller creature it is grabbing; +29 vs. Fortitude; on a hit, the target is swallowed and restrained (no save) and takes 20 damage plus 20 acid damage on subsequent rounds at the start of the elder purple worm's turn. The swallowed creature can make melee basic attacks only, and only with one-handed or natural weapons. If the elder purple worm dies, any creature trapped in its gullet can escape as a move action, ending that action in a square formerly occupied by the elder purple worm.

Alignment Unaligned   **Languages** –

Str 28 (+21)	**Dex** 18 (+16)	**Wis** 16 (+15)
Con 29 (+21)	**Int** 2 (+8)	**Cha** 10 (+12)

FRED HOOPER

QUICKLING

Quicklings are swift, wicked fey that kill other creatures for food, treasure, or sport. They like to set ambushes and outwit enemies, and they frequently ally with other creatures that share their desires. If their escapades enrage an adversary too strong to overcome, quicklings have no problem fleeing in a chorus of nervegrating laughter, leaving their so-called allies to fend for themselves.

Although quicklings are native to the Feywild, they also stray into the natural world to keep an eye out for interesting events and exploitable situations.

QUICKLING LORE

A character knows the following information with a successful Arcana check.

DC 15: Quicklings rely on their speed and wits to overcome their prey and elude their enemies. Devious and cruel, they delight in trapping, tormenting, and killing other creatures. They generally focus their attacks on weaker-looking creatures while dodging tougher adversaries.

ENCOUNTER GROUPS

Quicklings readily ally with other evil fey, including fomorians. Evil humanoids in the natural world value quicklings as allies and servants.

Level 9 Encounter (XP 2,150)
✦ 2 quickling runners (level 9 skirmisher)
✦ 1 eladrin twilight incanter (level 8 controller)
✦ 1 feymire crocodile (level 10 elite soldier)

Quickling Runner		Level 9 Skirmisher
Small fey humanoid		XP 400

Initiative +13   **Senses** Perception +7; low-light vision
HP 96; **Bloodied** 48
AC 24 (28 against opportunity attacks); **Fortitude** 20, **Reflex** 24, **Will** 20
Speed 12, climb 6; see also *fey shift* and *quick cuts*
🗡 **Short Sword** (standard; at-will) ✦ **Weapon**
   +14 vs. AC; 1d6 + 7 damage.
† **Quick Cuts** (standard; at-will) ✦ **Weapon**
   The quickling moves its speed. At any two points during its move, the quickling makes a melee basic attack at a -2 penalty. The quickling cannot use this power while immobilized or slowed.
Fey Shift (standard; encounter)
   The quickling runner shifts 10 squares.
Maintain Mobility (minor; recharge ⚁ ⚂ ⚃)
   An immobilized quickling runner is no longer immobilized.
Alignment Evil   **Languages** Elven
Skills Acrobatics +21, Bluff +9, Stealth +16
| **Str** 9 (+3) | **Dex** 24 (+11) | **Wis** 17 (+7) |
| **Con** 16 (+7) | **Int** 14 (+6) | **Cha** 10 (+4) |
Equipment short sword

QUICKLING RUNNER TACTICS

The quickling runner waits in ambush, hoping to catch enemies by surprise. It uses *fey shift* to slip past enemy defenders and attacks the weakest-looking opponent. It uses its *quick cuts* power as often as possible, relying on its high AC to dodge opportunity attacks.

Quickling Zephyr		Level 14 Lurker
Small fey humanoid		XP 1,000

Initiative +20   **Senses** Perception +10; low-light vision
HP 82; **Bloodied** 41
AC 30; **Fortitude** 26, **Reflex** 29, **Will** 23
Speed 12, climb 6; see also *blinding speed* and *unstoppable*
🗡 **Short Sword** (standard; at-will) ✦ **Weapon**
   +19 vs. AC; 1d6 + 9 damage.
Blinding Speed (move; recharge ⚁ ⚂ ⚃) ✦ **Illusion**
   The quickling zephyr moves up to 12 squares and becomes invisible until it attacks or until the end of its next turn.
Combat Advantage
   If the quickling zephyr has combat advantage against its target, it deals an extra 2d6 damage and dazes the target (save ends) on a successful melee attack.
Unstoppable
   The quickling zephyr ignores difficult terrain and can move across any solid or liquid surface.
Alignment Evil   **Languages** Elven
Skills Acrobatics +26, Bluff +13, Stealth +21
| **Str** 12 (+8) | **Dex** 28 (+16) | **Wis** 17 (+10) |
| **Con** 22 (+13) | **Int** 16 (+10) | **Cha** 12 (+8) |
Equipment short sword

QUICKLING ZEPHYR TACTICS

A quickling zephyr uses its *blinding speed* to maneuver so that it gains combat advantage against its enemies.

IZZY MEDRANO

RAKSHASA

DESPITE THEIR BESTIAL FEATURES, rakshasas are clever, malicious, and sophisticated. Although rakshasas come in many varieties, they all share some common traits, namely their feline heads, backward claws, and taste for luxury.

Rakshasas often conceal their true appearance, using illusion magic to adopt whatever disguises serve them best. They typically masquerade as nobles or wealthy merchants, lying and manipulating other creatures into doing their bidding. Rakshasas prefer to mislead would-be adversaries instead of fighting them, but if combat becomes necessary, rakshasas are fierce and ruthless.

A rakshasa has the head of a feline predator, usually a tiger, as well as a luxurious coat of fur and clawed hands. It is clothed in fine attire and expensive jewelry. A closer look at a rakshasa reveals that the palms of its hands are where the backs of the hands would be on a human—a subtle feature that adds to the creature's unsettling appearance.

RAKSHASA LORE

A character knows the following information with a successful Nature check.

DC 20: Rakshasas are malevolent, deceptive humanoids with a taste for luxury. They use powerful illusion magic to hide their true forms as they pose as nobles, merchant princes, crime lords, and other wealthy, influential individuals.

DC 25: Regardless of type, rakshasas all share one very peculiar trait. Their clawed hands are backwards from other humanoids, so that when a rakshasa stands with its arms at its side, its palms face outward instead of inward. This oddity does not detract from their manual dexterity or ability to wield weapons.

DC 30: According to some legends, rakshasas were spawned by demons that fled the Abyss and came to the natural world long ago. Many rakshasas discount these legends, proudly asserting that their species could never have such degenerate origins, yet their cruelty often suggests a demonic heritage.

Rakshasa warrior

Rakshasa Warrior	Level 15 Soldier
Medium natural humanoid	XP 1,200

Initiative +13   **Senses** Perception +16; low-light vision
HP 142; **Bloodied** 71
AC 31; **Fortitude** 29, **Reflex** 28, **Will** 28
Speed 6

⚔ **Longsword** (standard; at-will) ✦ **Weapon**
The rakshasa warrior makes two attack rolls and keeps the better result; +21 vs. AC; 1d8 + 5 damage, and the target is marked until the end of the rakshasa's next turn.

⚔ **Claw** (standard; at-will)
+21 vs. AC; 1d8 + 5 damage.

⚔ **Tiger Pounce** (immediate reaction, when a marked enemy within 5 squares of the rakshasa warrior shifts; at-will) ✦ **Weapon**
The rakshasa shifts to the nearest square adjacent to the enemy and makes a basic attack against it.

Deceptive Veil (minor; at-will) ✦ **Illusion**
The rakshasa warrior can disguise itself to appear as any Medium humanoid. A successful Insight check (opposed by the rakshasa's Bluff check) pierces the disguise.

Alignment Evil   **Languages** Common
Skills Athletics +15, Bluff +14, Intimidate +14
Str 20 (+12)   **Dex** 18 (+11)   **Wis** 18 (+11)
Con 14 (+9)   **Int** 12 (+8)   **Cha** 14 (+9)
Equipment scale armor, heavy shield, longsword

RAKSHASA WARRIOR TACTICS

A rakshasa warrior fights with its longsword, marking foes so that it can use *tiger pounce* on subsequent rounds.

Rakshasa Archer	Level 15 Artillery
Medium natural humanoid	XP 1,200

Initiative +13   **Senses** Perception +16; low-light vision
HP 110; **Bloodied** 55
AC 28; **Fortitude** 24, **Reflex** 26, **Will** 25
Speed 6

⚔ **Claw** (standard; at-will)
+19 vs. AC; 1d8 + 3 damage.

🏹 **Longbow** (standard; at-will) ✦ **Weapon**
Ranged 20/40; +20 vs. AC; 1d10 + 5 damage.

🏹 **Double Attack** (standard; at-will) ✦ **Weapon**
The rakshasa archer makes two longbow attacks against a single target or against two targets within 3 squares of one another.

🏹 **Ghost Arrow** (standard; recharge ⚄ ⚅) ✦ **Necrotic, Weapon**
Requires longbow; ranged 20/40; +20 vs. Reflex; 1d10 + 5 necrotic damage, and the target cannot spend healing surges (save ends).

Deceptive Veil (minor; at-will) ✦ **Illusion**
The rakshasa archer can disguise itself to appear as any Medium humanoid. A successful Insight check (opposed by the rakshasa's Bluff check) pierces the disguise.

Alignment Evil   **Languages** Common
Skills Bluff +14, Intimidate +14
Str 17 (+10)   **Dex** 20 (+12)   **Wis** 18 (+11)
Con 14 (+9)   **Int** 12 (+8)   **Cha** 14 (+9)
Equipment longbow, quiver of 30 arrows

Rakshasa assassin

RAKSHASA ASSASSIN TACTICS

A rakshasa assassin tries to attack from concealment in order to gain combat advantage. If it moves at least 2 squares on its turn, it can use *shadow form* to pass through solid barriers en route to its target. It then uses *phantom distraction* to gain combat advantage against its prey before making a *double attack*.

Rakshasa Noble	Level 19 Controller
Medium natural humanoid	XP 2,400

Initiative +14   **Senses** Perception +19; low-light vision
HP 178; **Bloodied** 89
AC 33; **Fortitude** 31, **Reflex** 33, **Will** 34; see also *phantom image*
Speed 7
ⓐ **Claw** (standard; at-will)
+22 vs. AC; 1d6 + 3 damage, and the target is blinded until the end of the rakshasa noble's next turn.
↗ **Mind Twist** (standard; at-will) ✦ **Psychic**
Ranged 20; +22 vs. Will; 3d6 + 7 psychic damage, and the target is dazed (save ends).
↗ **Phantom Lure** (standard; at-will) ✦ **Charm**
Ranged 10; +22 vs. Will; the target slides 5 squares.
↗ **Frightful Phantom** (standard; recharge ⚄ ⚅) ✦ **Fear**
Ranged 5; +22 vs. Will; 4d8 + 7 psychic damage, the target is pushed 5 squares, and the target is stunned (save ends).
Deceptive Veil (minor; at-will) ✦ **Illusion**
The rakshasa noble can disguise itself to appear as any Medium humanoid. A successful Insight check (opposed by the rakshasa's Bluff check) pierces the disguise.
Phantom Image (minor; recharge ⚄ ⚅) ✦ **Illusion**
Until the end of the rakshasa noble's next turn, any creature that attacks the rakshasa's AC or Reflex defense must roll twice and use the lower attack roll result. If either result is a critical hit, use that result instead.
Alignment Evil   **Languages** Common
Skills Arcana +20, Athletics +17, Bluff +21, Diplomacy +21, History +20, Insight +19, Intimidate +21

Str 16 (+12)	Dex 20 (+14)	Wis 20 (+14)
Con 18 (+13)	Int 22 (+15)	Cha 24 (+16)

RAKSHASA NOBLE TACTICS

A rakshasa noble disdains melee combat and prefers to use its *mind twist* power at range. It uses *frightful phantom* against an enemy who gets too close for comfort or *phantom lure* to lead the target into dangerous or entangling terrain. If forced into melee combat, it uses *phantom image* as often as it can to distort its true location while making claw attacks. If it successfully blinds a target with a claw attack, it tries to move away to a location where it can continue making ranged attacks.

RAKSHASA ARCHER TACTICS

The rakshasa archer keeps its distance and attacks with its bow, using *double attack* whenever possible and *ghost arrow* against bloodied foes.

Rakshasa Assassin	Level 17 Skirmisher
Medium natural humanoid	XP 1,600

Initiative +16   **Senses** Perception +16; low-light vision
HP 160; **Bloodied** 80
AC 31; **Fortitude** 29, **Reflex** 31, **Will** 29
Speed 6; see also *shadow form*
ⓐ **Short Sword** (standard; at-will) ✦ **Weapon**
+22 vs. AC; 1d6 + 6 damage.
† **Double Attack** (standard; at-will) ✦ **Weapon**
The rakshasa assassin makes two melee basic attacks.
↩ **Phantom Distraction** (minor; recharge ⚄ ⚅) ✦ **Illusion**
Close burst 1; +20 vs. Will; the target is dazed until the end of the rakshasa assassin's next turn.
Combat Advantage
The rakshasa assassin deals an extra 2d6 damage on melee and ranged attacks against any target it has combat advantage against.
Deceptive Veil (minor; at-will) ✦ **Illusion**
The rakshasa assassin can disguise itself to appear as any Medium humanoid. A successful Insight check (opposed by the rakshasa's Bluff check) pierces the disguise.
Shadow Form
If the rakshasa assassin moves at least 2 squares, it gains the phasing quality (see glossary) until the end of its turn.
Alignment Evil   **Languages** Common
Skills Acrobatics +18, Athletics +16, Bluff +17, Stealth +18

Str 18 (+12)	Dex 22 (+14)	Wis 16 (+11)
Con 16 (+11)	Int 12 (+9)	Cha 18 (+12)

Equipment chainmail, 2 short swords

RAKSHASA REINCARNATION

As fiendish spirits veiled in flesh, rakshasas are bound to the world. When they are killed, they reincarnate at some random spot elsewhere in the world after days, months, or sometimes years of tormented wandering as bodiless spirits. A reincarnated rakshasa awakens in full health, with complete possession of its memories and abilities. It often seeks vengeance later against those who killed it in its previous incarnation, but the world is wide and mortal lifetimes are short. It's said that rakshasas can be truly slain only by a specially blessed weapon that pierces its heart.

Rakshasa Dread Knight
Level 24 Soldier

Medium natural humanoid

XP 6,050

Initiative +18   **Senses** Perception +22; low-light vision

Aura of Doom aura 5; enemies in the aura regain half the normal amount of hit points when they spend a healing surge.

HP 220; **Bloodied** 110

AC 40; **Fortitude** 40, **Reflex** 37, **Will** 38

Speed 6

⊕ **Longsword** (standard; at-will) ✦ **Weapon**

The rakshasa dread knight makes two attack rolls and keeps the better result; +29 vs. AC; 1d8 + 7 damage, and the target is marked until the end of the rakshasa's next turn.

⊕ **Claw** (standard; at-will)

+29 vs. AC; 1d8 + 7 damage.

† **Triple Attack** (standard; at-will) ✦ **Weapon**

The rakshasa dread knight makes three melee basic attacks. If two or more attacks hit the same target, the target is dazed (save ends).

Deceptive Veil (minor; at-will) ✦ **Illusion**

The rakshasa dread knight can disguise itself to appear as any Medium humanoid. A successful Insight check (opposed by the rakshasa's Bluff check) pierces the disguise.

Knight's Move (move; recharge ⊡ ⊞)

The rakshasa dread knight can fly up to 6 squares. It must land at the end of this move or else it crashes.

Alignment Evil   **Languages** Common

Skills Athletics +22, Bluff +21, Insight +22, Intimidate +21

Str 25 (+19)	**Dex** 19 (+16)	**Wis** 21 (+17)
Con 20 (+17)	**Int** 15 (+14)	**Cha** 18 (+16)

Equipment scale armor, heavy shield, longsword

Rakshasa noble

RAKSHASA DREAD KNIGHT TACTICS

A rakshasa dread knight uses *triple attack* as often as it can while using *knight's move* to circumvent difficult, hindering, and hazardous terrain.

ENCOUNTER GROUPS

Rakshasas usually keep to themselves. They might also have allies and minions they've deceived or bullied into serving them.

Level 15 Encounter (XP 6,400)
✦ 2 rakshasa archers (level 15 artillery)
✦ 2 rakshasa warriors (level 15 soldier)
✦ 2 hellstinger scorpions (level 13 soldier)

Level 17 Encounter (XP 7,600)
✦ 1 rakshasa assassin (level 17 skirmisher)
✦ 1 yuan-ti malison disciple of Zehir (level 17 controller)
✦ 2 yuan-ti malison incanters (level 15 artillery)
✦ 2 yuan-ti abominations (level 14 soldier)

Level 17 Encounter (XP 7,600)
✦ 1 rakshasa noble (level 19 controller)
✦ 1 rakshasa assassin (level 17 skirmisher)
✦ 3 rakshasa warriors (level 15 soldier)

Level 18 Encounter (XP 9,600)
✦ 1 rakshasa noble (level 19 controller)
✦ 2 rakshasa warriors (level 15 soldier)
✦ 2 cambion hellfire magi (level 18 artillery)
✦ 2 shadow snakes (level 16 skirmisher)

Level 24 Encounter (XP 32,500)
✦ 2 rakshasa dread knights (level 24 soldier)
✦ 2 fell wyverns (level 24 skirmisher)
✦ 1 war devil (level 22 brute)

RAT

Rats prefer to live underground, venturing aboveground only at night. They skulk in the sewers and dark alleyways of towns and cities, drawn by the abundance of food, and occasionally inhabit dark caves, ruins, and dark thickets in the wilderness.

RAT LORE

A character knows the following information with a successful Nature check.

DC 15: Rats are sacred to Torog, the King That Crawls. Their presence signifies plague, decay, and collapse in decadent cities.

Giant Rat		Level 1 Minion
Small natural beast		XP 25

Initiative +3   **Senses** Perception +5; low-light vision
HP 1; a missed attack never damages a minion.
AC 15; **Fortitude** 13, **Reflex** 15, **Will** 12
Speed 6, climb 3
⊕ **Bite** (standard; at-will)
  +6 vs. AC; 3 damage.

Alignment Unaligned	**Languages** —	
Str 12 (+1)	**Dex** 17 (+3)	**Wis** 10 (+0)
Con 12 (+1)	**Int** 2 (-4)	**Cha** 6 (-2)

GIANT RAT TACTICS

Giant rats gang up on the nearest target, turning and fleeing when about half their number are slain.

Dire Rat		Level 1 Brute
Medium natural beast		XP 100

Initiative +2   **Senses** Perception +5; low-light vision
HP 38; **Bloodied** 19
AC 15; **Fortitude** 15, **Reflex** 13, **Will** 11
Immune filth fever (see below)
Speed 6, climb 3
⊕ **Bite** (standard; at-will) ✦ **Disease**
  +4 vs. AC; 1d6 + 2 damage, and the target contracts filth fever (see below).

Alignment Unaligned	**Languages** —	
Skills Stealth +7		
Str 14 (+2)	**Dex** 15 (+2)	**Wis** 10 (+0)
Con 18 (+4)	**Int** 3 (-4)	**Cha** 6 (-2)

DIRE RAT TACTICS

Dire rats are stealthy creatures that like to hunt in small packs, sneaking up on prey and ganging up on one creature at a time.

Rat Swarm		Level 2 Skirmisher
Medium natural beast (swarm)		XP 125

Initiative +6   **Senses** Perception +6; low-light vision
Swarm Attack aura 1; the rat swarm makes a basic attack as a free action against each enemy that begins its turn in the aura.
HP 36; **Bloodied** 18
AC 15; **Fortitude** 12, **Reflex** 14, **Will** 11
Resist half damage from melee and ranged attacks; **Vulnerable** 5 against close and area attacks
Speed 4, climb 2
⊕ **Swarm of Teeth** (standard; at-will)
  +6 vs. AC; 1d6 + 3 damage, and ongoing 3 damage (save ends).

Alignment Unaligned	**Languages** —	
Str 12 (+2)	**Dex** 17 (+4)	**Wis** 10 (+1)
Con 12 (+2)	**Int** 2 (-3)	**Cha** 9 (+0)

RAT SWARM TACTICS

Rat swarms are more determined and ferocious than common rats, simply overwhelming anything that looks like it might make a meal.

ENCOUNTER GROUPS

Kobolds and goblins sometimes use rats in fiendish traps to finish off hapless adventurers who fall into spiked pits or half-flooded caves. Monstrous rats also accompany wererats on raids.

Level 3 Encounter (XP 750)
✦ 2 kobold slingers (level 1 artillery)
✦ 2 rat swarms (level 2 skirmisher)
✦ 3 dire rats (level 1 brute)

Filth Fever	Level 3 Disease	**Endurance** stable DC 16, improve DC 21

◀ The target is cured.   **Initial Effect:** The target loses 1 healing surge.   ◀▶ The target takes a -2 penalty to AC, Fortitude defense, and Reflex defense.   ▶ **Final Effect:** The target takes a -2 penalty to AC, Fortitude defense, and Reflex defense. The target loses all healing surges and cannot regain hit points.

ROC

Rocs are enormous birds of prey with strong ties to the Elemental Chaos. Giants and titans value them as pets and allies.

The term "roc" refers to a number of related avians, each with their own unique traits and habitats.

COMMON ROC

COMMON ROCS LIVE IN SECLUDED MOUNTAIN AERIES beyond the reach of most nonflying creatures. They prefer to hunt horses and cattle, competing for food with other flying carnivores such as chimeras and manticores. A hungry roc attacks humanoids when easier game is scarce.

Roc	Level 14 Elite Skirmisher
Huge natural beast	XP 2,000

Initiative +16   **Senses** Perception +15
HP 288; **Bloodied** 144
AC 30; **Fortitude** 30, **Reflex** 30, **Will** 26
Saving Throws +2
Speed 4, fly 10 (clumsy), overland flight 15; see also *claw snatch*
Action Points 1
⊕ **Bite** (standard; at-will)
    Reach 2; +19 vs. AC; 2d6 + 7 damage.
† **Claw Snatch** (standard; at-will)
    The roc moves up to its fly speed and makes an attack against a Medium or smaller target at any point during its move; +17 vs. Reflex; 1d10 + 7 damage, and the target is grabbed, carried the rest of the roc's move, released, and knocked prone in a space adjacent to the roc.
Alignment Unaligned   **Languages** —
Str 25 (+14)   **Dex** 25 (+14)   **Wis** 16 (+10)
Con 24 (+14)   **Int** 2 (+3)   **Cha** 12 (+8)

ROC TACTICS

A flying roc likes to swoop down and use *claw snatch* to carry away a random adversary. It drops its victim somewhere a short distance away, and then lands to finish off the hapless soul with bite attacks. A bloodied roc usually flees unless it's particularly hungry.

ROC LORE

A character knows the following information with a successful Nature check.

DC 20: Rocs are enormous birds that live in mountainous nests, hunting large prey such as cattle and horses. Although they are natural beasts, rocs are closely related to elemental creatures such as thunderhawks and phoenixes. Like their more exotic kin, they are frequently found in the company of giants.

DC 25: Roc hatchlings can be trained to serve as guardians and mounts. A typical roc nest holds 1d4 eggs, each weighing close to 100 pounds. A roc egg is worth 10,000 gp on the open market, but few hunters consider the price worth the risk and trouble.

PHOENIX

THIS MIGHTY ELEMENTAL IS VIEWED AS A SYMBOL OF RESURRECTION AND IMMORTALITY because of its ability to recover from near death.

Phoenix	Level 19 Elite Brute
Huge elemental beast (fire)	XP 4,800

Initiative +15   **Senses** Perception +17
Fiery Body (**Fire**) aura 1; creatures in the aura at the start of their turns take 10 fire damage.
HP 300; **Bloodied** 150; see also *immolation*
AC 33; **Fortitude** 38, **Reflex** 31, **Will** 32
Resist 20 fire
Saving Throws +2
Speed 4, fly 10 (hover), overland flight 15
Action Points 1
⊕ **Bite** (standard; at-will) ✦ **Fire**
    Reach 2; +22 vs. AC; 2d6 + 6 damage, and ongoing 5 fire damage (save ends).
↞ **Radiant Burst** (standard; recharge ⚄) ✦ **Radiant**
    Close burst 5; +20 vs. Reflex; 2d10 + 7 radiant damage, and the target is dazed (save ends).
↞ **Immolation** (when first bloodied; daily) ✦ **Fire**
    Close burst 2; +20 vs. Reflex; 3d6 + 7 fire damage, and the phoenix dies. It automatically returns to life at the end of its next turn, with full normal hit points.
Alignment Unaligned   **Languages** —
Str 23 (+15)   **Dex** 22 (+15)   **Wis** 16 (+12)
Con 25 (+16)   **Int** 3 (+5)   **Cha** 24 (+16)

PHOENIX TACTICS

A phoenix usually begins a battle by dropping into the midst of its enemies like a blazing meteor and using *radiant burst*. It then makes bite attacks against groundbound foes from the air (taking advantage of its reach) until *radiant burst* recharges.

PHOENIX LORE

A character knows the following information with a successful Arcana check.

DC 20: Phoenixes have a fierce and inexplicable hatred of the undead. They attack undead foes in preference to any other, unless another enemy presents a drastically greater threat.

DC 25: When a phoenix is bloodied, it explodes in a ball of searing flame, only to be reborn at full strength moments thereafter.

DC 30: Although its body is composed of flame and not flesh, a single scarlet feather sometimes appears in the ashes left when a phoenix is finally slain. When used as a component in the Raise Dead ritual, the feather allows the ritual caster to raise a creature that has been dead for up to 1 year or grant 1 year of life to a creature that has died of old age (see *Player's Handbook* 311 for the description of the Raise Dead ritual).

THUNDERHAWK

THUNDERHAWKS ARE CREATURES OF STORM and favored pets of storm giants. Left to their own devices, they prefer to make their lairs on stormy mountaintops or remote coastal cliffsides.

Thunderhawk		Level 22 Elite Soldier
Huge elemental beast		XP 8,300

Initiative +21   **Senses** Perception +19
HP 420; **Bloodied** 210
AC 38; **Fortitude** 36, **Reflex** 36, **Will** 31
Resist 20 lightning, 20 thunder
Saving Throws +2
Speed 4, fly 10 (hover), overland flight 15
Action Points 1
⊕ **Bite** (standard; at-will) ✦ **Lightning, Thunder**
    Reach 2; +28 vs. AC; 2d8 + 6 damage plus 1d8 lightning damage, plus an extra 2d8 thunder damage when it charges.
↩ **Windrush** (minor 1/round; at-will)
    Close burst 2; +26 vs. Fortitude; the target is knocked prone.

Alignment Unaligned	**Languages** –	
Str 23 (+17)	**Dex** 26 (+19)	**Wis** 16 (+14)
Con 26 (+19)	**Int** 2 (+7)	**Cha** 14 (+13)

THUNDERHAWK TACTICS

A thunderhawk plummets out of the sky, charging the nearest foe and using *windrush* to knock enemies prone. On subsequent rounds, the thunderhawk hovers in the air as it continues to buffet foes with *windrush* and make bite attacks (taking advantage of its reach). Once bloodied, it flies off, only to return with another charge attack.

THUNDERHAWK LORE

A character knows the following information with a successful Arcana check.

    DC 25: Thunderhawks are the frequent companions of storm giants. Storm giants like to send their thunderhawks into melee, where the great birds can pin down opponents and render them vulnerable to the giants' ranged attacks.

ENCOUNTER GROUPS

Newly hatched rocs can be trained to serve as guards, mounts, and companions for various elemental creatures.

Level 14 Encounter (XP 4,800)
✦ 1 roc (level 14 elite skirmisher)
✦ 2 hill giants (level 13 brute)
✦ 2 galeb duhr rockcallers (level 11 controller)

Level 19 Encounter (XP 12,400)
✦ 1 phoenix (level 19 elite brute)
✦ 2 fire archon blazesteels (level 19 soldier)
✦ 1 fire archon ash disciple (level 20 artillery)

Level 22 Encounter (XP 21,400)
✦ 2 thunderhawks (level 22 elite soldier)
✦ 2 bralanis of the autumn winds (level 19 controller)

This subterranean creature grabs victims with its tentacles and drags them within reach of its monstrous, toothy maw.

A roper feeds on almost anything that blunders into its grasp. Its stony body makes it difficult to spot in natural caverns. It can move about at a slow creep and seek out good hunting spots. When it finds a suitable cave or passage, the roper blends in with the surrounding stalagmites and stalactites, waiting for fleshy prey to arrive.

Roper		Level 14 Elite Controller
Large elemental magical beast (earth)		XP 2,000

Initiative +8   **Senses** Perception +10; darkvision
HP 284; **Bloodied** 142
AC 30; **Fortitude** 29, **Reflex** 24, **Will** 26
Immune petrification
Saving Throws +2
Speed 2, climb 2 (spider climb)
Action Points 1

ⓐ **Tentacle** (standard; at-will) ✦ **Poison**
    Reach 10; +17 vs. Reflex; 2d10 + 4 damage, and the target is grabbed (until escape or until the tentacle is hit; see *tentacle grab*). While the target is grabbed, it is also weakened.

⬦ **Double Attack** (standard; at-will) ✦ **Poison**
    The roper makes two tentacle attacks.

⬦ **Reel** (minor 2/round; at-will)
    The roper makes an attack against a creature it has grabbed; +17 vs. Fortitude; on a hit, the target is pulled 5 squares. The roper can use this power only against a grabbed target once per turn.

⬦ **Bite** (standard; at-will)
    +19 vs. AC; 2d10 + 10 damage.

Stony Body
    A roper that does not move, retracts its tentacles, and keeps its eye and mouth closed resembles a jagged rock formation, stalagmite, or stalactite. In this form, the roper can be recognized with a successful DC 30 Perception check.

Tentacle Grab
    The roper can attack and grab with up to two tentacles at a time. While grabbing an enemy, it can act normally, but it can't use that tentacle for another attack. Enemies can attack the tentacle to make the roper let go of a grabbed creature; the tentacle's defenses are the same as the roper's. An attack that hits the tentacle does not harm the roper but causes it to let go and retract the tentacle.

Alignment Evil	**Languages** Primordial	
Skills Stealth +13		
Str 19 (+11)	**Dex** 12 (+8)	**Wis** 16 (+10)
Con 22 (+13)	**Int** 11 (+7)	**Cha** 9 (+6)

ROPER TACTICS

A roper has an excellent chance to surprise enemies using its *stony body* ability. When it attacks, it uses *double attack* to lash out with two of its tentacles, which secrete weakness-inducing venom. Sometimes it doubles up on the same target, but usually it tries to grab two meals at the same time. The roper then uses *reel* to drag grabbed prey within reach of its toothy maw. (Since *reel* is a minor action, a roper can use the power twice in the same round it uses *double attack*, but only once against each grabbed target.)

ROPER LORE

A character knows the following information with a successful Arcana check.

DC 20: Ropers are all too common in the vast caverns and tunnels of the Underdark. They are clever enough to strike bargains with other intelligent subterranean creatures, guarding tunnels and caves in exchange for food or treasure.

DC 25: Ropers swallow treasure they find, storing it in a spare gizzard. When a roper dies, the gizzard can be cut open to reveal what, if anything, the roper has collected over the years.

ENCOUNTER GROUPS

Ropers occasionally strike bargains with other Underdark dwellers, such as drow, troglodytes, and mind flayers, guarding chambers or passageways as long as their allies agree to provide regular meals—preferably live and screaming. Other Underdark predators such as balhannoths, grells, and umber hulks sometimes lurk near a roper's lair and fall upon hapless parties busy tangling with the roper.

Level 14 Encounter (XP 5,000)
✦ 1 roper (level 14 elite controller)
✦ 1 mind flayer infiltrator (level 14 lurker)
✦ 2 war trolls (level 14 soldier)

Level 14 Encounter (XP 5,200)
✦ 1 roper (level 14 elite controller)
✦ 1 drow arachnomancer (level 13 artillery)
✦ 4 drow warriors (level 11 lurker)

ROT HARBINGER

Sometimes known as angels of decay, rot harbingers are hateful winged undead that inflict a rotting curse with their touch.

Rot Harbinger	Level 20 Soldier
Medium elemental humanoid (undead)	XP 2,800

Initiative +18   **Senses** Perception +15
HP 193; **Bloodied** 96
AC 34; **Fortitude** 32, **Reflex** 32, **Will** 31
Immune disease, poison; **Resist** 10 necrotic
Speed 6, fly 8 (clumsy)
⊕ **Rotting Claw** (standard; at-will) ✦ **Necrotic**
   +25 vs. AC; 2d10 + 6 damage, and the target is marked until
   the end of the rot harbinger's next turn and takes ongoing 10
   necrotic damage (save ends).
Alignment Chaotic evil   **Languages** Abyssal
Str 22 (+16)   **Dex** 22 (+16)   **Wis** 20 (+15)
Con 25 (+17)   **Int** 17 (+13)   **Cha** 17 (+13)

ROT HARBINGER TACTICS

A clumsy flier, the rot harbinger usually lands to make attacks, raking enemies with its claws. When hard pressed, it takes to the air to escape and plots revenge against those who bested it.

Rot Slinger	Level 22 Artillery
Medium elemental humanoid (undead)	XP 4,150

Initiative +18   **Senses** Perception +21
HP 165; **Bloodied** 82
AC 37; **Fortitude** 37, **Reflex** 36, **Will** 34
Immune disease, poison; **Resist** 10 necrotic
Speed 6, fly 8 (clumsy)
⊕ **Rotting Claw** (standard; at-will) ✦ **Necrotic**
   +25 vs. AC; 2d10 + 5 damage, and the target takes ongoing 10
   necrotic damage (save ends).
⊙ **Orb of Decay** (standard; at-will) ✦ **Necrotic**
   Ranged 10; +25 vs. Fortitude; 2d8 + 8 necrotic damage, and the
   target is weakened and takes a −2 penalty to saving throws (save
   ends both).
Alignment Chaotic evil   **Languages** Abyssal
Str 20 (+16)   **Dex** 24 (+18)   **Wis** 20 (+16)
Con 27 (+19)   **Int** 17 (+14)   **Cha** 19 (+15)

ROT SLINGER TACTICS

The rot slinger hurls feculent globs of decaying matter at enemies, hoping to weaken them. Like the rot harbinger, it flees when the battle turns against it.

ROT HARBINGER LORE

A character knows the following information with a successful Religion check.

DC 20: Rot harbingers superficially resemble angels, but there's nothing angelic about them. Their touch causes living flesh to rot.

DC 25: Long ago, the gods tried to slay the demon lord Orcus while he was traveling outside of the Abyss. They sent a host of angels to slay the demon lord, but Orcus ultimately prevailed, killing every last one of them. When he returned to the Abyss, the demon lord of undeath created the first rot harbingers and rot slingers as mockeries of those he'd slain and sent them to the natural world to wreak havoc on the gods' creation.

DC 30: While many rot harbingers serve Orcus and Orcus's servitors, several more have escaped the demon lord's control. All that keeps them animate is their lust for agony and death.

ENCOUNTER GROUPS

Rot harbingers often join forces with other powerful undead creatures and various servants of Orcus.

Level 21 Encounter (XP 18,000)
✦ 2 rot harbingers (level 20 soldier)
✦ 1 deathpriest hierophant (level 21 elite controller)
✦ 3 slaughter wights (level 18 brute)

Level 22 Encounter (XP 19,000)
✦ 2 rot harbingers (level 20 soldier)
✦ 2 rot slingers (level 22 artillery)
✦ 1 voidsoul specter (level 23 lurker)

SAHUAGIN

ALSO KNOWN AS SEA DEVILS, sahuagin are vicious sea dwellers that share many traits with sharks. They slaughter and devour anything they can catch, raiding coastal settlements in the dead of night.

Sahuagin Guard — Level 6 Minion
Medium natural humanoid (aquatic) — XP 63

Initiative +5 **Senses** Perception +4; low-light vision
HP 1; a missed attack never damages a minion.
AC 20; **Fortitude** 18, **Reflex** 17, **Will** 16
Speed 6, swim 6
(+) **Trident** (standard; at-will) ✦ **Weapon**
+11 vs. AC; 5 damage; see also *blood frenzy*.
(↗) **Trident** (standard; at-will) ✦ **Weapon**
Ranged 3/6; +11 vs. AC; 5 damage. The sahuagin guard must retrieve its trident before it can throw it again.
Blood Frenzy
The sahuagin gains a +1 bonus to attack rolls and a +2 bonus to damage rolls against bloodied enemies.
Alignment Chaotic evil **Languages** Abyssal
Str 16 (+6) **Dex** 14 (+5) **Wis** 12 (+4)
Con 14 (+5) **Int** 10 (+3) **Cha** 10 (+3)
Equipment trident

SAHUAGIN GUARD TACTICS
Sahuagin guards viciously attack the weakest-looking enemy within reach, skewering it to death before moving on to the next foe.

Sahuagin Raider — Level 6 Soldier
Medium natural humanoid (aquatic) — XP 250

Initiative +7 **Senses** Perception +4; low-light vision
HP 70; **Bloodied** 35
AC 20; **Fortitude** 19, **Reflex** 16, **Will** 15
Speed 6, swim 6
(+) **Trident** (standard; at-will) ✦ **Weapon**
+11 vs. AC; 1d8 + 5 damage, and the target is marked until the end of the sahuagin raider's next turn; see also *blood frenzy*.
(↗) **Trident** (standard; at-will) ✦ **Weapon**
Ranged 3/6; +11 vs. AC; 1d8 + 5 damage. The sahuagin raider must retrieve its trident before it can throw it again.
‡ **Opportunistic Strike** (immediate reaction, when a flanked enemy shifts; at-will) ✦ **Weapon**
The sahuagin raider makes a melee basic attack against the enemy.
Blood Frenzy
The sahuagin gains a +1 bonus to attack rolls and a +2 bonus to damage rolls against bloodied enemies.
Alignment Chaotic evil **Languages** Abyssal
Str 20 (+8) **Dex** 14 (+5) **Wis** 12 (+4)
Con 14 (+5) **Int** 10 (+3) **Cha** 10 (+3)
Equipment trident

SAHUAGIN RAIDER TACTICS
Sahuagin raiders can be clever and patient hunters, but when the moment to strike arrives, they try to overwhelm their enemies quickly. They often fight in pairs, flanking enemies and making *opportunistic strikes* whenever possible.

Sahuagin Priest — Level 8 Artillery
Medium natural humanoid (aquatic) — XP 350

Initiative +8 **Senses** Perception +9; low-light vision
HP 70; **Bloodied** 35
AC 22; **Fortitude** 19, **Reflex** 20, **Will** 21
Speed 6, swim 8
(+) **Trident** (standard; at-will) ✦ **Weapon**
+12 vs. AC; 1d8 + 3 damage; see also *blood frenzy*.
(↗) **Trident** (standard; at-will) ✦ **Weapon**
Ranged 3/6; +12 vs. AC; 1d8 + 3 damage. The sahuagin priest must retrieve its trident before it can throw it again.
(↗) **Water Bolt** (standard; at-will)
Ranged 20 (10 out of water); +14 vs. AC; 2d8 + 5 damage (1d8 + 5 out of water); see also *blood frenzy*.
(↗) **Spectral Jaws** (standard; recharges when a target saves against this effect)
Ranged 20; spectral shark jaws appear and bite the target; +14 vs. Will; 3d6 + 5 damage, and the target takes ongoing 5 damage and takes a -2 penalty to all defenses (save ends both); see also *blood frenzy*.
Blood Frenzy
The sahuagin gains a +1 bonus to attack rolls and a +2 bonus to damage rolls against bloodied enemies.
Alignment Chaotic evil **Languages** Abyssal, Common
Skills Intimidate +12
Str 16 (+7) **Dex** 18 (+8) **Wis** 20 (+9)
Con 16 (+7) **Int** 12 (+5) **Cha** 16 (+7)
Equipment trident, holy symbol, kelp robe

SAHUAGIN PRIEST TACTICS
Sahuagin priests normally hang back from the fray, using their ranged powers to attack enemies that the raiders aren't engaging.

Sahuagin Baron — Level 10 Elite Brute (Leader)
Large natural humanoid (aquatic) — XP 1,000

Initiative +9 **Senses** Perception +6; low-light vision
Blood Healing (Healing) aura 10; any ally in the aura that starts its turn adjacent to a bloodied enemy regains 5 hit points.
HP 256; **Bloodied** 128
AC 26; **Fortitude** 25, **Reflex** 22, **Will** 23
Saving Throws +2
Speed 6, swim 8
Action Points 1
(+) **Trident** (standard; at-will) ✦ **Weapon**
Reach 2; +15 vs. AC; 2d4 + 6 damage; see also *blood hunger*.
(↗) **Trident** (standard; at-will) ✦ **Weapon**
Ranged 3/6; +15 vs. AC; 2d4 + 6 damage. The sahuagin baron must retrieve its trident before it can throw it again.
(+) **Claw** (standard; at-will)
Reach 2; +15 vs. AC; 1d6 + 6 damage, and ongoing 5 damage (save ends); see also *blood hunger*.
‡ **Baron's Fury** (standard; at-will) ✦ **Weapon**
The sahuagin baron makes a trident attack and two claw attacks.
Blood Hunger
The sahuagin baron gains a +2 bonus to attack rolls and a +5 bonus to damage rolls against bloodied enemies.
Alignment Chaotic evil **Languages** Abyssal, Common
Skills Intimidate +13
Str 22 (+11) **Dex** 18 (+9) **Wis** 12 (+6)
Con 18 (+9) **Int** 12 (+6) **Cha** 16 (+8)
Equipment trident, headdress

SHIFTER

DESCENDED FROM HUMANS AND LYCANTHROPES, shifters resemble humans with animalistic features. Some are ruthless brigands and wild brawlers, while others are heroes.

SHIFTER LORE

A character knows the following information with a successful Nature check.

DC 15: Shifters are sometimes called "the weretouched" because they're descended from lycanthropes. Shifters value their self-reliance, physical prowess, and freedom. They are spiritually drawn to gods of nature, the moon, and primal power.

Longtooth Hunter	Level 6 Soldier
Medium natural humanoid, shifter	XP 250

Initiative +7   **Senses** Perception +9; low-light vision
HP 71; **Bloodied** 35
AC 22; **Fortitude** 20, **Reflex** 17, **Will** 16
Speed 5
⚔ **Longsword** (standard; at-will) ✦ **Weapon**
   +12 vs. AC; 1d8 + 5 damage, and the target is marked until the end of the longtooth hunter's next turn.
⚔ **Hamstring** (standard; encounter) ✦ **Weapon**
   The longtooth hunter makes a longsword attack. If the attack hits, it makes a secondary attack against the same target. *Secondary Attack:* +9 vs. Reflex; the target is slowed (save ends).
Follow Quarry (immediate reaction, when an adjacent enemy shifts; at-will)
   The longtooth hunter shifts toward the enemy.
Longtooth Shifting (minor, usable only while bloodied; encounter) ✦ **Healing**
   For the rest of the encounter or until rendered unconscious, the longtooth hunter gains a +2 bonus to damage rolls. In addition, for as long as it is bloodied, the longtooth hunter gains regeneration 2.
Alignment Any   **Languages** Common
Skills Athletics +14, Endurance +11, Nature +9
| **Str** 20 (+8) | **Dex** 14 (+5) | **Wis** 13 (+4) |
| **Con** 15 (+5) | **Int** 10 (+3) | **Cha** 9 (+2) |
Equipment chainmail, light shield, longsword

LONGTOOTH HUNTER TACTICS

The longtooth hunter focuses on one enemy at a time. When its foe shifts away, it uses *follow quarry* to stay within striking distance. Against a highly mobile foe, the longtooth hunter uses *hamstring*.

Razorclaw Stalker	Level 7 Skirmisher
Medium natural humanoid, shifter	XP 300

Initiative +7   **Senses** Perception +9; low-light vision
HP 79; **Bloodied** 39
AC 21; **Fortitude** 20, **Reflex** 20, **Will** 18; see also *razorclaw shifting*
Speed 6; see also *razorclaw shifting*
⚔ **Short Sword** (standard; at-will) ✦ **Weapon**
   +13 vs. AC; 1d6 + 4 damage; see also *skirmish*.
⚔ **Short Sword Riposte** (free, when an enemy makes an opportunity attack against the razorclaw stalker; at-will) ✦ **Weapon**
   The razorclaw stalker makes a short sword attack against the enemy.
Skirmish +1d6
   If, on its turn, the razorclaw stalker ends its move at least 4 squares away from its starting point, it deals an extra 1d6 damage on its attacks until the start of its next turn.
Razorclaw Shifting (minor, usable only while bloodied; encounter)
   For the rest of the encounter or until rendered unconscious, the razorclaw stalker gains +2 speed and a +1 bonus to AC and Reflex defense.
Alignment Any   **Languages** Common
Skills Acrobatics +12, Stealth +12, Streetwise +8
| **Str** 18 (+7) | **Dex** 14 (+5) | **Wis** 13 (+4) |
| **Con** 15 (+5) | **Int** 12 (+4) | **Cha** 11 (+3) |
Equipment leather armor, short sword

RAZORCLAW STALKER TACTICS

The razorclaw stalker prefers a mobile, hit-and-run fight and doesn't mind provoking opportunity attacks to use *short sword riposte*.

ENCOUNTER GROUPS

Civilized shifters can be found living among humans and other humanoid creatures. Wild shifters roam the wilderness in the company of natural beasts, fey, and lycanthropes.

Level 6 Encounter (XP 1,250)
✦ 2 longtooth hunters (level 6 soldier)
✦ 1 werewolf (level 8 brute)
✦ 2 dire wolves (level 5 skirmisher)

SKELETON

Animated by dark magic and composed entirely of bones, a skeleton is emotionless and soulless, desiring nothing but to serve its creator.

Skeletons are often used as guardians in dungeons and tombs. They also serve as basic infantry in undead armies.

Decrepit Skeleton		Level 1 Minion
Medium natural animate (undead)		XP 25

Initiative +3   **Senses** Perception +2; darkvision
HP 1; a missed attack never damages a minion.
AC 16; **Fortitude** 13, **Reflex** 14, **Will** 13
Immune disease, poison
Speed 6
⊕ **Longsword** (standard; at-will) ✦ **Weapon**
    +6 vs. AC; 4 damage.
⊗ **Shortbow** (standard; at-will) ✦ **Weapon**
    Ranged 15/30; +6 vs. AC; 3 damage.

Alignment Unaligned	**Languages** –	
Str 15 (+2)	**Dex** 17 (+3)	**Wis** 14 (+2)
Con 13 (+1)	**Int** 3 (-4)	**Cha** 3 (-4)

Equipment heavy shield, longsword, shortbow, quiver of 10 arrows

DECREPIT SKELETON TACTICS

Decrepit skeletons make ranged basic attacks until enemies come within melee striking range, at which point they draw their swords and rush into battle.

Skeleton		Level 3 Soldier
Medium natural animate (undead)		XP 150

Initiative +6   **Senses** Perception +3; darkvision
HP 45; **Bloodied** 22
AC 18; **Fortitude** 15, **Reflex** 16, **Will** 15
Immune disease, poison; **Resist** 10 necrotic; **Vulnerable** 5 radiant
Speed 5
⊕ **Longsword** (standard; at-will) ✦ **Weapon**
    +10 vs. AC; 1d8 + 2 damage, and the target is marked until the end of the skeleton's next turn; see also *speed of the dead*.
Speed of the Dead
    When making an opportunity attack, the skeleton gains a +2 bonus to the attack roll and deals an extra 1d6 damage.

Alignment Unaligned	**Languages** –	
Str 15 (+3)	**Dex** 17 (+4)	**Wis** 14 (+3)
Con 13 (+2)	**Int** 3 (-3)	**Cha** 3 (-3)

Equipment chainmail, heavy shield, longsword

SKELETON TACTICS

A skeleton warrior charges fearlessly into battle, using *speed of the dead* to mercilessly attack enemies that try to slip past its guard.

Blazing Skeleton		Level 5 Artillery
Medium natural animate (undead)		XP 200

Initiative +6   **Senses** Perception +4; darkvision
Fiery Aura (**Fire**) aura 1; any creature starts its turn in the aura takes 5 fire damage.
HP 53; **Bloodied** 26
AC 19; **Fortitude** 15, **Reflex** 18, **Will** 16
Immune disease, poison; **Resist** 10 fire, 10 necrotic; **Vulnerable** 5 radiant
Speed 6

(Left to right) skeleton, boneshard skeleton, blazing skeleton, and decrepit skeleton

RALPH HORSLEY

- **Blazing Claw** (standard; at-will) ✦ **Fire**
  +8 vs. AC; 1d4 + 1 damage, and ongoing 5 fire damage (save ends).
- **Flame Orb** (standard; at-will) ✦ **Fire**
  Ranged 10; +8 vs. Reflex; 2d4 + 4 fire damage, and ongoing 5 fire damage (save ends).

Alignment Unaligned	Languages –	
Str 13 (+3)	Dex 18 (+6)	Wis 15 (+4)
Con 17 (+5)	Int 4 (–1)	Cha 6 (+0)

BLAZING SKELETON TACTICS

A blazing skeleton prefers to keep its distance from foes while hurling orbs of fire at them.

Boneshard Skeleton	Level 5 Brute
Medium natural animate (undead)	XP 200

Initiative +5   Senses Perception +4; darkvision
HP 77; **Bloodied** 38; see also *boneshard burst*
AC 17; **Fortitude** 16, **Reflex** 16, **Will** 15
Immune disease, poison; **Resist** 10 necrotic; **Vulnerable** 5 radiant
Speed 6

- **Scimitar** (standard; at-will) ✦ **Necrotic, Weapon**
  +9 vs. AC; 1d8 + 3 damage (crit 1d8 + 11) plus 5 necrotic damage.
- **Boneshard** (standard; at-will) ✦ **Necrotic**
  +9 vs. AC; 1d4 + 3 damage, and ongoing 5 necrotic damage (save ends).
- **Boneshard Burst** (when first bloodied and again when the boneshard skeleton is reduced to 0 hit points) ✦ **Necrotic**
  Close burst 3; +8 vs. Reflex; 2d6 + 3 necrotic damage.

Alignment Unaligned	Languages –	
Str 16 (+5)	Dex 16 (+5)	Wis 14 (+4)
Con 17 (+5)	Int 3 (–2)	Cha 3 (–2)

Equipment scimitar

BONESHARD SKELETON TACTICS

This skeleton alternates between slashing foes with its scimitar and impaling them with its *boneshard*.

Skeletal Tomb Guardian	Level 10 Brute
Medium natural animate (undead)	XP 500

Initiative +10   Senses Perception +12; darkvision
HP 126; **Bloodied** 63
AC 23; **Fortitude** 22, **Reflex** 23, **Will** 20
Immune disease, poison; **Resist** 10 necrotic; **Vulnerable** 5 radiant
Speed 8

- **Twin Scimitar Strike** (standard; at-will) ✦ **Weapon**
  The skeletal tomb guardian makes two scimitar attacks against the same target: +13 vs. AC; 1d8 + 4 damage (crit 1d8 + 12). This also holds true for opportunity attacks.
- **Cascade of Steel** (standard; at-will) ✦ **Weapon**
  The skeletal tomb guardian makes two *twin scimitar strike* attacks (four scimitar attacks total).
- **Sudden Strike** (immediate reaction, when an adjacent enemy shifts; at-will) ✦ **Weapon**
  The skeletal tomb guardian makes a melee basic attack against the enemy.

Alignment Unaligned	Languages –	
Str 18 (+9)	Dex 20 (+10)	Wis 14 (+7)
Con 16 (+8)	Int 3 (+1)	Cha 3 (+1)

Equipment 4 scimitars

SKELETAL TOMB GUARDIAN TACTICS

A skeletal tomb guardian hacks enemies to pieces with its scimitars.

SKELETON LORE

A character knows the following information with a successful Religion check.

DC 15: Skeletons are created by means of necromantic rituals. Locations with strong ties to the Shadowfell can also cause skeletons to arise spontaneously. These free-willed skeletons tend to attack any living creature they encounter. Skeletons have just enough intelligence to perceive obvious dangers, but they are easily fooled and lured into traps.

ENCOUNTER GROUPS

Skeletons often serve more powerful undead masters. Living beings can create and control skeletons as well.

Level 3 Encounter (XP 750)
- ✦ 1 hobgoblin warcaster (level 3 controller)
- ✦ 2 hobgoblin guards (level 3 soldier)
- ✦ 2 skeletons (level 3 soldier)

Level 5 Encounter (XP 1,100)
- ✦ 2 blazing skeletons (level 5 artillery)
- ✦ 2 boneshard skeletons (level 5 brute)
- ✦ 1 tiefling darkblade (level 7 lurker)

SKULL LORD

Skull lords marshal and command lesser undead. Left to their own devices, they seek knowledge of dark rituals to return their long-destroyed masters to existence, but they also serve living necromancers and more powerful undead.

Skull Lord		Level 10 Artillery (Leader)
Medium natural humanoid (undead)		XP 500

Initiative +8 — **Senses** Perception +7; darkvision

Master of the Grave (Healing) aura 2; undead allies in the aura gain regeneration 5 and a +2 bonus to saving throws. This aura ends when the *skull of death's command* is destroyed.

HP 40; **Bloodied** 20; see also *triple skulls*

AC 24; **Fortitude** 21, **Reflex** 22, **Will** 23

Immune disease, poison; **Resist** 10 necrotic; **Vulnerable** 5 radiant

Speed 6

ⓐ **Bone Staff** (standard; at-will) ✦ Necrotic, Weapon
+13 vs. AC; 1d8 + 2 damage plus 1d6 necrotic damage.

↗ **Skull of Bonechilling Fear** (minor 1/round; at-will) ✦ Cold, Fear
Ranged 10; +15 vs. Will; 1d6 + 3 cold damage, and the target is pushed 5 squares.

↗ **Skull of Death's Command** (minor 1/round; at-will) ✦ Necrotic
Ranged 10; the skull lord restores a destroyed undead minion within range. The restored undead minion's level must be no higher than the skull lord's level + 2. The restored minion stands in the space where it fell (or in any adjacent space, if that space is occupied) as a free action, has full normal hit points, and can take actions (as normal) on its next turn.

↗ **Skull of Withering Flame** (minor 1/round; at-will) ✦ Fire, Necrotic
Ranged 10; +15 vs. Fortitude; 2d6 + 3 fire and necrotic damage.

Triple Skulls ✦ Healing
When a skull lord is reduced to 0 hit points, one of its skulls (determined randomly from the three listed above) is destroyed, and it loses the ability to use that power. If the creature has any skulls remaining, it instantly heals to full hit points (40 hit points). When all three skulls are destroyed, the skull lord is destroyed as well.

Alignment Evil — **Languages** Common
Skills Bluff +15, Insight +12, Intimidate +15

Str 14 (+7)	Dex 16 (+8)	Wis 15 (+7)
Con 17 (+8)	Int 16 (+8)	Cha 21 (+10)

Equipment staff, 3 iron crowns

SKULL LORD TACTICS

A skull lord is almost always found with several lesser undead close by, especially skeleton and/or zombie minions. It avoid melee combat, preferring to use all three of its skulls in a given round.

SKULL LORD LORE

A character knows the following information with a successful Religion check.

DC 15: A skull lord is a formidable undead being with three skulls. Each skull has a different power, and a skull lord on the verge of destruction will sacrifice one of its skulls to keep the rest of its form intact. Once two of its skulls are destroyed, the creature loses the power to heal itself in this fashion.

DC 20: The first skull lords arose from the ashes of the Black Tower of Vumerion. None can say whether they were created intentionally by the legendary human necromancer Vumerion or came forth spontaneously from the foul energies of his fallen sanctum. The ritual for creating new skull lords also survived Vumerion's fall, eventually finding its way into the hands of Vumerion's rivals and various powerful undead creatures.

ENCOUNTER GROUPS

Skull lords lead troupes of lesser undead and occasionally serve as the lieutenants of even more powerful masters, both living and undead.

Level 10 Encounter (XP 2,500)
✦ 2 skull lords (level 10 artillery)
✦ 3 skeletal tomb guardians (level 10 brute)

Level 12 Encounter (XP 3,525)
✦ 1 skull lord (level 10 artillery)
✦ 2 zombie hulks (level 8 brute)
✦ 1 vampire lord (level 11 elite lurker)
✦ 9 vampire spawn bloodhunters (level 10 minion)

FRANZ VOHWINKEL

SLAAD

As CREATURES OF PURE ENTROPY, slaads exist to create disorder. Their hold on reality is tenuous at best. Their thoughts are clouded with maddening images, they seem aware of things beyond other creatures' perceptions, and they attack without provocation.

Slaads propogate by planting embryos in their victims. As each embryo grows, the host creature succumbs to madness. Left untreated, the embryo transforms into a slaad tadpole that burrows out of its host's skull, killing the host in the process. For this reason, most other intelligent creatures loathe and fear slaads.

A slaad tadpole matures into a full-sized adult slaad (of a random type) in 1d4 + 3 days. Until then, it feeds on whatever small prey it finds.

SLAAD LORE

A character knows the following information with a successful Arcana check.

DC 20: Slaads use their claws to plant embryos in living creatures—an infestation known as chaos phage. These embryos quickly grow into slaad tadpoles that kill their hosts and give rise to new slaads. Afflicted creatures typically succumb to madness before they die.

DC 25: Slaads worship no gods and believe they were the first creatures in the cosmos. Dull-witted slaads spread chaos instinctively, while intelligent slaads do so with intent.

DC 30: When a slaad becomes suffused with the entropic energies of the Abyss, its corporeal form is consumed and it transforms into a black slaad. Black slaads (also called void slaads) lose the ability to spread chaos phage, but they wield horrific entropic power.

Slaad Tadpole		Level 5 Lurker
Small elemental beast		XP 200

Initiative +7	**Senses** Perception +6; low-light vision	
HP 44; **Bloodied** 22		
AC 21; **Fortitude** 18, **Reflex** 20, **Will** 18; see also *chaos shift*		
Speed 4		

⊕ **Bite** (standard; at-will)
  +10 vs. AC; 1d8 damage, and the slaad tadpole becomes insubstantial until the start of its next turn.

Chaos Shift (immediate interrupt, when attacked by a melee attack; at-will)
  The slaad tadpole shifts 2 squares.

Alignment Chaotic evil	**Languages** —	
Skills Stealth +8		
Str 6 (+0)	**Dex** 12 (+3)	**Wis** 9 (+1)
Con 8 (+1)	**Int** 3 (-2)	**Cha** 7 (+0)

SLAAD TADPOLE TACTICS

A slaad tadpole avoids combat with creatures larger than itself. When cornered, it makes bite attacks. These attacks cause the creature to momentarily destabilize and become insubstantial. Both this and its *chaos shift* power are defense mechanisms that protect it against enemy attacks.

(Top left, clockwise) talon slaad, rift slaad, curse slaad, and blood slaad

Gray Slaad (Rift Slaad) — Level 13 Skirmisher

Gray Slaad (Rift Slaad)	Level 13 Skirmisher
Medium elemental humanoid	XP 800

Initiative +12 **Senses** Perception +7; low-light vision
HP 128; **Bloodied** 64; see also *planar flux*
AC 27; **Fortitude** 25, **Reflex** 26, **Will** 24
Immune chaos phage (see next page)
Speed 6, teleport 4

⊕ **Claws** (standard; at-will) ✦ **Disease**
+18 vs. AC; 2d8 + 2 damage, and the slaad makes a secondary attack against the same target. *Secondary Attack:* +16 vs. Fortitude; on a hit, the target contracts chaos phage (see sidebar).

↻ **Condition Transfer** (immediate interrupt, when hit by an attack that applies any conditions; recharge ⚄ ⚅)
Ranged 5; +16 vs. Fortitude; conditions applied by the triggering attack affect the target instead of the slaad.

↩ **Induce Planar Instability** (standard; encounter)
Close burst 3; +16 vs. Will; 1d8 + 2 damage, and the target shifts 3 squares and is knocked prone.

Planar Flux (free, when first bloodied; encounter) ✦ **Teleportation**
The slaad teleports 8 squares and becomes insubstantial until the end of its next turn.

Alignment Chaotic evil   **Languages** Primordial
Skills Athletics +13, Stealth +15
Str 15 (+8)   **Dex** 18 (+10)   **Wis** 12 (+7)
Con 16 (+9)   **Int** 9 (+5)   **Cha** 14 (+8)

Gray (Rift) Slaad Tactics

The gray slaad teleports into a flanking position and attacks with its claws. It uses *condition transfer* and *induce planar instability* as circumstances dictate.

When first bloodied, the slaad momentarily loses its grasp on reality, discorporating and then reforming in a new location.

Red Slaad (Blood Slaad) — Level 15 Soldier

Red Slaad (Blood Slaad)	Level 15 Soldier
Large elemental humanoid	XP 1,200

Initiative +13   **Senses** Perception +8; low-light vision
HP 146; **Bloodied** 73
AC 29; **Fortitude** 28, **Reflex** 29, **Will** 25
Immune chaos phage (see next page)
Speed 8, teleport 4

⊕ **Bite** (standard; at-will)
Reach 2; +21 vs. AC; 2d8 + 6 damage.

⊕ **Claw** (standard; at-will) ✦ **Disease**
Reach 2; +21 vs. AC; 1d6 + 3 damage, and the slaad makes a secondary attack against the same target. *Secondary Attack:* +19 vs. Fortitude; on a hit, the target contracts chaos phage (see sidebar).

↓ **Leaping Pounce** (standard; recharge ⚄ ⚅)
The slaad shifts 4 squares and makes two claw attacks. If either claw attack hits, the target is marked until the end of the slaad's next turn.

↩ **Horrid Croak** (standard; encounter) ✦ **Fear**
Close blast 5; +19 vs. Fortitude; the target is immobilized until the end of the slaad's next turn.

Alignment Chaotic evil   **Languages** Primordial
Skills Athletics +15, Stealth +16
Str 17 (+10)   **Dex** 19 (+11)   **Wis** 12 (+8)
Con 18 (+11)   **Int** 11 (+7)   **Cha** 15 (+9)

Red (Blood) Slaad Tactics

The red slaad springs into battle, using *leaping pounce* to attack two different targets if it can. It then uses *horrid croak* to immobilize enemies and makes bite attacks until it can make another *leaping pounce*.

Blue Slaad (Talon Slaad) — Level 17 Brute

Blue Slaad (Talon Slaad)	Level 17 Brute
Large elemental humanoid	XP 1,600

Initiative +10   **Senses** Perception +14; low-light vision
HP 200; **Bloodied** 100; see also *ravager's fury*
AC 29; **Fortitude** 29, **Reflex** 25, **Will** 24
Immune chaos phage (see next page)
Speed 6, teleport 2

⊕ **Claws** (standard; at-will) ✦ **Disease**
Reach 2; +20 vs. AC; 2d10 + 10 damage, and the slaad makes a secondary attack against the same target. *Secondary Attack:* +18 vs. Fortitude; on a hit, the target contracts chaos phage (see sidebar).

↓ **Fling** (standard; at-will)
Reach 2; +20 vs. AC; 1d10 + 10 damage, and the target slides 2 squares and is knocked prone.

↩ **Ravager's Fury** (standard, usable only while bloodied; encounter)
The slaad rakes all enemies within its reach: close burst 2; +20 vs. AC; 1d10 + 10 damage, and the slaad gains 20 temporary hit points.

Alignment Chaotic evil   **Languages** Primordial
Skills Athletics +19, Stealth +15
Str 22 (+14)   **Dex** 15 (+10)   **Wis** 13 (+9)
Con 20 (+13)   **Int** 9 (+7)   **Cha** 11 (+8)

Blue (Talon) Slaad Tactics

This slaad wades into combat, slashing with its claws. If it is bloodied and within reach of three or more enemies, it uses *ravager's fury*.

Green Slaad (Curse Slaad) — Level 18 Controller

Green Slaad (Curse Slaad)	Level 18 Controller
Large elemental humanoid	XP 2,000

Initiative +11   **Senses** Low-light vision; Perception +17
HP 173; **Bloodied** 86
AC 32; **Fortitude** 30, **Reflex** 29, **Will** 31
Immune chaos phage (see next page)
Speed 6, teleport 6

⊕ **Claws** (standard; at-will) ✦ **Disease**
Reach 2; +23 vs. AC; 2d10 + 3 damage, and the slaad makes a secondary attack against the same target. *Secondary Attack:* +21 vs. Fortitude; on a hit, the target contracts chaos phage (see sidebar).

↗ **Chaos Bolt** (standard; at-will)
Ranged 10; +21 vs. Will; 1d20 + 4 damage, and the target is dazed until the end of the slaad's next turn.

↻ **Transpose Target** (standard; recharge ⚅) ✦ **Teleportation**
Ranged 10; +21 vs. Reflex; 1d10 + 5 damage, and the target teleports 10 squares to an unoccupied space of the slaad's choosing (and in its line of sight).

↩ **Croak of Chaos** (standard; encounter)
Close burst 4; targets enemies; +21 vs. Fortitude; 1d10 + 6 damage, and the target slides 4 squares.

Alignment Chaotic evil   **Languages** Primordial
Skills Athletics +17, Bluff +18, Intimidate +18, Stealth +16
Str 17 (+12)   **Dex** 14 (+11)   **Wis** 17 (+12)
Con 21 (+14)   **Int** 15 (+11)   **Cha** 18 (+13)

GREEN (CURSE) SLAAD TACTICS

This slaad prefers to attack enemies at range, confounding them with *chaos bolt* and using *transpose target* as often as it can to teleport enemies into the midst of its allies. When surrounded by multiple foes, it uses *croak of chaos* to knock them back.

Black Slaad (Void Slaad)	**Level 20 Skirmisher**
Large elemental humanoid	XP 2,800

Initiative +10   **Senses** Perception +14; low-light vision
HP 191; **Bloodied** 95; see also *zone of oblivion*
AC 32; **Fortitude** 33, **Reflex** 30, **Will** 29
Immune disease; **Resist** insubstantial
Speed 6, teleport 3

⊕ **Claws** (standard; at-will)
   Reach 2; +25 vs. AC; 2d10 + 7 damage, and ongoing 10 damage (save ends). *Failed Save:* The target loses a healing surge.

⤢ **Ray of Entropy** (standard; at-will)
   Ranged 20; +23 vs. Reflex; 2d10 + 3 damage, and the target is surrounded by a shroud of crackling energy (save ends). Any time the target takes damage, the shroud deals 1d10 damage to the target.

⤡ **Zone of Oblivion** (when reduced to 0 hit points) ✦ **Zone**
   Close burst 2; +18 vs. Reflex; 2d10 + 6 damage. A black void fills the zone, blocking line of sight and dealing 2d10 + 6 damage to any creature that enters or starts its turn in the area. The zone lasts until the end of the encounter.

Alignment Chaotic evil   **Languages** Primordial
Skills Stealth +19

Str 24 (+17)	**Dex** 18 (+14)	**Wis** 13 (+11)
Con 23 (+16)	**Int** 11 (+10)	**Cha** 17 (+13)

BLACK (VOID) SLAAD TACTICS

The black slaad teleports from place to place, zapping foes with its *ray of entropy* or raking them with its claws.

ENCOUNTER GROUPS

Slaads most commonly appear with other slaads, but they have been known to form tenuous alliances with other creatures for reasons few understand.

Black slaad

Level 15 Encounter (XP 6,400)
✦ 2 gray slaads (level 13 skirmisher)
✦ 2 red slaads (level 15 soldier)
✦ 2 destrachan far voices (level 15 artillery)

Level 19 Encounter (XP 12,000)
✦ 1 black slaad (level 20 skirmisher)
✦ 2 rockfire dreadnought elementals (level 18 soldier)
✦ 1 fire giant forgecaller (level 18 artillery)
✦ 2 firebred hell hounds (level 17 brute)

CHAOS PHAGE

A creature implanted with a slaad embryo contracts chaos phage. To avoid repetition, the rules for the disease are presented here.

Chaos Phage	Level 16 Disease	Endurance stable DC 26, improve DC 31

| The target is cured. | ◀ | **Initial Effect:** A slaad embryo is implanted in the target. | ◀▶ | The target takes a −2 penalty to Will defense. While bloodied, the target succumbs to madness and attacks the nearest creature. | ▶ | The target dies, and a slaad tadpole burrows out of its skull. |

SNAKE

MONSTROUS SNAKES ARE STEALTHY, PATIENT HUNTERS that regard humanoids as prey. Most are simply dangerous animals, but the dark god Zehir blesses some serpents with evil intelligence.

Deathrattle Viper		Level 5 Brute
Medium natural beast (reptile)		XP 200

Initiative +6   **Senses** Perception +7; low-light vision
Death Rattle (Fear) aura 2; enemies in the aura take a -2 penalty to attack rolls.
HP 75; **Bloodied** 37
AC 17; **Fortitude** 16, **Reflex** 18, **Will** 16
Resist 10 poison
Speed 4, climb 4
⊕ **Bite** (standard; at-will) ✦ **Poison**
  +8 vs. AC; 1d6 + 4 damage, and the deathrattle viper makes a secondary attack against the same target. *Secondary Attack:* +6 vs. Fortitude; 1d8 + 2 poison damage, and ongoing 5 poison damage (save ends).
Alignment Unaligned   **Languages** –

Str 12 (+3)	**Dex** 19 (+6)	**Wis** 10 (+2)
Con 15 (+4)	**Int** 2 (-2)	**Cha** 14 (+4)

DEATHRATTLE VIPER TACTICS

A deathrattle viper spreads its bite attacks around and lets its venom do its work.

Crushgrip Constrictor		Level 9 Soldier
Large natural beast (reptile)		XP 400

Initiative +9   **Senses** Perception +12; low-light vision
HP 96; **Bloodied** 48
AC 25; **Fortitude** 25, **Reflex** 22, **Will** 22
Speed 6, climb 6, swim 6
⊕ **Bite** (standard; at-will)
  +15 vs. AC; 1d10 + 6 damage, and the target is grabbed (until escape).
↟ **Constrict** (standard; at-will)
  Affects a target the crushgrip constrictor has grabbed; +13 vs. Fortitude; 2d6 + 12 damage, and the target is dazed until the end of the crushgrip constrictor's next turn.
Alignment Unaligned   **Languages** –
Skills Stealth +12

Str 22 (+10)	**Dex** 16 (+7)	**Wis** 17 (+7)
Con 16 (+7)	**Int** 2 (+0)	**Cha** 10 (+4)

CRUSHGRIP CONSTRICTOR TACTICS

This snake fearlessly singles out prey even in the middle of large groups. The crushgrip bites its chosen victim, grabs him, and then tries to squeeze him to death in subsequent rounds.

Flame Snake		Level 9 Artillery
Medium elemental beast (fire, reptile)		XP 400

Initiative +9   **Senses** Perception +12
HP 74; **Bloodied** 37
AC 23; **Fortitude** 19, **Reflex** 22, **Will** 20
Resist 20 fire
Speed 6
⊕ **Bite** (standard; at-will) ✦ **Fire**
  +12 vs. AC; 1d6 + 5 damage plus 1d6 fire damage.
⊛ **Spit Fire** (standard; at-will) ✦ **Fire**
  Ranged 10; +13 vs. Reflex; 2d6 + 5 fire damage, and ongoing 5 fire damage (save ends).
Alignment Unaligned   **Languages** –

Str 11 (+4)	**Dex** 20 (+9)	**Wis** 16 (+7)
Con 14 (+6)	**Int** 2 (+0)	**Cha** 10 (+4)

FLAME SNAKE TACTICS

A flame snake instinctively tries to kill or incapacitate enemies at range, spitting fire at its prey. Only when its prey is badly burned does it slither in to kill with a bite.

Shadow Snake		Level 16 Skirmisher
Large shadow beast (reptile)		XP 1,400

Initiative +17   **Senses** Perception +13; darkvision
HP 158; **Bloodied** 79
AC 30; **Fortitude** 28, **Reflex** 29, **Will** 27
Resist 10 poison
Speed 7, climb 7; see also *shifting shadowstrike*
⊕ **Bite** (standard; at-will) ✦ **Poison**
  Reach 2; +21 vs. AC; 2d6 + 7 damage, and ongoing 10 poison damage (save ends).
↟ **Double Attack** (standard; at-will) ✦ **Poison**
  The shadow snake makes two bite attacks and shifts 1 square before, between, or after the attacks.
↟ **Shifting Shadowstrike** (standard; encounter) ✦ **Poison**
  The shadow snake shifts 7 squares and makes a bite attack against two different targets at any points during its move.
Vanish into the Night (standard; encounter)
  The shadow snake gains the insubstantial and phasing qualities, and is invisible in dim light, until the end of its next turn.
Alignment Evil   **Languages** –
Skills Stealth +20

Str 20 (+13)	**Dex** 25 (+15)	**Wis** 10 (+8)
Con 22 (+14)	**Int** 4 (+5)	**Cha** 20 (+13)

SHADOW SNAKE TACTICS

A shadow snake prefers to surprise foes using its natural stealth and cover of darkness. When it strikes, it uses *shifting shadowstrike* to weave through the front lines of its enemies while making bite attacks. On subsequent rounds, it uses *double attack* and tries to poison as many enemies as possible. When hard-pressed, the snake uses *vanish into the night* to escape.

SWORDWING

Swordwings are supreme collectors, gathering rare items and arranging them in galleries within their cavernous lairs.

A swordwing's collection defines it as an individual. A typical swordwing favors one particular collectable, while crownwings keep multiple collections. Typical "collectables" include skulls, weapons, gems, magic items, books, monster eggs, and victims' hearts.

Swordwing		Level 25 Soldier
Medium aberrant humanoid		XP 7,000

Initiative +21   **Senses** Perception +18; low-light vision
HP 234; **Bloodied** 117
AC 42; **Fortitude** 40, **Reflex** 38, **Will** 32
Speed 6, fly 10 (hover)
(+) **Armblade** (standard; at-will)
Reach 2; +30 vs. AC (+32 against a bloodied target); 2d6 + 9 damage (crit 2d6 + 21), and the target is marked until the end of the swordwing's next turn; see also *vicious opportunist*.
‡ **Sudden Strike** (immediate reaction, when an adjacent enemy shifts; at-will)
The swordwing makes a melee basic attack against the enemy. The attack deals an extra 2d6 damage if it hits.
Vicious Opportunist
The swordwing's opportunity attacks deal an extra 2d6 damage.
Alignment Evil   **Languages** Deep Speech
Skills Endurance +25, Stealth +24
Str 28 (+21)   **Dex** 24 (+19)   **Wis** 13 (+13)
Con 26 (+20)   **Int** 10 (+12)   **Cha** 10 (+12)

SWORDWING TACTICS

A swordwing swoops into battle and hacks enemies to pieces with its armblade, using its *sudden strike* power against those that try to shift away. The creature is incensed by the blood of its enemies and attacks bloodied foes with greater accuracy.

Crownwing	Level 26 Skirmisher (Leader)
Large aberrant humanoid	XP 9,000

Initiative +24   **Senses** Perception +20; low-light vision
HP 238; **Bloodied** 119
AC 40; **Fortitude** 36, **Reflex** 38, **Will** 32
Speed 6, fly 10 (hover); see also *flyby attack*
(+) **Armblade** (standard; at-will)
Reach 2; +31 vs. AC; 2d6 + 10 damage (crit 2d6 + 22) plus an extra 2d6 damage if the crownwing is flanking the target.
‡ **Flyby Attack** (standard; at-will)
The crownwing flies up to 10 squares and makes one melee basic attack at any point during that movement. The crownwing doesn't provoke opportunity attacks when moving away from the target of the attack.
➷ **Mark of Death** (standard; encounter)
Ranged 10; allies gain a +2 bonus to attack rolls and deal +10 damage against the target.
Alignment Evil   **Languages** Deep Speech
Skills Arcana +22, Endurance +24, Intimidate +21, Stealth +27
Str 30 (+23)   **Dex** 28 (+22)   **Wis** 15 (+15)
Con 22 (+19)   **Int** 18 (+17)   **Cha** 16 (+16)

CROWNWING TACTICS

The crownwing places its *mark of death* upon the foe it perceives as the most dangerous, then orders its underlings to attack that target while it takes out weaker prey using its armblade and *flyby attack* power.

SWORDWING LORE

A character knows the following information with a successful Dungeoneering check.

DC 25: Swordwings are insectoid creatures that inhabit the Underdark. One of their arms ends in a scimitarlike blade, hence the name.

DC 30: Swordwings live in clusters of tall "nesting spires" built from resources chewed out of the surrounding environment. From a distance, these towers resemble stalactites or stalagmites made of grayish-white paper, but in truth the structures are as hard as stone.

ENCOUNTER GROUPS

Swordwings occasionally ally with other Underdark dwellers such as mind flayers, beholders, and gibbering orbs.

Level 25 Encounter (XP 37,000)
✦ 4 swordwings (level 25 soldier)
✦ 1 crownwing (level 26 skirmisher)

Level 29 Encounter (XP 76,000)
✦ 3 swordwings (level 25 soldier)
✦ 1 gibbering orb (level 27 solo controller)

TIEFLING

Tieflings were once human, and they owe their fiendish bloodline to an infernal bargain made long ago. Sundered from humanity by their ancestors' overzealous ambitions, tieflings tend to be hardy, self-reliant opportunists.

Tiefling Heretic	Level 6 Artillery
Medium natural humanoid	XP 250

Initiative +8   **Senses** Perception +6; low-light vision
HP 60; **Bloodied** 30
AC 20; **Fortitude** 17, **Reflex** 18, **Will** 18
Resist 11 fire
Speed 6

⊕ **Dagger** (standard; at-will) ✦ **Weapon**
+10 vs. AC (+11 against a bloodied target); 1d4 + 2 damage.

⊙ **Balefire** (standard; at-will) ✦ **Fire**
Ranged 10; +9 vs. Reflex (+10 against a bloodied target); 1d8 + 5 fire damage, and ongoing 5 fire damage (save ends).

⤳ **Serpent Curse** (standard; encounter) ✦ **Illusion, Psychic**
Ranged 10; illusory snakes appear and attack the target; +9 vs. Will (+10 against a bloodied target); 1d6 + 5 psychic damage, and ongoing 5 psychic damage (save ends).

Cloak of Escape (immediate reaction, when the tiefling heretic is hit by a melee attack; at-will) ✦ **Teleportation**
The tiefling heretic teleports 5 squares.

Infernal Wrath (minor; encounter)
The tiefling heretic gains a +1 power bonus to its next attack roll against an enemy that hit it since the tiefling heretic's last turn. If the attack hits and deals damage, the tiefling heretic deals an extra 5 damage.

Alignment Any   **Languages** Common
Skills Bluff +15, Insight +11, Stealth +15

Str 15 (+5)	**Dex** 20 (+8)	**Wis** 16 (+6)
Con 18 (+7)	**Int** 13 (+4)	**Cha** 20 (+8)

Equipment dagger

TIEFLING HERETIC TACTICS
The tiefling heretic targets a potent foe with its *serpent curse* power, and then hurls *balefire* round after round. It avoids melee combat using its *cloak of escape* power.

TIEFLING LORE
A character knows the following information with a successful History check.

DC 15: The nobles of the ancient human empire of Bael Turath swore pacts to devils in return for the power to combat their enemies and conquer the world. These pacts corrupted not only the nobility but also their descendants. From this accord, the tiefling race was born.

ENCOUNTER GROUPS
Tieflings associate with anyone, although they rarely trust their so-called allies.

Level 8 Encounter (XP 1,650)
✦ 1 tiefling heretic (level 6 artillery)
✦ 1 tiefling darkblade (level 7 lurker)
✦ 2 cambion hellswords (level 8 brute)
✦ 1 succubus (level 9 controller)

Tiefling Darkblade	Level 7 Lurker
Medium natural humanoid	XP 300

Initiative +12   **Senses** Perception +5; low-light vision
HP 64; **Bloodied** 32
AC 20; **Fortitude** 17, **Reflex** 19, **Will** 17
Resist 12 fire
Speed 6; see also *cloak of lurking*

⊕ **Poisoned Short Sword** (standard; at-will) ✦ **Poison, Weapon**
+12 vs. AC (+13 against a bloodied target); 1d6 + 5 damage, and the tiefling darkblade makes a secondary attack against the same target. *Secondary Attack:* +10 vs. Fortitude; ongoing 5 poison damage (save ends).

Cloak of Lurking (move; recharge ⚅⚅) ✦ **Teleportation**
The tiefling darkblade teleports 5 squares and becomes invisible until the end of its next turn.

Infernal Wrath (minor; encounter)
The tiefling darkblade gains a +1 power bonus to its next attack roll against an enemy that hit it since the tiefling darkblade's last turn. If the attack hits and deals damage, the darkblade deals an extra 3 damage.

Alignment Any   **Languages** Common
Skills Bluff +13, Stealth +15

Str 13 (+4)	**Dex** 20 (+8)	**Wis** 14 (+5)
Con 16 (+6)	**Int** 13 (+4)	**Cha** 16 (+6)

Equipment leather armor, poisoned short sword

TIEFLING DARKBLADE TACTICS
A tiefling darkblade remains hidden long enough to coat its blade with infernal venom. It uses *cloak of lurking* at opportune times to gain combat advantage.

TREANT

A TREANT LOOKS LIKE AN ANIMATED TREE with a humanoid face blended into its trunk. When motionless, it is easily mistaken for an ordinary tree.

Treants consider themselves guardians of the forest. Some violently oppose all trespassers, while others battle only those who cut or burn down trees.

Blackroot Treant: This treant looks like a dead tree with brown, crumpled leaves clinging to its skeletal branches. Its bark and roots are black, and its eyes are cold, lifeless pits.

TREANT LORE

A character knows the following information with a successful skill check.

Nature DC 20: Treants are usually friendly to people who respect the wild.

Religion DC 25: A blackroot treant is an undead horror. Forests haunted by blackroot treants are blighted, forlorn places overrun with undead.

ENCOUNTER GROUPS

Elves, dryads, satyrs, and other fey commonly ally with treants and help them defend the forest. Undead are commonly encountered with blackroot treants.

Level 19 Encounter (XP 12,000)
✦ 1 blackroot treant (level 19 elite soldier)
✦ 2 slaughter wights (level 18 brute)
✦ 2 sword wraiths (level 17 lurker)

Treant		Level 16 Elite Controller
Huge fey magical beast (plant)		XP 2,800

Initiative +9   **Senses** Perception +15; low-light vision
Grasping Roots aura 3; nonflying enemies treat the area within the aura as difficult terrain.
HP 316; **Bloodied** 158
AC 32; **Fortitude** 32, **Reflex** 27, **Will** 32
Vulnerable fire (a treant takes ongoing 5 fire damage [save ends] when damaged by fire).
Saving Throws +2
Speed 8 (forest walk)
Action Points 1
⊕ **Slam** (standard; at-will)
    Reach 3; +21 vs. AC; 1d10 + 7 damage.
❋ **Awaken Forest** (standard; sustain minor; encounter) ✦ **Zone**
    Area burst 3 within 10; trees come alive and attack the treant's enemies within the zone; +21 vs. AC; 1d10 + 7 damage. The treant makes new attack rolls when it sustains the zone.
↙ **Earthshaking Stomp** (standard; encounter)
    Close burst 2; +19 vs. Fortitude; 2d6 + 7 damage, and the target is knocked prone if it's Medium or smaller. *Miss:* Half damage, and the target is not knocked prone.
Alignment Unaligned   **Languages** Elven
Skills Nature +20, Stealth +14

Str 24 (+15)	Dex 12 (+9)	Wis 24 (+15)
Con 22 (+14)	Int 14 (+10)	Cha 12 (+9)

TREANT TACTICS

A treant uses *awaken forest* at the start of battle and spends a minor action on subsequent rounds to sustain it. Meanwhile, it makes slam attacks. If surrounded by multiple melee combatants, the treant uses *earthshaking stomp*.

Blackroot Treant		Level 19 Elite Soldier
Huge fey magical beast (plant, undead)		XP 4,800

Initiative +13   **Senses** Perception +13; low-light vision
Blackroot Aura (Healing, Necrotic) aura 2; enemies in the aura at the start of their turns take 10 necrotic damage, while undead allies in the aura at the start of their turns regain 10 hit points.
HP 368; **Bloodied** 184
AC 36; **Fortitude** 34, **Reflex** 29, **Will** 32
Vulnerable fire (a blackroot treant takes ongoing 5 fire damage [save ends] when damaged by fire).
Saving Throws +2
Speed 6 (forest walk)
Action Points 1
⊕ **Slam** (standard; at-will) ✦ **Necrotic**
    Reach 3; +25 vs. AC; 1d12 + 8 damage, and ongoing 5 necrotic damage (save ends).
† **Entangling Roots** (minor; at-will)
    Reach 4; +23 vs. Reflex; the target is knocked prone and restrained (save ends). If the blackroot treant moves, slides, or is pushed more than 4 squares from the target, the target is no longer restrained.
Alignment Unaligned   **Languages** Elven
Skills Nature +18, Stealth +16

Str 27 (+17)	Dex 14 (+11)	Wis 18 (+13)
Con 24 (+16)	Int 16 (+12)	Cha 22 (+15)

BLACKROOT TREANT TACTICS

A blackroot treant uses *entangling roots* up to three times per round. It then makes slam attacks against creatures it has restrained.

TROGLODYTE

TROGLODYTES ARE SUBTERRANEAN SAVAGES descended from primitive reptiles. They launch raids against the surface world when food in the Underdark is scarce. Troglodytes secrete a foul musk, and in close quarters, the smell can be overpowering.

Troglodyte Warrior		Level 12 Minion
Large natural humanoid (reptile)		XP 175

Initiative +6   **Senses** Perception +5; darkvision
Troglodyte Stench aura 1; living enemies in the aura take a -2 penalty to attack rolls.
HP 1; a missed attack never damages a minion.
AC 25; **Fortitude** 25, **Reflex** 22, **Will** 21
Speed 5
(+) **Club** (standard; at-will) ✦ **Weapon**
  +15 vs. AC; 7 damage.
Alignment Chaotic evil   **Languages** Draconic
Skills Athletics +14, Endurance +13

Str 18 (+9)	**Dex** 12 (+6)	**Wis** 11 (+5)
Con 16 (+8)	**Int** 6 (+3)	**Cha** 8 (+4)

Equipment light shield, club

TROGLODYTE WARRIOR TACTICS

A troglodyte warrior pounds enemies with its club and relies on its horrid stench for added protection.

Troglodyte Mauler		Level 6 Soldier
Medium natural humanoid (reptile)		XP 250

Initiative +6   **Senses** Perception +5; darkvision
Troglodyte Stench aura 1; living enemies in the aura take a -2 penalty to attack rolls.
HP 74; **Bloodied** 37
AC 22; **Fortitude** 21, **Reflex** 18, **Will** 19
Speed 5
(+) **Greatclub** (standard; at-will) ✦ **Weapon**
  +12 vs. AC; 2d4 + 4 damage, and the target is marked until the end of the troglodyte mauler's next turn.
(+) **Claw** (standard; at-will)
  +10 vs. AC; 1d4 + 4 damage.
✟ **Bite** (minor 1/round; at-will)
  Requires combat advantage; +10 vs. Fortitude; 1d6 + 4 damage, and until the end of the troglodyte mauler's next turn, healing on the target restores only half the total amount.
↗ **Javelin** (standard; at-will) ✦ **Weapon**
  Ranged 10/20; +12 vs. AC; 1d6 + 4 damage.
Alignment Chaotic evil   **Languages** Draconic
Skills Athletics +12, Endurance +12

Str 18 (+7)	**Dex** 12 (+4)	**Wis** 15 (+5)
Con 18 (+7)	**Int** 6 (+1)	**Cha** 8 (+2)

Equipment greatclub, 2 javelins

TROGLODYTE MAULER TACTICS

A troglodyte mauler bludgeons foes to death with its stone greatclub and tries to flank enemies so that it can make bite attacks.

Troglodyte Impaler	Level 7 Artillery
Medium natural humanoid (reptile)	XP 300

Initiative +5   **Senses** Perception +9; darkvision
Troglodyte Stench aura 1; living enemies in the aura take a -2 penalty to attack rolls.
HP 69; **Bloodied** 34
AC 22; **Fortitude** 22, **Reflex** 19, **Will** 18
Speed 5
(+) **Spear** (standard; at-will) ✦ **Weapon**
  +11 vs. AC; 1d8 + 4 damage.
(+) **Claw** (standard; at-will)
  +9 vs. AC; 1d4 + 4 damage.
↗ **Javelin** (standard; at-will) ✦ **Weapon**
  Ranged 10/20; +12 vs. AC; 1d6 + 4 damage.
↗ **Impaling Shot** (standard; recharge ▫ ▫ ▫ ▫) ✦ **Weapon**
  Requires javelin; ranged 10; +12 vs. AC; 2d6 + 4 damage, and the troglodyte impaler makes a secondary attack against the same target. *Secondary Attack:* +10 vs. Fortitude; the target is restrained (save ends).
Alignment Chaotic evil   **Languages** Draconic
Skills Athletics +12, Endurance +13

Str 19 (+7)	**Dex** 14 (+5)	**Wis** 13 (+4)
Con 21 (+8)	**Int** 7 (+1)	**Cha** 9 (+2)

Equipment spear, quiver of 6 javelins

TROGLODYTE IMPALER TACTICS

A troglodyte impaler stays on the fringe of battle and hurls javelins at enemies, using *impaling shot* as often as it can. If it runs out of javelins, or if enemies enter melee range, it switches to its spear.

Troglodyte Curse Chanter	Level 8 Controller (Leader)
Medium natural humanoid (reptile)	XP 350

Initiative +5   **Senses** Perception +13; darkvision
Troglodyte Stench aura 1; living enemies in the aura take a -2 penalty to attack rolls.
HP 93; **Bloodied** 46
AC 23; **Fortitude** 22, **Reflex** 17, **Will** 22
Speed 5
(+) **Quarterstaff** (standard; at-will) ✦ **Weapon**
  +12 vs. AC; 1d8 + 2 damage.
(+) **Claw** (standard; at-will)
  +10 vs. AC; 1d4 + 2 damage.
↗ **Poison Ray** (standard; at-will) ✦ **Poison**
  Ranged 10; +11 vs. Fortitude; 1d6 + 5 poison damage, and the target is weakened (save ends).
↗ **Cavern Curse** (standard; recharge ▫ ▫ ▫ ▫) ✦ **Necrotic**
  Ranged 5; +11 vs. Fortitude; the target takes ongoing 5 necrotic damage and is slowed (save ends both).
◄ **Tunnel Grace** (minor 1/round; recharge ▫ ▫ ▫)
  Close burst 10; all allies in the burst gain +5 speed until the end of the troglodyte shaman's next turn.
◄ **Chant of Renewal** (standard; encounter) ✦ **Healing**
  Close burst 5; bloodied allies in the burst regain 15 hit points.
Alignment Chaotic evil   **Languages** Draconic
Skills Dungeoneering +13, Endurance +14, Religion +9

Str 15 (+6)	**Dex** 12 (+5)	**Wis** 18 (+8)
Con 21 (+9)	**Int** 10 (+4)	**Cha** 14 (+6)

Equipment robes, quarterstaff, skull mask

TROGLODYTE CURSE CHANTER TACTICS

A troglodyte curse chanter uses *tunnel grace* to grant its allies a sudden burst of speed while targeting foes with its *poison ray* and *cavern curse*. The curse chanter keeps its distance and waits until two or more of its fellows are bloodied before using *chant of renewal*.

TROGLODYTE LORE

A character knows the following information with a successful Nature or Dungeoneering check.

DC 15: Troglodytes are stocky, foul-tempered reptilian humanoids known for their powerful stench. Various powerful Underdark races such as drow and mind flayers often enslave troglodytes, using them as fodder in their armies.

Troglodytes dwell in subterranean warrens, gathering in tribes of no more than thirty adults. When opposing troglodyte tribes meet, a territorial fight usually ensues. Such battles end either with the annihilation of one tribe or the merging of two battered tribes into one under a single leader. Both genders partake equally in scavenging, raids, and attacks on weaker troglodyte tribes.

DC 20: Troglodytes lay their eggs in dank caverns. Of the hundreds of eggs laid, only a few dozen hatch and survive to adulthood. A hatchling reaches adulthood in two years.

Troglodytes have minimal culture and technology. They do not take slaves, and any captives that fall into their clutches are quickly devoured or sacrificed.

DC 25: Troglodytes worship a variety of loathsome deities, particularly Torog, "the King That Crawls." They strive to earn divine favor by torturing creatures in terrible rites lasting for hours. Troglodytes especially like to sacrifice intelligent creatures and brave enemies. They sometimes raid surface settlements for sacrificial victims.

ENCOUNTER GROUPS

Troglodyte raiding parties often include one or more drakes, and it's not unusual for a tribe of troglodytes to serve a dragon, naga, drow priest, or other powerful creature.

Level 6 Encounter (XP 1,300)
✦ 2 troglodyte maulers (level 6 soldier)
✦ 2 troglodyte impalers (level 7 artillery)
✦ 1 rage drake (level 5 brute)

Level 7 Encounter (XP 1,500)
✦ 2 troglodyte impalers (level 7 artillery)
✦ 3 gricks (level 7 brute)

Level 8 Encounter (XP 1,700)
✦ 3 troglodyte maulers (level 6 soldier)
✦ 2 troglodyte impalers (level 7 artillery)
✦ 1 troglodyte curse chanter (level 8 controller)

Level 11 Encounter (XP 3,200)
✦ 8 troglodyte warriors (level 12 minion)
✦ 3 drow warriors (level 11 lurker)

(Left to right) troglodyte impaler, troglodyte curse chanter, and troglodyte mauler

TROLL

A TROLL EATS ANYTHING THAT MOVES, from grubs to humans, and is rightly feared for its ravenous appetite, feral cunning, and remarkable regenerative power.

Trolls can be trained to serve in military units. Highly adaptable and resilient, they are found just about anywhere and in any climate.

TROLL LORE

A character knows the following information with a successful Nature check.

DC 15: Trolls hunt most other living creatures and are unconcerned about the size or numbers of their prey. They regenerate quickly, even after they are "slain." Their regeneration is so powerful, in fact, that trolls can regrow severed body parts. Only fire or acid can kill a troll, and trolls have a healthy fear of fire and acid for these reasons.

DC 20: Trolls travel in packs and without any migration pattern. They move until they discover an environment rich with prey, at which time they create a lair. Trolls then pillage the area for food until they've exhausted the resource. When trolls lair near an outpost or settlement, the result is the same: The trolls hunt until every living creature is devoured.

War trolls are more intelligent than the common troll, having been bred to wield weapons, wear armor, and employ tactics. War trolls typically travel from battle to battle in mercenary bands, selling their services to the highest bidder. War trolls are often fickle in their services, turning on a patron if the other side tempts them with a greater payment.

DC 25: Fell trolls are voracious carnivores that delight in gorging on humanoid prey. One or two such creatures can easily wipe out an entire village and devour all of its inhabitants in a single night.

Troll	Level 9 Brute
Large natural humanoid	XP 400

Initiative +7   **Senses** Perception +11
HP 100; **Bloodied** 50; see also *troll healing*
Regeneration 10 (if the troll takes acid or fire damage, regeneration does not function until the end of its next turn)
AC 20; **Fortitude** 21, **Reflex** 18, **Will** 17
Speed 8
(+) **Claw** (standard; at-will)
    Reach 2; +13 vs. AC; 2d6 + 6 damage; see also *frenzied strike*.
✦ **Frenzied Strike** (free, when the troll's attack bloodies an enemy; at-will)
    The troll makes a claw attack.
Troll Healing ✦ **Healing**
    If the troll is reduced to 0 hit points by an attack that does not deal acid or fire damage, it rises on its next turn (as a move action) with 10 hit points.
Alignment Chaotic evil   **Languages** Giant
Skills Athletics +15, Endurance +14

Str 22 (+10)	**Dex** 16 (+7)	**Wis** 14 (+6)
Con 20 (+9)	**Int** 5 (+1)	**Cha** 10 (+4)

TROLL TACTICS

A troll wades into the midst of its enemies, relying on regeneration to keep it alive. Trolls are not clever, and they usually attack whichever enemy last did the most harm. Trolls fight to the death, except when confronted by enemies using fire or acid. Trolls usually try to flee from such foes once bloodied.

War Troll	Level 14 Soldier
Large natural humanoid	XP 1,000

Initiative +12   **Senses** Perception +15
HP 110; **Bloodied** 55; see also *troll healing*
Regeneration 10 (if the war troll takes acid or fire damage, regeneration does not function until the end of its next turn)
AC 30; **Fortitude** 29, **Reflex** 25, **Will** 25
Speed 7
(+) **Greatsword** (standard; at-will) ✦ **Weapon**
    Reach 2; +20 vs. AC; 1d12 + 7 damage, and the target is marked until the end of the war troll's next turn.
(+) **Claw** (standard; at-will)
    Reach 2; +20 vs. AC; 2d6 + 7 damage.
(➔) **Longbow** (standard; at-will) ✦ **Weapon**
    Ranged 20/40; +20 vs. AC; 1d12 + 3 damage.
(↝) **Sweeping Strike** (standard; at-will) ✦ **Weapon**
    Requires greatsword; close blast 2; +20 vs. AC; 1d12 + 7 damage, and the target is knocked prone.
Blood Pursuit (immediate reaction, when a bloodied enemy within 2 squares of the war troll moves or shifts; at-will)
    The war troll shifts 1 square closer to the enemy.
Threatening Reach
    The war troll can make opportunity attacks against all enemies within its reach (2 squares).
Troll Healing ✦ **Healing**
    If the war troll is reduced to 0 hit points by an attack that does not deal acid or fire damage, it rises on its next turn (as a move action) with 15 hit points.
Alignment Chaotic evil   **Languages** Giant
Skills Athletics +17, Endurance +15

Str 24 (+14)	**Dex** 16 (+10)	**Wis** 16 (+10)
Con 20 (+12)	**Int** 10 (+7)	**Cha** 12 (+8)

Equipment plate armor, greatsword, longbow, quiver of 30 arrows

WAR TROLL TACTICS

War trolls control the battlefield with their *sweeping strike* power and their threatening reach. They don't like to give ground, using *blood pursuit* to keep after enemies that try to slink away. War trolls make claw attacks only when deprived of their swords.

Fell Troll — Level 20 Elite Brute
Huge natural humanoid — XP 5,600

Initiative +10   **Senses** Perception +16

HP 360; **Bloodied** 180

Regeneration 15 (if the fell troll takes acid or fire damage, regeneration does not function until the end of its next turn)

AC 32; **Fortitude** 38, **Reflex** 30, **Will** 31

Saving Throws +2

Speed 10

Action Points 1

(⊕) **Claw** (standard; at-will)

    Reach 3; +23 vs. AC; 2d10 + 7 damage; see also *blood frenzy*.

⨑ **Backhand Slam** (minor 1/round; at-will)

    Reach 3; +21 vs. Reflex; 2d6 + 7 damage, and the target is pushed 4 squares and knocked prone; see also *blood frenzy*.

Blood Frenzy

    The fell troll gains a +1 bonus to attack rolls and a +2 bonus to damage rolls against bloodied enemies.

Troll Healing ✦ Healing

    If the fell troll is reduced to 0 hit points by an attack that does not deal acid or fire damage, it rises on its next turn (as a move action) with 20 hit points.

Alignment Chaotic evil   **Languages** Giant

Skills Athletics +22, Endurance +23

Str 24 (+17)	**Dex** 10 (+10)	**Wis** 13 (+11)
Con 27 (+18)	**Int** 5 (+7)	**Cha** 7 (+8)

Fell Troll Tactics

A fell troll charges into battle, tearing foes apart with its claws and knocking them about with *backhand slam* attacks.

Encounter Groups

Trolls are usually encountered with other trolls, though sometimes brief alliances can spring up between trolls and other monstrous humanoids such as ogres and onis. Of all the troll varieties, war trolls are likely to be encountered in the widest variety of groups because they'll work with any creature for pay.

Level 9 Encounter (XP 2,000)
✦ 3 trolls (level 9 brute)
✦ 2 destrachans (level 9 artillery)

Level 16 Encounter (XP 7,050)
✦ 2 war trolls (level 14 soldier)
✦ 1 drow priest (level 15 controller)
✦ 1 drow blademaster (level 13 elite skirmisher)
✦ 1 night hag (level 14 lurker)
✦ 5 grimlock minions (level 14 minion)

Level 19 Encounter (XP 12,000)
✦ 1 fell troll (level 20 elite brute)
✦ 2 enormous carrion crawlers (level 17 elite controller)

(Left to right) troll, fell troll, and war troll

UMBER HULK

An umber hulk burrows through the earth and scours the Underdark in search of prey. As it burrows, it leaves rough-hewn tunnels in its wake.

Although it doesn't speak, an umber hulk understands Deep Speech.

Umber Hulk	Level 12 Elite Soldier
Large natural magical beast	XP 1,400

Initiative +11   **Senses** Perception +13; darkvision, tremorsense 5

HP 248; **Bloodied** 124

AC 30; **Fortitude** 33, **Reflex** 28, **Will** 27

Saving Throws +2

Speed 5, burrow 2 (tunneling)

Action Points 1

⊕ **Claw** (standard; at-will)
> Reach 2; +18 vs. AC; 2d6 + 8 damage.

† **Grabbing Double Attack** (standard; at-will)
> The umber hulk makes two claw attacks. If both claw attacks hit the same target, the target is grabbed (until escape). A grabbed target takes ongoing 10 damage from the umber hulk's mandibles until it escapes. The umber hulk cannot make any other attacks while grabbing a creature.

⬗ **Confusing Gaze** (minor 1/round; at-will) ✦ **Gaze, Psychic**
> Close blast 5; targets enemies; +16 vs. Will; the target slides 5 squares and is dazed (save ends).

Alignment Unaligned   **Languages** —

Str 26 (+14)	Dex 16 (+9)	Wis 14 (+8)
Con 20 (+11)	Int 5 (+3)	Cha 11 (+6)

Umber Hulk Tactics

An umber hulk charges into battle and makes a basic attack against its nearest foe, and then spends its action point to make a *grabbing double attack* against the same target. It uses *confusing gaze* as often as it can to confound its enemies.

Shadow Hulk	Level 17 Solo Soldier
Huge shadow magical beast	XP 8,000

Initiative +14   **Senses** Perception +16; darkvision, tremorsense 10

HP 860; **Bloodied** 430; see also *claw frenzy*

AC 35; **Fortitude** 38, **Reflex** 31, **Will** 30

Saving Throws +5

Speed 6, burrow 4 (tunneling); phasing

Action Points 2

⊕ **Claw** (standard; at-will)
> Reach 3; +23 vs. AC; 3d6 + 11 damage.

† **Grabbing Double Attack** (standard; at-will)
> The shadow hulk makes two claw attacks. If both claw attacks hit the same target, the target is grabbed (until escape). A grabbed target takes ongoing 15 damage from the shadow hulk's mandibles until it escapes. The shadow hulk cannot make any other attacks while grabbing a creature.

⬗ **Claw Frenzy** (standard, usable only while bloodied; recharge ⚅ ⚅)
> Close burst 3; +23 vs. AC; 3d6 + 11 damage.

⬗ **Maddening Gaze** (minor 1/round; at-will) ✦ **Gaze, Psychic**
> Close blast 5; targets enemies; +21 vs. Will; the target does nothing on its turn except attack its nearest ally, moving if necessary (save ends). The target makes only basic attacks while under this effect.

Alignment Unaligned   **Languages** —

Str 32 (+19)	Dex 18 (+12)	Wis 16 (+11)
Con 28 (+17)	Int 5 (+5)	Cha 13 (+9)

Shadow Hulk Tactics

The shadow hulk often hides from view and uses its tremorsense to detect prey. It then phases through a wall or other obstruction and attacks with surprise, using its *maddening gaze* and *grabbing double attack* every round until it successfully grabs a creature with its mandibles.

Umber Hulk Lore

A character knows the following information with a successful skill check.

Dungeoneering or Nature DC 20: Umber hulks use their thick claws to hew passages through earth and stone. Many deep caverns in the Underdark are linked together by umber hulk tunnels.

Arcana or Nature DC 25: An umber hulk's gaze causes confusion among its enemies, making them wander in a daze or, in the case of shadow hulks, attack their friends.

Encounter Groups

More intelligent Underdark races often enslave umber hulks. The creatures are loyal servitors as long as their masters keep them well fed.

Level 13 Encounter (XP 4,000)
✦ 2 umber hulks (level 12 elite soldier)
✦ 2 drow warriors (level 11 lurker)

UNICORN

Renowned for their grace and beauty, unicorns hail from the Feywild and are sometimes called to the natural world to guard forests or lakes.

Unicorn	Level 9 Skirmisher (Leader)	
Large fey magical beast		XP 400

Initiative +7 **Senses** Perception +10; low-light vision
Fey Warding aura 2; allies in the aura gain a +2 bonus to all defenses.
HP 93; **Bloodied** 46
AC 23; **Fortitude** 21, **Reflex** 21, **Will** 21
Speed 8; see also *fey step*
(+) **Hooves** (standard; at-will)
+14 vs. AC; 2d6 + 3 damage.
† **Piercing Charge** (standard; at-will)
The unicorn makes a charge attack: +15 vs. AC; 4d6 + 3 damage, and the target is pushed 1 square and knocked prone.
† **Horn Touch** (minor; encounter) ✦ **Healing**
An adjacent ally can spend a healing surge or make a saving throw against one effect that a save can end.
↗ **Fey Beguiling** (standard; recharges when no creature is affected by the power) ✦ **Charm**
Ranged 5; +12 vs. Will; the target cannot attack the unicorn, and the target must make opportunity attacks with a +2 bonus against any creature within reach that attacks the unicorn (save ends).
Fey Step (move; encounter) ✦ **Teleportation**
The unicorn can teleport 5 squares.

Alignment Unaligned		**Languages** Elven
Skills Nature +10		
Str 16 (+7)	**Dex** 13 (+5)	**Wis** 12 (+5)
Con 13 (+5)	**Int** 16 (+7)	**Cha** 17 (+7)

UNICORN TACTICS

A unicorn begins most encounters with a *piercing charge*. It then uses *fey beguiling* to prevent a nearby enemy from harming it while gaining a protector.

Dusk Unicorn	Level 12 Elite Controller (Leader)	
Large fey magical beast		XP 1,400

Initiative +8 **Senses** Perception +12; low-light vision
Fey Warding aura 2; allies in the aura gain a +2 bonus to all defenses.
HP 236; **Bloodied** 118
AC 28; **Fortitude** 28, **Reflex** 26, **Will** 28
Saving Throws +2
Speed 9; see also *fey step*
Action Points 1
(+) **Hooves** (standard; at-will)
+15 vs. AC; 2d8 + 5 damage.
† **Piercing Charge** (standard; at-will)
The dusk unicorn makes a charge attack: +15 vs. AC; 4d8 + 5 damage, and the target is pushed 1 square and knocked prone.
† **Horn Touch** (minor; encounter) ✦ **Healing**
An adjacent ally can spend a healing surge or make a saving throw against one effect that a save can end.
✳ **Fey Wisp** (standard; at-will) ✦ **Charm**
Area burst 5 within 10; +18 vs. Will; dancing lights appear in the origin square, and the target is pulled 3 squares toward the origin square.

⟵ **Twilight Teleport** (standard; encounter) ✦ **Teleportation**
Close burst 5; affects willing allies only; the target is teleported 5 squares, appearing in an unoccupied space in the dusk unicorn's line of sight.
Fey Step (move; encounter) ✦ **Teleportation**
The dusk unicorn can teleport 5 squares.

Alignment Unaligned		**Languages** Elven
Str 20 (+11)	**Dex** 14 (+8)	**Wis** 13 (+7)
Con 14 (+8)	**Int** 17 (+9)	**Cha** 20 (+11)

DUSK UNICORN TACTICS

A dusk unicorn likes to make *piercing charge* attacks. It uses *fey wisp* to lure enemies away from the battle, keeping them out of the fight as long as possible. The creature saves *twilight teleport* for when it needs to move its allies into positions where they can gain combat advantage.

UNICORN LORE

A character knows the following information with a successful Arcana check.

DC 15: Some mortals hunt unicorns for their horns, which are reputed to have powerful healing and magical properties.

DC 20: The dusk unicorn is a rare breed of unicorn with a dark coat and mane, and a black horn. The birth of a dusk unicorn is regarded as an auspicious omen among the fey.

ENCOUNTER GROUPS

Unicorns gather in small herds and sometimes ally with other fey creatures or animals.

Level 12 Encounter (XP 3,500)
✦ 1 dusk unicorn (level 12 elite controller)
✦ 3 banshrae warriors (level 12 skirmisher)

HEATHER HUDSON

VAMPIRE

Sustained by a terrible curse and a thirst for mortal blood, vampires dream of a world in which they live in decadence and luxury, ruling over kingdoms of mortals who exist only to sate their darkest appetites.

VAMPIRE LORE

A character knows the following information with a successful Religion check.

DC 15: Contrary to popular folklore, vampires are not hampered by running water or repelled by garlic, and they don't need invitations to enter homes. Wooden stakes hurt them, but no more so than any other sharp weapon. A vampire does not cast a shadow or produce a reflection in a mirror.

DC 20: A vampire lord can make others of its kind by performing a dark ritual (see the Dark Gift of the Undying sidebar). Performing the ritual leaves the caster weakened, so a vampire lord does not perform the ritual often.

ENCOUNTER GROUPS

A lone vampire lord might lead a retinue of vampire spawn and other undead creatures.

Level 12 Encounter (XP 3,850)
✦ 1 vampire lord (level 11 elite lurker)
✦ 1 battle wight commander (level 12 soldier)
✦ 3 battle wights (level 9 soldier)
✦ 6 vampire spawn bloodhunters (level 10 minion)

VAMPIRE LORD

Gifted and cursed with undead immortality, vampire lords trade many of the abilities they had in life for dark powers, including the power to create broods of vampire spawn.

Vampire lord is a monster template that can be applied to nonplayer characters. See the *Dungeon Master's Guide* for rules on creating new vampire lords using the template.

THE VAMPIRE'S COFFIN

Each vampire lord and vampire spawn is bound to a personal coffin, crypt, or gravesite. It must rest there at least 6 hours per day, at least 4 hours of which must be during daylight hours. (A vampire that did not receive a formal burial or did not have a coffin must instead lie under a foot or so of loose grave dirt or within a dark cave.) A vampire that doesn't rest in its personal coffin or gravesite is reduced to half normal hit points and is weakened until it does.

A vampire can change its personal coffin or gravesite by resting three consecutive times in the new one.

Vampires in coffins are light sleepers; they can make Perception checks (at a -5 penalty) to hear enemies approaching.

Vampire Lord (Human Rogue)	Level 11 Elite Lurker
Medium natural humanoid (undead)	XP 1,200

Initiative +12   **Senses** Perception +10; darkvision
HP 186; **Bloodied** 93
Regeneration 10 (regeneration does not function while the vampire lord is exposed to direct sunlight)
AC 29; **Fortitude** 30, **Reflex** 27, **Will** 25
Immune disease, poison; **Resist** 10 necrotic; **Vulnerable** 10 radiant
Saving Throws +2
Speed 8, climb 4 (spider climb)
Action Points 1

⚔ **Short Sword** (standard; at-will) ✦ **Weapon**
+13 vs. AC; 1d6 + 8 damage.

⚔ **Spiked Chain** (standard; at-will) ✦ **Weapon**
+13 vs. AC; 2d4 + 8 damage.

✦ **Deft Strike** (standard; at-will) ✦ **Weapon**
The vampire lord moves up to 2 squares and makes a melee basic attack at a +2 bonus.

✦ **Imperiling Strike** (standard; encounter)
+15 vs. Fortitude; 1d6 + 10 damage, and the target takes a -3 penalty to AC and Reflex defenses until the end of the vampire lord's next turn.

✦ **Blood Drain** (standard; recharges when an adjacent creature becomes bloodied) ✦ **Healing**
Requires combat advantage; +13 vs. Fortitude; 2d12 + 8 damage, the target is weakened (save ends), and the vampire lord regains 46 hit points; see also *combat advantage*.

➹ **Dominating Gaze** (minor; recharge ⚅) ✦ **Charm**
Ranged 5; +13 vs. Will; the target is dominated (save ends, with a -2 penalty on the saving throw). *Aftereffect:* The target is dazed (save ends). The vampire lord can dominate only one creature at a time.

Combat Advantage
The vampire lord deals an extra 3d6 damage with its attacks against any target it has combat advantage against.

Mist Form (standard; encounter) ✦ **Polymorph**
The vampire lord becomes insubstantial and gains a fly speed of 12, but cannot make attacks. The vampire lord can remain in mist form for up to 1 hour or end the effect as a minor action.

Second Wind (standard; encounter) ✦ **Healing**
The vampire lord spends a healing surge and regains 46 hit points. The vampire gains a +2 bonus to all defenses until the start of its next turn.

Alignment Evil   **Languages** Common
Skills Acrobatics +15, Athletics +18, Bluff +13, Intimidate +13, Stealth +15, Thievery +15
Str 26 (+13)	**Dex** 20 (+10)	**Wis** 11 (+5)
Con 13 (+6)	**Int** 12 (+6)	**Cha** 16 (+8)

Equipment leather armor, short sword

VAMPIRE LORD TACTICS

The vampire lord uses its *dominating gaze* at the start of combat to turn an enemy into a temporary ally. It uses *deft strike* unless it has combat advantage, in which case it uses *blood drain*. Once bloodied, it spends its action point to use *second wind*.

VAMPIRE SPAWN

Living humanoids slain by a vampire lord's blood drain are condemned to rise again as vampire spawn—relatively weak vampires under the dominion of the vampire lord that created them.

Vampire Spawn Fleshripper	Level 5 Minion
Medium natural humanoid (undead)	XP 50

Initiative +6	Senses Perception +4; darkvision

HP 1; a missed attack never damages a minion.
AC 20; **Fortitude** 17, **Reflex** 18, **Will** 17
Immune disease, poison; **Resist** 5 necrotic
Speed 7, climb 4 (spider climb)

⊕ **Claws** (standard, at-will) ✦ **Necrotic**
+11 vs. AC; 5 necrotic damage (7 necrotic damage against a bloodied target).

Destroyed by Sunlight
A vampire spawn that begins its turn in direct sunlight can take only a single move action on its turn. If it ends the turn in direct sunlight, it burns to ash and is destroyed.

Alignment Evil	**Languages** Common	
Str 14 (+5)	**Dex** 16 (+6)	**Wis** 12 (+4)
Con 14 (+5)	**Int** 10 (+3)	**Cha** 14 (+5)

Vampire Spawn Bloodhunter	Level 10 Minion
Medium natural humanoid (undead)	XP 125

Initiative +8	Senses Perception +6; darkvision

HP 1; a missed attack never damages a minion.
AC 25; **Fortitude** 22, **Reflex** 23, **Will** 22
Immune disease, poison; **Resist** 10 necrotic
Speed 7, climb 4 (spider climb)

⊕ **Claws** (standard, at-will) ✦ **Necrotic**
+16 vs. AC; 6 necrotic damage (8 necrotic damage against a bloodied target).

Destroyed by Sunlight
A vampire spawn that begins its turn in direct sunlight can take only a single move action on its turn. If it ends the turn in direct sunlight, it burns to ash and is destroyed.

Alignment Evil	**Languages** Common	
Str 14 (+7)	**Dex** 16 (+8)	**Wis** 12 (+6)
Con 14 (+7)	**Int** 10 (+5)	**Cha** 14 (+7)

VAMPIRE SPAWN TACTICS

Vampire spawn prefer to tear enemies apart with their claws rather than resort to using weapons.

CREATING VAMPIRE SPAWN

A living humanoid slain by a vampire lord's *blood drain* power rises as a vampire spawn of its level at sunset on the following day. This rise can be prevented by burning the body or severing its head.

A living humanoid reduced to 0 hit points or fewer—but not killed—by a vampire lord can't be healed and remains in a deep, deathlike coma. He or she dies at sunset of the next day, rising as a vampire spawn. A Remove Affliction ritual cast before the afflicted creature dies prevents death and makes normal healing possible.

DARK GIFT OF THE UNDYING

In the unholy name of Orcus, the Blood Lord, you transform another being into a vampiric creature of the night.

Level: 11 (caster must be a vampire lord)
Category: Creation
Time: 6 hours; see text
Duration: Permanent
Component Cost: 5,000 gp per level of the subject
Market Price: 75,000 gp
Key Skill: Religion (no check)

This ritual can be performed only between sunset and sunrise. As part of the ritual, you and the ritual's subject must drink a small amount of each other's blood, after which the subject dies and is ritually buried in unhallowed ground. After the interment, you invoke a prayer to Orcus and ask him to bestow the Dark Gift upon the subject. At the conclusion of the ritual, the subject remains buried, rising up out of its shallow grave as a vampire lord at sunset on the following day. (See the *Dungeon Master's Guide*, page 181, for rules on creating new vampire lords.) This ritual is ruined if a Raise Dead ritual is cast on the subject or if the subject is beheaded before rising as a vampire lord.

Performing the ritual leaves you weakened for 1d10 days (no save).

VINE HORROR

The vine horror is a cruel plant monster twisted into a vaguely humanoid form. It haunts swamps and jungles, indulging its murderous nature.

Vine Horror		Level 5 Controller
Medium natural humanoid (plant)		XP 200

Initiative +7   **Senses** Perception +9; blindsight 10
HP 67; **Bloodied** 33
AC 19; **Fortitude** 17, **Reflex** 18, **Will** 15
Speed 6 (forest walk, swamp walk), swim 6
⊕ **Claw** (standard; at-will)
  +8 vs. AC; 1d8 + 4 damage.
⟳ **Vicious Vines** (standard; encounter)
  Close burst 5; targets enemies; +10 vs. Reflex; the target is
  restrained and takes ongoing 10 damage (save ends both) as
  magical vines spring up out of the ground and crush it.
Malleability
  The vine horror can compress its body enough to squeeze
  through a 1-inch-wide crack. Cracks and other openings that are
  more than 1 inch wide do not slow the vine horror at all.
Alignment Evil   **Languages** Common, Elven
Skills Stealth +12

Str 18 (+6)	Dex 21 (+7)	Wis 14 (+4)
Con 19 (+6)	Int 9 (+1)	Cha 10 (+2)

VINE HORROR TACTICS

The vine horror waits for enemies to come within 5 squares, at which point it uses *vicious vines* to restrain them. It then makes claw attacks against restrained foes, gaining combat advantage.

Vine Horror Spellfiend		Level 7 Artillery
Medium natural humanoid (plant)		XP 300

Initiative +7   **Senses** Perception +10; blindsight 10
HP 65; **Bloodied** 32
AC 19; **Fortitude** 18, **Reflex** 17, **Will** 15
Speed 6 (forest walk, swamp walk), swim 6
⊕ **Claw** (standard; at-will)
  +10 vs. AC; 1d8 + 4 damage.
⊗ **Shock Orb** (standard; at-will) ✦ **Lightning**
  Ranged 10; +12 vs. AC; 1d8 + 4 lightning damage.
⊁ **Lashing Vine of Dread** (standard; at-will) ✦ **Fear**
  Ranged 5; +10 vs. Reflex; 1d6 + 4 damage, and the target is
  pushed 5 squares.
✳ **Caustic Cloud** (standard; recharge ⚄ ⚅) ✦ **Acid**
  Area burst 1 within 10; +10 vs. Fortitude; 1d6 + 3 acid damage,
  and the target takes ongoing 5 acid damage and is blinded (save
  ends both).
Malleability
  The vine horror can compress its body enough to squeeze
  through a 1-inch-wide crack. Cracks and other openings that are
  more than 1 inch wide do not slow the vine horror at all.
Alignment Evil   **Languages** Common, Elven
Skills Stealth +12

Str 18 (+7)	Dex 18 (+7)	Wis 14 (+5)
Con 17 (+6)	Int 11 (+3)	Cha 10 (+3)

VINE HORROR SPELLFIEND TACTICS

The spellfiend drops a *caustic cloud* on multiple foes before hurling *shock orbs* at individual targets. Any enemy that gets too close is driven back by the creature's *lashing vine of dread*.

VINE HORROR LORE

A character knows the following information with a successful Nature check.

DC 15: Vine horrors are created naturally through an unusual sequence of events. When an evil humanoid dies in a wilderness location touched by the Shadowfell, its blood sometimes saturates the earth and infuses the local plant life. These plants twist and writhe into the form of one or more vine horrors.

DC 20: A vine horror often takes on aspects of the humanoid whose blood gave it life. For example, if the individual was a wizard, the vine horror might gain abilities similar to spells. The vine horror spellfiend is such a creature.

ENCOUNTER GROUPS

Vine horrors share the same hunting grounds as shambling mounds and have been known to hunt alongside them. They also serve hags, greenscale marsh mystic lizardfolk, and other intelligent swamp dwellers.

Level 8 Encounter (XP 1,900)
✦ 2 vine horror spellfiends (level 7 artillery)
✦ 1 bog hag (level 10 skirmisher)
✦ 2 trolls (level 9 brute)

WARFORGED

WARFORGED ARE A RACE OF MAGICAL CONSTRUCTS built for war and gifted with sentience.

WARFORGED LORE

A character knows the following information with a successful Arcana or Nature check.

DC 15: Warforged are sexless and cannot reproduce. They are created in magical factories called creation forges and given sentience by means of an elaborate ritual.

ENCOUNTER GROUPS

Warforged are built for war, fighting for whatever side created them. In times of peace, they serve as guards and mercenaries, working for any creature that shares their ideals and disposition.

Level 4 Encounter (XP 875)
✦ 1 warforged captain (level 6 soldier)
✦ 1 warforged soldier (level 4 soldier)
✦ 3 human guards (level 3 soldier)

EVA WIDERMANN

Warforged Soldier		Level 4 Soldier
Medium natural humanoid (living construct)		XP 175

Initiative +6   **Senses** Perception +3
HP 56; **Bloodied** 28; see also *warforged resolve*
AC 20; **Fortitude** 17, **Reflex** 15, **Will** 14
Saving Throws +2 against ongoing damage
Speed 5
⊕ **Longsword** (standard; at-will) ✦ **Weapon**
    +9 vs. AC; 1d8 + 4 damage, and the target is marked until the end of the warforged soldier's next turn; see also *battlefield tactics*.
Battlefield Tactics
    The warforged soldier gains a +1 bonus to melee attacks if it has an ally adjacent to the target.
Warforged Resolve (minor, usable only while bloodied; encounter)
    The warforged soldier gains 14 temporary hit points.
Alignment Any   **Languages** Common
Skills Endurance +8, Intimidate +7
Str 18 (+6)   **Dex** 14 (+4)   **Wis** 12 (+3)
Con 16 (+5)   **Int** 10 (+2)   **Cha** 10 (+2)
Equipment plate armor, heavy shield, longsword

WARFORGED SOLDIER TACTICS

Warforged soldiers cooperate with each other, employing *battlefield tactics* to edge in and defeat foes.

Warforged Captain		Level 6 Soldier (Leader)
Medium natural humanoid (living construct)		XP 250

Initiative +7   **Senses** Perception +4
Aura of Command aura 10; allies in the aura gain a +1 power bonus to attack rolls.
HP 72; **Bloodied** 36; see also *warforged resolve*
AC 22; **Fortitude** 20, **Reflex** 17, **Will** 18
Saving Throws +2 against ongoing damage
Speed 5
⊕ **Glaive** (standard; at-will) ✦ **Weapon**
    Reach 2; +11 vs. AC; 2d4 + 5 damage, and the target is marked until the end of the warforged captain's next turn; see also *battlefield tactics*.
† **Tactical Switch** (standard; recharge ⚅ ⚄ ⚃) ✦ **Weapon**
    The warforged captain makes a melee basic attack. On a hit, the target slides 1 square, and the warforged captain or an ally within 10 squares of the warforged captain shifts 1 square.
Battlefield Tactics
    The warforged captain gains a +1 bonus to melee attacks if it has an ally adjacent to the target.
Warforged Resolve (minor, usable only while bloodied; encounter)
    The warforged captain gains 18 temporary hit points.
Alignment Any   **Languages** Common
Skills Endurance +11, Intimidate +11
Str 20 (+8)   **Dex** 14 (+5)   **Wis** 12 (+4)
Con 16 (+6)   **Int** 10 (+3)   **Cha** 16 (+6)
Equipment plate armor, glaive

WARFORGED CAPTAIN TACTICS

A warforged captain uses *tactical switch* to pull enemies out of their fighting formation, creating holes that its allies can exploit. It tries to stay within 10 squares of its allies so that they benefit from its aura.

WIGHT

A WIGHT DEVOURS THE LIFE FORCE of living creatures to assuage its hunger for the soul it has lost and can never retrieve.

Deathlock Wight — Level 4 Controller
Medium natural humanoid (undead)   XP 175

Initiative +4   **Senses** Perception +1; darkvision
HP 54; **Bloodied** 27
AC 18; **Fortitude** 15, **Reflex** 16, **Will** 17
Immune disease, poison; **Resist** 10 necrotic; **Vulnerable** 5 radiant
Speed 6

(+) **Claw** (standard; at-will) ✦ Necrotic
+9 vs. AC; 1d6 necrotic damage, and the target loses 1 healing surge.

↗ **Grave Bolt** (standard; at-will) ✦ Necrotic
Ranged 20; +6 vs. Reflex; 1d6 + 4 necrotic damage, and the target is immobilized (save ends).

↗ **Reanimate** (minor; encounter) ✦ Healing, Necrotic
Ranged 10; affects a destroyed undead creature of a level no higher than the deathlock wight's level + 2; the target stands as a free action with a number of hit points equal to one-half its bloodied value. This power does not affect minions.

↚ **Horrific Visage** (standard; recharge ⚄ ⚅ ⚅) ✦ Fear
Close blast 5; +7 vs. Will; 1d6 damage, and the target is pushed 3 squares.

Alignment Evil   **Languages** Common
Skills Arcana +10, Religion +10

| Str 10 (+2) | Dex 14 (+4) | Wis 9 (+1) |
| Con 14 (+4) | Int 16 (+5) | Cha 18 (+6) |

DEATHLOCK WIGHT TACTICS
A deathlock wight uses *grave bolt* to immobilize enemies and *horrific visage* to keep them at a distance. When its most powerful ally or bodyguard falls in battle, it uses *reanimate* to put it back in play.

Wight — Level 5 Skirmisher
Medium natural humanoid (undead)   XP 200

Initiative +7   **Senses** Perception +0; darkvision
HP 62; **Bloodied** 31
AC 19; **Fortitude** 18, **Reflex** 17, **Will** 16
Immune disease, poison; **Resist** 10 necrotic; **Vulnerable** 5 radiant
Speed 7

(+) **Claw** (standard; at-will) ✦ Necrotic
+10 vs. AC; 1d6 + 4 necrotic damage, the target loses 1 healing surge, and the wight shifts 3 squares.

Alignment Evil   **Languages** Common
Skills Stealth +10

| Str 18 (+6) | Dex 16 (+5) | Wis 6 (+0) |
| Con 14 (+4) | Int 10 (+2) | Cha 15 (+4) |

WIGHT TACTICS
A wight charges its enemies and tears them apart with its claws, shifting gleefully through their ranks and trying to flank them whenever possible.

Battle Wight — Level 9 Soldier
Medium natural humanoid (undead)   XP 400

Initiative +7   **Senses** Perception +3; darkvision
HP 98; **Bloodied** 49
AC 25; **Fortitude** 22, **Reflex** 18, **Will** 22
Immune disease, poison; **Resist** 10 necrotic; **Vulnerable** 5 radiant
Speed 5

(+) **Souldraining Longsword** (standard; at-will) ✦ Necrotic, Weapon
+15 vs. AC; 1d8 + 5 necrotic damage, and the target loses 1 healing surge and is immobilized (save ends).

↗ **Soul Reaping** (standard; recharge ⚄ ⚅) ✦ Healing, Necrotic
Ranged 5; affects an immobilized target only; +12 vs. Fortitude; 2d8 + 5 necrotic damage, and the battle wight regains 10 hit points.

Alignment Evil   **Languages** Common
Skills Intimidate +14

| Str 20 (+9) | Dex 13 (+5) | Wis 9 (+3) |
| Con 18 (+8) | Int 12 (+5) | Cha 20 (+9) |

Equipment plate armor, heavy shield, longsword

BATTLE WIGHT TACTICS
This creature brazenly wades into battle, swinging its longsword decisively. It shifts away from enemies to use *soul reaping*, targeting foes who are immobilized by its longsword attacks.

Battle Wight Commander — Level 12 Soldier (Leader)
Medium natural humanoid (undead)   XP 700

Initiative +12   **Senses** Perception +12; darkvision
HP 106; **Bloodied** 53
AC 28; **Fortitude** 26, **Reflex** 23, **Will** 26
Immune disease, poison; **Resist** 10 necrotic; **Vulnerable** 5 radiant
Speed 5

(+) **Souldraining Longsword** (standard; at-will) ✦ Necrotic, Weapon
+18 vs. AC; 1d8 + 7 necrotic damage, and the target is immobilized and weakened (save ends both) and loses 1 healing surge.

↗ **Soul Harvest** (standard; recharge ⚄ ⚅ ⚅) ✦ Healing, Necrotic
Ranged 5; affects an immobilized target only; +15 vs. Fortitude; 2d8 + 7 necrotic damage, and the battle wight commander and all undead allies within 2 squares of it regain 10 hit points.

Alignment Evil   **Languages** Common
Skills Intimidate +18

| Str 24 (+13) | Dex 19 (+10) | Wis 14 (+7) |
| Con 22 (+12) | Int 15 (+7) | Cha 24 (+13) |

Equipment plate armor, heavy shield, longsword

BATTLE WIGHT COMMANDER TACTICS
A battle wight commander is a clever, resolute, and patient foe. The creature uses *soul harvest* as often as it can, positioning itself so that its undead allies can reap the healing benefits of the power as well.

Slaughter Wight — Level 18 Brute
Medium natural humanoid (undead) — XP 2,000

Initiative +14   **Senses** Perception +13; darkvision
HP 182; **Bloodied** 91; see also *death wail*
AC 30; **Fortitude** 30, **Reflex** 27, **Will** 26
Immune disease, poison; **Resist** 20 necrotic; **Vulnerable** 10 radiant
Speed 7

⊕ **Claw** (standard; at-will) ✦ **Healing, Necrotic**
+21 vs. AC; 3d6 + 8 necrotic damage, the target loses 1 healing surge and is weakened (save ends), and the slaughter wight regains 15 hit points.

⟵ **Death Wail** (when reduced to 0 hit points) ✦ **Necrotic**
Close burst 5; targets enemies; +21 vs. Fortitude; 2d6 + 4 necrotic damage. Undead allies in the burst can make a basic attack as a free action.

Alignment Chaotic evil   **Languages** Common
Str 26 (+17)   **Dex** 20 (+14)   **Wis** 9 (+8)
Con 22 (+15)   **Int** 12 (+10)   **Cha** 18 (+13)

Slaughter Wight Tactics

A slaughter wight revels in combat and attack ferociously with its claws, tending to single out weak or disadvantaged enemies. When slain, it unleashes a horrible *death wail* that spurs nearby undead allies.

Wight Lore

A character knows the following information with a successful Religion check.

DC 15: Wights are restless undead that savagely attack the living, draining their life energy. They often serve more powerful undead creatures as soldiers and lieutenants.

Wights typically inhabit the places where they died, although they are by no means bound to these locations. They also haunt tombs and catacombs, greedily hoarding any treasure they find.

Encounter Groups

Wights associate with other undead creatures as well as living denizens of the Shadowfell, including shadar-kai and dark creepers. Some wights—deathlock wights and battle wights in particular—gather other undead creatures to their service. A battle wight commander or slaughter wight might serve as a lieutenant to a more powerful creature, such as a lich or vampire.

Level 3 Encounter (XP 778)
✦ 1 deathlock wight (level 4 controller)
✦ 3 zombies (level 2 brute)
✦ 6 zombie rotters (level 3 minion)

Level 11 Encounter (XP 3,100)
✦ 1 battle wight commander (level 12 soldier)
✦ 4 battle wights (level 9 soldier)
✦ 1 shadar-kai witch (level 7 controller)
✦ 2 shadar-kai chainfighters (level 6 skirmisher)

Level 18 Encounter (XP 10,200)
✦ 2 slaughter wights (level 18 brute)
✦ 3 abyssal ghouls (level 16 skirmisher)
✦ 1 nabassu gargoyle (level 18 lurker)

(Left to right) battle wight, deathlock wight, slaughter wight, and wight

WOLF

Wolves are pack hunters that hunt all kinds of prey and are common across a wide variety of terrains and climates.

Gray Wolf		Level 2 Skirmisher
Medium natural beast		XP 125

Initiative +5   **Senses** Perception +7; low-light vision
HP 38; **Bloodied** 19
AC 16; **Fortitude** 14, **Reflex** 14, **Will** 13
Speed 8
⊕ **Bite** (standard; at-will)
   +7 vs. AC; 1d6 + 2 damage, or 2d6 + 2 damage against a prone target.
Combat Advantage
   If the gray wolf has combat advantage against the target, the target is also knocked prone on a hit.
Alignment Unaligned   **Languages** —
Str 13 (+2)   **Dex** 14 (+3)   **Wis** 13 (+2)
Con 14 (+3)   **Int** 2 (–3)   **Cha** 10 (+1)

GRAY WOLF TACTICS

Gray wolves work together to take down an enemy, usually focusing on the weakest in a group. They flank prey so that successful bite attacks knock the victim prone, allowing other wolves to deal greater damage.

Dire Wolf		Level 5 Skirmisher
Large natural beast (mount)		XP 200

Initiative +7   **Senses** Perception +9; low-light vision
HP 67; **Bloodied** 33
AC 19; **Fortitude** 18, **Reflex** 17, **Will** 16
Speed 8
⊕ **Bite** (standard; at-will)
   +10 vs. AC; 1d8 + 4 damage, or 2d8 + 4 damage against a prone target.
Combat Advantage
   The dire wolf gains combat advantage against a target that has one or more of the dire wolf's allies adjacent to it. If the dire wolf has combat advantage against the target, the target is also knocked prone on a hit.
Pack Hunter (while mounted by a friendly rider of 5th level or higher; at-will) ✦ **Mount**
   The dire wolf's rider gains combat advantage against an enemy if it has at least one ally other than its mount adjacent to the target.
Alignment Unaligned   **Languages** —
Str 19 (+6)   **Dex** 16 (+5)   **Wis** 14 (+4)
Con 19 (+6)   **Int** 5 (–1)   **Cha** 11 (+2)

DIRE WOLF TACTICS

Dire wolves use tactics similar to gray wolves, although they don't necessarily need to flank an enemy to knock it prone.

WOLF LORE

A character knows the following information with a successful Nature check.

DC 15: Members of a wolf pack growl, howl, bark, and use body language to communicate. These sounds can warn a traveler in wolf territory, but howls can carry many miles.

DC 20: Larger and more aggressive than gray wolves, dire wolves supplant gray wolves in regions of the wild where more dangerous and monstrous predators also hunt. They often hunt alongside werewolves and shifters.

ENCOUNTER GROUPS

Many different humanoids domesticate wolves to one degree or another. Wolves can also be corrupted into serving unwholesome monsters.

Level 3 Encounter (XP 825)
✦ 3 gray wolves (level 2 skirmisher)
✦ 2 hobgoblin archers (level 3 artillery)
✦ 1 hobgoblin warcaster (level 3 controller)

Level 5 Encounter (XP 1,100)
✦ 3 dire wolves (level 5 skirmisher)
✦ 2 longtooth hunter shifters (level 6 soldier)

WORG

This enormous, evil relative of the wolf savors the taste of humanoid flesh and likes to stalk people over other prey.

Worg	Level 9 Brute
Large natural magical beast	XP 400

Initiative +7   **Senses** Perception +9; darkvision
Frightful Growl (Fear) aura 3; enemies in the aura take a -1 penalty to attack rolls, and allies in the aura gain a +1 power bonus to attack rolls.
HP 120; **Bloodied** 60
AC 20; **Fortitude** 20, **Reflex** 18, **Will** 18
Speed 8
✦ **Bite** (standard; at-will)
   +12 vs. AC; 2d6 + 5 damage, and ongoing 5 damage (save ends).
Alignment Chaotic evil   **Languages** Abyssal
Skills Stealth +12
Str 21 (+9)   **Dex** 17 (+7)   **Wis** 10 (+4)
Con 20 (+9)   **Int** 7 (+2)   **Cha** 16 (+7)

WORG TACTICS

Worgs don't cooperate particularly well, as each seeks to slake its own thirst for slaughter.

Guulvorg	Level 16 Elite Brute
Huge natural magical beast	XP 2,800

Initiative +11   **Senses** Perception +13; darkvision
AC 31; **Fortitude** 34, **Reflex** 29, **Will** 28
HP 384; **Bloodied** 192
Saving Throws +2
Speed 9
Action Points 1
✦ **Bite** (standard; at-will)
   Reach 2; +19 vs. AC; 2d12 + 8 damage, and the target is knocked prone.
✦ **Tail Slam** (standard; at-will)
   Reach 2; +17 vs. Reflex; 2d8 + 8 damage, and the target is knocked prone and dazed (save ends).
✢ **Guulvorg Fury** (standard; at-will)
   The guulvorg makes a bite attack against one target and tail slam against another; both attacks are made at a -2 penalty.
Alignment Chaotic evil   **Languages** Abyssal
Str 26 (+16)   **Dex** 16 (+11)   **Wis** 10 (+8)
Con 22 (+14)   **Int** 5 (+5)   **Cha** 15 (+10)

Guulvorg

GUULVORG TACTICS

A guulvorg prefers to make bite attacks against single foes. If engaged by two or more enemies, it uses *guulvorg fury*.

WORG LORE

A character knows the following information with a successful Nature check.

DC 15: Worgs live in catacomblike warrens with many exits. Each pack keeps grisly trophies and treasures in its lair. Worgs get along well with goblins and often carry them into battle.

DC 20: Guulvorgs are often encountered in pairs (a male and a female). They are capable of bearing Large riders into battle.

ENCOUNTER GROUPS

Worgs hunt in packs, while guulvorgs usually hunt alone or in pairs. Both worg strains willingly ally with evil humanoids.

Level 10 Encounter (XP 2,500)
✦ 3 worgs (level 9 brute)
✦ 2 razorclaw stalker shifters (level 7 skirmisher)
✦ 1 oni night haunter (level 8 elite controller)

Level 17 Encounter (XP 8,400)
✦ 2 guulvorgs (level 16 elite brute)
✦ 2 cyclops hewers (level 16 soldier)

Worg

WRAITH

Wraith		Level 5 Lurker
Medium shadow humanoid (undead)		XP 200

Initiative +10   **Senses** Perception +2; darkvision
HP 37; **Bloodied** 18
Regeneration 5 (if the wraith takes radiant damage, regeneration
     is negated until the end of the wraith's next turn)
AC 16; **Fortitude** 13, **Reflex** 16, **Will** 14
Immune disease, poison; **Resist** 10 necrotic, insubstantial;
     Vulnerable 5 radiant (see also *regeneration* above)
Speed fly 6 (hover); phasing ; see also *shadow glide*
⊕ **Shadow Touch** (standard; at-will) ✦ **Necrotic**
     +8 vs. Reflex; 1d6 + 4 necrotic damage, and the target is
     weakened (save ends).
Combat Advantage ✦ **Necrotic**
     The wraith deals an extra 1d6 necrotic damage against any
     target it has combat advantage against.
Shadow Glide (move; encounter)
     The wraith shifts 6 squares.
Spawn Wraith
     Any humanoid killed by a wraith rises as a free-willed wraith
     at the start of its creator's next turn, appearing in the space
     where it died (or in the nearest unoccupied space). Raising the
     slain creature (using the Raise Dead ritual) does not destroy the
     spawned wraith.
Alignment Chaotic evil   **Languages** Common
Skills Stealth +11

Str 4 (-1)	**Dex** 18 (+6)	**Wis** 10 (+2)
Con 13 (+3)	**Int** 6 (+0)	**Cha** 15 (+4)

THIS RESTLESS APPARITION LURKS IN THE SHADOWS, thirsting
for souls. Those it slays become free-willed wraiths as hateful
as their creator.

WRAITH LORE

A character knows the following information with a successful
Religion check.

    DC 15: Infused with the necromantic essence of the Shad-
owfell, a wraith is a spirit bereft of soul and body—a hollow
vessel containing minimal personality and knowledge, if any.
It usually remains near where its physical form fell or was
buried.

    The touch of a wraith usually causes weakness. A mad
wraith weakens the mind instead of the body, and its touch
can even drive a creature to attack its allies.

    DC 20: When a wraith slays a humanoid, that creature's
spirit rises as a free-willed wraith of the same kind. With the
aid of magic or ritual, and with the proper components, a necromancer can summon or even create a wraith. Other wraiths
are born on the Shadowfell, and many remain there or enter
the natural world through planar rifts and gates.

    DC 25: When many people die abruptly, a dread wraith
can coalesce from their collected spirits. Common wraiths
can also evolve into larger, more malevolent wraiths over time.

WRAITH TACTICS

A wraith uses hit-and-run tactics and flanking to gain combat
advantage, phasing through walls, doors, and other obstacles
to break line of sight. When bloodied, the wraith flees, only to
return after it has regenerated most or all of its damage.

Mad Wraith		**Level 6 Controller**
Medium shadow humanoid (undead)		XP 250

Initiative +8   **Senses** Perception +6; darkvision
Mad Whispers (**Psychic**) aura 3; deafened creatures are immune;
     any enemy in the aura at the start of its turn takes 5 psychic
     damage and is dazed until the start of its next turn. (If the mad
     wraith takes radiant damage, the aura is negated until the end of
     the mad wraith's next turn.)
HP 54; **Bloodied** 27
AC 18; **Fortitude** 15, **Reflex** 18, **Will** 17
Immune disease, poison; **Resist** 10 necrotic, insubstantial;
     Vulnerable 5 radiant (see also *mad whispers* above)
Speed fly 6 (hover); phasing
⊕ **Touch of Madness** (standard; at-will) ✦ **Psychic**
     +8 vs. Will; 1d6 + 5 psychic damage, and the target takes a -2
     penalty to Will defense (save ends).
✦ **Touch of Chaos** (standard; recharge ⚄ ⚅) ✦ **Psychic**
     +9 vs. Will; 2d6 + 4 psychic damage, and the target moves up
     to its speed and makes a basic attack against its nearest ally as a
     free action.
Spawn Wraith
     Any humanoid killed by a mad wraith rises as a free-willed mad
     wraith at the start of its creator's next turn, appearing in the
     space where it died (or in the nearest unoccupied space). Raising
     the slain creature (using the Raise Dead ritual) does not destroy
     the spawned wraith.
Alignment Chaotic evil   **Languages** Common
Skills Stealth +13

Str 6 (+1)	**Dex** 20 (+8)	**Wis** 6 (+1)
Con 12 (+4)	**Int** 11 (+3)	**Cha** 19 (+7)

MAD WRAITH TACTICS

A mad wraith likes to float over difficult terrain, making it hard for enemies to escape its *mad whispers* aura. It uses *touch of chaos* against an enemy whose Will defense is reduced by the creature's *touch of madness*.

Sword Wraith	Level 17 Lurker
Medium shadow humanoid (undead)	XP 1,600

Initiative +19   **Senses** Perception +14; darkvision
Regeneration 10 (if the sword wraith takes radiant damage, regeneration is negated until the end of the sword wraith's next turn)
HP 90; **Bloodied** 45; see also *death strike*
AC 30; **Fortitude** 29, **Reflex** 30, **Will** 32
Immune disease, poison; **Resist** 20 necrotic, insubstantial;
   Vulnerable 10 radiant (see also *regeneration* above)
Speed fly 8 (hover); phasing ; see also *shadow glide*
(↻) **Shadow Sword** (standard; at-will) ✦ **Necrotic**
   +20 vs. Reflex; 2d8 + 7 necrotic damage, and the target is weakened (save ends).
‡ **Death Strike** (when reduced to 0 hit points) ✦ **Necrotic**
   The sword wraith shifts 4 squares and makes a melee basic attack, dealing an extra 2d8 necrotic damage on a hit.
Combat Advantage ✦ **Necrotic**
   The sword wraith deals an extra 2d6 necrotic damage against any target it has combat advantage against.
Shadow Glide (move; encounter)
   The sword wraith shifts 6 squares.
Spawn Wraith
   Any humanoid killed by a sword wraith rises as a free-willed sword wraith at the start of its creator's next turn, appearing in the space where it died (or in the nearest unoccupied space). Raising the slain creature (using the Raise Dead ritual) does not destroy the spawned wraith.
Alignment Chaotic evil   **Languages** Common
Skills Stealth +20

Str 14 (+10)	**Dex** 24 (+15)	**Wis** 12 (+9)
Con 18 (+12)	**Int** 11 (+8)	**Cha** 24 (+15)

SWORD WRAITH TACTICS

A sword wraith attacks from hiding, striking foes with its *shadow sword* and maneuvering into a flanking position whenever possible (perhaps with the aid of its *shadow glide* power). When bloodied, it uses its phasing ability to escape, returning once it has regenerated.

Dread Wraith	Level 25 Lurker
Large shadow humanoid (undead)	XP 7,000

Initiative +25   **Senses** Perception +18; darkvision
Shroud of Night aura 5; bright light in the aura is reduced to dim light, and dim light becomes darkness.
HP 124; **Bloodied** 62; see also *death strike*
Regeneration 20 (if the dread wraith takes radiant damage, regeneration is negated until the end of the wraith's next turn)
AC 37; **Fortitude** 33, **Reflex** 37, **Will** 37
Immune disease, fear, poison; **Resist** 30 necrotic, insubstantial;
   Vulnerable 15 radiant (see also *regeneration* above)
Speed fly 10 (hover); phasing ; see also *shadow glide*
(↻) **Dread Blade** (standard; at-will) ✦ **Necrotic**
   Reach 2; +28 vs. Reflex; 2d10 + 9 necrotic damage, and the target is weakened (save ends).
↤ **Death Shriek** (when reduced to 0 hit points) ✦ **Psychic**
   Close blast 3; targets enemies; +27 vs. Will; 4d6 + 9 psychic damage, and the target is dazed (save ends). *Miss:* Half damage, and the target is not dazed.
Combat Advantage ✦ **Necrotic**
   The dread wraith deals an extra 3d6 necrotic damage against any target it has combat advantage against.
Shadow Glide (move; encounter)
   The dread wraith shifts 6 squares.
Spawn Wraith
   Any humanoid killed by a dread wraith rises as a free-willed dread wraith at the start of its creator's next turn, appearing in the space where it died (or in the nearest unoccupied space). Raising the slain creature (using the Raise Dead ritual) does not destroy the spawned wraith.
Alignment Chaotic evil   **Languages** Common
Skills Stealth +26

Str 18 (+16)	**Dex** 28 (+21)	**Wis** 12 (+13)
Con 20 (+17)	**Int** 14 (+14)	**Cha** 28 (+21)

DREAD WRAITH TACTICS

Dread wraiths are fearless combatants that like to flank enemies, using *shadow glide* or phasing through walls (as needed) to maneuver into position. If it takes radiant damage, it angrily attacks the source of that damage above all other targets.

ENCOUNTER GROUPS

Wraiths pollute their surroundings with necrotic energy, giving rise to or attracting other undead. Although wraiths are without motivation, they are intelligent and sometimes choose to serve other creatures.

Level 5 Encounter (XP 1,100)
✦ 2 wraiths (level 5 lurker)
✦ 4 dark creepers (level 4 skirmisher)

Level 6 Encounter (XP 1,250)
✦ 1 mad wraiths (level 6 controller)
✦ 4 evistro demons (level 6 brute)

Level 17 Encounter (XP 7,600)
✦ 4 sword wraiths (level 17 lurker)
✦ 1 immolith demon (level 15 controller)

Level 25 Encounter (XP 35,000)
✦ 3 dread wraiths (level 25 lurker)
✦ 1 death titan (level 25 elite brute)

WYVERN

SIMILAR IN APPEARANCE TO A DRAGON, a wyvern uses its venomous tail to sting prey to death before snatching its prize and flying off to devour it.

Despite appearances, a wyvern is more closely related to drakes than dragons, lacking the cunning and intelligence of the latter.

Wyvern	Level 10 Skirmisher
Large natural beast (mount, reptile)	XP 500

Initiative +10   **Senses** Perception +12; low-light vision
HP 106; **Bloodied** 53
AC 24; **Fortitude** 24, **Reflex** 20, **Will** 19
Speed 4, fly 8 (hover); see also *flyby attack*

⊕ **Bite** (standard; at-will)
Reach 2; +15 vs. AC; 1d8 + 7 damage.

⊕ **Claws** (standard; at-will)
The wyvern can attack with its claws only while flying; +15 vs. AC; 1d6 + 7 damage, and the target is knocked prone.

† **Sting** (standard; at-will) ✦ **Poison**
Reach 2; +15 vs. AC; 1d6 + 4 damage, and the wyvern makes a secondary attack against the same target. *Secondary Attack:* +13 vs. Fortitude; ongoing 10 poison damage (save ends).

† **Flyby Attack** (standard; at-will)
The wyvern flies up to 8 squares and makes one melee basic attack at any point during that movement. The wyvern doesn't provoke opportunity attacks when moving away from the target of the attack.

Aerial Agility +2 (while mounted by a rider of 10th level or higher; at-will) ✦ **Mount**
While flying, the wyvern grants its rider a +2 bonus to all defenses.

Alignment Unaligned   **Languages** —
Str 24 (+12)   **Dex** 17 (+8)   **Wis** 15 (+7)
Con 18 (+9)   **Int** 2 (+1)   **Cha** 8 (+4)

WYVERN TACTICS

The wyvern begins combat by using its *flyby attack* power to swoop down and knock an enemy prone with its claws. The creature then lands and alternates between sting and bite attacks. When bloodied, the wyvern takes to air again.

Fell Wyvern	Level 24 Skirmisher
Large shadow beast (reptile)	XP 6,050

Initiative +19   **Senses** Perception +19; darkvision
HP 228; **Bloodied** 114
AC 38; **Fortitude** 42, **Reflex** 34, **Will** 31
Resist 10 necrotic; **Vulnerable** 5 radiant
Speed 6, fly 12 (hover); see also *flyby attack*

⊕ **Bite** (standard; at-will)
Reach 2; +29 vs. AC; 2d8 + 10 damage.

⊕ **Claws** (standard; at-will)
The fell wyvern can attack with its claws only while flying; +29 vs. AC; 2d6 + 10 damage, and the target is knocked prone.

† **Necrovenom Sting** (standard; at-will) ✦ **Necrotic, Poison**
Reach 2; +29 vs. AC; 2d6 + 9 damage, and the fell wyvern makes a secondary attack against the same target. *Secondary Attack:* +27 vs. Fortitude; ongoing 20 necrotic and poison damage (save ends).

† **Flyby Attack** (standard; at-will)
The fell wyvern flies up to 12 squares and makes one melee basic attack at any point during that movement. The fell wyvern doesn't provoke opportunity attacks when moving away from the target of the attack.

↞ **Pestilent Breath** (standard; recharge ⚃ ⚅) ✦ **Necrotic**
Close blast 5; +27 vs. Fortitude; 2d10 + 9 necrotic damage, and ongoing 10 necrotic damage (save ends).

Alignment Unaligned   **Languages** —
Str 30 (+22)   **Dex** 20 (+17)   **Wis** 15 (+14)
Con 28 (+21)   **Int** 2 (+8)   **Cha** 6 (+10)

FELL WYVERN TACTICS

A fell wyvern uses tactics similar to those of the common wyvern, except that it uses *pestilent breath* as often as it can.

WYVERN LORE

A character knows the following information with a successful skill check.

Nature DC 15: To domesticate a wyvern, a humanoid master must handle the creature from its birth.

Arcana DC 25: Fell wyverns are native to the Shadowfell but are found throughout the natural world, especially in areas with strong ties to the Shadowfell.

ENCOUNTER GROUPS

Wyverns live and hunt in small groups called flights. Despite the unruly nature of wyverns, some humanoids make an effort to capture and tame them.

Level 10 Encounter (XP 2,500)
✦ 2 wyverns (level 10 skirmisher)
✦ 1 venom-eye basilisk (level 10 artillery)
✦ 1 ettin marauder (level 10 elite soldier)

HEATHER HUDSON

YUAN-TI

YUAN-TI ARE CRUEL SERPENTINE TYRANTS descended from a powerful prehistoric race of snake people. Their ancient sprawling empires were corrupted and fell to ruin eons ago. Today, these empires are mostly forgotten.

Yuan-ti inhabit the jungles of the natural world, hiding amid crumbling ruins, building secret temples to Zehir (the god of poison and serpents), taking slaves, making sacrifices, and plotting to retake the world.

YUAN-TI MALISON

MALISONS REPRESENT THE BULK OF YUAN-TI SOCIETY. They are highly intelligent and manipulative, and they create powerful auras to aid their minions and allies. They regard their various bodyguards, cultists, and pets as their primary weapons, using them with care and precision.

Malisons have serpentine heads. Roughly half of them are born with legs, and the other half are born with snakelike lower torsos.

Yuan-ti Malison Sharp-eye	Level 13 Artillery
Medium natural humanoid (reptile)	XP 800

Initiative +12   **Senses** Perception +13
HP 98; **Bloodied** 49
AC 27; **Fortitude** 23, **Reflex** 25, **Will** 23; see also *chameleon defense*
Resist 10 poison
Speed 7

(+) **Scimitar** (standard; at-will) ✦ **Weapon**
  +16 vs. AC; 1d8 + 4 damage (crit 2d8 + 12).

(↗) **Longbow** (standard; at-will) ✦ **Poison, Weapon**
  Ranged 20/40; +18 vs. AC; 1d10 + 6 damage, and the yuan-ti malison sharp-eye makes a secondary attack against the same target. *Secondary Attack:* +16 vs. Fortitude; ongoing 5 poison damage, and the target is dazed (save ends both).

Chameleon Defense
  The yuan-ti malison sharp-eye has concealment against attacks that originate more than 3 squares away.

Alignment Evil   **Languages** Common, Draconic
Skills Bluff +15, History +12, Insight +13, Stealth +17
Str 18 (+10)   **Dex** 23 (+12)   **Wis** 14 (+8)
Con 14 (+8)   **Int** 12 (+7)   **Cha** 18 (+10)
Equipment scimitar, longbow, quiver of 30 arrows

YUAN-TI MALISON SHARP-EYE TACTICS

A malison sharp-eye uses ranged attacks in preference to all other attacks. Its *chameleon defense* allows it to make Stealth checks to remain hidden while shooting.

Yuan-ti Malison Incanter	Level 15 Artillery (Leader)
Medium natural humanoid (reptile)	XP 1,200

Initiative +13   **Senses** Perception +13
Zehir's Shield aura 10; allies in the aura gain a +2 power bonus to all defenses.
HP 118; **Bloodied** 59; see also *poisoned domination* and *slither away*
AC 29; **Fortitude** 26, **Reflex** 27, **Will** 27; see also *deflect attack* and *slither away*
Resist 10 poison
Speed 7; see also *slither away*

(+) **Bite** (standard; at-will) ✦ **Poison**
  +16 vs. Fortitude; 1d6 + 6 damage, and ongoing 5 poison damage (save ends).

(↗) **Mindwarp** (standard; at-will) ✦ **Psychic**
  Ranged 20; +20 vs. AC; 2d6 + 7 psychic damage, and the target is dazed (save ends).

↗ **Poisoned Domination** (standard; recharges when first bloodied) ✦ **Charm**
  Ranged 5; affects a creature taking ongoing poison damage; +20 vs. Will; the target is dominated until the end of the incanter's next turn. *Aftereffect:* The target is dazed (save ends).

↗ **Zehir's Venom** (standard; recharge ⚄ ⚅ ⚅) ✦ **Poison**
  Ranged 10; affects a creature taking ongoing poison damage; +20 vs. Fortitude; 2d10 + 6 poison damage, and the target is dazed (save ends).

Deflect Attack (immediate interrupt, when hit by an attack; recharge ⚄ ⚅)
  The yuan-ti malison incanter transfers the attack's damage and effects to an adjacent ally.

Slither Away
  While bloodied, the yuan-ti malison incanter gains +2 speed and a +5 bonus to all defenses.

Alignment Evil   **Languages** Common, Draconic
Skills Arcana +19, Bluff +19, History +19, Insight +18, Stealth +18
Str 16 (+10)   **Dex** 22 (+13)   **Wis** 22 (+13)
Con 22 (+13)   **Int** 25 (+14)   **Cha** 25 (+14)

Yuan-ti Malison Incanter Tactics

A yuan-ti malison incanter uses *mindwarp* until one or more enemies are poisoned by its allies, at which point it targets them with *poisoned domination* and *Zehir's venom*. The incanter remains adjacent to an ally at all times so that it can use *deflect attack* to avoid taking damage. If it is bloodied and defeat seems inevitable, the incanter uses *slither away* to escape.

Yuan-ti Malison Disciple of Zehir	Level 17 Controller
Medium natural humanoid (reptile)	XP 1,600

Initiative +13   **Senses** Perception +12
Zehir's Favor (Healing, Poison) aura 10; allies in the aura at the start of their turns regain 5 hit points, while enemies in the aura at the start of their turns take 5 poison damage.
HP 164; **Bloodied** 82
AC 31; **Fortitude** 29, **Reflex** 29, **Will** 32
Resist 10 poison
Speed 7
⊕ **Morningstar** (standard; at-will) ✦ **Poison, Weapon**
  +22 vs. AC; 1d10 + 3 damage, and the yuan-ti malison disciple of Zehir makes a secondary attack against the same target. *Secondary Attack:* +20 vs. Fortitude; ongoing 10 poison damage (save ends).
↗ **Soothing Words** (standard; recharge ⚁ ⚂ ⚃ ⚄ ⚅) ✦ **Charm**
  Ranged 5; the target must be able to hear the disciple of Zehir; +24 vs. Will; the target is dominated (save ends). *Aftereffect:* The target is dazed (save ends).
Alignment Evil   **Languages** Common, Draconic
Skills Bluff +21, History +18, Insight +17, Religion +18, Stealth +18
Str 16 (+11)   **Dex** 20 (+13)   **Wis** 18 (+12)
Con 20 (+13)   **Int** 20 (+13)   **Cha** 26 (+16)
Equipment morningstar

Disciple of Zehir Tactics

A disciple of Zehir uses *soothing words* to dominate its enemies, turning them against one another.

Yuan-ti Abomination

The yuan-ti abomination lives for battle, crushing enemies in the name of Zehir and on the orders of its malison superiors.

Yuan-ti Abomination	Level 14 Soldier
Large natural humanoid (reptile)	XP 1,000

Initiative +13   **Senses** Perception +10
HP 140; **Bloodied** 70
AC 30; **Fortitude** 30, **Reflex** 28, **Will** 27
Resist 10 poison
Speed 7, climb 7
⊕ **Bastard Sword** (standard; at-will) ✦ **Poison, Weapon**
  Reach 2; +20 vs. AC; 1d12 + 6 damage (crit 2d12 + 18), and the target is marked until the end of the yuan-ti abomination's next turn and takes ongoing 5 poison damage (save ends).
↓ **Grasping Coils** (minor 1/round; at-will)
  +18 vs. Reflex; the target is pulled 1 square and grabbed (until escape). The yuan-ti abomination can grab only one creature at a time.
↓ **Bite** (standard; at-will) ✦ **Poison**
  Grabbed target only; +18 vs. Fortitude; 1d12 + 5 poison damage, and ongoing 10 poison damage (save ends).
Alignment Evil   **Languages** Draconic
Skills Endurance +15, Intimidate +14, Stealth +14
Str 22 (+13)   **Dex** 18 (+11)   **Wis** 16 (+10)
Con 20 (+12)   **Int** 12 (+8)   **Cha** 14 (+9)
Equipment heavy shield, bastard sword

Yuan-ti Abomination Tactics

A yuan-ti abomination attacks with its scimitar and its *grasping coils* every round. If it succeeds in grabbing an enemy and there are no other foes opposing it, it bites the grabbed foe. Otherwise, it holds that enemy in place while it attacks another target with its scimitar.

YUAN-TI ANATHEMA

Anathemas ruled the yuan-ti as kings until they were stricken with madness and imprisoned. Lesser yuan-ti still revere them as emissaries of the god Zehir, placating them with daily sacrifices.

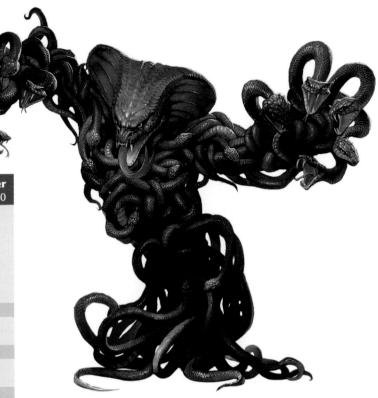

Yuan-ti Anathema	Level 21 Elite Skirmisher
Huge natural magical beast (reptile)	XP 6,400

Initiative +18   **Senses** Perception +17
HP 412; **Bloodied** 206
AC 37; **Fortitude** 39, **Reflex** 35, **Will** 35
Resist 20 poison
Saving Throws +2
Speed 8; see also *swarm of snakes* and *trample*
Action Points 1

(+) **Slam** (standard; at-will) ✦ **Poison**
    Reach 3; +26 vs. AC; 2d6 + 7 damage, and ongoing 10 poison damage (save ends).

⸸ **Double Attack** (standard; at-will) ✦ **Poison**
    The yuan-ti anathema makes two slam attacks, each against a different target.

⸸ **Bite** (standard; at-will) ✦ **Poison**
    Reach 3; +26 vs. AC; 2d8 + 7 damage, and the yuan-ti anathema makes a secondary attack against the same target. *Secondary Attack:* +24 vs. Fortitude; the target takes ongoing 15 poison damage and a –4 penalty to attack rolls (save ends both).

⸸ **Trample** (standard; at-will)
    The yuan-ti anathema can move up to its speed and enter enemies' spaces. This movement provokes opportunity attacks, and the anathema must end its move in an unoccupied space. When it enters an enemy's space, the anathema makes a trample attack: +24 vs. Reflex; 2d6 + 7 damage, and the target is knocked prone.

⟳ **Horde of Snakes** (standard; recharges when the yuan-ti anathema uses *swarm of snakes*) ✦ **Poison**
    Close burst 1; +26 vs. Fortitude; 2d4 + 6 damage, and ongoing 10 poison damage (save ends).

Swarm of Snakes (move; at-will)
    The yuan-ti anathema collapses into hundreds of snakes, which shift up to 8 squares away and then re-form as the anathema in an unoccupied space. The anathema ignores difficult terrain while moving in this fashion.

Alignment Evil	**Languages** Draconic	
Str 25 (+17)	**Dex** 23 (+16)	**Wis** 15 (+12)
Con 30 (+20)	**Int** 5 (+7)	**Cha** 22 (+16)

YUAN-TI ANATHEMA TACTICS

The anathema normally begins battle by trampling several foes, and then spends its action point to bite the nearest enemy. On subsequent rounds, it alternates between biting a single enemy and using its *double attack* against two targets. If closely pressed by three or more foes, the anathema uses *horde of snakes* and *swarm of snakes* to attack all nearby targets, slither away, and reform in a new spot.

YUAN-TI LORE

A character knows the following information with a successful Nature check.

DC 20: Yuan-ti malisons represent the bulk of yuan-ti society, accounting for 90 percent or more of a yuan-ti settlement's population (excluding nonyuan-ti slaves and worshipers). Some malisons are born with humanoid lower bodies while retaining an ophidian head. Whether they possess legs or a long serpent tail, malisons make superb intermediaries between races. They often work with human cultists who revere the snake god Zehir.

DC 25: Yuan-ti abominations are the elite troops and champions of yuan-ti society, overcoming threats that yuan-ti malisons, human cultists, and slaves are unable to defeat.

DC 30: Both the yuan-ti and their enemies fear yuan-ti anathemas. Anathemas were regarded as kings among their lesser kindred. However, they went mad and turned upon their own kind, savagely butchering their followers until they were overthrown. Anathemas are kept in subterranean prisons. Other yuan-ti regard them as holy creatures but fear that the anathemas would swarm, slay, and eat everything if released. Living sacrifices are dropped from high temple ziggurats down into anathema dens to placate them, lest they grow restless.

SNAKETONGUE CULTISTS

SNAKETONGUE CULTISTS ARE HUMAN WORSHIPERS OF ZEHIR who believe that the yuan-ti are Zehir's blessed emissaries in the natural world. Zehir and the yuan-ti reward the cultists' devotion with ritual transformations, bestowing upon the cultists minor reptilian traits.

Snaketongue cultists are fanatics, eager to die in Zehir's name. They take great risks to protect their yuan-ti allies from harm.

Snaketongue Initiate		Level 7 Minion
Medium natural humanoid, human		XP 75

Initiative +5   **Senses** Perception +4
HP 1; a missed attack never damages a minion.
AC 20; **Fortitude** 18, **Reflex** 17, **Will** 17
Speed 6
✦ **Greatsword** (standard; at-will) ✦ **Poison, Weapon**
   +11 vs. AC; 5 damage, and the snaketongue initiate makes a secondary attack against the same target. *Secondary Attack:* +9 vs. Fortitude; ongoing 2 poison damage (save ends).

Alignment Chaotic evil	**Languages** Common, Draconic	
Str 16 (+6)	**Dex** 14 (+5)	**Wis** 12 (+4)
Con 13 (+4)	**Int** 12 (+4)	**Cha** 14 (+5)

Equipment leather armor, poisoned greatsword

SNAKETONGUE INITIATE TACTICS

Poison drips from the blade of the initiate's sword, which it swings with great zeal. The initiate gladly sacrifices itself to protect its yuan-ti masters.

Snaketongue Zealot		Level 12 Minion
Medium natural humanoid, human		XP 175

Initiative +7   **Senses** Perception +6
HP 1; a missed attack never damages a minion.
AC 25; **Fortitude** 23, **Reflex** 22, **Will** 22
Speed 6
✦ **Greatsword** (standard; at-will) ✦ **Poison, Weapon**
   +16 vs. AC; 6 damage, and the snaketongue zealot makes a secondary attack against the same target. *Secondary Attack:* +14 vs. Fortitude; ongoing 3 poison damage (save ends).

Alignment Chaotic evil	**Languages** Common, Draconic	
Str 16 (+8)	**Dex** 14 (+7)	**Wis** 12 (+6)
Con 13 (+6)	**Int** 12 (+6)	**Cha** 14 (+7)

Equipment leather armor, poisoned greatsword

SNAKETONGUE ZEALOT TACTICS

The snaketongue zealot tries to strike down Zehir's hated enemies, cutting deep into infidels with its poisoned greatsword.

Snaketongue Warrior		Level 8 Brute
Medium natural humanoid, human		XP 350

Initiative +6   **Senses** Perception +5
HP 106; **Bloodied** 53
AC 20; **Fortitude** 18, **Reflex** 17, **Will** 17
Resist 10 poison
Speed 6
✦ **Greatsword** (standard; at-will) ✦ **Poison, Weapon**
   +13 vs. AC; 1d10 + 3 damage (1d10 + 5 damage while bloodied) and the snaketongue warrior makes a secondary attack against the same target. *Secondary Attack:* +11 vs. Fortitude; ongoing 5 poison damage (save ends).

Alignment Evil	**Languages** Common, Draconic	
Skills Religion +10		
Str 16 (+7)	**Dex** 14 (+6)	**Wis** 12 (+5)
Con 16 (+7)	**Int** 12 (+5)	**Cha** 14 (+6)

Equipment leather armor, poisoned greatsword

SNAKETONGUE WARRIOR TACTICS

Snaketongue warriors charge into battle, doing their utmost to keep their vile masters safe.

Snaketongue Assassin — Level 9 Lurker
Medium natural humanoid (shapechanger), human — XP 400

Initiative +13 **Senses** Perception +8
HP 80; **Bloodied** 40
AC 23; **Fortitude** 21, **Reflex** 21, **Will** 20; see also *crowd shield*
Resist 10 poison
Speed 7

(+) **Dagger** (standard; at-will) ✦ **Poison, Weapon**
+14 vs. AC; 1d4 + 3 damage, and ongoing 10 poison damage (save ends).

Crowd Shield
The snaketongue assassin gains a +2 bonus to its AC and Reflex defense if it has one creature adjacent to it, or a +4 bonus if two or more creatures are adjacent to it.

Serpent Form (move; at-will) ✦ **Polymorph**
The snaketongue assassin transforms into a crushgrip constrictor (page 240). Any equipment the assassin is carrying merges with the new form. The assassin uses the crushgrip constrictor's statistics instead its own, except for hit points. Reverting to its true form is a minor action.

Alignment Evil   **Languages** Common, Draconic
Skills Religion +11, Stealth +14
Str 16 (+7)   **Dex** 20 (+9)   **Wis** 18 (+8)
Con 20 (+9)   **Int** 14 (+6)   **Cha** 14 (+6)
Equipment leather armor, poisoned dagger

Snaketongue Assassin Tactics

A snaketongue assassin stealthily approaches an enemy in human form and usually remains in this form until bloodied, at which point it transforms into a crushgrip constrictor. While in human form, it tries to stay close to its allies and enemies to gain the benefits of *crowd shield*.

Snaketongue Celebrant — Level 11 Controller
Medium natural humanoid (shapechanger), human — XP 600

Initiative +9   **Senses** Perception +14
HP 117; **Bloodied** 58
AC 24; **Fortitude** 22, **Reflex** 20, **Will** 24
Resist 10 poison
Speed 7

(+) **Scimitar** (standard; at-will) ✦ **Poison, Weapon**
+14 vs. AC; 1d8 + 3 damage (crit 2d8 + 11), and the snaketongue celebrant makes a secondary attack against the same target.
Secondary Attack: +12 vs. Fortitude; ongoing 5 poison damage (save ends).

⌁ **Serpent's Lash** (standard; recharge ⚁ ⚂ ⚃) ✦ **Psychic**
Ranged 5; a whip of amber-colored energy lashes the target; +14 vs. Will; 1d8 + 5 psychic damage, and the target grants combat advantage to all of its enemies until the end of the yuan-ti celebrant's next turn.

✳ **Coils of Despair** (standard; recharge ⚄ ⚅)
Area burst 5 within 10; targets enemies; +14 vs. Reflex; the target is restrained (save ends) by writhing coils of green energy.

Serpent Form (move; at-will) ✦ **Polymorph**
The snaketongue celebrant transforms into a crushgrip constrictor (page 240). Any equipment the celebrant is carrying merges with the new form. The celebrant uses the crushgrip constrictor's statistics instead its own, except for hit points. Reverting to its true form is a minor action.

Alignment Evil   **Languages** Common, Draconic
Skills Diplomacy +15, Insight +14, Intimidate +15, Religion +13
Str 17 (+8)   **Dex** 19 (+9)   **Wis** 19 (+9)
Con 21 (+10)   **Int** 16 (+8)   **Cha** 21 (+10)
Equipment hooded robe, poisoned scimitar

Snaketongue Celebrant Tactics

The celebrant uses *coils of despair* to restrain foes, saving *serpent's lash* for enemies that its allies cannot reach easily. In melee combat, the celebrant prefers to fight in *serpent form*.

Snaketongue Cultist Lore

A character knows the following information with a successful Nature check.

DC 15: Human cultists of Zehir are often found living among yuan-ti as second-class citizens. The cultists bow to the needs of yuan-ti, and they often serve as spies in human cultures where yuan-ti are hated and feared.

DC 20: Snaketongue cultists typically wield envenomed blades, proudly referring to them as "the fangs of Zehir."

Encounter Groups

Yuan-ti encounters usually consist of a mixed group of yuan-ti malisons, yuan-ti abominations, and snaketongue cultists. Occasionally they are joined by other reptilian monsters and humanoid slaves.

Level 9 Encounter (XP 2,025)
✦ 1 snaketongue celebrant (level 11 controller)
✦ 1 snaketongue warrior (level 8 brute)
✦ 9 snaketongue initiates (level 7 minion)
✦ 1 flame snake (level 9 artillery)

Level 11 Encounter (XP 3,100)
✦ 1 yuan-ti abomination (level 14 soldier)
✦ 1 yuan-ti malison sharp-eye (level 13 artillery)
✦ 4 snaketongue zealots (level 12 minion)
✦ 1 snaketongue assassin (level 9 lurker)

Level 16 Encounter (XP 6,800)
✦ 1 yuan-ti malison disciple of Zehir (level 17 controller)
✦ 2 yuan-ti malison incanters (level 15 artillery)
✦ 2 shadow snakes (level 16 skirmisher)

Level 22 Encounter (XP 19,200)
✦ 1 yuan-ti anathema (level 21 elite skirmisher)
✦ 2 dark nagas (level 21 elite controller)

ZOMBIE

A ZOMBIE IS THE ANIMATED CORPSE of a living creature. Imbued with the barest semblance of life, this shambling horror obeys the commands of its creator, heedless of its own wellbeing.

A typical zombie is made of the corpse of a Medium or Large creature.

Zombie Rotter	Level 3 Minion
Medium natural animate (undead)	XP 38

Initiative -2   **Senses** Perception -1; darkvision
HP 1; a missed attack never damages a minion.
AC 13; **Fortitude** 13, **Reflex** 9, **Will** 10
Immune disease, poison
Speed 4
⊕ **Slam** (standard; at-will)
   +6 vs. AC; 5 damage.

Alignment Unaligned	**Languages** –	
Str 14 (+2)	**Dex** 6 (-2)	**Wis** 8 (-1)
Con 10 (+0)	**Int** 1 (-5)	**Cha** 3 (-4)

ZOMBIE ROTTER TACTICS

Zombie rotters swarm the nearest living target and beat it to death.

Zombie	Level 2 Brute
Medium natural animate (undead)	XP 125

Initiative -1   **Senses** Perception +0; darkvision
HP 40; **Bloodied** 20; see also *zombie weakness*
AC 13; **Fortitude** 13, **Reflex** 9, **Will** 10
Immune disease, poison; **Resist** 10 necrotic; **Vulnerable** 5 radiant
Speed 4
⊕ **Slam** (standard; at-will)
   +6 vs. AC; 2d6 + 2 damage.
⊥ **Zombie Grab** (standard; at-will)
   +4 vs. Reflex; the target is grabbed (until escape). Checks made to escape the zombie's grab take a -5 penalty.
Zombie Weakness
   Any critical hit to the zombie reduces it to 0 hit points instantly.

Alignment Unaligned	**Languages** –	
Str 14 (+3)	**Dex** 6 (-1)	**Wis** 8 (+0)
Con 10 (+1)	**Int** 1 (-4)	**Cha** 3 (-3)

ZOMBIE TACTICS

When two or more zombies attack a single foe, one of them uses *zombie grab* to prevent the foe's escape.

Gravehound	Level 3 Brute
Medium natural animate (undead)	XP 150

Initiative +2   **Senses** Perception +1; darkvision
HP 54; **Bloodied** 27; see also *death jaws* and *zombie weakness*
AC 14; **Fortitude** 14, **Reflex** 12, **Will** 11
Immune disease, poison; **Resist** 10 necrotic; **Vulnerable** 5 radiant
Speed 8
⊕ **Bite** (standard; at-will) ✦ **Necrotic**
   +7 vs. AC; 1d6 + 3 damage, and the target takes ongoing 5 necrotic damage (save ends) and is knocked prone if it is Medium size or smaller.
⊥ **Death Jaws** (when reduced to 0 hit points) ✦ **Necrotic**
   The gravehound makes a bite attack against a target within its reach.

Zombie Weakness
   Any critical hit to the gravehound reduces it to 0 hit points instantly.

Alignment Unaligned	**Languages** –	
Str 16 (+4)	**Dex** 13 (+2)	**Wis** 10 (+1)
Con 14 (+3)	**Int** 1 (-4)	**Cha** 3 (-3)

GRAVEHOUND TACTICS

A gravehound uses its speed to overtake prey. When it dies, it makes one final bite attack against a living creature within reach.

Corruption Corpse	Level 4 Artillery
Medium natural animate (undead)	XP 175

Initiative +3   **Senses** Perception +3; darkvision
Grave Stench aura 1; living enemies in the aura take a -5 penalty to attack rolls.
HP 46; **Bloodied** 23; see also *death burst*
Regeneration 5 (if the corruption corpse takes radiant damage, regeneration doesn't function on its next turn)
AC 17; **Fortitude** 16, **Reflex** 14, **Will** 14
Immune disease, poison; **Resist** 10 necrotic; **Vulnerable** 5 radiant
Speed 4
⊕ **Slam** (standard; at-will)
   +8 vs. AC; 1d6 + 3 damage.
⤳ **Mote of Corruption** (standard; at-will) ✦ **Necrotic**
   The corruption corpse hurls a black glob of necrotic filth. Ranged 10; +7 vs. Reflex; 2d6 + 3 necrotic damage, and the target is weakened (save ends).
⇐ **Death Burst** (when reduced to 0 hit points) ✦ **Necrotic**
   The corruption corpse explodes. Close burst 1; +7 vs. Fortitude; 2d6 + 3 necrotic damage.

Alignment Unaligned	**Languages** –	
Str 16 (+5)	**Dex** 13 (+3)	**Wis** 12 (+3)
Con 16 (+5)	**Int** 4 (-1)	**Cha** 3 (-2)

CORRUPTION CORPSE TACTICS

The corruption corpse hurls globs of necrotic matter at living creatures until one or more living creatures close to within melee range, at which point it makes slam attacks.

Rotwing Zombie	Level 4 Skirmisher
Medium natural animate (undead)	XP 175

Initiative +6   **Senses** Perception +2; darkvision
HP 54; **Bloodied** 27; see also *zombie weakness*
AC 17; **Fortitude** 16, **Reflex** 16, **Will** 14
Immune disease, poison; **Resist** 10 necrotic; **Vulnerable** 5 radiant
Speed 4, fly 4 (clumsy)
⊕ **Slam** (standard; at-will)
   +9 vs. AC; 1d8 + 2 damage.
Flying Charge
   When flying, the rotwing zombie deals an extra 2d6 damage on a successful charge attack.
Zombie Weakness
   Any critical hit to the rotwing zombie reduces it to 0 hit points instantly.

Alignment Unaligned	**Languages** –	
Str 14 (+4)	**Dex** 14 (+4)	**Wis** 10 (+2)
Con 14 (+4)	**Int** 1 (-3)	**Cha** 3 (-2)

ROTWING ZOMBIE TACTICS

The rotwing zombie often perches silently on a ledge or precipice. It swoops down and makes a *flying charge* against the nearest enemy.

Monster	Level and Role	Page
Cambion Hellfire Magus	18 Artillery	39
Fire Giant Forgecaller	18 Artillery	123
Mordant Hydra	18 Solo Brute	164
Slaughter Wight	18 Brute	263
Aboleth Overseer	18 Elite Controller (L)	8
Dracolich	18 Solo Controller	72
Gibbering Abomination	18 Controller	126
Green Slaad (Curse Slaad)	18 Controller	238
Mind Flayer Mastermind	18 Elite Controller	188
Elder Black Dragon	18 Solo Lurker	76
Nabassu Gargoyle	18 Lurker	115
Abyssal Ghoul Hungerer	18 Minion	119
Dire Bulette	18 Elite Skirmisher	38
Medusa Shroud of Zehir	18 Skirmisher	187
Death Hag	18 Soldier	151
Bodak Reaver	18 Soldier	36
Fire Giant	18 Soldier	123
Greater Helmed Horror	18 Elite Soldier	155
Rockfire Dreadnought (Elemental)	18 Soldier	104
Beholder Eye Tyrant	19 Solo Artillery	32
Angel of Vengeance	19 Elite Brute	17
Goristro (Demon)	19 Elite Brute	55
Phoenix (Roc)	19 Elite Brute	220
Bralani of Autumn Winds (Eladrin)	19 Controller	102
Elder Green Dragon	19 Solo Controller	80
Fomorian Painbringer	19 Elite Controller	110
Rakshasa Noble	19 Controller	217
Fire Archon Blazesteel	19 Soldier	19
Ice Archon Rimehammer	19 Soldier	20
Blackroot Treant	19 Elite Soldier	251
Elder Blue Dragon	20 Solo Artillery	79
Fire Archon Ash Disciple	20 Artillery	19
Fell Troll	20 Elite Brute	255
Nightwalker	20 Elite Brute	197
Ice Archon Frostshaper	20 Controller (L)	21
Black Slaad (Void Slaad)	20 Skirmisher	239
Rimefire Griffon	20 Skirmisher	147
Ice Devil (Gelugon)	20 Soldier	63
Rot Harbinger	20 Soldier	223
Soulspike Devourer	20 Elite Soldier (L)	69
Ghaele of Winter (Eladrin)	21 Artillery	103
Larva Mage	21 Elite Artillery	175
Giant Mummy	21 Brute	193
Dark Naga	21 Elite Controller	194
Deathpriest Hierophant (Orcus)	21 Elite Controller	209
Tormenting Ghost	21 Controller	117
Angel of Valor Legionnaire	21 Minion	16
Legion Devil Legionnaire	21 Minion	64
Wild Hunt Hound	21 Skirmisher	161
Yuan-ti Anathema	21 Elite Skirmisher	271
Fire Titan (Giant)	21 Elite Soldier	124
Marut Blademaster	21 Soldier	185
Rot Slinger	22 Artillery	223
Bluespawn Godslayer (Dragonspawn)	22 Elite Brute	89
Death Giant	22 Brute	120
Hezrou (Demon)	22 Brute	56
War Devil (Malebranche)	22 Brute (L)	67
Marut Concordant	22 Elite Controller	185
Astral Stalker (Abomination)	22 Elite Lurker	10
Grimlock Follower	22 Minion	148

Monster	Level and Role	Page
Efreet Fireblade	22 Soldier	98
Elder Red Dragon	22 Solo Soldier	83
Thunderhawk (Roc)	22 Elite Soldier	221
Efreet Cinderlord	23 Artillery	98
Glabrezu (Demon)	23 Elite Brute	54
Blackfire Dracolich	23 Solo Controller	73
Earthwind Ravager (Elemental)	23 Controller	104
Voidsoul Specter	23 Lurker	244
Abyssal Ghoul Myrmidon	23 Minion	119
Efreet Flamestrider	23 Skirmisher	99
Blood Fiend (Abomination)	23 Soldier	12
Chuul Juggernaut	23 Elite Soldier	43
Great Flameskull	24 Artillery	109
Ancient White Dragon	24 Solo Brute	85
Aspect of Orcus	24 Elite Brute	208
Lich, Eladrin Wizard	24 Elite Controller	176
Storm Giant	24 Controller	124
Fell Wyvern	24 Skirmisher	268
Marilith (Demon)	24 Elite Skirmisher	57
Elder Purple Worm	24 Solo Soldier	214
Rakshasa Dread Knight	24 Soldier	218
Primordial Naga	25 Solo Artillery	195
Death Titan (Giant)	25 Elite Brute	120
Primordial Hydra	25 Solo Brute	165
Efreet Pyresinger	25 Controller	99
Dread Wraith	25 Lurker	267
Sorrowsworn Soulripper	25 Skirmisher	242
Death Knight, Dragonborn	25 Elite Soldier	51
Swordwing	25 Soldier	249
Thunderblast Cyclone (Elemental)	26 Elite Artillery	105
Phane (Abomination)	26 Elite Controller	13
Ancient Black Dragon	26 Solo Lurker	76
Lich Vestige	26 Minion	176
Crownwing (Swordwing)	26 Skirmisher (L)	249
Storm Gorgon	26 Skirmisher	143
Dragonborn Champion	26 Soldier	87
Pit Fiend (Devil)	26 Elite Soldier (L)	65
Balor (Demon)	27 Elite Brute	53
Shadowraven Swarm (Sorrowsworn)	27 Brute	243
Ancient Green Dragon	27 Solo Controller	81
Gibbering Orb	27 Solo Controller	127
Storm Titan (Giant)	27 Elite Controller	125
Doresain, the Ghoul King (Orcus)	27 Elite Skirmisher	208
Sorrowsworn Reaper	27 Soldier	242
Ancient Blue Dragon	28 Solo Artillery	79
Atropal (Abomination)	28 Elite Brute	11
Earthrage Battlebriar	28 Elite Brute	28
Sorrowsworn Deathlord	28 Lurker (L)	242
Efreet Karadjin	28 Soldier (L)	100
Godforged Colossus	29 Elite Brute	44
Runescribed Dracolich	29 Solo Controller	73
Tarrasque (Abomination)	30 Solo Brute	13
Ancient Red Dragon	30 Solo Soldier	83
Orcus	33 Solo Brute (L)	206

Combat Improves When You Add a Mouse

BRING EVEN MORE TO YOUR GAME TABLE WITH D&D INSIDER.™

With quick access to exclusive material and digital tools D&DI™ will help enhance every aspect of your tabletop game. And, with D&DI, you can take your game online, so you can play with friends anywhere—wherever they live, wherever you go.

GET A 10-DAY FREE*TRIAL AT:
DNDINSIDER.COM

POWERED BY
GLEEMAX

GET MORE AT
D&D INSIDER
www.dndinsider.com